web publishing

with QuarkImmedia

web publishing

with QuarkImmedia

For Windows & Macintosh

The Ultimate Guide to Designing
Interactive Multimedia

Roger Sperberg & Martha Leinroth

VENTANA

Library of Congress Catalog Card Number: 96-61797

First Edition 9 8 7 6 5 4 3 2 1

Printed in the United States of America

Ventana Communications Group, Inc.
P.O. Box 13964
Research Triangle Park, NC 27709-3964
919.544.9404
FAX 919.544.9472
http://www.vmedia.com

About the Authors

Roger Sperberg

Roger Sperberg is director of creative services at Ballantine Books/Random House and a principal in K/S Motion Arts, a multimedia design shop. He has written for nearly every computer magazine and was for many years the editor of *Electronic Directions*, an award-winning magazine on electronic publishing. A long-time educator, he has taught designers and editors at magazine and book publishing houses in New York. He lives in Brooklyn, N.Y., with his wife and son.

Martha Leinroth

Martha Leinroth is a digital artist, photographer, and experienced instructor in desktop, multimedia, and Internet publishing. She has taught QuarkXPress and other desktop publishing applications to numerous art directors, designers, and production artists in the publishing industry. An alpha tester for QuarkImmedia, she created an online training module that has been distributed by Quark on several QuarkImmedia prototype disks.

Her computer art and photographs have been exhibited internationally and she has received several grants and awards for her art, including a National Endowment for the Arts Visual Artists Grant and fellowships at the MacDowell Colony. A member of the faculty of the Rochester Institute of Technology for almost ten years, she has also taught at Northeastern University and The New School for Social Research.

Acknowledgments

Martha Leinroth

The writing of this book was more than a collaboration between two people; we had the assistance of many talented folks.

Thanks to our editors at Ventana—Neweleen Trebnik, Jennifer Huntley, Karen Stewart, and technical editor, Marian Hartsough. Their perseverance and patience were instrumental in the creation of this book.

Diane Chavan, Tony Freeman, and Ron Lockhart of Publication Directions started us off on this adventure by giving us the opportunity to be part of the QuarkImmedia Early Adopters program.

A number of people from Quark were excellent resources and teachers. We especially want to thank Terry Ficke, David Anderson, Aaron Templer, Molly Gookin, Jonathan Levitt, Gary Fluitt, Mark Schwenk, and Ryan House. We appreciate the time and support they gave us.

Thanks to Megan Reid—her great illustrations, buttons, and ideas are an important part of the exercises in this book.

Christopher Bishop was an invaluable resource for Chapter 8, "Sound." He also learned both Quark and Photoshop just to help out with the screenshots for the book.

I would like to thank individually the following people for the assistance they gave me: Tony Freeman, who created the Publica Support Center. He wrote the outline and text for the project that we produced as part of the Early Adopter Program for QuarkImmedia. Without his help I would not have been able to learn this program and produce the project in such a short time. Stewart McBride at United Digital Artists, who provided me with the opportunity to be the first teacher of the release version of Immedia. And finally, David Anderson, who participated in the class and has been a valuable resource. (And thanks to Camille Collett, the best teaching assistant.)

My nieces, Alexandra and Abigail, danced and sang for several of the exercises in this book. They also managed to do without my 'puter for most of the fall.

No one who starts a first book understands how much time and effort it will take and how little time is left for anything else. My family and friends were amazingly patient and supportive over the months it took to complete this project.

Roger Sperberg

I would like to thank Fred Dodnick, Steve Palmer, Ruth Ross, Betsy Elias, and George Davidson at Ballantine Books for their support and encouragement while I was working on this book. I would never have finished it without their assistance. At different stages along the way, the efforts of Steve Kortch, Chester Sullivan, Julie Gandy, Pam Walker, Jay Monday, Bill Hoffman, John Deckert, Janet Bernstein, Bob Halsell, Todd Katz, Bob Hobson, Christel Nordhausen, Joe King, Katherine Showalter, Jason Kiffer, Ilsa Lee Kaye, Pat Robinson, Barbara Lambrecht, Fritz Sperberg, and Ron Sperberg enabled me to complete this book, and I would like to thank each of them. I also want to express my gratitude to many others who helped me but whom I cannot thank here.

I know that no one does this alone. Specifically, in my case, Martha Leinroth has been a true partner, sharing the work and the delights. It was a lucky day when she first brought her photos into our offices. But most of all, I owe the deepest debt to my wife, Jill Kimball, who sacrificed and labored far beyond what was asked. This book is as much hers as mine. Thank you, darlin.

Dedications

For Jill.

—*R. S.*

To Alexandra and Abigail, and the next generation of 'puter users.

—*M. L.*

Contents

Web Publishing With QuarkImmedia

Introduction

In this book you will learn how to create interactive multimedia presentations using QuarkImmedia, as well as how to publish them on the Web. It includes a Companion CD-ROM with tutorial files and interactive examples so you can learn to use multimedia from actual multimedia.

You will need to know the basics of using QuarkXPress—how to create text and picture boxes, how to draw lines and move items around the page, and how to format text. Actually, you can pick up these essentials quickly on your own, but they're not covered here at all. In any case, you must have version 3.32 or later of QuarkXPress to run Immedia. If you don't have QuarkXPress, we've provided a save-disabled version for you on the Companion CD-ROM. You can try out all of the exercises and create your own projects—in both QuarkXPress and QuarkImmedia—but you won't be able to save them. If you're hazy about some features in XPress or need to learn it, check Appendix B, "QuarkXPress References," for a list of books about the program.

Who Is This Book For?

As the World Wide Web gets better at delivering multimedia pages, the need increases for every designer, not just Web specialists, to be able to create interactive (or just plain active) pages.

We've designed this book for those who know the basics of QuarkXPress and want to be involved in interactive media—designers and producers who are planning projects for the World Wide Web, corporate intranets, CD-ROMs, or computer-based presentations but who don't want to invest the time and effort it takes to master professional authoring programs or to learn a programming language such as Lingo or Java.

It's also for designers and producers who are frustrated with the limitations of HyperText Markup Language (HTML) and most multimedia authoring programs. They want the typographic and layout capabilities of Quark-XPress: to be able to use any font, to control the look of type, and to be sure that what the viewer sees onscreen is exactly what they created.

Intranet use is the fastest-growing area of the Web. As more businesses put their documents online, designers face the daunting tasks of converting Quark documents for online use and of learning to design in HTML. This book shows them how to take what they've created in Immedia and use it directly on their corporate intranet.

We designed this book to explain things in a way that is clear and direct and that provides plenty of hands-on experience. Learning from example is one of the best ways to learn, so we've included plenty of exercises and finished projects with which to work.

How This Book Is Organized

Web Publishing With QuarkImmedia is structured so you can make projects from the beginning, using the simpler concepts first and then tackling the more complicated. After the introductory section explaining Immedia's logic, the techniques chapters all include bountiful illustrations so you can easily follow the explanations while reading, and exercises, so you can learn by doing. One exercise in each chapter uses simple shapes and designs so you can focus on the concept being covered. An additional exercise utilizes material included on the accompanying CD-ROM for more sophisticated-looking projects.

Chapter 1, "The Challenge of Multimedia," provides an introduction to multimedia and interactivity from the perspective of QuarkImmedia, and explains how Immedia relates to the Web and to its parent environment, Quark-XPress. We also discuss the Companion CD-ROM that comes with this book and its special features, including a demonstration of effects and techniques, so you'll be able to use multimedia to learn multimedia. We also discuss some of the projects you will be able to make once you've learned the basics of QuarkImmedia.

Immedia is designed to make interactive presentations easy for those who have spent time in the print world. QuarkImmedia works and thinks like a page layout program, which is why it's so easy to learn and use. In Chapter 2, "The QuarkImmedia Methodology," we'll look at the basic elements of Immedia: interactive objects, which are made from QuarkXPress items, and events, the actions that make a project interactive.

The QuarkImmedia palette is the heart of this program. This is where all of the objects are created and events are defined. It's surprisingly easily to use. We'll take you step by step through the panels and menus of the palette in Chapter 3, "The QuarkImmedia Palette & Menu."

In Chapter 4, "Creating Multimedia: Making a Project," we'll go through the elements and concepts of working with QuarkImmedia, starting with how to set up a project and following with how to create interactive Immedia objects from QuarkXPress items. Adding interactivity means understanding user events, how to assign actions with mouse clicks.

Windows are a special category of objects. They can be opened from a page, be moved anywhere onscreen, and stay open when the project moves to a new page. In Chapter 5, "Window Objects," we'll look at how to create windows and special characteristics of the different window types.

In film, TV, video, even slide presentations, you can control the transition from scene to scene, make dissolves, wipes, and other effects. You can't do this on the Web. But QuarkImmedia has transitions you can assign to page entries and to the opening of windows and other objects. We'll examine these transitions one by one and talk about customizing them in Chapter 6, "Transitions & Pages."

What's exciting and unique about electronic media is hypertext, linking to other pages and documents from words in text. Having looked at interactive objects, it's time to look at interactive text, which we'll do in Chapter 7, "Hot Text Links." We see how to make headlines or text interactive, using words as navigation or to open windows and start other events.

Although QuarkXPress puts only images and text on a page, Immedia is not just for eyes only. Sound has a great role to play, even in Internet projects. We explore adding sound effects and background music in Chapter 8, "Sound."

Immedia is more than just a page layout program that links pages, objects, and sound. We've only talked about static images, but Immedia has many ways of working with moving images. The simplest is sliding or moving still images and objects around a page. In Chapter 9, "Movement," we look at sliding objects and using Quark-XPress lines, text boxes, and picture boxes as paths for moving items.

On many Web pages the viewer often doesn't know if anything has happened in response to a mouse click. Immedia's buttons can provide feedback to a viewer. Because they have several looks or states which change in relation to action and mouse events, buttons add a new level of interactivity to Immedia. Buttons are made in Immedia's own paint program—we'll show you how in Chapter 10, "Buttons."

While Immedia isn't able to work with video directly, it's great with QuickTime movies. As you'll see in Chapter 11, "Playing Movies," these can be made from video and animation. They can even record MIDI music tracks, providing high sound quality with very little file size.

We said that there's no programming in QuarkImmedia. Well, there are times when interactive objects and their associated events can't provide all the interactivity that one wants. How do you start at the entry to a page or create a number of actions that work in sequence? Immedia can do this without programming. As we'll see in Chapter 12, "Scripts," you can select scripting actions directly from menus. It's as easy as clicking on the action you want.

Not only can Immedia play QuickTime movies, but it can also make and play animation. We've seen how still objects can move about a page. Animation can provide even more movement—filling your screen with moving objects. And it's easier in Immedia than in most animation programs. In Chapter 13, "Playing Animations," we'll go over different ways of importing and playing animations.

Immedia can do more than just play animation. There's an editing window with a paint program; it works just like the window in which you make buttons. Chapter 14, "Making Animations," shows you how to construct your own animation. Animated objects, cartoons, and flip books are just a few of the things you can make.

System cursors can get boring. In Chapter 15, "Cursors," we'll show you how to use Immedia to make your own. You can even make animated cursors, a blinking light or beating heart, for instance. These are made just like buttons and animation in their own editing window.

Not only can Immedia present information, pictures, movies, animation, and sound, but it also has the capability to send and receive text information and to search through it as well. Chapter 16, "Text Box Objects," describes how to use editable text boxes for forms and surveys and scrollable text boxes for lengthy documents. We'll also show you how text box objects make it easy to update your Web site at any time.

The mouse isn't the only way to interact with an Immedia project. You can make custom menus in the menu bar and place pop-up menus anywhere in your project. Immedia also has the capability to add custom keyboard commands to a project. We'll show you how to do this in Chapter 17, "Menus & Keys."

We've been talking about Web and multimedia publishing through most of the book. But printing is an important part of publishing, it's been the main publishing medium for over 500 years! Immedia doesn't neglect print. We'll take you through some of the things you need to consider when printing your projects in Chapter 18, "Printing."

In QuarkImmedia you can preview to your heart's content. But there will come a time when you want to share your work with others. Many of them won't have Immedia or won't want to take the time to open QuarkXPress. Immedia projects can be exported in several formats: as standalone projects, for CD-ROMs, and for the Internet. In Chapter 19, "Exporting a Project," we'll take you through some of the issues you have to consider in designing and exporting for different delivery methods.

To look at exported projects you'll need a Viewer. The QuarkImmedia Viewer is free. The Macintosh Viewer is included on the Companion CD-ROM, and the beta Windows version is available from Quark's Web site, http://www.quark.com. Of course, you can also distribute the Viewer with your projects. It's easy to use, as you'll see in Chapter 20, "Using the QuarkImmedia Viewer." Note that you'll have to configure some parts of the Viewer if you want to look at Web sites that aren't written for Immedia. Refer to this chapter to see how easy it is to do.

The QuarkImmedia Viewer has controls for navigating the Internet and intranets as well. You can also program navigation controls into your project, as well as controls for sending and receiving documents and information. We'll show you how to customize the Viewer in Chapter 21, "Internet Controls." Designing for the limited bandwidth of the Internet can be tricky. We also have tips on designing sites for optiumum viewing in this chapter.

We've now gone through all the basics of using Immedia. For many projects, this is all you'll need to know. But if you want to delve into some of Immedia's advanced features, we'll get you started.

Chapter 22, "Advanced Features," covers conditional statements, some of the programming-like options in Immedia. We'll show you how to program Immedia to play a sound while an animation is playing and stop when the animation stops or to close all windows on the screen before opening another. Like scripting, it's a matter of choosing the programming action you want from a list.

Online Updates

As we all know, the Internet and its related technologies are constantly changing. As hard as we've tried to make the information in this book current, the reality is that some of it will need updating soon after this book goes to press. Ventana provides an easy way to meet this challenge: the *Web Publishing With QuarkImmedia* Online Updates. You can access this valuable resource via Ventana's World Wide Web site at http://www.vmedia.com/updates. Once there, you'll find updated material relevant to this book as well as material relevant to changes that will appear in Quark-Immedia version 1.1, to be released later this year.

We also have our own Web site, www.immediacy.com, which has updates to the book, new projects and exercises, as well as techniques and tips to make your work with Immedia more productive. You can access our site with the QuarkImmedia Viewer or an HTML browser such as Netscape Navigator or Microsoft Internet Explorer.

■ Moving On

That's the book. But it's not the end of what we have for you. On the Companion CD-ROM there are files and completed projects for all of the exercises that accompany each chapter. If you don't have QuarkXPress or the Quark-Immedia XTension, don't worry. There's a save-disabled version of XPress with the Immedia XTension for Macintosh on the CD-ROM. We've included some tips and techniques that we've discovered in the projects we've done in the last year, since we first were given the opportunity to work with the earliest pre-release versions of Immedia.

We've found Immedia to be fun to learn and delight-fully easy to work with. Without any multimedia back-ground you can start projects in just a few days. We know, we've seen it happen with designers we've taught! The world of WYSDOWYC is at your fingertips.

chapter 1

The Challenge of Multimedia

WYSDOWYC: that's our new acronym to explain interactivity onscreen: What You See Depends On Where You Click. Clicking on one or another object onscreen might cause a video to play, start an animation, jump you to another page, bring up a form, flash an information window, play music, download a file, or link you some-where—anywhere!—on the World Wide Web.

Interactive Multimedia, the World Wide Web & QuarkImmedia

Being interactive is what computers do best. Movies, books, TV shows, records—these media are linear: start at the beginning and continue in a straight line to the end. But a WYSDOWYC project uses a computer's interactive capabilities so the viewer (reader; user; interactivist?) can map more than one route through the information.

Studies have shown that learning is much more successful when several senses are involved. Presentations with visuals are much more effective than just plain talk. Interactive media requires physical involvement, too. Because it combines sight, hearing, and movement, interactive media can boost recall up to 85%.

And since people want to look into things in their own way, at their own pace, WYSDOWYC provides the broadest means of presentation for getting your message across (read, seen, or heard) in its entirety.

That said, making interactive presentations hasn't ever been easy—or inexpensive. Until recently, learning to use the tools available basically meant a career shift: mastery wasn't guaranteed for anyone who couldn't devote full time to the job.

Still, as the World Wide Web gets better at delivering multimedia pages, the need has increased for every designer, not just multimedia and Web specialists, to create interactive—or just plain active—pages. That's what brings us to QuarkImmedia.

QuarkImmedia offers a nonmultimedia designer a quick boost into multimedia expertise. Conceived as an extension to the page-layout program QuarkXPress, and not as a stand-alone application, it lets print designers create multimedia screens with the industry-standard layout application they already know.

Laying out a screen "project" in QuarkXPress with Immedia doesn't require a designer to learn new tools or, more importantly, how to work around a new program's limitations. Creating interactivity—triggering a pop-up window, a transition to a new page, music, or a video—is easy. There is no programming language to learn. Plus Immedia is constructed so you can put your project on the Web or a CD as easily as you can put it on that sales rep's laptop computer—Mac or Windows.

Of course, QuarkImmedia doesn't do everything. Those big-budget productions will still use the steep-learning-curve applications. But the professional multimedia-ist will want to add QuarkImmedia to his or her toolbox for the bulk of jobs because of the speed and simplicity with which they can assemble projects.

QuarkXPress

Figure 1-1: You must have version 3.32 or later of QuarkXPress installed to run the QuarkImmedia XTension.

You cannot author a project in QuarkImmedia unless you already have a copy of QuarkXPress, version 3.32, installed on your computer, as shown in Figure 1-1. Immedia is not a stand-alone product. Immedia extends the capabilities of QuarkXPress. And yes, Immedia is bigger than its parent program, and costs just as much.

CD-ROM

If you don't have QuarkXPress already installed on your computer, you can still work most of the exercises in this book. The Companion CD-ROM contains a save-disabled copy of QuarkXPress with the Immedia XTension for Macintosh.

TIP

Software that comes with Immedia will update QuarkXPress to 3.32 rev 5 from 3.32 rev 0 through rev 4. If you are using an earlier version of QuarkXPress, you will need to obtain the updates to bring you to at least 3.32 rev 0. You can download updates for your version of QuarkXPress from the file library located at http://www.quark.com. The minimum system requirements are System 7.1.2, Sound Manager 3.1 (which is included on the disk if you don't have it already), and 4 MB of RAM available for the Immedia design tool.

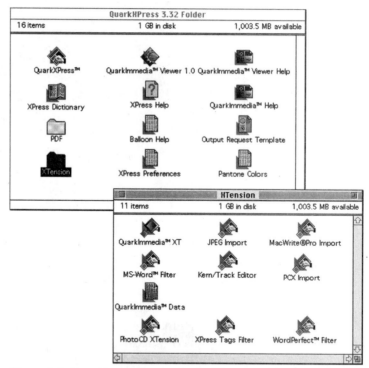

Figure 1-2: QuarkImmedia goes in the XTension folder.

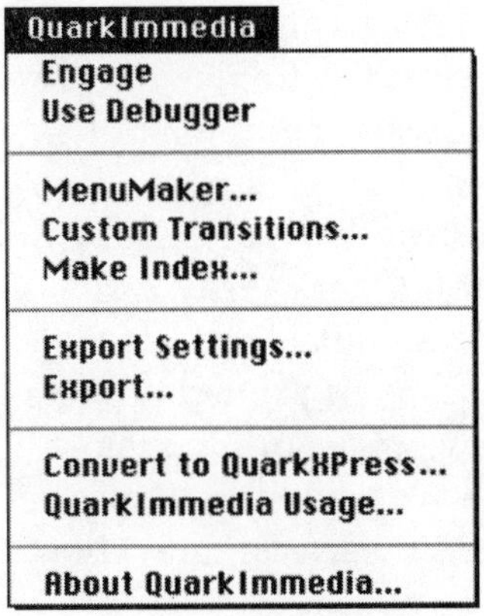

QuarkImmedia

Engage
Use Debugger

MenuMaker...
Custom Transitions...
Make Index...

Export Settings...
Export...

Convert to QuarkXPress...
QuarkImmedia Usage...

About QuarkImmedia...

Figure 1-3: A QuarkImmedia menu is added to the menu bar.

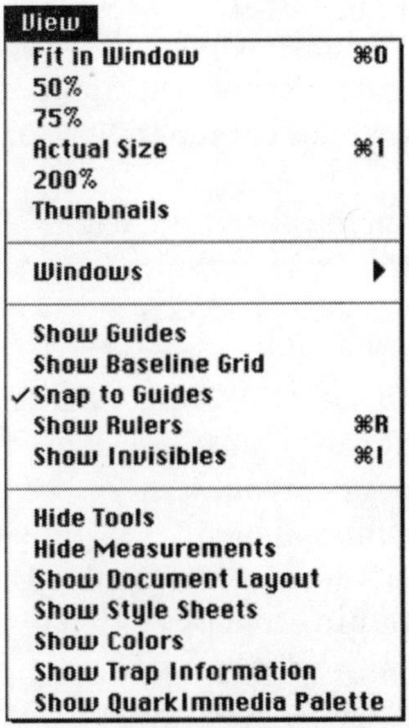

View

Fit in Window   ⌘0
50%
75%
Actual Size   ⌘1
200%
Thumbnails

Windows   ▶

Show Guides
Show Baseline Grid
✓Snap to Guides
Show Rulers   ⌘R
Show Invisibles   ⌘I

Hide Tools
Hide Measurements
Show Document Layout
Show Style Sheets
Show Colors
Show Trap Information
Show QuarkImmedia Palette

Figure 1-4: The Quark-Immedia palette is displayed from a new command at the bottom of the View menu.

As an XTension, Immedia should be located in the XTensions folder that is itself located in the parent QuarkXPress folder (Figure 1-2). As long as it's located there (or in the same folder as QuarkXPress itself), Immedia will be available whenever you launch QuarkXPress. An additional menu—headed QuarkImmedia, appropriately enough (Figure 1-3), another palette at the bottom of the View menu (Figure 1-4), and additional choices in the File | New and Edit | Preferences submenus, shown in Figures 1-5 and 1-6, comprise the visible differences in QuarkXPress with Immedia.

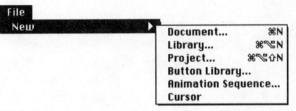

Figure 1-5: Four new options have been added to the File | New submenu.

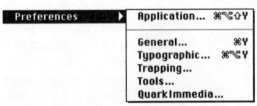

Figure 1-6: Immedia has its own set of preferences in the Edit | Preferences submenu.

For the more than one million users of QuarkXPress, Immedia's subservient role to QuarkXPress means they don't need to learn a new set of tools and methods to lay out a design, put pictures and text on a page, adjust these objects' positioning, and fine tune the type's appearance. Nor do they have to learn yet another method for adjusting the viewing size of the project onscreen, moving from page to page, or setting up reused layouts in master pages or repeated type specs in style sheets. The framework for building a document in QuarkXPress becomes the framework for building a project in Immedia.

Even for users new to QuarkXPress this is a reason for rejoicing: The superior type controls QuarkXPress has available for print purposes become available to us for screen projects. When we have to convert printed projects to onscreen projects—or the reverse, make printed versions of our multimedia projects—we have everything we need in QuarkXPress, which means the least aggravation for this none-too-easy task.

What About the Web?

Immedia projects can be played from a hard disk—for a presentation or in a kiosk-type situation—which will always occasion the fewest hitches or hiccups when playing and which requires the least amount of preparation for the presenter.

But Immedia was designed from the beginning with a full awareness of the need to distribute your multimedia projects on CD-ROM and over the World Wide Web. Simple settings allow you to export your projects for optimal playback from hard disk, CD-ROM, or over the Web. The no-charge-to-distribute QuarkImmedia Viewer plays an Immedia project. Or you can, if you wish, embed the Viewer to make a stand-alone presentation.

This Viewer is Web and browser aware, and downloads, caches, and plays the parts of your project in pieces. That means the person viewing your site on the Web doesn't have to wait for your whole project to be downloaded before interacting with it; while one page is being read, other pages, videos, and so on, can be sent and kept at the ready. This makes Immedia the friskiest and most interactive venue on the Internet.

The QuarkImmedia Viewer has the standard controls for opening a Web URL (Uniform Resource Locator), moving back and forth among pages, adding to a hot list, and so on. But the QuarkImmedia Viewer will be used *with* and not *in place of* browsers like Netscape Navigator and Microsoft Explorer. Why? Because Immedia doesn't read HTML, the hypertext linking language of these browsers. Typically, someone will use the QuarkImmedia Viewer to play Web-accessed Immedia projects and link to other sites. They may use either the Viewer or their browser to see the new site, depending on whether it uses Immedia or HTML to construct its pages. You'll probably want to add the capability for visitors to your site to download QuarkImmedia Viewer, or link to Quark's own site to do the same. Of course, once they've downloaded the Viewer at any site, they won't ever have to do it again. All in all, QuarkImmedia's Web capabilities make it the most viable approach to multimedia publishing on the Internet.

Is that important? Well, people who had never heard of the World Wide Web a year ago now are demanding interactive pages for their company right away, lest they lose the electronic initiative to their competitors. The consequent demand for electronic design—which is far greater than what the current supply of experienced interactive-screen designers can handle—is devolving on print designers.

Let's see. Print designers have to design interactive pages. They already know how to lay out designs in QuarkXPress. QuarkImmedia uses those same tools for layout, is easy to learn, and makes for the most active pages possible on the Web. Deciding that Immedia is the right tool is a no-brainer.

Won't people use HTML or Adobe Acrobat? you ask yourself. Yes, for limited interaction. Immedia won't drive them away. It will just supplant them for anything worth checking out.

Immedia on the Companion CD-ROM

This book comes with a save-disabled version of Quark-XPress with the QuarkImmedia XTension for Macintosh, so you can see how things work, rather than just read about it. You'll be able to construct every one of the exercises in the book, getting firsthand experience with the program if you don't yet own a copy.

Instructions on how to install the save-disabled version of QuarkXPress appear in the installation folder on the Companion CD-ROM. The version of XPress that comes on this CD-ROM can't be used to save the Immedia projects you construct. If you don't complete an exercise and have to quit this version of the program, when you come back to it, you'll have to begin from scratch.

At the time this book went to press, the final version of the Immedia Viewer for Windows was not yet available, so it is not included on the Companion CD-ROM. However, the beta version is downloadable for free from the Quark Web site: http://www.quark.com.

Using Multimedia to Learn Multimedia

The exercises in these chapters and on the Companion CD-ROM operate on a basic principle: writing can't do justice to multimedia. That's almost a self-evident proposition—if reading about a picture (or music or animation) had the same impact as the picture (or music or animation) itself, there'd be no call for multimedia at all. So where this book describes a specific effect, you can see that effect demonstrated in the exported version of the exercise.

Seeing a technique demonstrated is not the same as learning how to do it. Exported QuarkImmedia projects are closed—you can't look inside to see how they're put together. That's why we've included unexported, completed versions of the exercises on the Companion CD-ROM. You can open and examine each one. If you have a question about a technique in an exercise or what to check what you've just done, take a look at the finished version.

After all, some explanations just make more sense in multimedia. Isn't that the whole point of programs like QuarkImmedia?

Immedia-Built Examples

The Companion CD-ROM contains finished QuarkImmedia projects, including two example projects from Quark—Connect With QuarkImmedia and Electronic Launch Brochure—which describe the program's features while illustrating the very same features in the project design.

All of the exercises in the book have been placed on the Companion CD-ROM in completed form, so you can compare your efforts with the intended result. Independent versions of the exercises are also on the Companion CD-ROM, in case you want to study the exercises but aren't at a computer with the Immedia XTension installed.

We'll also post exercises and tips or techniques relating to them on our Web site, www.immediacy.com. You can use the Immedia Viewer or an HTML browser such as Netscape Navigator or Microsoft Internet Explorer to visit the site.

Viewers for 68000 Macintoshes and PowerPC Macintoshes are also included on the Companion CD-ROM. The beta version of the Windows Viewer is downloadable from the Quark Web site: http://www.quark.com. You may distribute these freely with your projects.

Moving On

In this chapter, we've tried to explain what multimedia, as seen through the lens of QuarkImmedia, is all about. We explore where Immedia fits in the scheme of things, and how it makes sense for a lot of different people, particularly the nonmultimedia designer, to whom it offers a quick boost into multimedia expertise. The World Wide Web puts its own spin on things, and part of Immedia's appeal stems from its being tailored for publishing on the Web as easily as to a CD-ROM or kiosk.

We've explained what we're trying to do in our efforts at teaching you Immedia. We've noted how techniques chapters always involve two hands-on exercises, one made from scratch and one using files located on the Companion CD-ROM.

In Chapter 2, "The QuarkImmedia Methodology," we take a look at how Immedia approaches multimedia—and in particular, how Immedia thinks.

The QuarkImmedia Methodology

QuarkImmedia sets out on the multimedia fandango from an unexpected position. It thinks the static structure of the printed page provides the best footing for someone building a complex of *interactivity*. Slideshow, animation-score, and stage metaphors all have their advantages, but you know what? Immedia has it right. The printed page does work best.

Why is that?

Well, basically, laying out a page for print is easy to master, and most of you are probably already familiar with how it's done.

Changing what's onscreen can be like turning pages—clicking on one button takes us to one page, on a different button to a different page. We see this sort of thing every day when we use our bank's ATM machine. Throwing in awkwardly grasped ideas like time segments and looping and puppets muddles things rather quickly even before we get to the complexity of the information we want to transmit. So the page metaphor works because it's going to let us structure the mass of our information without getting lost ourselves.

Of course, there's a reason why QuarkImmedia begins with the page: Immedia is an add-on product—an XTension—to the page-layout program, QuarkXPress.

How QuarkImmedia Thinks

Using Immedia, you can design any part of the page layout to trigger an event that causes a box to pop up, start animation or video playing, jump to another page, or literally to perform a hundred other actions.

When we lay out a page, we add text and picture boxes and lines, what QuarkXPress calls "items." We go a step further, of course, putting pictures and text in the boxes and adjusting them. To *our eyes* the pictures and words constitute the design, but XPress makes a distinction between the items we've put on the page and their contents. You could even say, without too much misrepresentation, that it's the items that matter to XPress. And, to a large extent, Immedia thinks the same way.

When Immedia looks at a page or screen of our project, it sees all the items we've put on the page and classifies them either as plain old QuarkXPress items, or as items that we identify as special Immedia "objects." An object is special in this way: it can have an action associated with it. For example, we can identify a picture box as an object, then set things up so that clicking on the picture plays a video.

First we identify the special Immedia objects—anything else is just background as far as Immedia is concerned. Then we establish the initiating act that will trigger the action, what Immedia calls a "user event." Clicking, double-clicking, or just moving the mouse on top of an object are the primary user events.

Then Immedia wants to know what action (or series of actions) should take place. Each of the user events for an object can have a separate action associated with it.

So we pick parts of our page layout—pictures or "hot" text or special buttons we've placed there—and they sit on our page waiting for an initiating action. If your project is an interactive catalog, moving the mouse on top of a picture of something for sale might bring up a detailed description, while clicking on the picture would cause a dialog box to appear, allowing the viewer to select color, size, and quantity, and transfer that information to an order form. The page would have navigation buttons to display other pages or sections or the table of contents. After 30 seconds, say, the next page would automatically be displayed. While the static images of catalog pages might be the easiest to envision, there's nothing inherent in Immedia that means your page has to be static. The action of entering a new page might trigger the playing of a video or animation, which perhaps loops endlessly, while different objects traverse paths on the page, awaiting the viewer's initiating actions from mouse or keyboard.

QuarkImmedia Objects

The starting point for working with Immedia is the object.

QuarkXPress has three types of items: text boxes, picture boxes, and lines. QuarkImmedia has a number of object types—items that have been given identifying names and new multimedia attributes. You can make any item (Figures 2-1, 2-2, and 2-3) a basic object or an animation object. You can make any box (but not a line) a window object or a pop-up menu object, as well. Only text boxes can be specified as text box objects and only picture boxes can be movie objects. By their names, you can understand what sort of thing the object types contain.

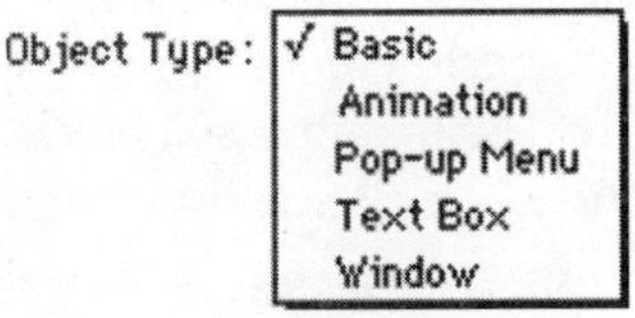

Basic Objects

The basic object is the default object type. Making a QuarkXPress item into a QuarkImmedia object requires only that, while the item is selected, you give it a name in the Immedia palette and assign it basic multimedia attributes. An Immedia object continues to be an item. You can still put a TIFF image into a picture box that's an Immedia object and spec'd type in text boxes. But now when a viewer clicks on the object, the action has interactive significance.

Figure 2-1: A text box can become one of these five types of objects in Immedia.

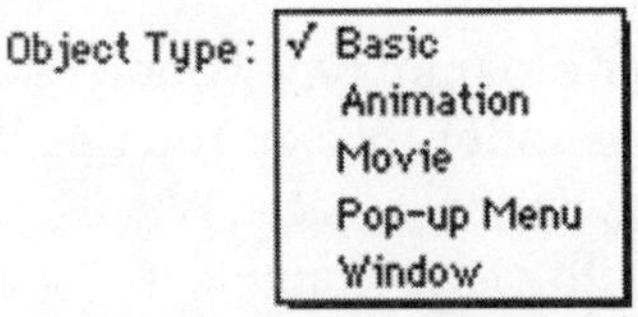

Figure 2-2: A picture box can become one of these five types of objects in Immedia.

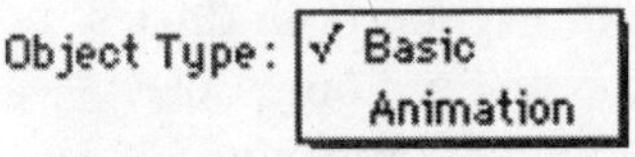

Figure 2-3: A line can become only a basic or an animation object.

Use the basic object for most multimedia tasks. When you need to play movies or animation, create a pop-up menu or a dialog box, use multi-state buttons, or accept text input from your user, you'll need to work with the other object types.

If you need to make the text in your text box searchable or scrollable onscreen, or if you want the user to enter information, you'll use the text box object rather than the basic object.

Animation Objects

There are really two types of animation objects in Immedia, a box that plays an animation, and an item that you can "animate" by moving it around the screen. You can define a picture box identified as an animation object as a container where an animation sequence plays. Immedia's own animation capabilities are somewhat limited. You can send items careering along a path created by the perimeter of some box or along a line. It works very simply. The text in a text box, a line, an arrow, or a picture in a picture box all traverse the path you identify when the box or line is made an animation object. Interestingly enough, an animation sequence inside an animation object, for example, does the same.

Window Objects

When you need to create computer program type windows, palettes, and dialog boxes, use the window object. You can use both text and picture boxes as window objects. Window objects can also simply be boxes with pictures and text placed not on the page but on the pasteboard and then called up by a user event, such as a click on some other object that is on the page.

Window objects have the unique property of unifying all the items and objects placed within their boundaries. Window objects float in front of the rest of your project surface, and you can choose the level of computer "windowness" that you want, from just an information box to standard windows with title bars and close buttons, to dialog boxes to floating palettes. You'll be astonished at how easily you can make floating palettes that contain a project's navigation controls and provide your project with a level of interactivity that you might have thought unattainable without learning computer programming.

Pop-Up Menu Objects

Both text and picture boxes can serve as pop-up menu objects. This might seem counter to logic—how does a picture box contain the text of a menu? Either type of item acts as a place holder for a menu made in the MenuMaker utility (located in the QuarkImmedia menu). The options in a pop-up menu have scripts associated with them. Thus, when a viewer clicks on a pop-up menu object next to a picture of a refrigerator, a script appears. Each menu option might be the name of a manufacturer, with a script that causes the picture to change to a model for that manufacturer.

Movie Objects

To play a QuickTime movie in your project, make a picture box into a movie object. The movie's poster (often the first frame) will display in the picture box. As with any picture box contents, the image size and cropping can be adjusted at will. But you can't flip, rotate, or skew the movie, nor can you make the box nonrectangular.

Text Box Objects

The text box object provides you with several capabilities that a text box made into a plain old basic object doesn't have. First off, this is the right type if you want the user to be able to search the text or edit it (before exporting). If the text is so long that it extends beyond the boundaries of the box onscreen, the text box object type can have scroll bars and arrows. Additionally, when you need to capture user input, you want to use the text box object, as you do when you want to read in a text file from outside the project to provide updated information.

Button Objects

In general computer use, a button can be any shape or appearance. Clicking on a button initiates some action. In Immedia, of course, you can set things up so that any object can be clicked on to initiate an action. But sometimes, especially for navigation and movie controls, you want the button to really look like a button, and by its appearance to indicate the state of some activity—you're depressing the button now, or the button is depressed and the movie is playing. For these instances in which a button needs to display several states, Immedia has an additional object type: the button object.

Immedia makes it easy to construct multi-state buttons and to assign different actions to the states. However, unlike these other object types, you don't create a QuarkXPress item and make it an object. Instead, all button objects are created and stored in an Immedia button library and dragged onto your page like any other library object.

Events

The other half of understanding Immedia comes from what you can make Immedia do. Immedia calls what your viewer does a "user event." Any user event can trigger one of more than a hundred "actions," (covered in more detail in later chapters). We'll call the combination of user event and action an "event." Having created a page and made Immedia objects out of QuarkXPress items, you next set up events, such as:

- When the viewer moves the mouse on top of the object (and then, when it moves off).

- When the viewer clicks on the object (you can distinguish between the pressing down and the release or Click up).

■ When the viewer right-clicks on the object (on their PC) or holds down the Option key (on their Mac).

■ When the viewer double-clicks on the object.

■ When the viewer does nothing for a set period of time.

One of Immedia's idiosyncrasies is that each user event gets one and only one action. So when you need a series of actions to occur, you create a "script"—which is simply a list of actions—and thus you maintain the one-to-one correspondence Immedia expects.

What actions can Immedia take?

■ **Display another page.** This can be the next page, the previous page, the first page, the last page, the most recently looked-at page, or any specific page. You can specify a transition effect and its duration as the page changes. That is, you choose whether you want a dissolve, a wipe, or one of the other effects and just how long it takes for one page to change to another.

■ **Play a sound.** This might be a simple beep or a full-fledged concerto. You can have clicking sounds for your user events and provide user feedback, in addition to having the click initiate the playing of an audio segment. You might have a narrator reading the text on-screen. And don't forget, you can have music playing in the background while other things are going on, letting the viewer (in this case, listener) adjust the volume.

■ **Display an information window.** You can display the information window wherever you want onscreen, with or without a title bar or close box, containing text, pictures, and buttons.

■ **Hide a visible object and make a hidden object visible.** The logic of this action makes more sense when you envision it as one of a series of actions in a script.

■ **Slide an object onscreen, offscreen, or following the outline of an object.** Immedia's movement capabilities are limited but you can slide objects to exact locations on- or offscreen.

- **Change the cursor shape.** This might be only one action that occurs during the progress of a script. Changing the cursor shape provides immediate, visible feedback to the user that something is happening, for example while the user loads a large video.

- **Play a QuickTime movie.** Video often seems to be what gives a multimedia project that multimedia feel. You have all the controls for starting, pausing, resuming, or stopping the video and adjusting the volume. And, of course, you can enlarge or shrink the display and crop it as desired.

- **Play an animation.** Using a flip-book type approach, with a succession of still images, Immedia gives you an animation-creating studio. You can also play standard PICS animation. But one of Immedia's best tricks is to play an animation in an object while sliding the object around the screen.

- **Pause a video, animation, or sound.** Hey, just starting it playing isn't really sufficient. With Immedia's multi-state buttons, you can assign the obvious actions—play, pause, resume, stop—to the different states.

- **Print the page or some file or collected information.** Print is one of the media in multimedia, in case you've forgotten, and is usually a very handy one for carrying information around.

- **Open another project.** Handy for chaining—playing one project after another—and for modularizing your work.

- **Open a Web URL and perform the usual navigation.** You can permanently assign, or "hard wire," URLs to objects, or accept user input or create your own "buttons" (they can be pictures or text) to move back and forth among URLs.

■ **Update the information in your project from the Web in real-time.** A nifty feature allows you to grab text from an outside file and display it in your project. So a newspaper's West Coast correspondents could add late scores to the appropriate on-line file and instantly they show up in the *On-Line Daily*'s sports page. Or think of it as a way for non-Immedia trained personnel to update sales prices. Or stock availability. Or schedules for executives or sales reps. Or any other constantly fluctuating information that a variety of people need access to.

■ **Disable the keyboard or buttons onscreen (and re-enable them).** Well, for times when you *don't* want user input.

■ **Search the text of your project for user-specified words.** Say my project contains maps of my company's 33 floors and it locates each person's desk on those floors. With this feature, you can find John in Accounting at extension 1234 without having to scan through those 2,000 employee names listed alphabetically by last name.

■ **Add a menu to the project page or to the Viewer menu bar.** Since each option on a menu activates a script, the menu becomes the easiest way to aggregate options in a single place.

■ **Collect user information in a file.** Since you have user-fillable text fields, you can also easily save the information entered—and use it in your project. A simple example: asking for the user's name on startup, so you can personalize certain screens.

Macintosh & Windows

The initial release of Immedia occurred in September 1996 on the Macintosh platform, while we were working on this book. Projects intended to be played in Windows, as of this writing, have to be constructed on a Macintosh. That may not last for long. A Windows version of the Immedia-authoring XTension is currently under development. Will you be able to take a QuarkImmedia project put together on a Mac and open it in Windows Immedia, the way you can a QuarkXPress document? That will clearly be a goal of the Immedia design team.

And will Windows Immedia look the same and act identically to the Mac Immedia pictured and described in these pages? Again, if XPress is any guide, you would expect only cosmetic differences, with perhaps keyboard discrepancies being the most significant.

Whatever the differences—extra or missing features— you'll be able to go online to Ventana's World Wide Web site (www.vmedia.com/updates.html) and find them described fully. You can also visit our Web site at www.immediacy.com to get information about Immedia for both Mac and Windows users.

Moving On

In this chapter we've taken a look at how QuarkImmedia approaches the issue of representing a multimedia plan. It relies naturally enough on the page as the basic construct— easy to understand and to put together. More important from our inexperienced eyes is getting the hang of what *we* are expected to do—where we should start and what should be the sequence.

Soon enough, these procedures will be old-hat. But for now we isolate the object that the user is going to interact with, the manner of that interaction (what Immedia calls the user event), and how it triggers some activity or action.

Immedia has its variety of objects, which we must begin to distinguish from the start, since we will use a specific object type for each type of multimedia flash. For the minimum level of interactive properties there is the basic object. For animation the animation object, for movies the movie object, for buttons the button object. For forms and user-supplied text the text box object. For custom and user-customizable menus the pop-up menu object. And for windows—computer screen windows with title bars, dialog boxes, floating palettes—the window object.

The user interacts with the object, triggering some activity. It could be almost anything you might imagine, from going to another page, to playing a sound or a video or an animation. Accessing a site on the World Wide Web. Collecting information. Activities too numerous to mention yet again. In Immedia you have the tools to make a whole environment, and a structure that prevents it from overwhelming you. What a concept.

The heart of Immedia is the Immedia palette. In its six tabbed panels you will find an elegantly simple method of processing the scores of details necessary to make things move and talk and interact. In the next chapter, "The QuarkImmedia Palette & Menu," we will take a look at how all these pieces fit together.

chapter 3

The QuarkImmedia Palette & Menu

The QuarkImmedia XTension alters the appearance of QuarkXPress by adding a new menu (the QuarkImmedia menu), as well as by adding commands to the View menu and File | New and Edit | Preferences submenus. The main working area is the QuarkImmedia palette, a 4 ¾" by 4 ⅜" floating palette—a window that floats above XPress document and Immedia project windows.

Before we begin project making, we'll go over the palette's structure, so you know where things are and how best to set things up. As you will soon see, Immedia's multimedia actions are bundled in the ubiquitous Action pop-up menu. We'll briefly go over it and the other Immedia-related commands. The Action pop-up menu is so central to what you are doing in Immedia that virtually every submenu has its own chapter in this book. In this chapter, we want to spell out what you can expect to find in each area of the palette and program.

About the Palette

To display the Immedia palette onscreen, choose the View | Show QuarkImmedia Palette command (Figure 3-1).

Figure 3-1: As with other palettes, the command to display the QuarkImmedia palette is found in the View menu.

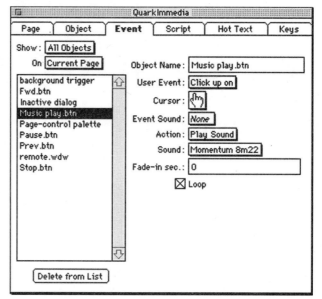

Figure 3-2: The QuarkImmedia Palette, with the Event panel active.

Take a look at Figure 3-2. Across the top of this palette are six tabs, identifying the different aspects of Immedia's controls. When you click a tab, a panel for that type of control displays. Each panel has a scrollable window on its left with the settings displayed on the panel's right-hand side.

Page Panel

Controls relating to pages, especially how they "enter" and "exit" the screen appear on the Page panel (Figure 3-3).

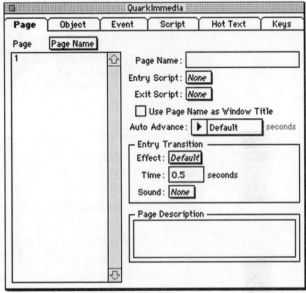

Figure 3-3: The Page panel.

On the left is the Page scrollable list. All of the project's pages, or its master pages, are listed here. Since every page in a project can be identified by a name as well as by number (Figure 3-4), the scrollable list displays both the page name for your project's pages and the sequential page number—that is, numbering from the first page (the same as QuarkXPress's document layout palette). Using the Page | Section command to "renumber" pages doesn't affect this numbering.

You can double-click on any entry in the Page scrollable list to jump the project to that page. This method of moving around your project is useful, since the lists for the other panels always reflect the active page. Of course,

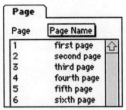

Figure 3-4: You can name pages and refer to them by name or page number.

using keyboard commands, the project window scroll bar, the Page menu commands, and the document layout palette remain available as ways to navigate your project.

Naming a page is simple. Select the appropriate page, enter the name in the Page Name text field, and press the Return or Enter key to give the page its name. Clicking on another page entry also adds your page name. Whenever you highlight a page name in the scrollable list, that name appears in the Page Name field, so you can alter it at any time.

TIP

Since much of your project design consists of moving from one page to another with different information, naming pages has great advantages in project construction. Adding, deleting, and moving pages necessarily alters page numbering, so you can make all your references—especially including jumps to a page—by page name rather than number, that is, to "Company Info" rather than "Page 28." That way even last-minute adds or cuts don't alter your page flow unexpectedly or necessitate changes in other references to pages.

The pop-up menu at the scrollable list's head (refer to Figure 3-4) lets you choose between listing page names and the master pages on which each page is based. To work on a master page, you use one of the standard methods of switching the display. You can't access a master page from this scroll window.

Page Entry & Exit

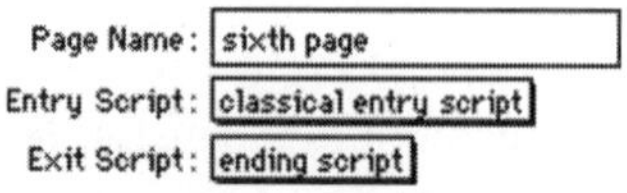

Page Name: | sixth page
Entry Script: | classical entry script
Exit Script: | ending script

Figure 3-5: Specify Page entry and exit scripts here.

Below the Page Name field, as illustrated in Figure 3-5, you specify if you want a script to run when entering and/or when exiting the page. Since this script runs every time a page displays (or closes) and consists of any number of actions, which may involve movement in an animation or video and which may loop endlessly, the static nature of project construction in no way leads to static projects.

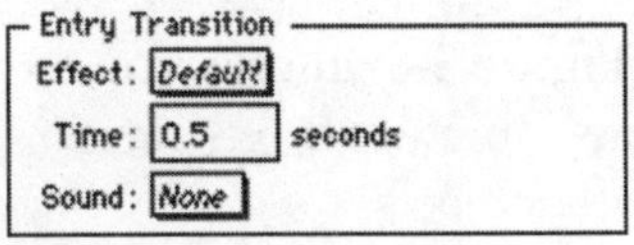

Entry Transition
Effect: [Default]
Time: [0.5]   seconds
Sound: [None]

Figure 3-6: The Entry Transition area.

Actually, before you see a page, the page must be projected onto your screen. The manner in which the page first appears—special effects such as a fade, dissolve, or wipe—Immedia calls a transition. You choose the specific transition and how long it should last (and any accompanying sound) a little lower down the panel, as shown in Figure 3-6.

A check box labeled "Use Page Name as Window Title" is a special control that pertains only when your project pages have title bars and you want to override the usual title with the specific name of your page. Unless you want their computer-application look, you probably will only want to use title bars with projects distributed over the Web.

The last control on the page—Auto Advance—lets you specify whether the project will automatically move on to the next page after a certain amount of time has passed without the user having triggered a move by clicking some button. You can choose a standard value for all pages, setting it as a default, or choose 5, 15, 30, 45, or 60 seconds from the pop-up menu. You can enter any value you prefer, in seconds. And, of course, you can choose "None," which means the page will remain onscreen until either the user initiates movement to another page, or the script does.

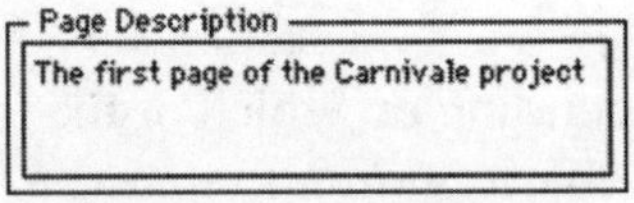

Page Description
The first page of the Carnivale project

Figure 3-7: The Page description area.

A box at the bottom of the Page panel provides you with a place to enter a description of the page (Figure 3-7). This description is limited to 255 characters. This text can be grabbed and displayed in a text box object (as can the page name) and can also be included as part of a user-initiated search—the kind of thing you might do to allow users to literally look before they link.

Object Panel

Object Type in the Object panel (Figure 3-8) allows you to define standard QuarkXPress items—picture boxes, text boxes, and lines—as QuarkImmedia objects.

Figure 3-8: The Object panel.

There are different controls depending on which of the seven types of objects you select—basic, animation, movie, pop-up menu, text box, window, and button.

As with the other panels, the left side contains a scrollable list. As a default, the list displays the names of objects on the current page, plus its pasteboard. You can restrict the display to only objects of a particular object type—and you can enlarge the scope to include the entire project. In that case, the page where the object is located appears in parentheses after the name.

Double-clicking any object listed in the scrollable list will make the object active, which will be indicated by the appearance of selection handles (Figure 3-9). If the object lies outside the display, say on the pasteboard, then the

Figure 3-9: Double-clicking on an object name makes the object active on your page.

display will shift so you can see it. If the object is on another page, the display will necessarily have to jump to that page.

QuarkXPress items on your page don't show up in this scrollable list, as you must first define them as Quark-Immedia objects. When you manually select an item on your page, simply clicking in the Object Name field and typing in a name does the trick. Pressing Return or Enter, or choosing one of the object types from the pop-up menu will complete the action, as will clicking outside the palette or on another tab. Objects on the same page must be uniquely named, but two objects, such as buttons, can have the same name if they're on different pages.

The name you enter can have upper and lowercase characters, spaces, numbers, accented letters, and punctuation in it. Be wary of using characters you obtain by pressing Option and Shift-Option, since many of them are missing from the Geneva font, which is used for displaying names in the dialog box. All you'll get for these missing letters is an indecipherable box. The name can be as long as you need, over a hundred characters if you must, but only the first 20 or so characters will display in the scrollable list.

Remember, making an item into an object is what gives it multimedia functionality.

You establish your choice of object types in the Object Type pop-up menu (Figure 3-10). Only the permissible types of objects display for the selected item. When a line is selected, you can choose only the basic and animation object types. A picture box can be a basic object, an animation object, a window object, a pop-up menu object, or a movie object. A text box can be a basic object, an animation object, a window object, a pop-up menu object, or a text-box object. Button objects are created in a button library and dragged onto the page from there. You don't convert them the way you do the other object types from items.

Once you set the object type, the panel's controls reflect the specific capabilities of the different object types.

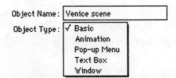

Figure 3-10: The Object Type pop-up menu options.

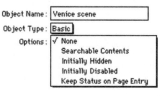

Figure 3-11: Basic object options.

Basic Object

The Options pop-up menu essentially identifies the display options for the object (Figure 3-11). These options are available with other types of objects as well, so we'll look at them now.

■ Searchable Contents (for text boxes only)—check this option to include the text in this box when a user searches for specific words in the project.

■ Initially Hidden—when the viewer first enters the page you can choose to have the object hidden from view, and have it revealed only when triggered by some action (a click, a mouse passing over an object, and so on) or script.

■ Initially Disabled—you may choose to have the multimedia functionality of the object turned off when the page initially displays, waiting for an action or script to activate the object.

■ Keep Status on Page Entry—when the user leaves this page and then returns, should the Hidden/ Shown and Disabled/Enabled options return to their original state? Or reflect the state when the user left? Check this option if you want the latter.

If no options are chosen, the pop-up displays "None," if more than one, "Multiple Options" displays. Choosing "None" turns off any options that have previously been checked.

The Initially at pop-up menu (Figure 3-12) specifies whether an object should start out at its "home" position, where it has been positioned on the page, or on one of the pasteboards outside the page. Home is defined in this fashion, and the initial position so indicated, because for many objects you will want them to end up—and not begin—at home.

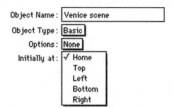

Figure 3-12: Initially at pop-up menu options.

Animation Object

Making something an animation object in Immedia means one of two things: either it will serve as a display box for the flip-book type animation created by Immedia or converted from PICS animation, or it will itself be moved around the screen following the outline of a QuarkXPress box or line.

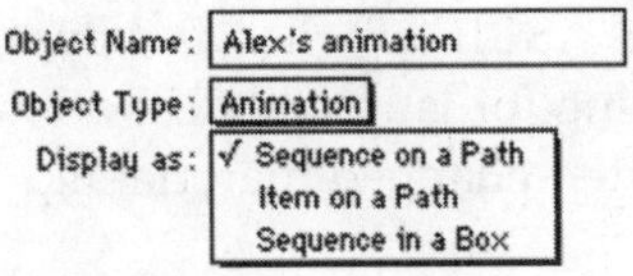

The Display as pop-up (Figure 3-13) uses what seem like non-intuitive names, but they are in fact fairly descriptive of the options. An animation object can be:

■ Item on a Path—a line, text box, or picture box that moves around the screen.

■ Sequence in a Box—a box that contains an animation sequence.

■ Sequence on a Path—this same type box being moved around the screen while the animation inside it is playing.

Of course, the path being followed, how fast the animation plays, and how fast it moves around the screen are all specified here, as well.

Figure 3-13: Animation object options.

Movie Object

Only picture boxes can be movie objects (Figure 3-14). When the movie object is defined, you can specify a particular movie that will play inside that box. However, and this proves confusing when first working with movie objects, you will also have to identify the movie when you choose the play action. Why? Because Immedia actually allows you to play any movie in this box. This first identification is just naming a default movie, and its poster (or identifying frame) will be displayed in the box on your screen.

On this panel you also indicate whether you want the movie object to have QuickTime controls displayed with it, loop continuously, be preloaded, or be treated as a button so that clicking and passing the mouse over the box have interactivity significance.

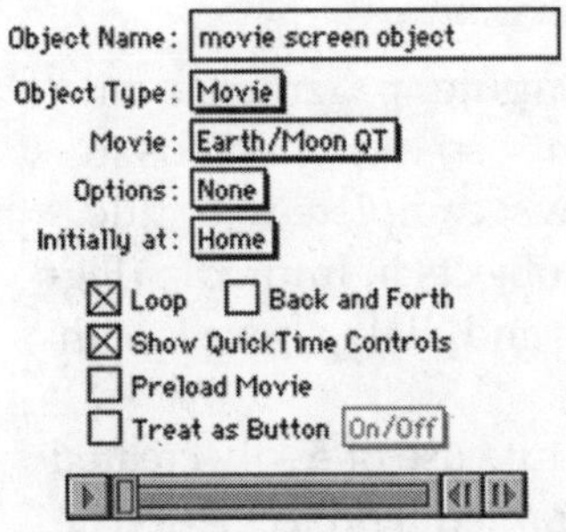

Figure 3-14: Movie object options.

Figure 3-15: Text box object options.

Text Box Object

Only text boxes can be text box objects (Figure 3-15). Regular text that the reader won't interact with at all goes in plain QuarkXPress text boxes. You use text box objects for fields that users can enter text in, or for boxes that have scroll bars (to cut down on the space they occupy on the page), or for lists.

Immedia can also grab external ASCII text files and put them into a text box object, allowing for laughably easy updating of time-sensitive and often-changed material like schedules or news items.

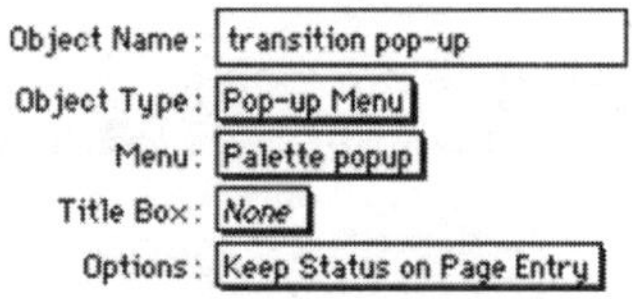

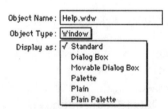

Figure 3-16: Pop-up menu object options.

Pop-Up Menu Object

You use pop-up menu objects in your projects for space-saving reasons. Immedia accepts both text and picture boxes as pop-up menu objects (Figure 3-16). The box made into a pop-up menu object actually only serves to define the location and width of the pop-up menu.

Menus are constructed using the QuarkImmedia | MenuMaker command. The main option here is simply to specify which menu goes with which pop-up menu object.

Window Object

Multimedia projects resemble computer programs even more than they do print documents, so it only stands to reason that you can make windows, complete with title bar, title, and close box. Window objects in Immedia (Figure 3-17) include floating palettes and dialog boxes, with their varying display priorities.

More than any other feature, astute use of easily created window objects will stamp your Immedia project as a true multimedia effort and not simply converted print material.

Figure 3-17: Window object options.

Object Name: Play Button
Object Type: On/Off Button
Key Alias:
☐ Initially On
☐ Initially Disabled
☐ Initially Hidden
☐ Keep Status on Page Entry

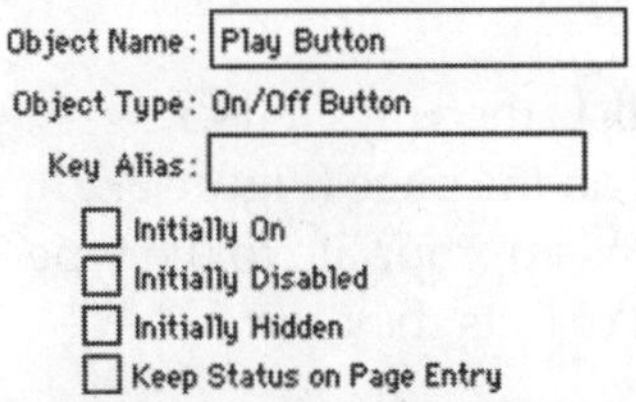

Figure 3-18: Button object options.

Button Object

Button objects are created in a button editing window in a button library and dragged onto the page from there. You don't convert them from QuarkXPress items the way you do the other object types.

Buttons are listed in the Object scrollable list, however, with various options (Figure 3-18). You can assign a keyboard equivalent to the action of clicking a button, either here in the Object panel, or in the Keys panel.

Event Panel

Much of the action in Immedia occurs in the Event panel (Figure 3-19) because here is where you connect the object on the page, the user's interaction with that object, and what action Immedia undertakes.

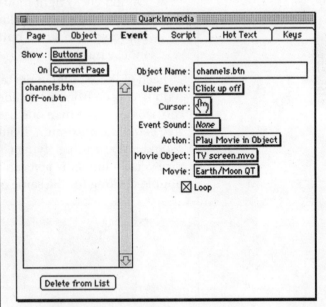

Figure 3-19: The Event panel.

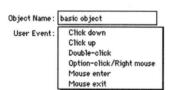

Figure 3-20: The User event pop-up menu.

The scrollable list on the left and the Object Name field duplicate that in the Object panel, enabling you to create or rename an object here, as well.

The User Event pop-up menu lists the ways a user's mouse can interact with an object on the page (Figure 3-20). This pop-up menu displays options appropriate to the type of object that is selected. For most objects they are:

■ Click down—when the user presses the mouse button.

■ Click up—when the user releases the mouse button.

■ Mouse enter—when the pointer passes over the object onscreen.

■ Mouse exit—when the pointer moves off of the object.

■ Double-click—pressing and releasing twice in succession.

■ Option-click/right mouse—on the single-mouse-button Macintosh, clicking while the Option key is depressed; on a two-button PC, clicking the right mouse button.

Each of these user events can have one action associated with it, chosen from the Action pop-up menu below. You can activate more than one user event for any object, with five being the maximum. Double-clicking can't be assigned if you are specifying Click up or Click down, and vice versa—Immedia just can't handle both single and double-clicking for the same object.

Note that buttons and some text box objects have fewer user events, pop-up menu objects have no assignable user events at all (although they respond to pressing the mouse), and window objects have two unique user events: window open and window close.

You can assign a sound to accompany any of these user events. A nice solid *click!* sound supplies a useful confirmation that your program has accepted a user's mouse click.

And you can change the cursor shape, too—which occurs as a matter of course when the user's mouse passes over a clickable object, when it changes from the standard back-pointing arrow to a finger-pointing hand. You might prefer to design your own cursor. For instance, you might set up an animated cursor that is used while the mouse pointer is passing over the object.

The *pièce de résistance* of the Event panel is the Action pop-up menu, from which you can choose one, and only one, action from its 17 submenus (Figure 3-21). This apparent limitation serves to simplify the interface without actually restricting your options. Whenever you require more than one action for any specific user event, you simply gather them up in a script, and choose "Run Script" as your "single" action.

The Event panel then changes once you choose any of the more than one hundred actions, adding fields as appropriate, so you can specify the page, object, script, and so on, that you mean.

We'll pass over explaining the Action pop-up menu until we've gotten through all of the panels in the QuarkImmedia palette.

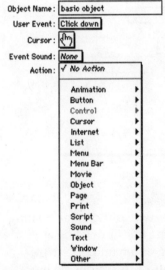

Figure 3-21: The Action pop-up menu.

Script Panel

Like the Event panel, the Script panel has an Action pop-up menu (Figure 3-22). Except here, the Action scrollable list can contain many actions, each of which accesses one command from the Action pop-up menu.

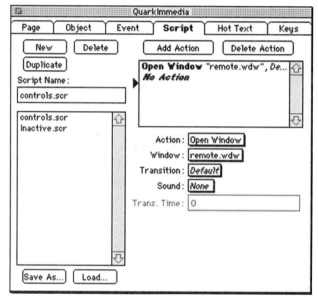

Figure 3-22: The Script panel.

The panel's left side lists scripts, with buttons for creating a new script, duplicating an existing one or deleting any script, as well as a field for naming or renaming a script.

The buttons on the right side affect the scrollable list there. Clicking Add inserts a *No Action* place holder. Since a script is simply a list of actions, you put as many place holders in the scrollable list as you want actions, then replace each place holder with a specified action. The insertion triangle on the scrollable list's left side lets you insert a place holder between existing actions. Dragging an action up or down rearranges the order the actions take place in, and the Delete button removes an action. Scripts are covered in Chapter 12.

Hot Text Panel

Individual words or phrases in running text can be set up with interactive links in much the same way as objects. But since one XPress text box might have more than one interactive text link, we can't simply use the interactive properties of the box by turning it into an object.

Instead, Immedia provides another class of interactive object: the hot text string.

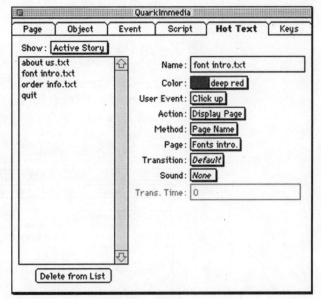

Figure 3-23: The Hot Text panel.

The Hot Text panel (Figure 3-23) in fact operates much the same as the Event panel, with:

- A scrollable listing of all the instances of interactive text in one text box, one story, one page, or all the project's pages.

- A field for naming the hot text string.

- A field to specify the color of the text.

- A pop-up menu containing the same six user events as for most objects.

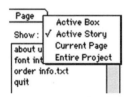

Figure 3-24: The Show pop-up menu categories for hot text strings.

- A pop-up menu to specify the action to take.
- Other fields appearing as appropriate to the action chosen.

Note that unlike the Event panel for objects, here we don't have a Sound pop-up menu. The Color pop-up menu appears here but not in the Event panel.

You'll use the Show pop-up menu (Figure 3-24) more in this panel than elsewhere. The option to display all the hot text in one story, of course, will extend across as many pages in your project as the story itself.

Keys Panel

In the Keys panel (Figure 3-25), you identify keyboard commands that direct Immedia to run scripts, perform the operations associated with button states, or activate any commands in a menu.

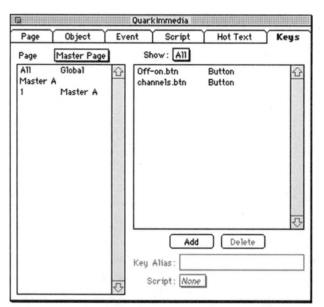

Figure 3-25: The Keys panel.

You might do this as an alternative to some standard user event with the mouse, or as a stand-alone event, such as using Shift-Home to jump to the project's first page.

Because you can make keyboard commands that work on only one page, on all pages, or with a master page (and consequently, all pages that use that master page for their design), the Keys panel works a little differently than the other panels.

The scrollable list on the left side contains the different bounds possible for a keyboard command:

- Global, that is, all pages
- Each master page used in your project
- Each individual page of your project

When you highlight one of these categories on the left side, the right side scrollable list identifies all the existing applicable keyboard commands. To add a new one, simply click the Add button in the panel's lower right and press the key or key combination you want. To display the combination, Immedia uses these symbols:

⇧   Shift

⌘   Command

⌥   Option

⌃   Control

You can specify any key on your keyboard excepting only the Power on, Escape, Delete, and Del keys, singly or in combination with any of the shifting keys—Shift, Command, Option, and Control. That is, you can use the letter z or Command-Option-Shift-z, the Page-Down key, or Control-Option-comma.

Of course, it wouldn't make sense to use standard keyboard commands—Command-period for cancel, Command-Z for undo, Command-Q for quit, Command-S for save, among others—for something other than what users already expect.

Having chosen an individual key or some combination of keys, you then specify the script you want to run when that key or combination is pressed.

■ The Action Pop-Up Menu

The Action pop-up menu appears in the Event, Script, and Hot Text panels, with only slight differences. Of course, this makes sense, because each of these panels provides the opportunity for you to associate a user's mouse activity with an Immedia response. In the Event and Hot Text panels, interaction with an object or interactive text string triggers the action specified in the Action pop-up menu. The Script panel is where you gang up a batch of actions and give this batch a single name, which you can then access in the Event and Hot Text panels, as well as in the Page panel entry and exit scripts and in the QuarkImmedia Preferences' startup, quit, and inactivity scripts.

The Action pop-up menu (refer to Figure 3-21) is divided into 17 submenus, listed alphabetically (except for the grab bag "Other," which comes last).

- Animation
- Button
- Control
- Cursor
- Internet
- List
- Menu
- Menu bar
- Movie
- Object
- Page
- Print
- Script
- Sound
- Text
- Window
- Other

The Animation submenu (Figure 3-26) contains commands for playing, pausing, resuming, and stopping animation. It also has commands that tell Immedia to play an animation while moving the box along a path and that permit more than one animation to play in an animation object (seriatim, not simultaneously). Immedia's ability to play many animations simultaneously is one of the chief advantages of the program. These actions are discussed in Chapter 13, "Playing Animations." How to make animation is explained in Chapter 14, "Making Animations."

The Button submenu (Figure 3-27) is used to change button states to on or off, as well as to temporarily enable or disable buttons. The ease with which sophisticated buttons can be created and "programmed" also sets Immedia apart. Buttons are explored in Chapter 10.

The Control submenu provides for limited programming-like features for use only with scripts. Standard loop, while, and if tests are available; you can test for a variety of conditions, such as whether an animation or movie or sound is playing, paused, or stopped, or whether a window is open or a download is progressing, and so on, for most of the other submenu activities. The Control submenu is discussed fully in Chapter 22, "Advanced Features."

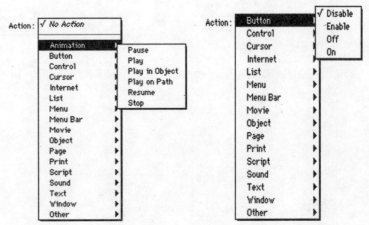

Figure 3-26: The Animation submenu.

Figure 3-27: The Button submenu.

The Cursor submenu (Figure 3-28) provides for changing, hiding, or redisplaying specific cursors. This is discussed in Chapter 15, "Cursors," as is the creation of animated cursors.

The Internet submenu commands (Figure 3-29) perform the range of activities a project or user needs to interact with the World Wide Web, such as downloading a file, opening a URL, moving back and forth among previously opened addresses, uploading text from your forms, and hiding and displaying the Immedia Web browser. These commands are discussed in Chapter 21, "The Internet Controls."

The List submenu (Figure 3-30) permits sophisticated gathering of information into lists and manipulation of the lists. How to use this capability is covered in Chapter 22, "Advanced Features."

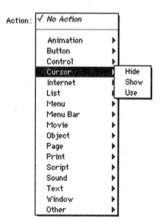

Figure 3-28: The Cursor submenu.

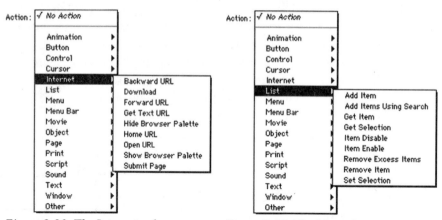

Figure 3-29: The Internet submenu.   *Figure 3-30: The List submenu.*

Menu commands (Figure 3-31) let you add or remove, enable, or disable commands on a menu, as well as copy text to or from a command. Immedia's ability to place a pop-up menu anywhere in your project provides exceptional flexibility in providing interactivity.

The Menu Bar commands (Figure 3-32) are used with menus that you add to the QuarkImmedia Viewer menu bar in your exported projects. You can add or remove a menu to the menu bar, enable or disable it, place check marks next to commands and remove them, and hide or display the menu bar. Menu and menu bar commands are covered in Chapter 17, "Menus & Keys."

Commands in the Movie submenu (Figure 3-33) let you play and stop playing, pause, and resume a QuickTime movie. You can show or hide a QuickTime movie controller, set the movie volume, and set a specific movie to play in a Movie object. Chapter 11, "Playing Movies," reviews movie commands.

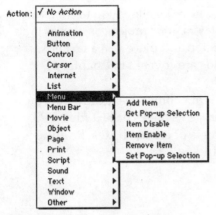

Figure 3-31: The Menu submenu.

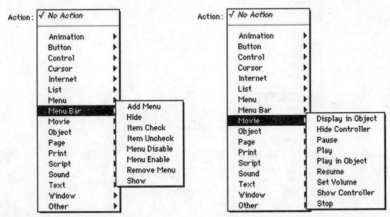

Figure 3-32: The Menu Bar submenu.

Figure 3-33: The Movie submenu.

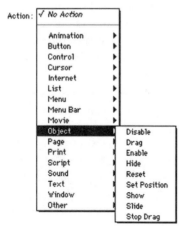

Figure 3-34: The Object submenu.

Figure 3-34 shows the Object submenu commands which you use to manipulate Immedia objects—hiding or showing them, enabling or disabling them, moving them, making them capable of being dragged around the screen. Chapter 4, "Creating Multimedia: Making a Project," introduces many of the Object actions.

Page commands (Figure 3-35) allow you to choose different pages to display in your project, as well as grab a page name or description and place it in a text box. Most of these commands are covered in Chapter 6, "Transitions & Pages."

Commands in the Print submenu (Figure 3-36) control printing of your project's pages or text files, EPS graphics, and the contents of certain boxes. Printing is discussed in Chapter 18.

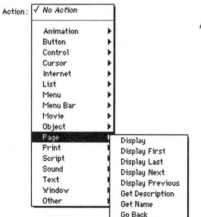

Figure 3-35: The Page submenu.

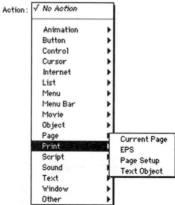

Figure 3-36: The Print submenu.

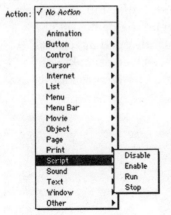

Figure 3-37: The Script submenu.

Scripts in Immedia, which are discussed in Chapter 12, are simply lists of the other actions described here. Commands in the submenu (Figure 3-37) manipulate these scripts, activating or deactivating them, running, and stopping them.

The commands in the Sound submenu, shown in Figure 3-38, play, stop, pause, and resume audio files, differentiating them from background audio, and permit you to adjust the volume of any sound playing. Chapter 8 discusses sound commands.

Chapter 16, "Text Box Objects," covers the text commands shown in Figure 3-39. These commands permit the contents of text boxes to be searched, written to a file, selected, cut, copied, and pasted, and external text files to be put into Immedia boxes.

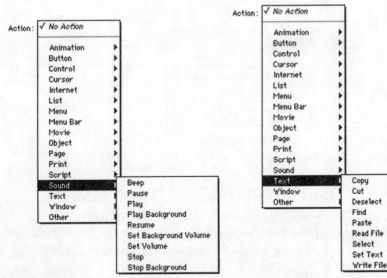

Figure 3-38: The Sound submenu.

Figure 3-39: The Text submenu.

Windows in Immedia are the stuff of computer application windows, floating palettes, and dialog boxes. The Window actions (Figure 3-40) include opening, closing, and setting the title for windows, as well as making a window that you can drag around onscreen. Windows are covered in Chapter 5.

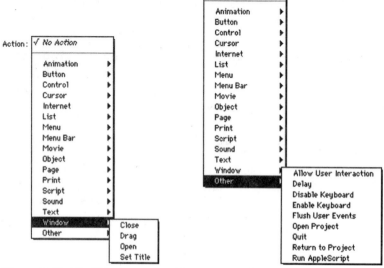

Figure 3-40: The Window submenu.

Figure 3-41: The Other submenu.

A miscellany of commands have been placed in the Other submenu (Figure 3-41). These commands provide a delay between actions, enable or disable the keyboard, run an AppleScript script, account for certain user actions, and open another project. The Other commands are located in the submenu. You can also find the command for quitting your Immedia project here.

The QuarkImmedia Menu

QuarkImmedia

Engage
Use Debugger

MenuMaker...
Custom Transitions...
Make Index...

Export Settings...
Export...

Convert to QuarkXPress...
QuarkImmedia Usage...

About QuarkImmedia...

Figure 3-42: The QuarkImmedia menu.

Immedia adds the QuarkImmedia menu to the Quark-XPress menu bar, with four groupings of commands (Figure 3-42).

Engage & Use Debugger

Engage lets Immedia emulate how the project will behave in the Viewer. Use Debugger activates a window that displays a line for each action occurring in a running project, enabling you to identify exactly what is happening in those situations when things aren't working as you expected.

MenuMaker

MenuMaker, discussed in Chapter 17, is used to create new menus and set up the commands that appear on the menus (Figure 3-43). Each command in a menu runs a script created in the Immedia palette's Script panel.

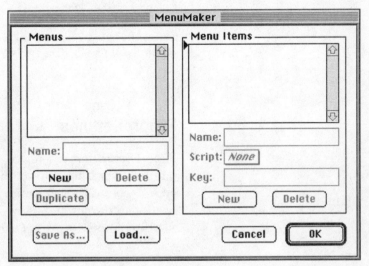

Figure 3-43: The MenuMaker dialog box.

Custom Transitions

Custom Transitions (Figure 3-44) lets you adjust the 17 standard transitional effects (such as dissolve and fade) in Immedia, as well as make permanent variations.

In Immedia you can use Make Index to create a searchable index of text files in your project, which you can use to facilitate certain List actions.

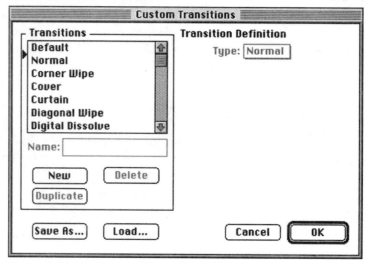

Figure 3-44: The Custom Transitions dialog box.

Export Settings

Export Settings is where you choose compression settings (Figure 3-45). These are settings for audio and video in your exported project, and where you enter creator identification information (Figure 3-46). You then create a freestanding Immedia project using the Export command.

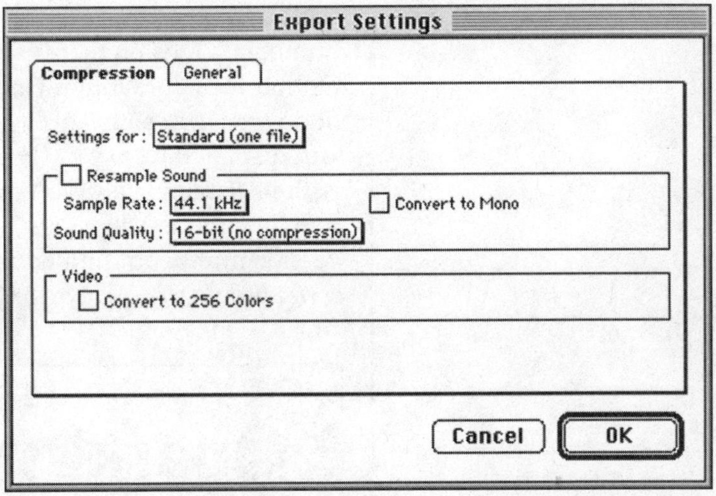

Figure 3-45: Export settings for compression.

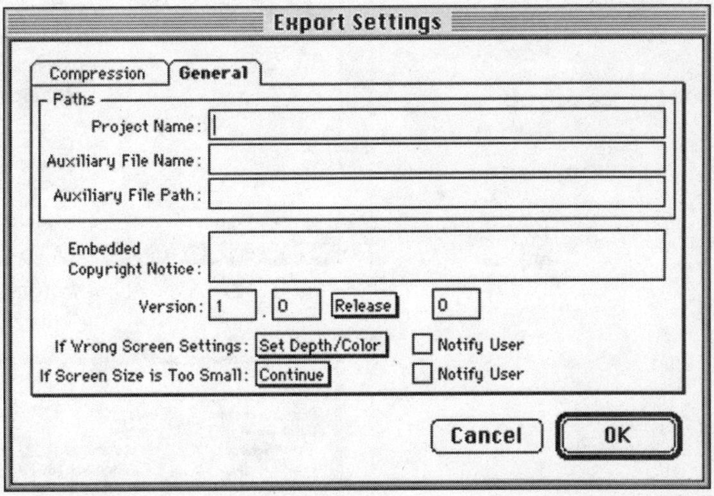

Figure 3-46: Export settings for text.

Use Convert to QuarkXPress (when an Immedia project is active) or Convert to QuarkImmedia (with a QuarkXPress document active) when you're working with a file intended for screen or print but you need it in the other medium. Fully realized documents and projects require significant adjustment with this type of conversion; there are no free lunches here.

About QuarkImmedia identifies the version of the Immedia XTension that is active (Figure 3-47). Pressing Option-Help, or Option-Command-?, or depressing Option when choosing Apple Menu | About QuarkXPress, will display the QuarkXPress Environment dialog box, with its list of installed XTensions. Highlighting Quark-Immedia in the XTensions list will identify not only the version number of Immedia you are using but also the serial number (Figure 3-48).

Figure 3-47: About QuarkImmedia.

QuarkXPress® Environment		
XPress Version :	3.32	**XTensions :**
Patch Level :	5	QuarkImmedia
Serial Number :	XA40008226	
Machine Type :	Power Mac 6100/60	
32-bit QuickDraw :	Yes	
Floating Point Unit :	No	
Main Monitor Depth :	8	
Keyboard Type :	Extended Keybd	
Memory :	4624096/	
System Version :	7.5.5	
Language :	U.S. English	
Script Manager Version :	7.1.0	
Printer Name :	–	
Color SW 2400 :	7.0	XTension Serial # : IA1001
Max Files Open :	40	©1996 Quark, Inc. – 1.0

`OK` `User Reg. Info.` `Create Reg. Disk`

Figure 3-48: QuarkXPress Environment dialog box.

QuarkImmedia Preferences

In addition to having application, general, typographic, trapping, and tools preferences, you now also have certain default settings, or preferences, in effect with QuarkImmedia. These pertain to your project—such things as what scripts to run when you begin and end the project, or when nothing is happening, and whether or not to display a menu bar—and to the appearance of interactive text and text that isn't rasterized on export (Figure 3-49). As you might expect, changing these preferences with a project open affects only that project. With no project open, new settings become the default for every new project.

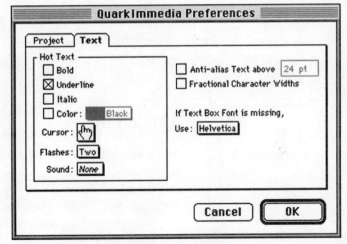

Figure 3-49: QuarkImmedia text preferences.

Buttons, Animation & Cursors

Immedia's multi-state buttons, flip book style animation, and animated cursors are all created in similar grid-style editing windows (and discussed in detail in Chapters 10, 14, and 15, respectively). You get to the appropriate window using File | New | Animation and File | New | Cursor for animation and cursors (Figure 3-50), but buttons are created using a button library (Figure 3-51).

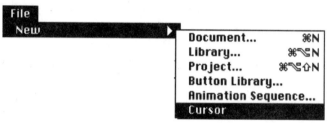

Figure 3-50: File | New submenu.

Figure 3-51: A button library.

Moving On

Since Immedia relies on QuarkXPress for its interface and design tools and follows an intuitive approach to making multimedia actions, most people will find learning Immedia easy going in the initial stages. In our experience teaching Immedia to new users, elation bordering on ecstatic reverence greets the first day or so of material. We have also seen that, eventually, the new users are overwhelmed by the many features in the program. The features have been split up between menus and palettes and then divided among the six panels in the palette; also, these panels have a never-static structure. Any quirky or non-obvious steps seem to pass into incomprehensibility.

Rest assured, after time to digest the details, comprehension rules again.

In this book, we have taken pains to emphasize the central line in every action, stressing what you are doing and why. In the chapters that follow, two (and sometimes more) exercises translate "features" into procedures—not "what this is" but "here's what you use this for" and "here's how to use this" and "this is what it looks like." We know you'll learn more by doing the exercises than by reading explanations, so we've included step-by-step illustrations so you won't go astray. And, of course, the finished exercises are located on the Companion CD-ROM so you can study each aspect in case you have problems.

The overview of features in this chapter, primarily of the QuarkImmedia palette and the centrally important Action pop-up menu, provides you with the lay of the land, so you know in general what's out there.

Now it's time to really get our hands on the program and begin making projects. We try to make each exercise focus on the features covered in that chapter, and that means we have struggled to find content that lends itself to particular approaches. Usually the exercises are independent of each other. We've found that the big project that uses every feature in the program only muddles things up in the beginning user's head.

In the next chapter, we'll begin with the most basic steps: how to begin a new project, create Immedia objects, and make user activity (like clicking) trigger Immedia multimedia activity.

chapter 4

Creating Multimedia: Making a Project

Now it's time to get down to brass tacks: mastering the Immedia tools and making multimedia projects. Part of your QuarkXPress work methods will not change. Creating for electronic publication is similar to creating for print. You still need to lay out pages with text and picture boxes, spec type, and crop and size pictures. One thing has changed though—you have to look at your project page differently, imagining it from your user's perspective: What size screen will they have? How fast is the computer they're using? Can they tell what parts of the page to interact with? Will they react as we expect them to, or have we done something ambiguous or misleading?

You'll have to develop new visual cues to let your projects' users know where to click and how to navigate from page to page.

In this book, we'll start with simple projects of only a few pages, but as you go through the various exercises, and as you begin your own projects, you'll want to map out what links exist and how best to display the nonlinear information. You'll need to determine which of the following ways you want to present the information.

- On a new page—accessible from every other page?
- In a box that pops up next to an object—which requires you to "program" the box to remove it from the display?
- In a window—so it can be around the screen, and remain visible until its close box is clicked?

Where once you could sketch out a design as a sequence of thumbnail images, now you'll diagram multipath flow charts, with many arrows from any one page leading to many other pages. By the end of this book you'll be designing sound and motion, too. How you "diagram" that is up to you. Take note now that you have to keep many more considerations in mind as you proceed.

For now, we'll start with the basics—how to begin, how to create objects, how to get from page to page, and how to pop up information. Let's get started.

Beginning a Project

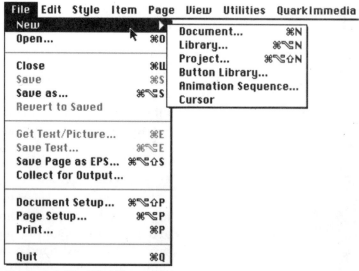

Figure 4-1: The File | New submenu.

Starting a project in QuarkImmedia begins naturally with the File | New submenu. As you can see in Figure 4-1, the QuarkXPress menu has sprouted four new options:

- Project
- Button Library
- Animation Sequence
- Cursor

You'll choose the first of these new options—Project. We'll defer discussion of the other choices until Chapter 10, "Buttons," and Chapter 13, "Playing Animations."

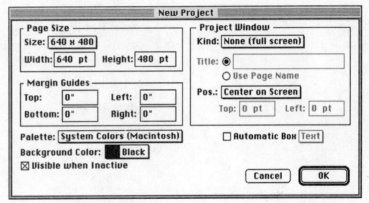

Figure 4-2: The New Project dialog box.

As with a new QuarkXPress document, the command to start a new project requires you to specify the page size and margins (Figure 4-2). You also choose whether you want text and picture boxes to appear on the page automatically. These settings should be familiar; they're almost the same as they are in XPress.

Options more specific to a screen project and not print publication are also set here. The Project Window area, which takes the place of the Column Guide area, has settings for displaying the project window. Other settings you can select include a specific color palette and the color to display around your project; you can also specify whether the project window will remain visible when the user opens another application.

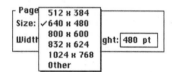

Figure 4-3: Page Size pop-up menu.

Selecting a Page Size

Let's go through the options for selecting a page size, one by one. The Page Size field settings (Figure 4-3) include five preset screen sizes. You can enter other dimensions, measured in points, in the Width and Height fields. Of course, screens are measured using pixels and most monitors have a resolution of 72 pixels to the inch, but since 72 points—a point is a standard printing unit—equals 1 inch, and most monitors have a resolution of 72 pixels to the inch (or thereabouts), for our purposes a point equals a pixel. This "screen point," to coin a label, will shrink at higher resolutions as pixels get smaller, and you won't be able to translate reliably between screen points (or pixels) and inches. But due to the availability of these preset page size options, you won't often need to translate between pixels and inches. The preset page size options are:

- 512 x 384
- 640 x 480
- 800 x 600
- 832 x 624
- 1024 x 768

Beware of choosing sizes larger than 640 x 480 unless you know specifically the monitor on which your project/presentation is playing. While PC users can display higher resolutions on a 14-inch monitor, many Mac users with that size monitor are restricted to a resolution of 640 x 480. Remember, too, that laptop computers may use different proportions, for instance, 640 x 440. You'll have to manually enter those dimensions—or any others for your project—in the Width and Height fields.

Specifying a Background Color

If your project doesn't use the full size of the user's screen, you can specify a color to display between the edge of the page and the edge of the monitor using the Background

Color pop-up menu (Figure 4-4). Black is the factory-set default, but like the other options in the New Project Setup dialog box, and like those in the New Document dialog box in XPress, the setting you use in one project becomes the default value for the next. Unless you change the settings that come with the program, the colors available in the Background Color pop-up menu include the standard screen colors of black, white, red, green, and blue, as well as colors intended for print purposes: cyan, yellow, magenta, and registration. To make a color part of your own default preferences, it must be added while no document or project is open. Do this the same way you add colors in XPress. Use Edit | Colors to open the Default Colors dialog box and add new colors.

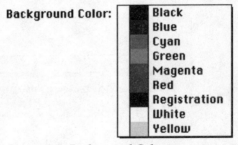

Background Color:

- Black
- Blue
- Cyan
- Green
- Magenta
- Red
- Registration
- White
- Yellow

Figure 4-4: Background Color pop-up menu.

Choosing a Color Palette

Immedia restricts the number of colors you can use in a project to 256 colors or shades of gray. As you see in Figure 4-5, you may use the standard Macintosh system palette, either color or grayscale, the standard Windows system palette, or a custom palette of 256 colors or less, which you've created using an application like Adobe Photoshop or Equilibrium DeBabelizer.

Figure 4-5: Choosing a color palette for your project.

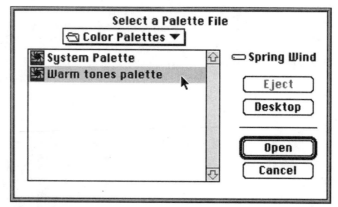

Figure 4-6: Accessing custom palettes using the Select a Palette File dialog box.

Figure 4-7: A custom palette appearing in the Palette pop-up menu.

You can choose a custom color palette for your project using the Custom Colors option in the Palette pop-up menu (Figure 4-5). This calls up the Select a Palette File dialog box (Figure 4-6), from which you can navigate to any location on your local drive or network. Once you choose a custom color palette, it will be displayed in the Palette pop-up menu (Figure 4-7) as an available choice for this project.

Creating Custom Color Palettes

While Photoshop can create a palette that is best suited for a particular color image, DeBabelizer has a capability well-suited to your needs. It can create a color palette that's optimized for all of the images in your project. Of course, the more diverse the color range of your photos, the less satisfactory any single group of 256 colors is going to be for any specific image. Any color in the image that does not appear in the palette will be replaced by a color that does, which may change the way the image looks. In general, for the best results you'll want to use images that share color characteristics.

For the sake of convenience, you may want to place all your color palettes in a standard location. While an adaptive palette may suit one photo or a set of related photos, you may also find over time that certain standard palettes that you develop work best for a variety of images. Putting them all together makes it easier for you to access a color palette for subsequent projects.

Note that a pixel of the color mapped to, say, number 100, may display as red in one palette, and green or yellow (or any color) in other palettes. The use of a single palette for your project is a limitation you can only surmount by much experimentation and planning.

TIP

The system palettes for both Windows and Macintosh contain 256 colors, but 40 of them are not the same. Because Mac and Windows computers display different colors for these 40, your images may not look the same on both platforms.

We've included a color palette with the 216 colors that are the same on both platforms on the Companion CD-ROM.

CD-ROM

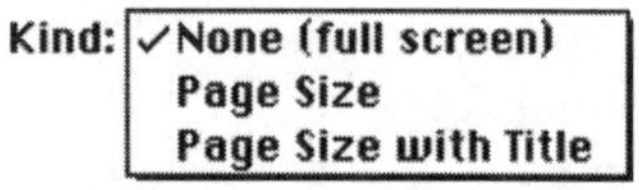

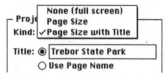

Figure 4-8: Controls regarding the appearance of your project window in the Kind pop-up menu.

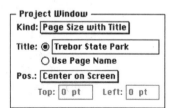

Figure 4-9: Setting a title for your project window.

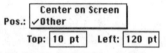

Figure 4-10: Centering the project window on the user's screen.

Figure 4-11: Positioning the project window on the user's screen.

Deciding on a Kind of Project Window

Since your project will display in a window on the viewing user's computer screen, you must also make some decisions regarding this window's looks and behavior. The Project Window area has several controls affecting this. If you want the plainest possible window, occupying the full page size you have already established, choose the first option "None (full screen)" from the Kind pop-up menu (see Figure 4-8). Full screen might be the best choice for a presentation running from a local hard disk or CD-ROM drive.

Adding a Title to Your Project Window

An intranet or Internet project would probably be better served by a window that includes a title bar, so that it can be moved around the screen as the user interacts with other programs. The title bar can be unlabeled, or display a label or title that you specify in the Title area (see Figures 4-9 and 4-10). You also have the option of using as a title the name that you give to an individual page in the QuarkImmedia palette's Page panel. This will, of course, enable the title bar to assist the user in distinguishing among your pages.

Positioning Your Project Window on the Screen

Use the Pos. (for position) pop-up menu in the Project Window area of the New Project Setup dialog box to position your project window on the screen. You can specify whether the window is centered on the screen where the project plays, or whether the upper-left corner of the project should be positioned at an exact location as shown in Figure 4-11. The Top and Left fields specify the distance from the top of the user's screen and from its left side, in pixels (or "screen points"), when the project window is smaller than the monitor.

Indicating the Visibility of Your Project Window

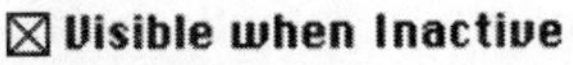

A related control, Visible when Inactive, lets you specify whether your project window displays in the background on-screen when another application is active. It does this when the check box is checked (see Figure 4-12). Otherwise the project window will be hidden when inactive.

Setting Page Margins

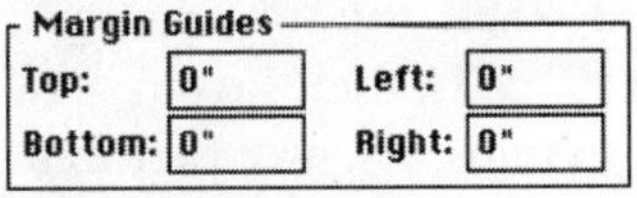

Setting margins in your project (Figure 4-13) works the same as it does with a new QuarkXPress document. In the Margin Guides area you can enter numbers in a variety of measurement units, as long as you also specify the unit you are using in the following manner:

"	inches
p	picas
pt	points
m	millimeters
cm	centimeters
c	ciceros (a French typesetting measure)

If the default unit of measurement is inches, say, then you don't have to enter the inch mark. But be alert, because even when you choose inches as your default, Immedia and XPress specify other units for some fields.

TIP

As you know from QuarkXPress, the default units are set in the General Preferences, which you get to using the Edit | Preferences | General command. Because of the equivalence between "screen points" and pixels, you may want to try using points as your default unit of measurement.

In the margin fields, as in all numeric fields in dialog boxes and the Measurements palette, you can enter arithmetic phrases, such as 1" + 18 pt, and the program will perform the calculation for you and then translate the result into your default measurement unit.

☒ **Visible when Inactive**

Figure 4-12: Does the project window disappear when another program window becomes active?

Margin Guides
Top: 0" Left: 0"
Bottom: 0" Right: 0"

Figure 4-13: The Margin Guides area.

Using the Automatic Text or Picture Feature

With a QuarkXPress document, using the automatic text box implies some sort of running text (since the boxes on your pages are typically linked together sequentially), and hence, the need for margins.

In your Immedia project, the automatic text box (Figure 4-14) behaves as it does in a document, linking automatically from page to page when the default settings are in effect. However, since you can now place a picture box on the page automatically (Figure 4-15), you may prefer to eliminate margins, setting the value in the Margin Guides area fields to zero. With no margins, any pictures used as backgrounds will fill the active page area without manual adjustment.

Figure 4-14: Check here to place a text or picture box on your page automatically.

Figure 4-15: Setting up an automatic picture box.

Changing a Project's Setup

Once set, you can modify any of these settings—except the margins and automatic boxes—using the File | Project Setup command (Figures 4-16 and 4-17). As you might expect, margins are changed in the Master Guides dialog box, which you access using the Page | Master Guides command. As you may remember from QuarkXPress, you can only access the Master Guides dialog box when a master page is active.

Figure 4-16: Project Setup command.

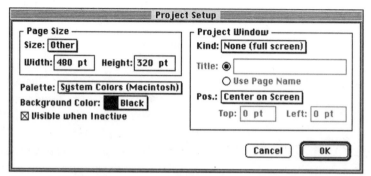

Figure 4-17: The Project Setup dialog box.

Laying Out a Page

You lay out an Immedia page the same way you do an XPress document page. Place text boxes wherever you want copy or headlines, enter or import the text, then select type and spec it (set font, size, and leading) using the Style menu or Measurement palette controls. Graphics go into picture boxes, including those made with the Polygon Picture Box tool, which makes it possible for you to make many-sided boxes of any shape. With polygon picture boxes, a face can appear through the shape of a star, or a skyscraper can appear in silhouette.

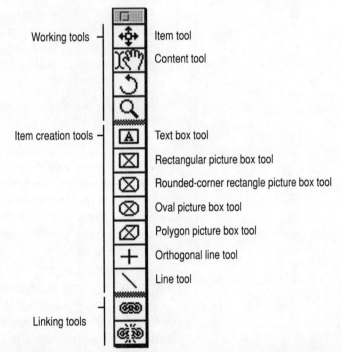

Working tools — Item tool
Content tool

Item creation tools — Text box tool
Rectangular picture box tool
Rounded-corner rectangle picture box tool
Oval picture box tool
Polygon picture box tool
Orthogonal line tool
Line tool

Linking tools —

Figure 4-18: The QuarkXPress tool palette. The Item Creation tools add items to your page. They can then be identified as Immedia objects.

The Easiest Method to Size Pictures

QuarkXPress has a superb method for sizing pictures that doesn't use a menu command, and which consequently doesn't seem to be widely known. It's simple though and quickly gets you what you want.

1. Use the Get Picture command to put a picture inside a picture box.

2. Drag the box handles or the picture itself until you have the precise cropping you want (nudging the graphic with the keyboard arrow keys provides easy fine tuning).

3. Depress the Command, Shift, and Option keys and, at the same time, drag any box handle toward or away from the center of the box to enlarge or shrink the picture and the box simultaneously.

Result: your graphic will be exactly the size you want with exactly the cropping you want.

While constructing the page is the same, the flow of a project is unlike that of a QuarkXPress document. Sequencing is multipath, since any one page can lead to other pages. And you can literally keep peripheral information on the periphery—that is, on the pasteboard and off of the page still at hand, popping up at a mouse click or other initiating event. Constructing the Immedia project page involves many steps irrelevant to a print project.

As described in Chapter 2, "The QuarkImmedia Methodology," in the section "How Immedia Thinks," you will identify some of the text and some of the graphics on your page as Immedia objects. This simply means you're giving them the right to have interactive properties when the project is played. Any items—QuarkXPress text boxes, picture boxes, or lines—not specifically named in the Immedia palette as an object are treated as background as far as our project is concerned. They are visible, but not interactive.

A user can interact with an object in a handful of ways:

- Clicking
- Double-clicking
- Pressing the Option key (or, if running Windows, clicking with the right mouse button)
- Rolling the mouse over the object

Actually, Immedia makes even more of these user events by separating the pressing down and the release of the mouse button when the user is clicking (click down and click up), and by distinguishing between the mouse pointer passing over the object and then passing off the object (mouse enter and mouse exit).

Thus a user can interact with an object in six different ways, and any interaction—what Immedia calls a user event—can trigger any of the more than 100 different types of actions that Immedia provides.

So, after we know what our page should look like, and have planned the paths through our information for the user, and prepared our audio and video and animations, and then actually created the pages and put the boxes on the page and the text and pictures into the boxes, our work in Immedia breaks down into these simple steps:

- Give our objects names.
- Associate specific user events (clicking, mouse enter, and so on) with specific actions (display next page, play video, and so on).

And you'll always start this process by selecting a QuarkXPress item and giving it a name in the Immedia palette.

To follow the discussion below, choose the File | New | Project command now to create a new project. If you don't have QuarkImmedia, there is a demo version on the Companion CD-ROM that you can use as you go through the following sections.

Creating Objects

To give a QuarkXPress item interactive properties, you must display the QuarkImmedia palette. Choose the View | Show QuarkImmedia Palette command (Figure 4-19) if your palette is not currently visible. If the command reads "Hide QuarkImmedia Palette," then the palette is already onscreen and choosing the command will remove it. With the advent of the WindowShade control panel, you might have lost sight of the minimized palette. Choosing first Hide, then Show redisplays the palette at full size.

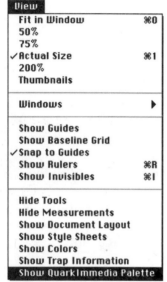

Figure 4-19: To display the QuarkImmedia palette onscreen, choose the Show QuarkImmedia Palette command in the View menu.

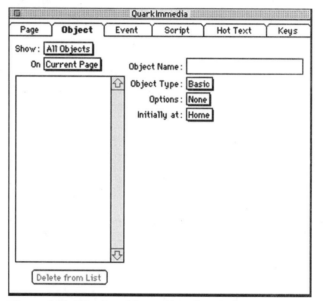

Figure 4-20: The QuarkImmedia palette before any objects have been created.

The QuarkImmedia palette has six tabs across its top as seen in Figure 4-20. Click the Object tab to open the Object palette. The Object scrollable list appears blank. (All of the options for this and the other panels were discussed in detail in Chapter 3, "The QuarkImmedia Palette & Menu.") You can make any text box, picture box, or line on your page into an object. If your page is blank, add picture and text boxes to your page now.

TIP

Don't be confused if you find you can make items into objects in a standard QuarkXPress document. Obviously, print documents can't have interactive properties, but this isn't a mistake. Sometimes, you'll want to convert existing documents into projects. There's a special command for this—QuarkImmedia | Convert to QuarkImmedia. (There's a reverse action too, a command for making a project into a document—Convert to QuarkXPress.) Making objects before you have a project is just a way of giving you a head start on the conversion. Creating an object requires only that you select an item on your page, then click in the Object Name field in the Immedia palette and enter a name. Pressing Return or Enter completes the action and adds the name to the Object scrollable list. Clicking in the scroll list, on another tab, or outside the palette, or choosing one of the Object Type options also adds the name.

TIP

The Object Type pop-up menu omits one category: the button object. You can't create a button object from a QuarkXPress item. Instead you use the tools in the editing windows of a button library to create or modify buttons. The creation and use of buttons is discussed in full in Chapter 10, "Buttons."

Naming Objects

The name you enter can have upper and lowercase characters, spaces, numbers, accented letters, and punctuation in it. Some characters, such as those made with the Shift and Option keys, are missing from the font used in the QuarkImmedia palette and will show up here as an indecipherable box. You can make the name as long as you need, over a hundred characters if you must, but only the first 20 or so characters will display in the scrollable list.

Consistency in capitalization, as well as use of hyphens and spaces and the like will help you stay in control of a complex project. As you'll learn, the events you'll construct consist of a variety of parts, of which the object is only the first. You may find it easiest to add the word "object" or "obj" when you name an object to distinguish it from these other parts, all of which you'll want to give similar names because of their association with each other. This will help you distinguish among the steps you take for the most complex activities, at least until you have mastered the full logic of Immedia.

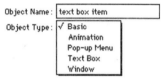

Figure 4-21: Object types for a text box.

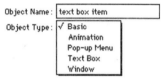

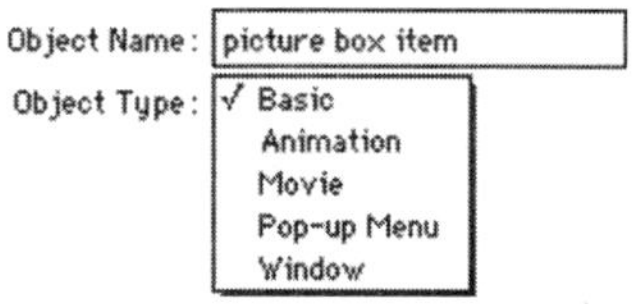

Figure 4-22: Object types for a picture box.

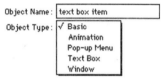

Figure 4-23: Object types for a line.

The second step in making an object is to specify what type of object it will be. Text boxes (Figure 4-21), picture boxes (Figure 4-22), and lines (Figure 4-23) can all be converted to objects, but not all object types can be made from every type of item. That is, you can't put a movie in a text box or line.

In this chapter we'll look at just two types: basic and window, reserving discussion of the other types for later chapters.

A basic object is an item that now can have multimedia properties assigned to it. You might regard the basic object type as the core set of properties and the other types—animation object, movie object, and so on—as having additional properties.

The basic object type is assigned by default to a new object when you create it. At any time you can switch the object type by choosing one of the other options in the Object Type pop-up menu.

You assign properties to a basic object in the Options and Initially at pop-up menu in the Object panel as shown in Figure 4-24. Depending on whether (and when) you want the user to interact with your basic object, or if it's intended simply to display information, you may choose to make it

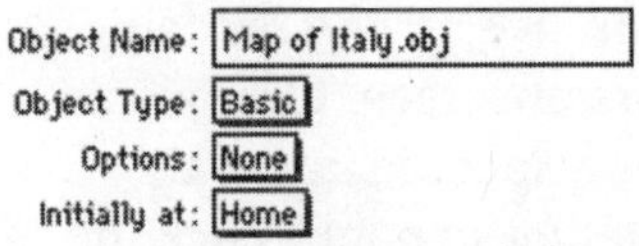

Object Name: Map of Italy .obj
Object Type: Basic
Options: None
Initially at: Home

Figure 4-24: Default settings for a newly created object.

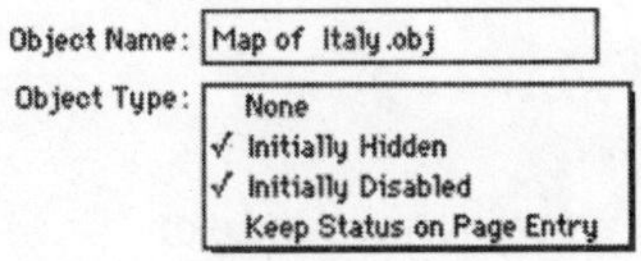

Object Name: Map of Italy .obj
Object Type:
  None
  √ Initially Hidden
  √ Initially Disabled
  Keep Status on Page Entry

Figure 4-25: Options for a basic object (picture box).

Options: √ None
  Searchable Contents
  Initially Hidden
  Initially Disabled
  Keep Status on Page Entry

Figure 4-26: Options for a basic object (text box).

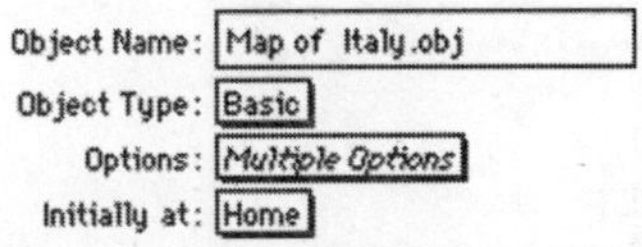

Object Name: Map of Italy.obj
Object Type: Basic
Options: Multiple Options
Initially at: Home

Figure 4-27: "Multiple Options" appears when more than one option is chosen.

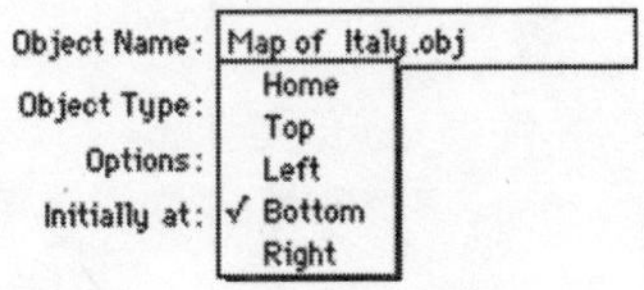

Object Name: Map of Italy .obj
Object Type:
  Home
  Top
  Left
Options:
  √ Bottom
Initially at: Right

Figure 4-28: Choosing which pasteboard should hold an object.

invisible, or hidden, when the page is first entered, or as well as to disable its features (see Figure 4-25). Then some subsequent activity will reveal or activate it.

Of course, this raises the issue of what to do with the object if the user leaves the page and then comes back—should things stay as they are or should they revert to their original state? "Keep Status on Page Entry" provides for the former. Otherwise, conditions revert.

TIP

Assigning and changing multimedia properties in the Immedia palette is as direct as changing the settings displayed in the pop-up menus and text fields for the highlighted entry in the scrollable list. You don't have to execute a change, such as clicking an OK button, in any way.

This means there's no going back to previous settings by canceling your actions, because there's no Cancel button, either.

Clicking outside the Immedia palette and saving your project provides you with a modicum of reversibility since you have recourse to the File | Revert to Saved command. This command will discard every change you have made since you last saved your project.

A text box made into a basic object has an additional option. If you provide the user with the ability to search through your project, you have to specify which of your objects have content that should be examined during the user search. That's why you would declare the object has "searchable contents" (Figure 4-26).

When check marks appear beside more than one option, the single-line pop-up menu indicates this by displaying "*Multiple Options*" as shown in Figure 4-27.

Rather than hide an object, it may make more sense to position it off the page on the pasteboard when the page is first entered. The Initially at pop-up menu lets you specify which pasteboard—on the left or right, above or below the page—should hold the object (Figure 4-28).

Then something the user does can trigger the reposition-
ing of the object so that it appears onscreen. Or you can
program the item to appear after a specific interval.

Having created an object in the Object panel, click the
Event tab to set up what happens when a user interacts
with your object.

Events

We are always distinguishing between what the user
does—the user event—and how the project responds—the
action. But since, practically speaking, you don't have one
without the other, we'll term the two activities together as
simply an "event."

The Event panel shown in Figure 4-29 puts the controls
for both ends of an event in one place. It adds the finishing
touches of specifying certain sounds and cursor shapes to
aurally and visually indicate an event. But we will defer
discussion of these aspects for now. What we're interested
in are the User Event and Action pop-up menus.

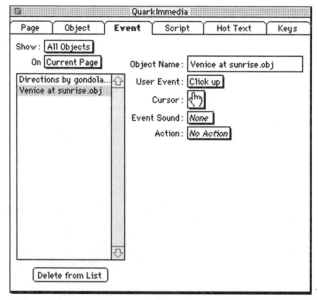

*Figure 4-29: The Event tab allows you to determine what happens
when a user interacts with your object.*

As we said earlier in this chapter, the user can do a handful of things with the mouse to interact with your project—press the mouse button and release it, double-click, move the mouse onto or off of the object, click the right mouse button on a PC, or click while depressing the Option key on a Macintosh.

Each of these activities can have a separate action associated with it in your project, and its own sound and its own cursor. And the user can interact with any object in more than one way. With the scrollable list of objects on the left side, the six different user events and the more than one hundred potential actions in the Action pop-up menu, the Event panel is a happening place. And one in which you will have to be alert in order to keep everything straight.

User Events

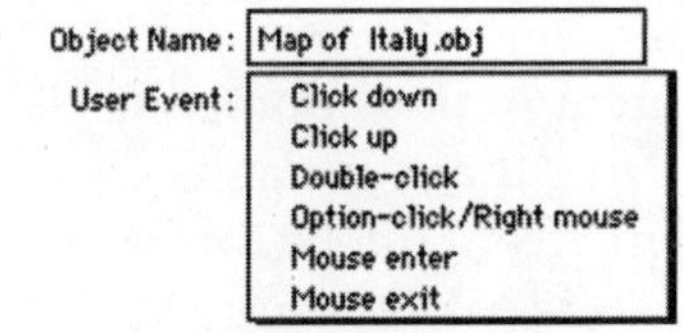

Immedia defines the user events precisely (Figure 4-30). A mouse click is divided into two components: depressing the mouse—click down—and releasing—click up. Use click up when you want your action triggered by a mouse click, and reserve click down for times when you want your action to occur only while the mouse button stays depressed (what is widely known as a mouse "press"). Then you'll halt or reverse your action with the click up.

Clicking with the Option key depressed (Macintosh) or with the right mouse button (PC) lacks the same distinctions: a click is just a click.

Double-clicking and the click up and click down user events are mutually exclusive—designating one grays out the other in the pop-up menu. Usually double-clicking means a specific type of action—opening or launching. And single clicking usually indicates selection. However, with the advent of our hyperlinks and buttons, most users will expect a single click to initiate an action. Use double-clicking only in those circumstances where a single click might be ambiguous, or users would, by experience, anticipate double-clicking.

Object Name: | Map of Italy .obj

User Event:
- Click down
- Click up
- Double-click
- Option-click/Right mouse
- Mouse enter
- Mouse exit

Figure 4-30: User events: ways the user can interact with the object.

Mouse enter and mouse exit comprise the two parts of a mouse "rollover." When a pointer moves on top of an object, you have the mouse enter user event. If you want the action to halt or disappear when the pointer is no longer on top of the object, you specify that in conjunction with the mouse exit.

Actions

If user events are what makes a project interactive, then actions are what make it multimedia. The Action pop-up menu consists of 17 submenus and one singular item: *No Action* (see Figure 4-31).

"No Action" means, for the mouse action showing in the User Event pop-up menu, nothing will occur. It's what you choose when you want to deactivate a user event.

By default, all the user events are set to *No Action* for a newly created object (Figure 4-32).

We will be discussing the different Action submenus through the course of this book. Note that you can't access the Action | Control submenu from the Event panel. It's meant only for scripts and is always gray here (Figure 4-31).

For now let's look at just two of the submenus—Page and Object.

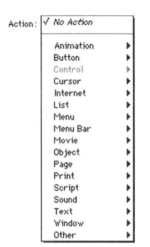

Figure 4-31: The Action pop-up menu.

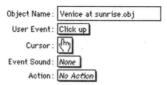

Figure 4-32: Default view and settings for a newly created object.

Display a Page

Six of the choices in the Page submenu (Figure 4-33) jump the project display to another page.

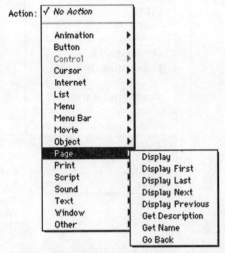

Figure 4-33: Actions you can perform with a page.

Display First, Display Last, Display Next, and Display Previous coincide with the XPress Page menu commands First, Last, Next, and Previous and switch the display to the first page of the project, the last page of the project, the next page, or the previous page. You may well associate these actions with standard buttons placed on every page.

If you check the Page Wraparound check box in the Immedia Preferences dialog box (see Figures 4-34 and 4-35), then the first and last pages of the project will be connected. On the last page, Display Next takes the user to the first page, and vice versa. Otherwise, on the first and last pages, Display Previous and Display Next have no effect.

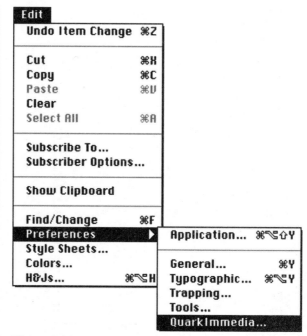

Figure 4-34: How to access QuarkImmedia preferences.

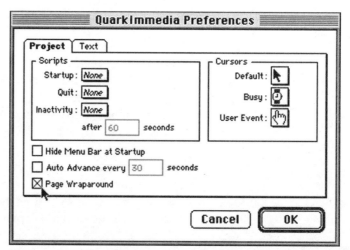

Figure 4-35: Check Page Wraparound to connect the first and last pages of your project.

Go Back returns the user to whatever page was previously viewed. Of course, in a hyperlink world, this could be any page.

Two options, Get Name and Get Description, are used in grabbing information from the Page panel—either the page name or the text you use to describe it—and inserting it into a text box object in your project.

The submenu's first option allows you to make the project jump to a particular page. You can identify the page by number or name (see Figure 4-36). As discussed in the next chapter, giving a page a name prevents a variety of problems and is the preferred option.

Any of these commands relating to page display permit a sound to be associated with a page change, with any of the 18 built-in transitions (or any custom ones you create), and with the amount of time it takes to make the transition. Transitions are discussed in full in Chapter 5, "Window Objects."

The simplest type of interactivity you can build into your project is to create an object, then associate the click up user event with the command to display a specific page. From this directability springs the multipath essence of multimedia.

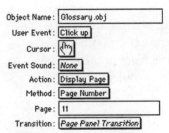

Figure 4-36: Display a specific page, identified by number.

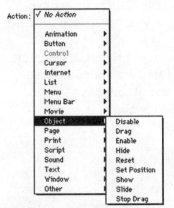

Figure 4-37: Actions you can perform with an object.

Display an Object

Since you can choose to place an object off to the side on the pasteboard when you first create it, you might wonder why you would do that and how you bring the object back "home" (the spot where it was placed on the page).

Use the Set Position option on the Action | Object submenu, shown in Figure 4-37, to shift objects back home and to the side of the page. A variety of options are presented to you when you choose this action, chiefly what object you want to position and by what method. We'll focus on Home and To Sides, but you can also move it to an exact location using (x,y) Position, away from its current position using (x,y) Offset, or to align with another object (Figure 4-38). As you would expect, the exact options in the display vary depending on the method you choose.

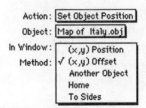

Figure 4-38: Methods of positioning an object.

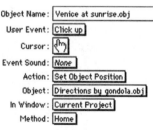

Object Name: Venice at sunrise.obj
User Event: Click up
Cursor: 🖑
Event Sound: None
Action: Set Object Position
Object: Directions by gondola.obj
In Window: Current Project
Method: Home

Figure 4-39: Event panel options with Set Object Position as the action.

Keep in mind that the user's interaction with one object will initiate an action with a second object—the one you want to move. So you begin by highlighting that first object in the scrollable list (making the name visible in the Object Name field), designating one of the user events, and identifying the action as Set Object Position.

With that done, you then choose the object to move and the method (Figure 4-39). As with other actions, you can switch cursors and accompany the action with a sound if you desire. You can also move an object in the current project window or within a window object.

Exercise 4-1

Now it's your turn. You'll create a project from scratch, performing the operations we've just discussed—making objects, adding events, changing the display from one page to another, and moving an object. No special files are needed for this exercise.

And of course, you'll run the project to test it, using the Engage command in the QuarkImmedia menu. Engage enables you to operate the project without having to formally export it and test it in the Viewer.

Set Up the Project

1. To begin a new project, Select the File | New | Project command. Set the page size to 480 points wide by 320 points high.

    You can leave the other settings as they are: margins zero for all, palette set to Macintosh system colors, background color of black, Visible when Inactive checked, the Project Window Kind set to None, the position to Center on Screen, and the Automatic Box unchecked (Figure 4-40).

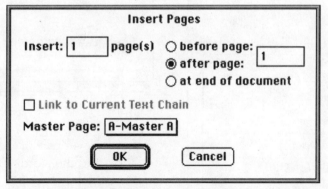

New Project

┌ Page Size ─────────────
Size: [Other]
Width: [480 pt]   Height: [320 pt]

┌ Margin Guides ─────
Top: [0p]   Left: [0p]
Bottom: [0p]   Right: [0p]

Palette: [System Colors (Macintosh)]
Background Color: [■] [Black]
☒ Visible when Inactive

┌ Project Window ─────
Kind: [None (full screen)]
Title: ◉ [   ]
○ Use Page Name
Pos.: [Center on Screen]
Top: [0 pt]   Left: [0 pt]

☐ Automatic Box [Text]

[Cancel] [OK]

Figure 4-40: Settings for Exercise 4-1 in the New Project dialog box.

2. Once you have the project page displayed, choose the Page | Insert command (Figure 4-41) and insert another page, following page 1 (Figure 4-42).

Page
Insert...
Delete...
Move...

Master Guides...
Section...

Previous
Next
First
Last
Go to...   ⌘J

Display   ▶

Figure 4-41: Use Page | Insert to add an extra page to the project.

Insert Pages

Insert: [1]   page(s) ○ before page:
                         ◉ after page: [1]
                         ○ at end of document

☐ Link to Current Text Chain

Master Page: [A-Master A]

[OK]   [Cancel]

Figure 4-42: The default settings in Insert Pages add new pages after the current page.

Set Up the Content

Page
Insert...
Delete...
Move...

Master Guides...
Section...

Previous
Next
First
Last
Go to...   ⌘J

Display   ▶ ✓ *Document*
              A-Master A

Figure 4-43: Use Page | Display | A-Master A to work on the project's master page.

3. Now switch to the project's master page, using the Page | Display | A-Master A command (Figure 4-43). Whatever we add to this page will appear on all our project pages.

4. Use the polygon picture box tool to draw a park-shaped object, occupying the center and upper-right portion of the page. Give it a green background color by selecting green in the Colors palette (View | Show Colors, if the palette isn't visible). Then add a lake-shaped object, colored blue, on top.

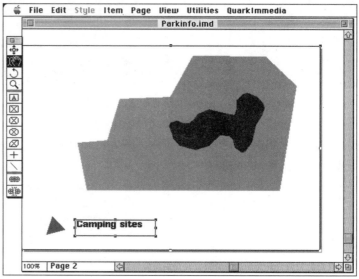

Figure 4-44: Adding in our background shapes.

5. In the lower part of the page, add a small red triangle and the words **Camping sites**, as shown in Figure 4-44.

6. You don't want to perform too many steps without saving your document. We gave our example the name Parkinfo.imd. When you save, click outside the QuarkImmedia palette in your project window to ensure that QuarkXPress recognizes the action.

7. Use Page | Display | Document to switch the display back to page 1.

8. Use the View | Show QuarkImmedia Palette command to display the Immedia palette if it's not already visible (Figure 4-45).

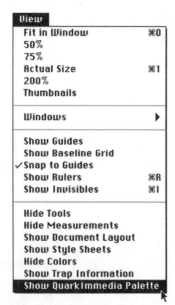

Figure 4-45: The Show QuarkImmedia Palette command.

Now we'll create an Immedia object using the red triangle on page 1 and have it switch the display to page 2 when the user clicks on it. Then we'll perform a similar operation with the triangle on page 2 and make it switch the display back to the first page.

Create Objects & Assign Events

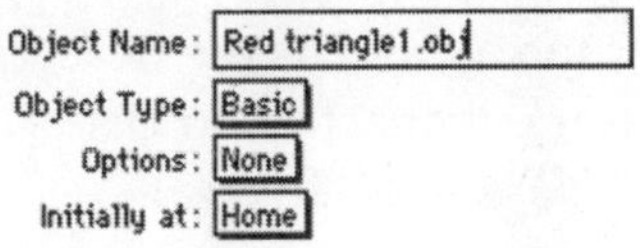

Object Name: Red triangle1.obj
Object Type: Basic
Options: None
Initially at: Home

Figure 4-46: Create an object called "Red triangle1.obj."

9. Select the red triangle on page 1. Click the Object tab in the Immedia palette and click in the Object Name field. Enter a name that clearly identifies the object. We used the name "Red triangle1.obj" (Figure 4-46).

10. Click the Event tab. The Click up user event is already chosen. In the Action pop-up menu, as shown in Figure 4-47, choose the Display command from the Page submenu.

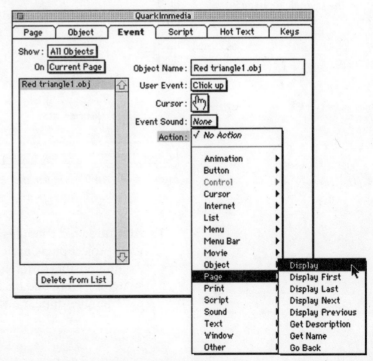

Figure 4-47: Set the action to display a page.

Object Name: Red triangle1.obj
User Event: Click up
Cursor: ⟨ʰᵐ⟩
Event Sound: None
Action: Display Page
Method: Page Number
Page: 2
Transition: Page Panel Transition
Sound: None
Trans. Time: 0

Figure 4-48: Identify page 2.

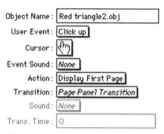

Object Name: Red triangle2.obj
User Event: Click up
Cursor: ⟨ʰᵐ⟩
Event Sound: None
Action: Display First Page
Transition: Page Panel Transition
Sound: None
Trans. Time: 0

*Figure 4-49: Event settings
for the triangle on page 2.*

11. The default method of identifying pages uses page numbers. Enter **2** as the page number (Figure 4-48). This means that when the red triangle on page 1 is clicked, the display will jump to page 2.

12. Now switch to page 2. We'll do the same thing again, only making the action here take us to the first page.
    Select the red triangle at the bottom of the project page. Create an object called "Red triangle2.obj"; you can do this in the Event tab as well as the Object tab. Now set the Click up user event action to Display First Page.

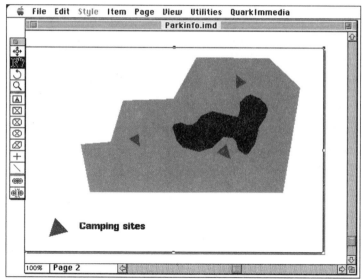

Figure 4-50: Adding information to the map.

13. Add three red triangles to the green park area on your project page, indicating camping sites. This is the only visible difference between pages 1 and 2, so switching from one page to the other will make the red triangles appear and disappear.

Figure 4-51: Choose QuarkImmedia | Engage to see how your project will play in the Viewer.

Test the Links

14. Return to page 1. Before testing, save your project.
   a. Press function key F15 or choose QuarkImmedia | Engage to test the project so far (Figure 4-51).
   b. Click the red triangle at the bottom of page 1 to display the second page—identical to the first with the addition of the camping sites. Click the red triangle on the bottom of the page to return the project to the first page.
   c. To stop or disengage the project, press function key F15 or Command-Q.

Move an Object From the Pasteboard

Now it's time to look at moving an object off the pasteboard and onto the page so we can see it. And when we're done, we'll look at returning the object to the pasteboard.

15. On page 1, add a text box with the words **Lake Perry Como** next to the blue lake, as shown in Figure 4-52.

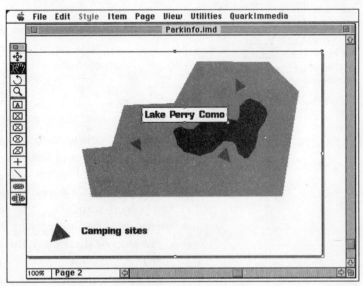

Figure 4-52: Add a text box identifying the lake.

Figure 4-53: Create an object from the box, positioning it initially on the right pasteboard.

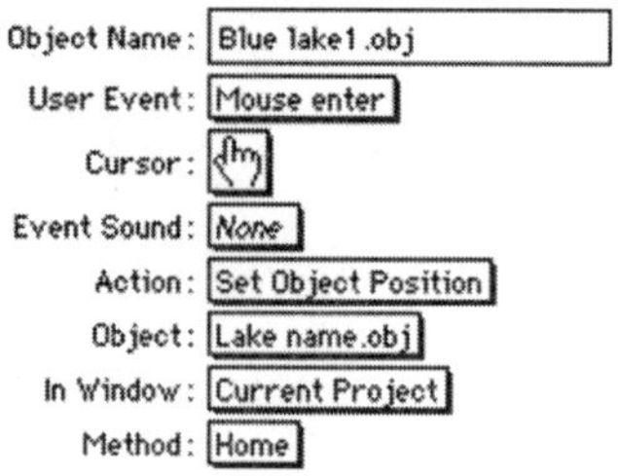

Figure 4-54: Settings for the Mouse enter user event.

Object Name: Blue lake1.obj
User Event: Mouse exit
Cursor:
Event Sound: None
Action: Set Object Position
Object: Lake name.obj
In Window: Current Project
Method: To Sides
Pasteboard: Right

Figure 4-55: Settings for the Mouse exit user event.

In the Object panel, create an object with the name "Lake name.obj." In the Initially at pop-up menu, select Right (see Figure 4-53). The box won't be visible when page 1 is displayed.

16. Select the blue lake. Create an object with the name "Blue lake1.obj."

   In the Event panel, select the user event Mouse enter. In the Action pop-up menu, choose Set Position from the Object submenu. You use the Object pop-up menu to select Lake name.obj; to set the position, choose Home in the Method pop-up menu.

   These settings mean that when the user's mouse enters the lake, the text box with the lake name will move to its home position on the page (where it will be visible).

17. To make the text box disappear when the mouse no longer appears over the lake, you activate another user event.

   a. In the User Event pop-up menu, choose Mouse exit. Again, in the Action pop-up menu, choose Set Position from the Object submenu and Lake name.obj in the Object pop-up menu.

   b. To set the position, choose To Sides in the Method pop-up menu, and Right in the Pasteboard pop-up menu.

Final Test

The final test is to save the project and engage. Move the mouse pointer over the lake to display the name.

   Note that the way we set things up, the name only displays when the user is looking at the first page. Copying objects from page 1 to page 1 allows for shortcut methods of setting up duplicated behavior.

   To stop or disengage the project, press Command-Q or F15.

Problems?
If your project doesn't seem to work right, try running the finished project located on the Companion CD-ROM. It's located in the Exercise folder, in the folder called Exer04-1.

In QuarkXPress, you simply open the project called Exer04-1.imd. You can engage the project to see exactly what is intended. And you can click any object name and study the settings in the Object and Event panels to guide you in locating any place you may have gone astray.

■ Exercise 4-2

Let's do it again, this time using the same features to a different effect. We'll work with material that's been created for this exercise, located on the Companion CD-ROM. The elements for this project are located in the Exercise folder, in the folder called Exer04-2.

The project you'll complete has three pages. Instead of a park and lake, we'll take a tour of Venice, a city on a lagoon with a canal running through it.

The project is designed so that when the mouse moves over a location on the map, its name appears on the map. Clicking the name takes the viewer to a page with a photograph of the site. A small image of the map on that page gets the viewer back to the first page.

Open the Project

1. Open the project file called Exer04-2.qxd, and display the first page in its entirety using the View | Fit in Window command (Figure 4-56). The project page is set to 640 points (or pixels) wide by 480 points high.

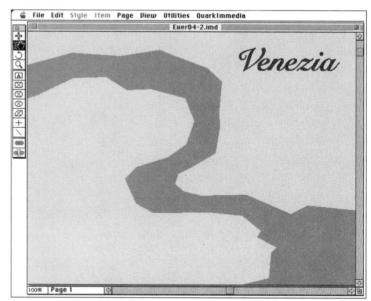

Figure 4-56: Page 1 of the project: a map of Venice.

The map on page 1 was made with QuarkXPress picture boxes, one blue area representing the Grand Canal, and two shapes made with the Polygon Picture Box tool representing the land areas of Venice. Right now the map has a title but no other description or labels.

Create Objects

2. On top of the blue Grand Canal, add a polygon picture box with edges that follow the contour of the canal down to where it joins the sea in the lower right. Don't worry about being too precise with the edges. The viewer will probably click right in the middle of the canal. But if you just have to, you can use the Item | Reshape Polygon command to adjust its shape.

   After it's made, give it a background color of None (Figure 4-57).

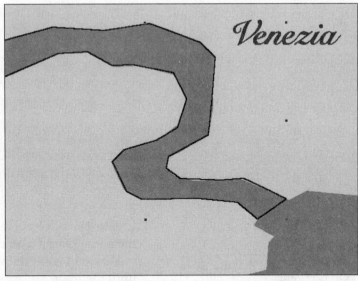

Figure 4-57: Add a polygon picture box over the canal.

This shape will be a trigger, both for displaying the site name and for changing the display to the page with the picture of the Grand Canal.

If the QuarkImmedia Palette is not already displayed, choose the View | Show QuarkImmedia Palette command to display it. Click the Object tab to open the Object panel.

To create an object from this canal-shaped polygon, first select it on the page.

Then, in the Object panel's Object Name field enter this name: **Grand Canal.obj**. Keep the default settings for the three pop-up menus: Basic for Object Type, None for Options, and Home for Initially at (Figure 4-58).

3. Next is the label. Add a text box directly on top of the canal. Enter this text: **The Grand Canal**. We've used 21-point Galliard in our example, but you can spec this type with any font from your system you think appropriate. Again, give this box a background color of None (Figure 4-59).

Object Name: Grand Canal.obj
Object Type: Basic
Options: None
Initially at: Home

Figure 4-58: Create a basic object.

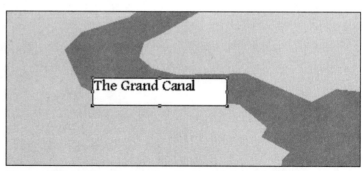

Figure 4-59: Add a text box for the Grand Canal label.

Object Name: Grand Canal label.obj
Object Type: Basic
Options: None
Initially at: Right

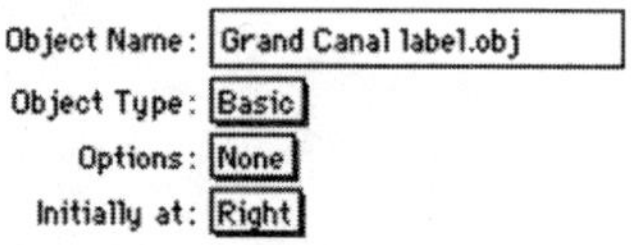

Figure 4-60: Create an object from the label box.

4. Create a basic object from this box as well. Give it the name **Grand Canal label.obj**.

We don't want the viewer to see these objects until the mouse moves over them, so we'll use the same technique we used in Example 1 to hide them on the right pasteboard until the mouse action sets them on the page. Leave the Options pop-up menu at None. Choose Right in the Initially pop-up menu (Figure 4-60).

Before proceeding any further, save your work. Obviously if you opened the project directly from the Companion CD-ROM, you'll need to save your version to your local drive.

5. If you click on the page just above where the Grand Canal connects to the sea and below the word Venezia, you'll find another polygon box whose shape and location defines the area of the Piazza San Marco (Figure 4-61). Create a basic object called San Marco.obj, with the default settings.

6. Make a label for this box in the same fashion as you did in step 3 for the Grand Canal: Make a box, enter the text **Piazza San Marco**, spec the type, and give the box a transparent background (Figure 4-62).

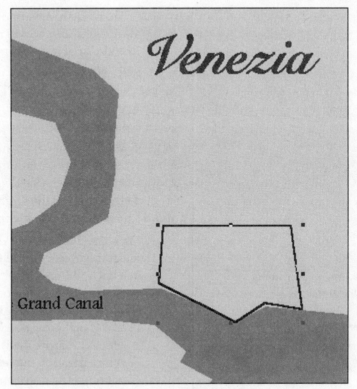

Figure 4-61: Locating the Piazza San Marco polygon box.

Figure 4-62: Add a text box for the Piazza San Marco label.

Then create a basic object. Call this object San Marco label.obj. It will have the same settings as the Grand Canal label.obj—Options set to None, Initially at set to Right.

Add Interactivity

In the Event panel we'll create user events to display a name when the mouse moves onto one of the map's hot spots and make the name disappear when the mouse exits. We'll do this first for the Grand Canal, then test the project and do the same for the Piazza San Marco.

7. Click the Event tab, and in the Event scrollable list select the object Grand Canal.obj.

  Choose Mouse enter in the User Event pop-up menu. In the Action pop-up menu, select Object | Set Position. Next identify the object you want to move, Grand Canal label.obj. Make sure the Method Home is selected (Figure 4-63).

  When the user moves the mouse over the Grand Canal.obj—the polygon box shaped like the canal—the box with the label moves onto the page.

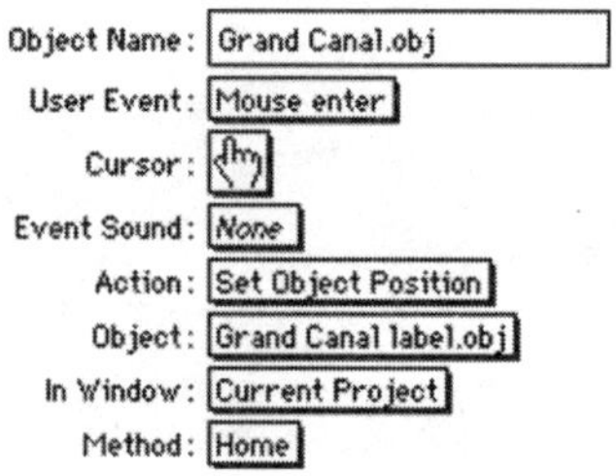

Next we want to make the label disappear when the mouse leaves the object area.

8. Select Mouse exit in the User Event pop-up menu and select Object | Set Position in the Action pop-up menu. Make sure you identify which object to hide, the Grand Canal label.obj.

  This time, because we're sending the text object back to the side of the document, choose Method To Sides and Pasteboard Right, as shown in Figure 4-64.

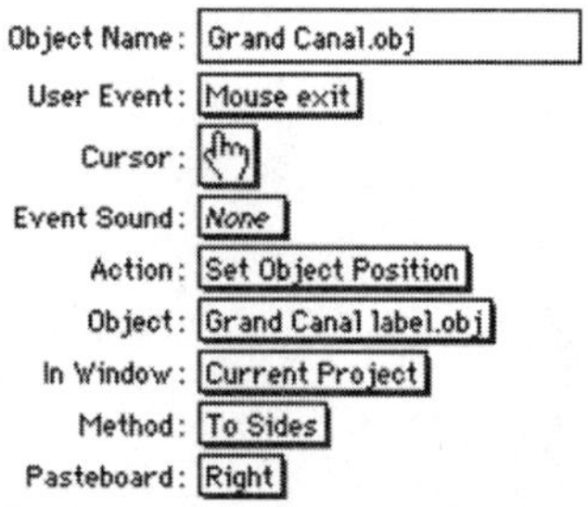

Object Name: Grand Canal.obj
User Event: Mouse enter
Cursor:
Event Sound: None
Action: Set Object Position
Object: Grand Canal label.obj
In Window: Current Project
Method: Home

Figure 4-63: Settings for the Mouse enter user event.

Object Name: Grand Canal.obj
User Event: Mouse exit
Cursor:
Event Sound: None
Action: Set Object Position
Object: Grand Canal label.obj
In Window: Current Project
Method: To Sides
Pasteboard: Right

Figure 4-64: Settings for the Mouse exit user event.

Finally, we want the page to change to page 2 when the viewer clicks the mouse.

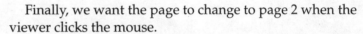

Object Name:	Grand Canal.obj
User Event:	Click up
Cursor:	🖑
Event Sound:	None
Action:	Display Page
Method:	Page Number
Page:	2
Transition:	Page Panel Transition
Sound:	None
Trans. Time:	0

Figure 4-65: Settings for the Click up user event

9. With Grand Canal.obj still active, select Click up in the User Event pop-up menu. For the Action choose Page | Display. By selecting Method Page Number and typing **2** into the Page Number field, you'll send the viewer to page 2 whenever the mouse is clicked (Figure 4-65).

Repeat steps 7, 8, and 9 for the San Marco.obj. For the Mouse enter and Mouse exit user events, you need to specify the San Marco label.obj. For the Click up user event, specify page **3**.

Test the Links

We've done a lot of work, so let's save the project at this point and take a look. In the QuarkImmedia menu select Engage to preview the project.

Moving your mouse over the canal or piazza area will bring up the appropriate label, which disappears when you move the mouse away. When you click on these same spots, you'll go to one of the other pages. But there's no way now to get back to the first page. We'll have to make one.

Create a Return to the First Page

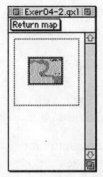

Figure 4-66: Open the Exer04-2.qxl library, with its small graphic of the map.

10. Open the library for this exercise, Exer04-2.qxl. In it you'll find a tiny graphic of the map page as shown in Figure 4-66. Drag the graphic onto page 2 and position it in the lower-right corner (Figure 4-67).

File Edit Style Item Page View Utilities QuarkImmedia

Exer04-2.imd

100% Page 2

Figure 4-67: Position the graphic on page 2, in the lower-right corner.

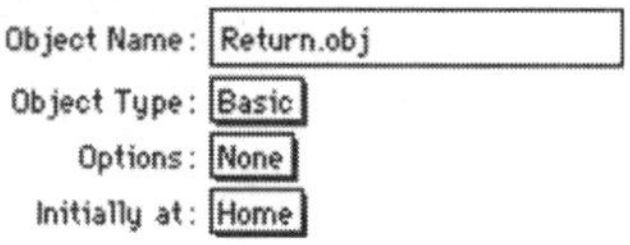

Object Name: Return.obj
Object Type: Basic
Options: None
Initially at: Home

Figure 4-68: Creating a basic object for the return.

Object Name: Return.obj
User Event: Click up
Cursor:
Event Sound: None
Action: Display First Page
Transition: Page Panel Transition
Sound: None
Trans. Time: 0

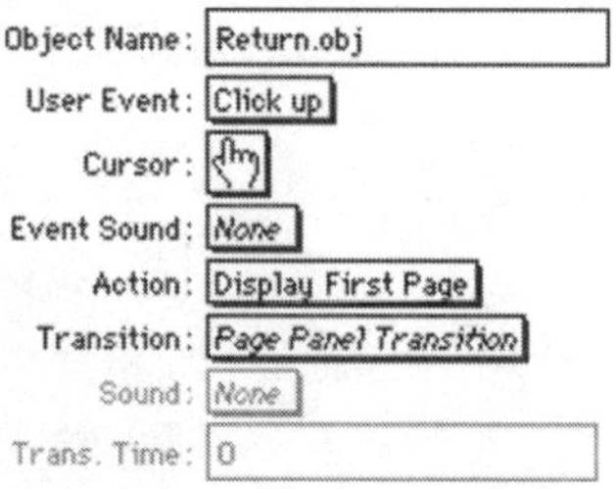

Figure 4-69: Settings for the Click up user event for Return.obj.

Since we want to return to the map of Venice when we click this image, let's name this object in the Name field of the Object panel Return.obj. Retain the default settings: Basic in the Object Type pop-up menu, None in the Options pop-up menu, and Home in the Initially at pop-up menu (Figure 4-68).

11. Now, go to the Event panel to create the way to get back to the map. In the User Event pop-up menu, select Click up.

    Since we know the map will always be the first page of this project, in the Action menu select Page | Display First (Figure 4-69). Clicking on this map image returns the document to the first page.

12. To make a similar return button on the page for San Marco, copy Return.obj on page 2 and paste it into the same spot on the next page. Note that it will have the same name on page 3 as the original did on page 2, and that it has the properties we want already set.

Since we in fact want this button to do exactly the same thing as it did on the previous page—return to the first page—there's no need to change anything in either the Object or Events panels.

13. Save and test the project again, using Quark-Immedia | Engage.

Problems?

If your project doesn't seem to work right, try running the finished project located on the Companion CD-ROM. It's located in the Exercise folder, in the folder called Exer04-2.

In QuarkXPress, you simply open the project called Done04-2.imd. You can engage the project to see exactly what is intended. And you can click any object name and study the settings in the Object and Event panels to guide you in locating any place you may have gone astray.

Moving On

Getting started in Immedia involves the usual procedures of any document—inserting pages, adding text and picture boxes, styling type and pictures, and so on. Of course, our new project has different considerations when being set up:

- What size screen should it be designed for?
- Will it fill the screen or include a title bar?
- What color palette should be used?
- Should you have a picture box or text box placed on the page automatically?

More than that, a project takes us to a new level of activity. For this, we turn to the QuarkImmedia palette.

In the Immedia palette, we create objects from QuarkXPress items. So far, we have made only basic objects. But in later chapters we'll use the Object panel, where we give objects their names and initial properties, to make objects specifically for animations, movies, buttons, pop-up menus, and windows. In this panel, we indicated that some objects might not appear initially at "home" (the spot where it was placed on the page); instead they may appear on one of the pasteboards above, below, or to the side of the page.

The real interest in making an object is that it gives the item interactive properties. And it's in the Event panel that we make those connections, setting up the user events— what the user does with the mouse to interact with the object—with the actions Immedia takes.

So far we've looked at Page actions, displaying the first, last, next, or previous page, and displaying a specific page. And we've looked at the Object | Set Position action, positioning an object at its home and then back on the pasteboard, keying these actions to Mouse enter and Mouse exit user events.

Next, in Chapter 5, "Window Objects," we'll look at window objects, for displaying information in a way that gives the user greater control over its position and removal.

Window Objects

With your previous experience in making QuarkXPress documents and working with text and picture boxes, you've probably found that you can make that mental translation and see how they'll work as basic objects in Immedia.

But in the mental gearing up for multi- and not just single media, you probably haven't made a place for dialog boxes, floating palettes, and windows.

These concepts don't belong to the print world, though you're probably familiar with them from using programs like QuarkXPress. Yet, in a sense, making a project is akin to making a program or application. It's no different really from any you run on your computer, so you now have the tools to display (and collect) information in screen-traditional ways. Immedia refers to dialog boxes, floating palettes, and windows—all of which you can now display at will—as window objects.

Types of Window Objects

When you use a window object, you must determine just what sort of interaction you want to have with the user. Text boxes and picture boxes can be made into window objects of different sorts, each used for a different purpose. They are:

- **Standard window with title bar and close box (Figure 5-1).** Yes, these are windows like you use every day in every application on your computer. The user can drag these around the screen by grabbing the title bar, and they stay onscreen until the close box is clicked, which means you don't have to program the user event to close it. As a window, it will stay in front of your Immedia page, but behind a newly made active window.

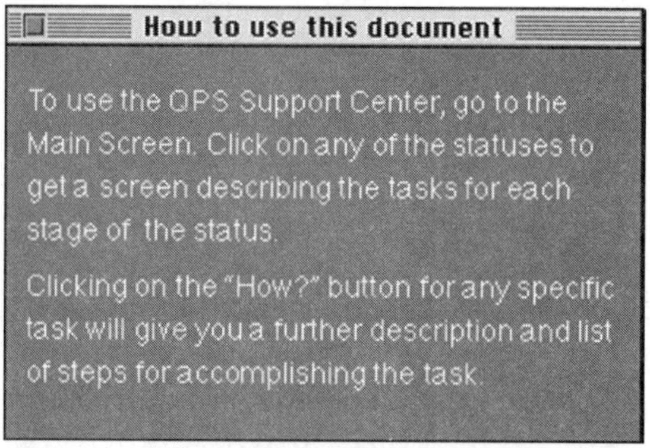

Figure 5-1: Standard window boxes can be moved around the screen and closed using a close box.

- **Plain window, without title bar (Figure 5-2).** Because it lacks a title bar, this type of window physically resembles a basic object. But window objects lasso everything inside them into a group. This means you can use the set position action, as we did in Chapter 4, "Creating Multimedia: Making a Project," to bring a group of items onscreen. You might expect that lacking a title bar, this plain window wouldn't be draggable—but Immedia allows the viewer to drag the window by using any object inside the window to make the whole window draggable.

To use the QPS Support Center, go to the Main Screen. Click on any of the statuses to get a screen describing the tasks for each stage of the status.

Clicking on the "How?" button for any specific task will give you a further description and list of steps for accomplishing the task.

Figure 5-2: Plain window objects resemble basic objects.

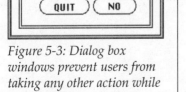

Figure 5-3: Dialog box windows prevent users from taking any other action while they are open.

- **Dialog box (Figure 5-3).** This window form prevents users from acting outside its boundaries, so users have to respond to it and dismiss it before proceeding. Dialog boxes appear on top of all windows and palettes.

- **Floating palette (Figure 5-4).** Well, since it has a title bar, and close box, a palette behaves and looks like a regular window with a thin title bar. But a palette stays in front of all windows, even when the user clicks outside its boundaries. Palettes are naturals for controls.

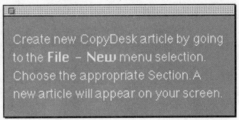

Create new CopyDesk article by going to the **File** – **New** menu selection. Choose the appropriate Section. A new article will appear on your screen.

Figure 5-4: Palette windows stay in front of all other windows.

■ **Plain palette without title bar (Figure 5-5).** Perhaps the reason to get rid of the title bar is for looks. Still, you can allow the viewer to make this type of palette draggable, even though it lacks the title bar.

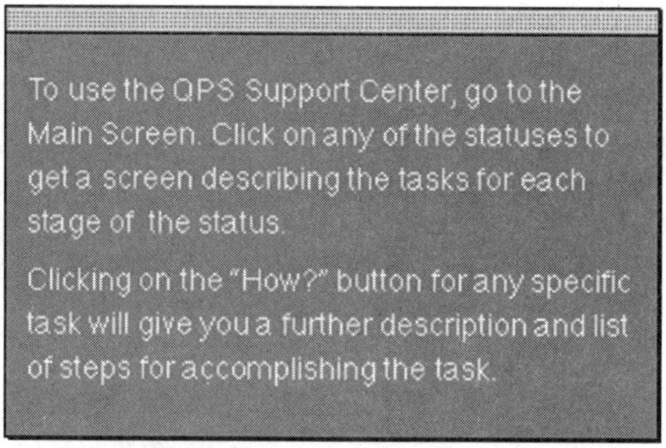

To use the QPS Support Center, go to the Main Screen. Click on any of the statuses to get a screen describing the tasks for each stage of the status.

Clicking on the "How?" button for any specific task will give you a further description and list of steps for accomplishing the task.

Figure 5-5: A palette doesn't have to include a close box.

Windows, palettes, and dialog boxes not only give your project an interactive feel, but they also provide you with the full panoply of ways to present information and give control to your viewer. What may be the most surprising feature is how easily windows are set up.

TIP

Having a box or window with additional information appearing onscreen is one of the ways you make all the information available without cluttering up a low-resolution screen with too much text. So when should you use a basic object for this, as discussed in Chapter 4, and when a window object? Well, window objects provide two advantages for this type of presentation. The title bar, with close box, means the information can stay onscreen as long as the user wants, and can be moved over if desired. And when you need to display more than one box—for instance, a picture and text—the window object serves to group the boxes.

Creating a Window Object

You create a window object in the standard fashion that you use to create all objects other than button objects. That is, with either a text box or picture box active on your page, you click the Object tab and enter a name in the Object Name field (Figure 5-6). Although any object on your project page can be made into a window object, it must be placed on the pasteboard before you preview or export the project.

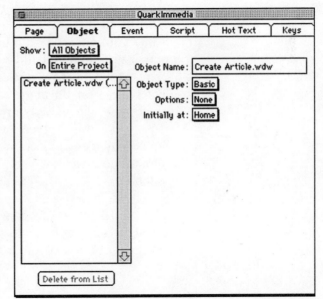

Figure 5-6: As with other objects, you create window objects in the Object panel.

The options in the Object panel change depending on the type of object you choose. When you choose a window object, you next choose which type of window, as identified above: standard, plain, dialog box, movable dialog box, palette, plain palette.

Standard and palette window objects can include (or omit) a close box. They can also include a title in their title bars, as can a movable dialog box.

When you can move a window object around your screen, you will also be presented with the option of having Immedia "remember window position"—that is, not return the window object to its default position when the project is closed and reopened, but instead keep track of the spot where it was moved.

Names in Immedia

While you're learning Immedia, it may help you keep things straight if you add an identifying "extension" to page, object, hot text, and script names. For a basic object, we tack on .obj at the end of the name. For window objects, we use .wdw. For movie objects, animation objects, and text box objects, we use .mvo, .ano, and .tbo. For pop-up menu objects, we use .pu; for button objects, .btn; for hot text, .txt.

Instead of filename-like extensions, you might prefer to tack on uppercase letters at the end of the name: O, W, M, A, TB, P, B, HT. Neither is strictly necessary, but we strongly support anything that helps you keep related features separate in your accounting.

Exercise 5-1

Now let's use these different types of windows in an Immedia project. No special files are needed for this exercise.

In this first exercise, we'll create a multi-page project and construct a simple page-control palette that allows us to move to the next or previous page. This palette will be something we can use in later projects.

Set Up the Project

1. Begin a new project (File | New | Project), and set the
   Page Size to 480 points wide and 320 points high.
   Check the Automatic Picture Box. You can leave the
   other settings as they are: margins zero for all, palette set to Macintosh system colors, background
   color of black, the project window kind set to None
   (Figure 5-7).

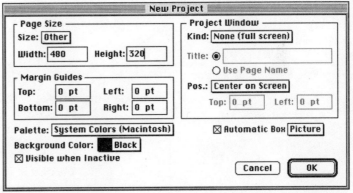

Figure 5-7: Settings for Exercise 5-1 in the New Project dialog box.

2. In Edit | Preferences | QuarkImmedia, check the Page
   Wraparound box (Figure 5-8), and Hide Menu Bar at
   Startup.

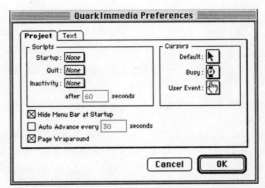

*Figure 5-8: Hide the Menu Bar and select Page Wraparound in the
Preferences.*

3. Use Page | Insert to add three pages to the end of the document.

4. We won't actually put content on these pages, so we'll differentiate them by giving them different colors and adding a page number to each. Select the picture box on the first page and give it a blue background color.

Then give the box on page 2 a background color of magenta, on page 3 green, and page 4 yellow.

Now we'll give each page a page number.

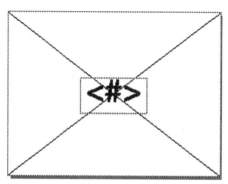

Figure 5-9: Add page numbers on the master page.

5. Use the Page | Display | A-Master A command to display master page A.

6. Add a text box that's 2" square, center it on the page, and enter the keyboard command to display the current page number: Command-3 (Figure 5-9).

Select the type and make it 72 points and bold. Set the background color of this box to None.

7. Return to page 1 of the project, using Page | Display | Document.

Now we'll construct a simple page-control palette:

8. In the pasteboard located off to the side of page 1, add a picture box that's 1.5" wide and .8" tall. Give this box a 2-point red border (Figure 5-10).

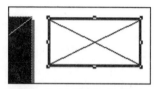

Figure 5-10: To make the page-control palette, create a picture box with a red border on the pasteboard.

9. Display the Object panel of the QuarkImmedia palette. Create a window object from this box. Give it the name "Page-control palette" and specify Palette in the Display as pop-up.

   Because we centered the page numbers on the page, we don't want this palette to be centered and cover up the page numbers.

Object Name: Page-control palette
Object Type: Window
Display as: Palette
Position: At Absolute Position
144 from left   -72 from top

Figure 5-11: In the Object panel, make the picture box into a palette window object.

10. Choose At Absolute Position in the Position pop-up, and enter 2" (144 pt) for the From Left position—which will center the box horizontally on the page—and -1" (-72 pt) for the From Top position, to position the palette above the page.

    Make sure that Include Close Box is not checked. We won't want to accidentally remove these controls (Figure 5-11).

11. Using the polygon-picture box tool, add a left-pointing triangle and right-pointing triangle inside the box we'll be using as the Page-control palette.

    Use the Item | Space Align command to align these triangles and center them in the box.

    Give the triangles each a cyan background.

Make the Next Page & Previous Page Buttons

Object Name: Previous page.obj
User Event: Click up
Cursor: 🖑
Event Sound: None
Action: Display Previous Page

Figure 5-12: For the left triangle, set the action to Display Previous Page.

12. Select the left triangle. Create a basic object called "Previous page.obj." Leave Initially at set to Home, and Options to None.

13. Display the Event panel, making certain Previous page.obj is highlighted.

    For the Click Up user event, choose Page | Display Previous in the Action pop-up menu (Figure 5-12).

14. Similarly for the right triangle, create a basic object called "Next page.obj."

    In the Event panel, for the Click Up user event, set the action to Display Next Page (Figure 5-13).

Object Name: Next page.obj
User Event: Click up
Cursor: 🖑
Event Sound: None
Action: Display Next Page

Figure 5-13: For the right triangle, set the action to Display Next Page.

Figure 5-14: Use the blue box on page 1 to display the palette.

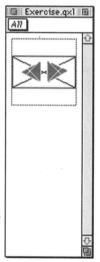

Figure 5-15: Put the palette in a library for use in subsequent projects.

These simple controls allow us to navigate from page to page, but we have to bring this page-control palette onto the screen manually. We'll do that by using the picture box on page 1 as a trigger to display this window.

15. Select the blue picture box on page 1. Create a basic object called "Blue box.obj."

16. In the Event panel, set the User Event pop-up menu to "Mouse enter." In the Action pop-up menu, choose Window | Open and specify the page-control palette in the Window pop-up (Figure 5-14).

17. Save the project using the name Paging.imd.

We will want to use the page-control palette in other projects. Create a new library called Exercise.qxl, and put the palette in the library (Figure 5-15).

18. To test the project, choose QuarkImmedia | Engage or press function key F15. (If the Use Debugger command has a check mark beside it, you may prefer to turn that feature off for now.)

Figure 5-16: The page-control palette appears above and not over the page.

Note how moving the mouse over the blue box on page 1 displays the page-control palette, and how this palette appears above and not over the page (Figure 5-16). Drag the palette by its title bar to any position on your screen. One of the strengths of Immedia is that it can assume control over the full display no matter what other applications might be running.

Click on the triangles to move from page to page. Because you checked Page Wraparound in QuarkImmedia Preferences, clicking on the next-page triangle takes you from the last page to the first page, and the previous-page triangle from the first page to the last page.

Press Command-Q or function key F15 to disengage the project.

Exercise 5-2

This exercise contains two pages from a larger project that was developed as an online training module. This is actually one of the first projects we did with Immedia and it was used on two CDs distributed by Quark to illustrate Immedia's capabilities before the program had been released. In fact, we learned Immedia and created this document in three days. It shows what can be made with simple means—the interactivity is created with basic and window objects. You can take a look at the finished version on the Companion CD-ROM.

Open the Project

1. Locate the files for this exercise in the folder for Exercise 05-2.

2. Open Exer05-2.qxd and take a look at the project.

The project contains two pages, which have been labeled for you in the Page panel. Page 1 is called "Main Screen" and Page 2 "First Edit" (Figure 5-17).

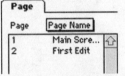

Figure 5-17: The pages for the project have been labeled in the Page panel.

The first page is a diagram of the different stages in Quark Publishing System copy flow for a magazine called *Publica*. Each of the colored boxes links to a page that describes the tasks for that stage. You'll create the action that links the first box to the second page.

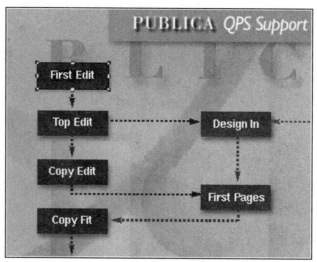

Figure 5-18: Select the text box labeled First Edit on page 1 of the project.

Create the First Interactive Object

Figure 5-19: Make the First Edit text box into a basic object.

3. Select the first box in the left column, the one labeled First Edit (Figure 5-18). In the Object panel of the QuarkImmedia palette, name this box First Edit.obj. It's a basic object, so select Basic in the Object Type field. In the Options field choose None and Initially at set to Home (Figure 5-19).

Now, let's create the user event that will display the next page.

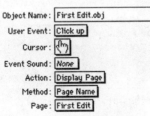

Figure 5-20: Set the user events in the Event panel to include an action that displays the next page.

4. In the Event panel, make sure that the object you just created, First Edit.obj, is highlighted in the scrollable list and its name is displayed in the Name field. Go to the User Event pop-up menu. To make this page change to First Edit when the user releases the mouse, make sure Click up is selected.

In the Action pop-up menu, choose Page | Display (Figure 5-20).

5. As we've said before (and we'll probably say it again), it's a good idea to identify pages by name rather than by number, so select Page Name in the Method pop-up menu and the name of the page, First Edit, in the Page pop-up menu beneath. Now, no matter how many pages you add before this one, or how much you rearrange the order, the page First Edit will always be linked to this object.

Make a Window Object to Display Instructions

We'd like to display instructions for using this project. The user may want to move the object with these instructions to the side and keep it open while going through the project. A window object is a great way to do this.

6. Open the library for this exercise, Exer05.qxl, located in the Exer05 folder.

7. Using the Label pop-up menu at the top of the library for this project, find the item labeled Help. Drag this text box onto the pasteboard of this page (Figure 5-21). Why isn't it placed on the page, where we want the viewer to see it? Because window objects always stay out of sight on the pasteboard until a user event activates them.

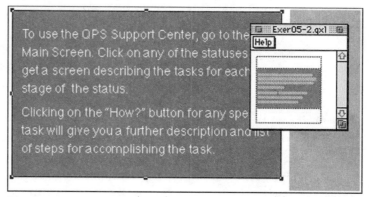

Figure 5-21: Take the first text box from the library and place it on the pasteboard.

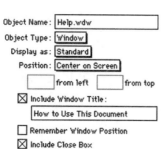

Figure 5-22: Turn the text box into a standard window object.

8. Make this text box a Window object, naming it Help.wdw (Figure 5-22). If you make it a standard Window object, it will float in front of the project but not obscure any other windows the user might open.

   In the Display as field choose Standard and for Position, select Center on Screen.

9. The user may want to put this window on the side of the screen while going through the project. To make it easy to identify when other windows are open, you should put a title on it. Check Include Window Title and type **How to Use this Document** in the Title field.

   Don't forget to include a close box.

Make an Interactive Object to Open the Window

How do you open this window? It would be nice to click on the word "Help" at the bottom of the page to open the window. Interactive text is the subject of Chapter 7, "Hot Text Links," so we won't go into hot text here. But there is a simple way of doing this that you can use right now. It's easy to put a transparent object over the word "Help" and make that box interactive.

Figure 5-23: Put a text box with background of None *over the word "Help" to make it appear to be clickable.*

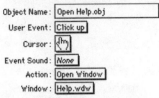

Figure 5-24: Select the object Help.wdw in the Window pop-up menu.

10. Make a text box 60 points wide by 20 points high. Place this over the word "HELP" at the bottom of the page and, using Item | Modify or the Colors palette, set the background to None (Figure 5-23).

    Name the object Open Help.obj (Figure 5-24) and use the default settings for an object: Object Type Basic, Options None, Initially at Home.

11. In the Event panel, select Click up for the user event, in the Action pop-up menu choose Window | Open.

    When the Window pop-up menu appears, select the one made in steps 6 through 9, Help.wdw.

Save & Preview the Project

This is a good time to save your project. *Publica* is the name of the magazine, so you can call it Publica.qxd.

    Having saved the project, let's take a look:

12. Use QuarkImmedia | Engage to preview the project. Open the Help window first, and try moving it around the screen. Close the window, then click on the First Edit object to go to the next page.

13. Close this preview with function key F15 or by using the keyboard command Command-Q.

Create Window Objects for the Second Page

The second page of the project explains the different tasks involved with one of the stages of producing this magazine. Some readers may want more explanation than the one or two sentences which describe each step, so now we'll make several windows they can open for more information.

14. In the Page panel, double-click on the second page, First Edit, in the scrollable list. This makes page 2 active.

    Next, in the library find the item called Create Article. Drag it to the pasteboard beside the First Edit page (Figure 5-25).

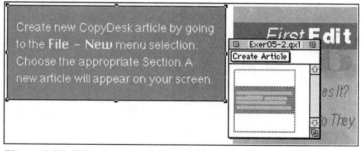

Figure 5-25: Take the second text box from the library and place it on the pasteboard.

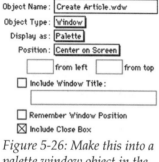

Figure 5-26: Make this into a palette window object in the Object panel.

15. Just as you did with the Help window, make this text box into a window object in the Object panel, naming it Create Article.wdw (Figure 5-26).

This time make it a palette window object, which has a smaller title bar than a standard window. So, in the Display as pop-up menu select "Palette." For position, Center on Screen is fine.

This palette won't need a title, but you do want to provide a way to close it, so check Include Close Box.

Now go through the same process to make two additional windows.

16. The second window is made from the text box labeled Edit Print. Find it in the library and place it on the pasteboard (Figure 5-27).

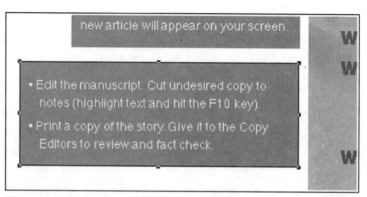

Figure 5-27: Create another window object from a library text box.

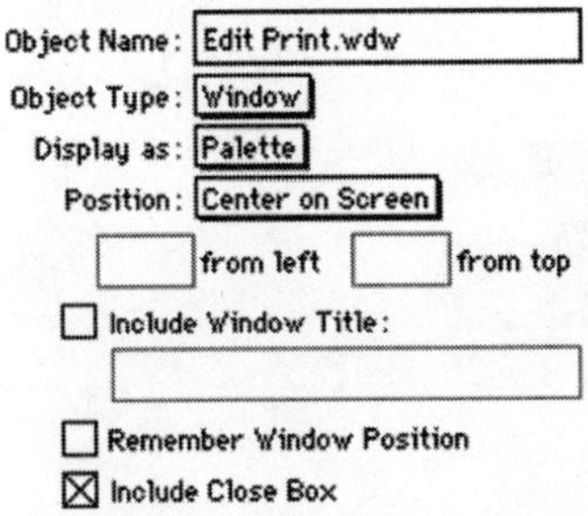

Object Name: Edit Print.wdw
Object Type: Window
Display as: Palette
Position: Center on Screen
☐ from left ☐ from top
☐ Include Window Title:
☐ Remember Window Position
☒ Include Close Box

Figure 5-28: This object will be a palette window object also.

17. Name it Edit Print.wdw in the Object panel. To make it an interactive window, select Window in the Object Type pop-up menu.

In the Display as pop-up menu, choose palette. Make sure you give the viewer a way to close this by checking the Include Close Box check box (Figure 5-28).

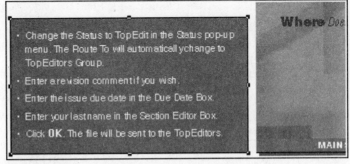

Figure 5-29: Make the last window for this page.

18. Go back to the library to get the text box for one more window. This one's labeled Route To. Place it on the pasteboard (Figure 5-29).

19. Make the box a window object, naming it Route To.wdw. Use the same settings as before: Display as Palette, check Include Close Box (Figure 5-30).

Object Name: Route To.wdw
Object Type: Window
Display as: Palette
Position: Center on Screen
☐ from left ☐ from top
☐ Include Window Title:
☐ Remember Window Position
☒ Include Close Box

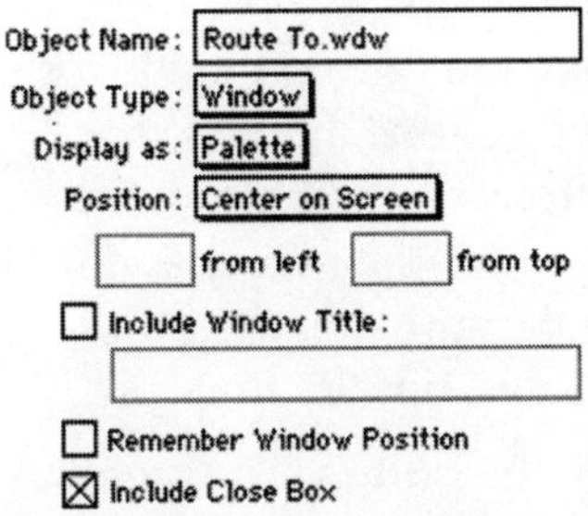

Figure 5-30: It, too, will be a palette window object.

Create an Interactive Object to Open the Window

You won't have to do anything for the window objects in the Event panel. They don't do anything to other objects, so there's no need to make a user event and assign an action. You will, however, need to make objects to open these windows.

20. In the library, there's an image of a button with the word "How?" on it. Drag it onto the project page and place it after the sentence "Create a new Copy Desk article" (Figure 5-31).

Figure 5-31: Place the image of a button on the page.

21. Make this a basic object, naming it How.obj. Use the default settings: Option None, Initially at Home.

22. To open the first window with this object, select Click up in the User Event pop-up menu of the Event panel.

23. Choose Action | Window | Open. What window? The one you just created, Create Article.wdw (Figure 5-32).

Figure 5-32: For the Click up user event select the action Open Window.

Use Duplicates of the Object to Open the Other Windows

You'll need another button just like the one you made for the first window. Now that you've got one, it's easy to make a second one. When you duplicate the button, the picture boxes are duplicated, but so are the names and the user events. You'll just have to make sure that the duplicated buttons open the new windows, not the first.

24. Use Item | Duplicate to copy the button. The name of the new button becomes How.obj copy. To make the name consistent with the other objects, let's rename this one "How2.obj."

25. Place How2.obj at the end of the sentence "Edit the story and print for the Copy Editors."
    Keep the other settings on the Object panel.

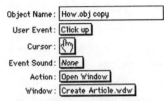

Figure 5-33: A duplicate of the How? object will have the same user events.

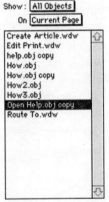

Figure 5-34: Copy the Help object from page 1 and paste it in the same place on page 2.

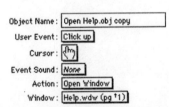

Figure 5-35: Use the window from page 1 for the help window on page 2.

26. In the Event panel the user event, Click up, is already selected, as is the Action. The Window pop-up menu, however, says Create Article.wdw (Figure 5-33). You'll need to change that to Edit Print.wdw.

27. Make another copy of the button and rename it How3.obj.
    Put How3.obj at the end of the final sentence in the last section of the page.

28. You don't need to change the other settings on the Object panel. In the Event panel, however, make sure the Window pop-up menu displays the name of the third window object, Route To.wdw.

Make a Help Window for This Page

29. It's easy to create a help window for this page. Just as you did with the How? object, you can duplicate the text box over the word "Help" on page 1 and paste it over the same word at the bottom of page 2 (Figure 5-34).

This time you won't need to change any of the settings for the object. You want this object to open a window just like the one on page 1. Look at the Event panel—you'll see that Action is set to open Help.wdw (pg. †1). Click on the Help object on this page and it will open the Help window on page 1 (Figure 5-35).

Save & Preview Your Project

Let's try this all out.

30. Save your project. Then preview the project using QuarkImmedia | Engage.
    Open the help window on page 1 and leave it open when you go to page 2. You'll see how you can use windows to keep information in front of a viewer no matter what page the project is on.

Moving On

Multimedia presentations differ from print presentations in more than just the addition of movement, sound, and interactivity. When you design your projects, you can use the full range of windows, palettes, and dialog boxes that any software program has.

Window objects in Immedia can be used as information pop-ups. They have a grouping capability and can carry a title bar, which means they can stay onscreen until closed by the user and can be dragged over to some other area of the screen. They can even be accessed from other pages.

Window objects can also take the form of palettes, which stay open and stay above all windows—perfect for floating controls—and of dialog boxes, which force users to respond to them before allowing things to proceed.

Now that we have a few projects under our belt, with the notion of objects in the forefront of our attention, let's take a look at how Immedia uses pages in Chapter 6, "Transitions & Pages."

Transitions & Pages

We saw in the last chapter that for purposes of creating and manipulating, Immedia pages onscreen act like XPress pages on paper. But the onscreen page gives us a rich environment for movement from one page to another, as well as a wealth of ways to present information without even having to leave a page.

In this chapter, we'll discuss the basics of working with Immedia pages, how to set up transitions from one page to another, and how to put information up on the screen using Window objects.

Pages

The scrollable list on the Page panel lists not only page numbers, but also the names you give your pages (Figure 6-1). It's safer to use names. Why? Using a name generally provides insurance that your project won't have to be redirected if you want to insert, delete, or move pages.

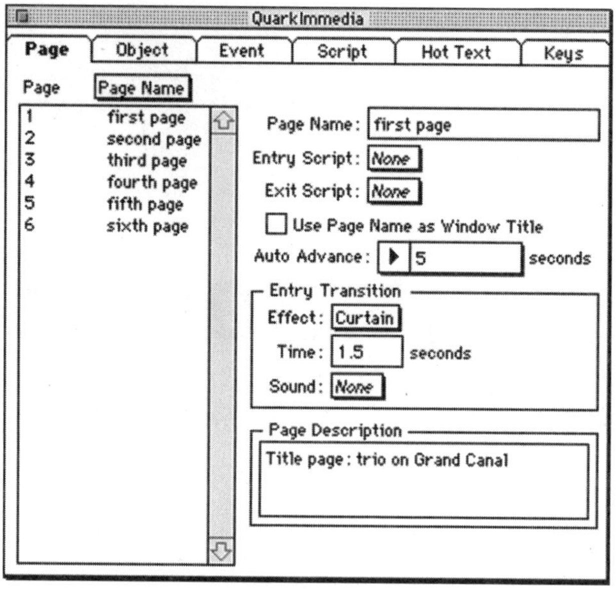

Figure 6-1: The Page panel lists your pages, by number and name.

Naming a page in the Page panel is similar to the way you name an object. In this case, however, any pages added to your project show up automatically in the Page scrollable list. You simply click the page number in the list, then enter a name in the Page Name field. Press Return or Enter to complete the naming.

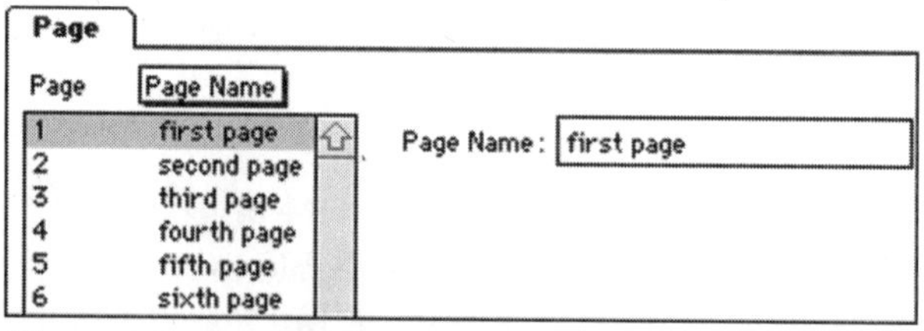

Figure 6-2: The Page Name field.

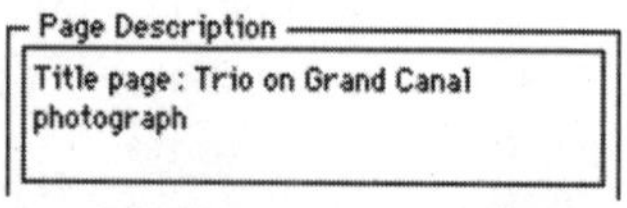

Figure 6-3: The Page Description field provides information about a page that can be accessed by the user.

As you might expect, changing the name is no more complicated than highlighting the page in the scrollable list and altering the name in the Page Name field (Figure 6-2).

A field called Page Description, available for each page, provides you with more than just a way of identifying what happens on each page. You can arrange the page so that the user can access the contents of the Page Description field (Figure 6-3). The field is limited to a maximum of 255 characters, or about 40 words.

TIP

Double-clicking a page name or number in the Page scrollable list makes that the active page on your display. In this respect, double-clicking a page listing is similar to double-clicking a page icon in the Document Layout palette.

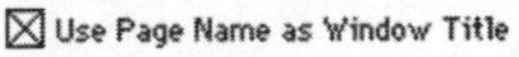

☒ Use Page Name as Window Title

Figure 6-4: Override the default Window Title setting here.

If your project includes a title bar—as determined initially in the New Project dialog box and changeable using File | Project Setup—the title bar can include the page name for each individual page, or just for those pages for which you check the box labeled Use Page Name as Window Title (Figure 6-4).

Auto Advance

Changing the display from one page to another may be initiated by a user event, as we saw in the last chapter. Alternatively, you can have the page automatically advance to the next page after a set length of time, like a self-running slide-show.

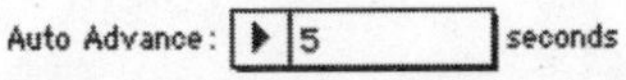

Auto Advance : ▶ 5   seconds

Figure 6-5: Auto Advance changes pages after a period of inactivity.

You can set your project to advance to the next page automatically from every page in QuarkImmedia Preferences (Figure 6-5). In the Page panel, setting Auto Advance to Default uses the value entered in QuarkImmedia Preferences (Figure 6-6); choosing None or any time value overrides the Preferences setting.

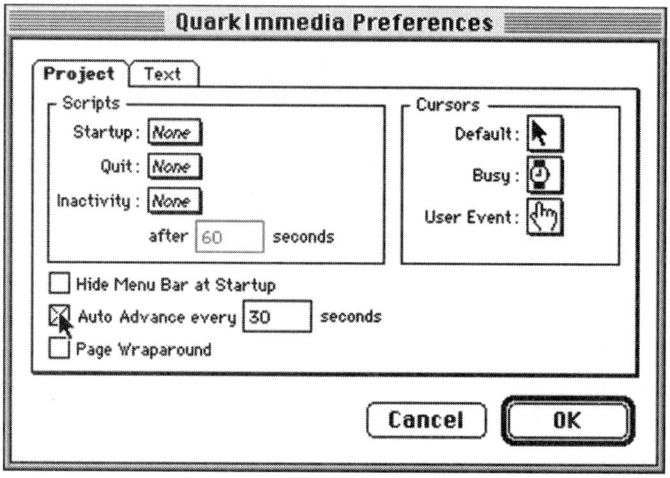

Figure 6-6: The QuarkImmedia Preferences default Auto Advance setting.

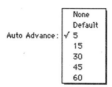

Figure 6-7: Auto Advance pop-up menu.

The preset times in the pop-up menu are 5, 15, 30, 45, and 60 seconds. However, you can enter any time value—simply highlight the current value and replace it with the length of time you want (Figure 6-7).

> **TIP**
>
> *Unlike the other pop-up menus, you find the selections in the Auto Advance pop-up menu by clicking on the triangle that precedes it. You highlight whatever's displayed in the pop-up menu and type in the number you want.*

Transitions

As noted in Chapter 4, "Creating Multimedia: Making a Project," you can specify the speed, sound, and type of transition from one page to another as part of the displaying page action. Now you can design not only what pages look like, but also what they look like in transition to another page.

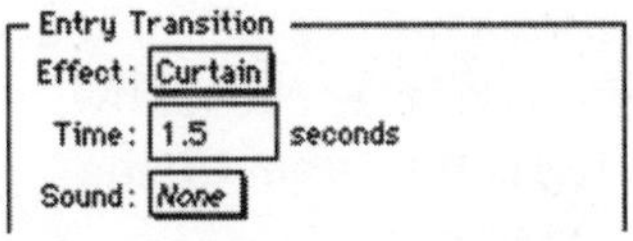

Entry Transition
Effect: Curtain
Time: 1.5   seconds
Sound: None

Figure 6-8: Entry Transition area.

QuarkImmedia

Engage
Use Debugger

MenuMaker...
Custom Transitions...
Make Index...

Export Settings...
Export...

Convert to QuarkXPress...
QuarkImmedia Usage...

About QuarkImmedia...

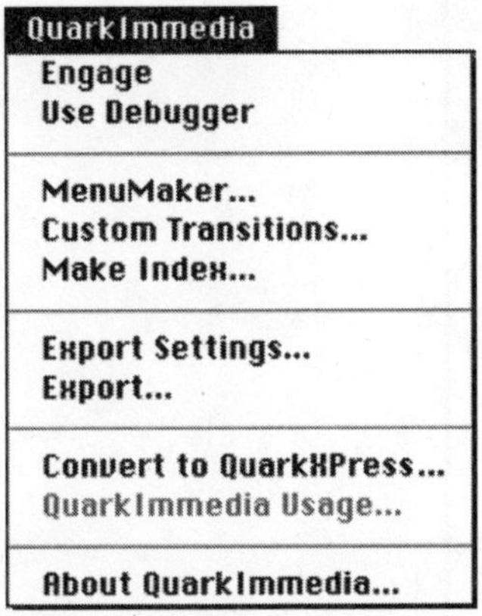

Figure 6-9: The QuarkImmedia menu.

In the Page panel, you can also specify these features in the Entry Transition area (Figure 6-8). Event panel settings override settings on the Page panel—unless you specify Page Panel Transition there; that's Immedia's way of telling you to use the transition chosen in the Page panel.

Using disparate transitions throughout your project can be as jarring to the sensibilities as too-many or ill-chosen fonts in a print document; the transitions in Immedia provide pacing and atmosphere lacking in other programs that provide hyperlinking, such as HTML documents and Acrobat PDF files.

The Transitions pop-up menu appears in several places in Immedia, including at certain times when actions display or hide objects. We'll discuss the transitions here as they are set when you first install Immedia. Note, however, that you can use the QuarkImmedia | Custom Transitions command (Figure 6-9) to alter any of the 18 transitions listed here in a variety of predefined ways to make your own versions (Figure 6-10). Moreover, you can delete entries from the list of transitions, so they don't appear in the pop-up menu, rearrange their order and rename them, as well as add your own.

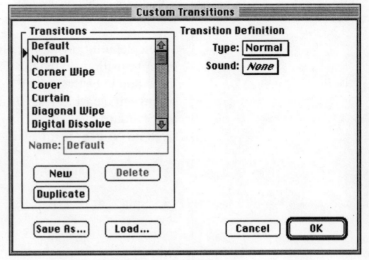

Figure 6-10: Custom Transitions dialog box.

When you select a sound and enter a new value for the transition's duration in the definition, your entries show up as default entries in the Entry Transition area. Changing them in the Page panel then overrides them.

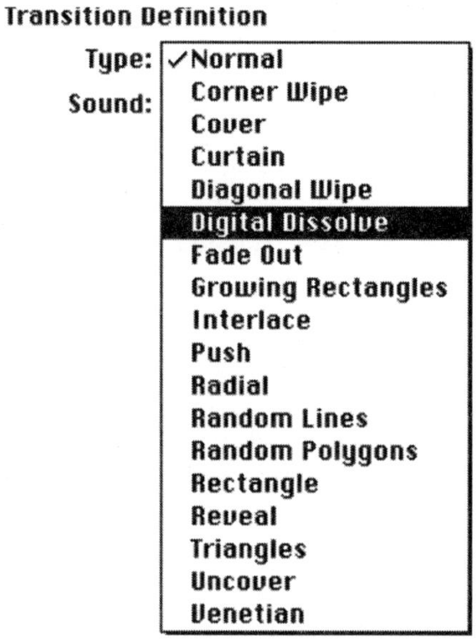

Transition Definition

Type:　✓Normal
Sound:　Corner Wipe
　　　　Cover
　　　　Curtain
　　　　Diagonal Wipe
　　　　Digital Dissolve
　　　　Fade Out
　　　　Growing Rectangles
　　　　Interlace
　　　　Push
　　　　Radial
　　　　Random Lines
　　　　Random Polygons
　　　　Rectangle
　　　　Reveal
　　　　Triangles
　　　　Uncover
　　　　Venetian

Figure 6-11: Defining which transition to use as a default, in the Custom Transitions dialog box.

The default transition is always taken from one of the other transitions in the list (Figure 6-11). You can set any transition to be the default for your project. Like other settings in QuarkXPress, such as the Normal style sheet or the Standard H&J table, changes made with no project open become the settings used for any new project.

Listed here are the packaged transitions and their effects. Some of the aspects you can customize are also described. In the following exercise, we will actually see what each of these transitions looks like. Static images picturing the transitions accompany the exercise.

- ■ Normal—Direct cut from one page to the next.

- ■ Corner Wipe—Like a second-hand sweep, from 9 o'clock to 12 o'clock, with the focal point in the lower-right corner. You can switch to a counter-clockwise direction, and start at any corner (Figures 6-12 and 6-13).

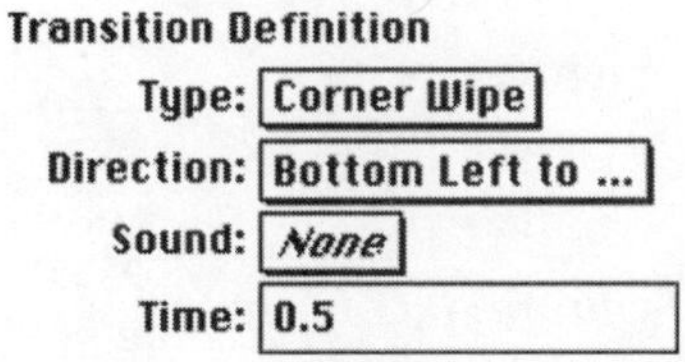

Transition Definition

Type:	Corner Wipe
Direction:	Bottom Left to ...
Sound:	*None*
Time:	0.5

Figure 6-12: Corner Wipe settings.

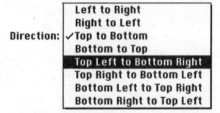

Direction:
- Left to Right
- Right to Left
- ✓Top to Bottom
- Bottom to Top
- **Top Left to Bottom Right**
- Top Right to Bottom Left
- Bottom Left to Top Right
- Bottom Right to Top Left

Figure 6-13: In which direction should the wipe go?

■ Cover—The new page comes in like a window shade dropping down from above. You can change the transition to any direction, including diagonals (Figures 6-14 and 6-15), and split the screen horizontally and/or vertically when the effect occurs, so that you might have the screen divide into 16 equal-sized rectangles, each showing that segment of the new page covering up that portion of the old.

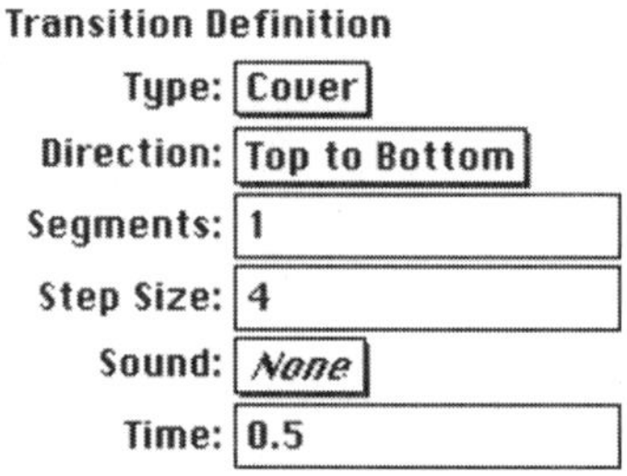

Transition Definition

Type:	Cover
Direction:	Top to Bottom
Segments:	1
Step Size:	4
Sound:	*None*
Time:	0.5

Figure 6-14: Cover settings.

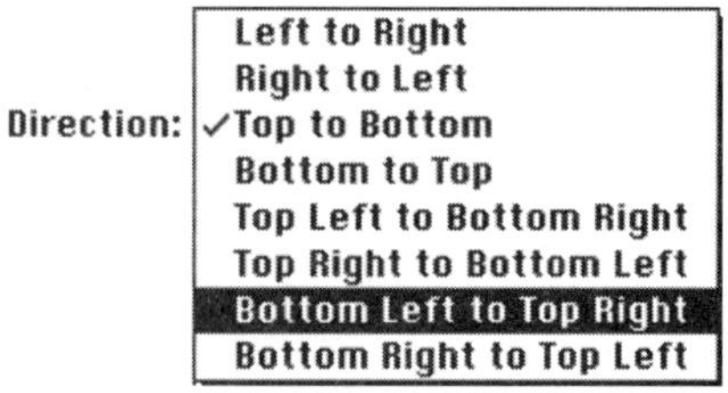

Direction:	
	Left to Right
	Right to Left
	✓Top to Bottom
	Bottom to Top
	Top Left to Bottom Right
	Top Right to Bottom Left
	Bottom Left to Top Right
	Bottom Right to Top Left

Figure 6-15: Set the direction of the transition.

■ Curtain—The new page appears from the center, with the old page acting like a curtain opening. Alternatively, as Figure 6-16 shows, you can have the new page come in from the outsides instead of opening from the center and speed up the transition on slower machines by using bigger steps for the advancing edges.

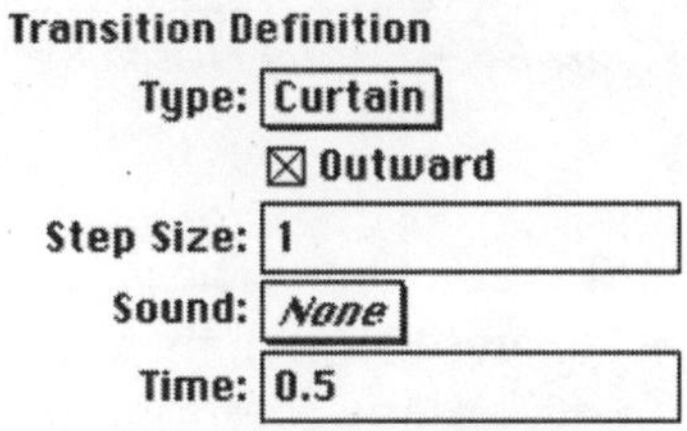

Transition Definition

Type: [Curtain]

☒ Outward

Step Size: [1   ]

Sound: [*None*]

Time: [0.5   ]

Figure 6-16: Curtain settings.

■ Diagonal Wipe—Sweeping from one corner to the other. The original is from the lower left to the upper right, but you can pick any diagonal direction (Figures 6-17 and 6-18).

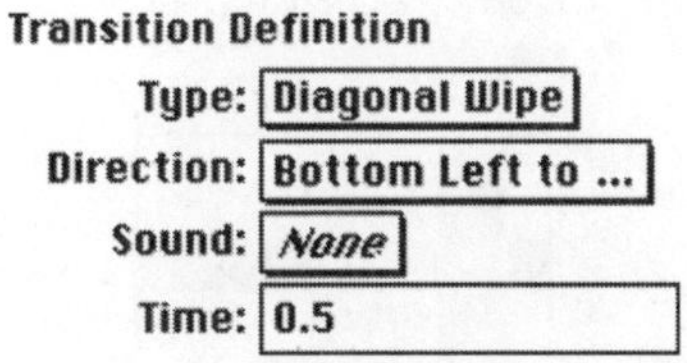

Transition Definition

Type: [Diagonal Wipe]

Direction: [Bottom Left to ...]

Sound: [*None*]

Time: [0.5   ]

Figure 6-17: Diagonal Wipe settings.

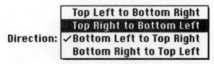

Direction:
- Top Left to Bottom Right
- **Top Right to Bottom Left**
- ✓Bottom Left to Top Right
- Bottom Right to Top Left

Figure 6-18: What direction should the Diagonal Wipe take?

■ Digital Dissolve—A pixelly transition from one page to the next, the image forming in a Pointillist fashion (Figure 6-19).

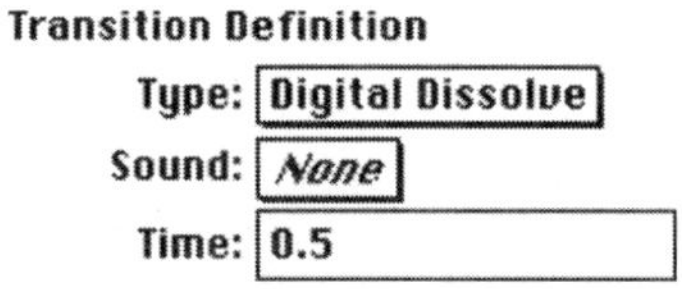

Transition Definition

Type: Digital Dissolve
Sound: *None*
Time: 0.5

Figure 6-19: Digital Dissolve settings.

■ Fade Out—The whole screen fades to black (the preset color), then fades in the new page. You can pick any color (Figures 6-20 and 6-21).

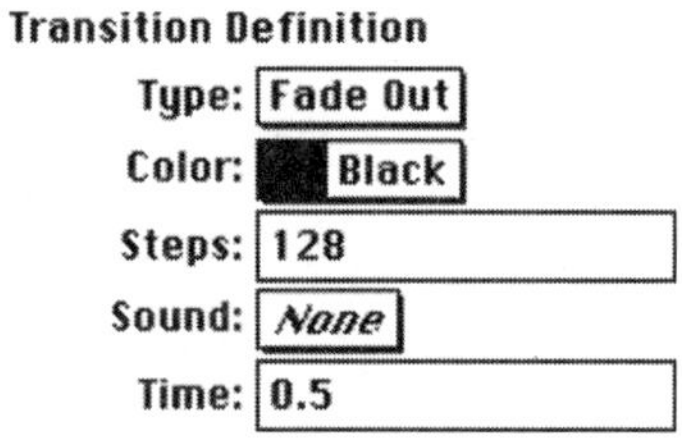

Transition Definition

Type: Fade Out
Color: Black
Steps: 128
Sound: *None*
Time: 0.5

Figure 6-20: Fade Out settings.

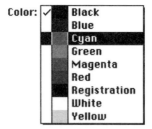

Color: ✓ Black
Blue
Cyan
Green
Magenta
Red
Registration
White
Yellow

Figure 6-21: What color should the transition fade to?

■ Growing Rectangles—Tiny rectangles, offset from each other in a honeycomb fashion, appear and grow ever larger until they merge with each other, with ever-smaller areas of the old page shrinking until completely gone (Figure 6-22).

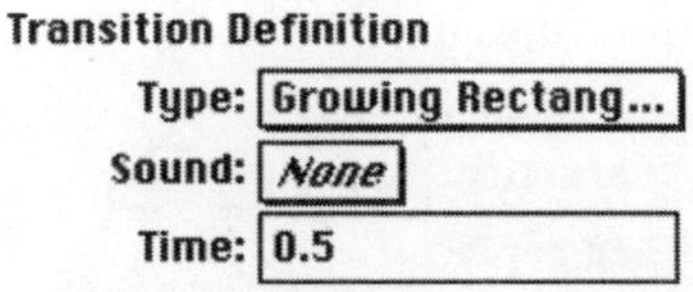

Transition Definition
Type: `Growing Rectang...`
Sound: `None`
Time: `0.5`

Figure 6-22: Growing Rectangles settings.

■ Interlace—Horizontal bands appear, growing from 1 pixel to 4 pixels, as the old page's image is covered up by the new image. You can make the striations from 1 to 16 pixels wide, and have them grow up or down, or have vertical stripes that grow to the left or right (Figure 6-23).

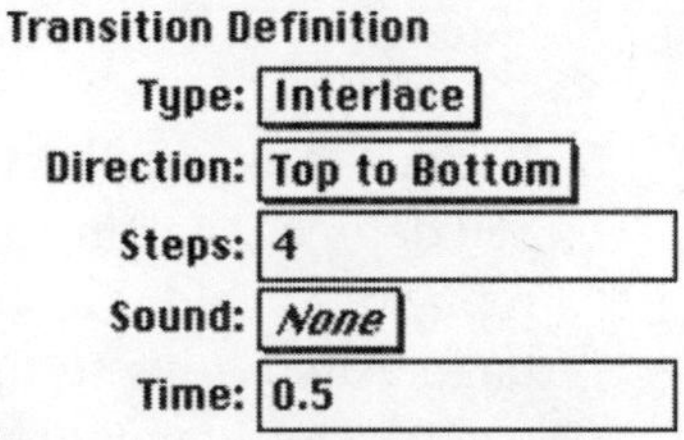

Transition Definition
Type: `Interlace`
Direction: `Top to Bottom`
Steps: `4`
Sound: `None`
Time: `0.5`

Figure 6-23: Interlace settings.

■ Push—Like Cover, the new page comes down onto
the screen, but now the old page is pushed off, not
covered up. The direction, and how many segments
are happening simultaneously, can be adjusted
(Figures 6-24 and 6-25).

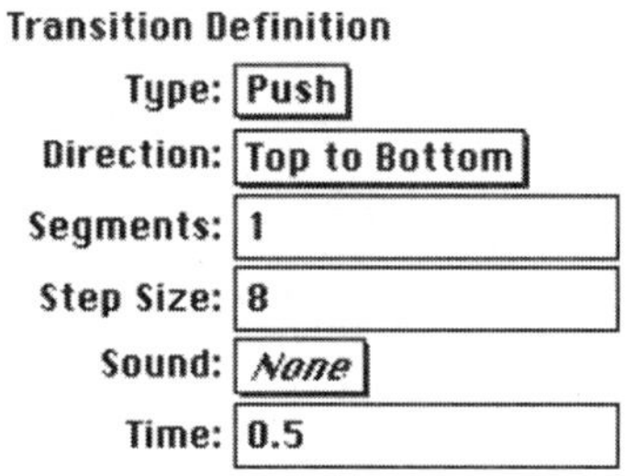

Transition Definition

Type:	Push
Direction:	Top to Bottom
Segments:	1
Step Size:	8
Sound:	*None*
Time:	0.5

Figure 6-24: Push settings.

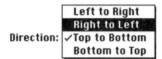

Direction:
Left to Right
Right to Left
✓Top to Bottom
Bottom to Top

Figure 6-25: Push the old page from what direction?

■ Radial—The initial setting is a clockwise sweep of
360 degrees, starting at 12 o'clock, as the new page
replaces the old. The focal point is the center of your
page. Alternative settings sweep from 6 and 12
o'clock simultaneously, in the same direction (circu-
lar) and in opposite directions (bow tie); and from 12
o'clock towards 6 o'clock both clockwise and
counter-clockwise simultaneously—like a fan opening into a full circle (Figures 6-26 and 6-27).

Transition Definition

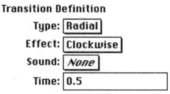

Type:	Radial
Effect:	Clockwise
Sound:	*None*
Time:	0.5

Figure 6-26: Radial settings.

```
Effect:  ✓Clockwise
Sound:    Fan
          Circular
Time:     Bow Tie
```

Figure 6-27: Different Radial types.

■ Random Lines—Vertical bands appear over the old page until it is completely covered. You can make the bands thicker and horizontal (Figure 6-28).

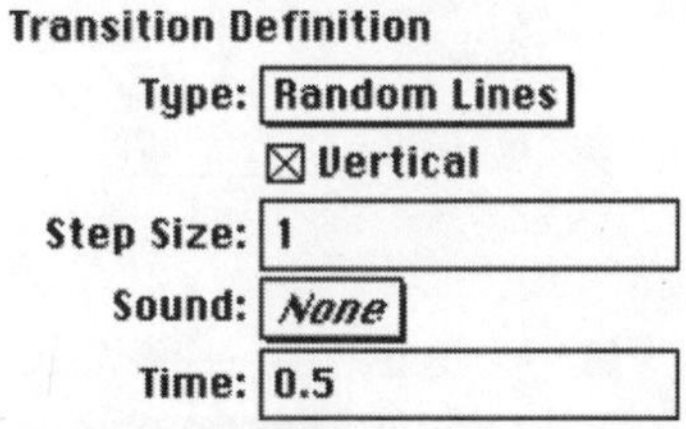

Transition Definition

Type: Random Lines
      ☒ Vertical
Step Size: 1
Sound: *None*
Time: 0.5

Figure 6-28: Random Lines settings.

■ Random Polygons—Like the Rectangle transition (see below), except Random Polygons uses a randomly generated polygon shape that doesn't appear at the exact screen center. It grows larger until the full area of the screen has been encompassed (Figure 6-29).

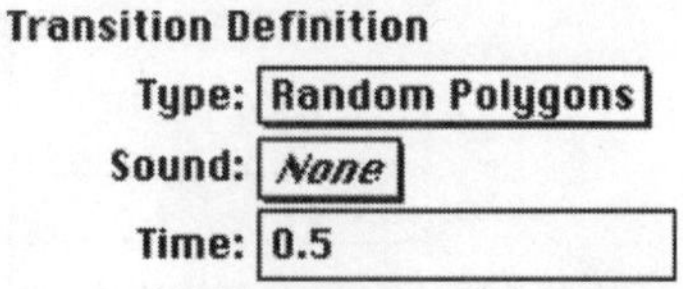

Transition Definition

Type: Random Polygons
Sound: *None*
Time: 0.5

Figure 6-29: Random Polygon settings.

■ Rectangle—A rectangle grows out from the center of your screen and replaces the old page. You can alternatively have the old page be a continually reduced rectangle that disappears in the center of the screen (Figure 6-30).

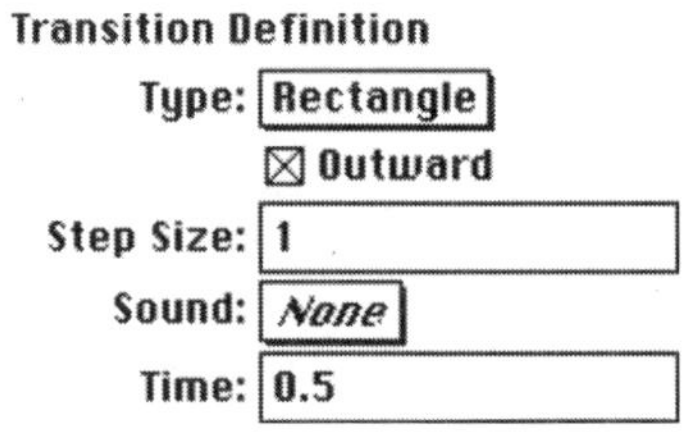

Transition Definition

Type: [Rectangle]

☒ Outward

Step Size: [1]

Sound: [*None*]

Time: [0.5]

Figure 6-30: Rectangle settings.

■ Reveal—As originally set, 13 vertical bands gradually grow wider, revealing the new page (Figure 6-31). This is related to Cover and Venetian, which you can set similarly. In Cover, however, the edge of the band marches across the width, while Reveal peels away the width. In Venetian, the band increases width from both edges.

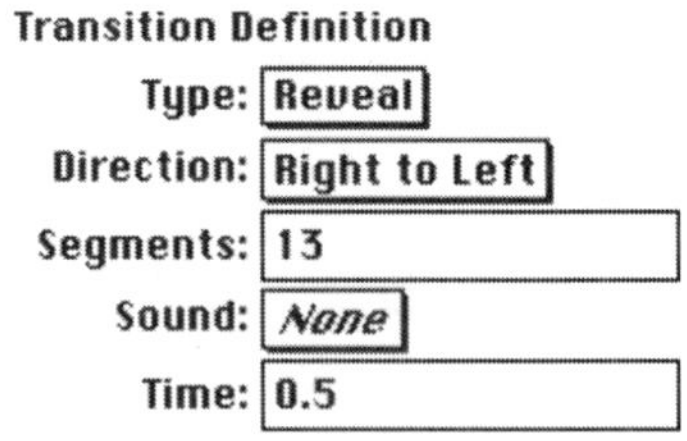

Transition Definition

Type: [Reveal]

Direction: [Right to Left]

Segments: [13]

Sound: [*None*]

Time: [0.5]

Figure 6-31: Reveal settings.

■ Triangles—Rows of adjacent triangles are added from the top of the screen. Halfway through, the rows cover the screen from top to bottom, and the old page peeks through the areas between the triangles. As the transition continues, this see-through area is filled in with the new page.

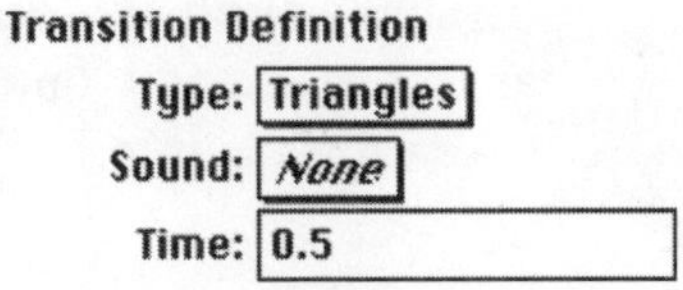

Transition Definition

Type:	Triangles
Sound:	None
Time:	0.5

Figure 6-32: Triangles settings.

■ Uncover—The old page drops down the screen, uncovering the new page. The process can be divided into segments and the direction changed so that it begins from any side or corner (Figures 6-33 and 6-34).

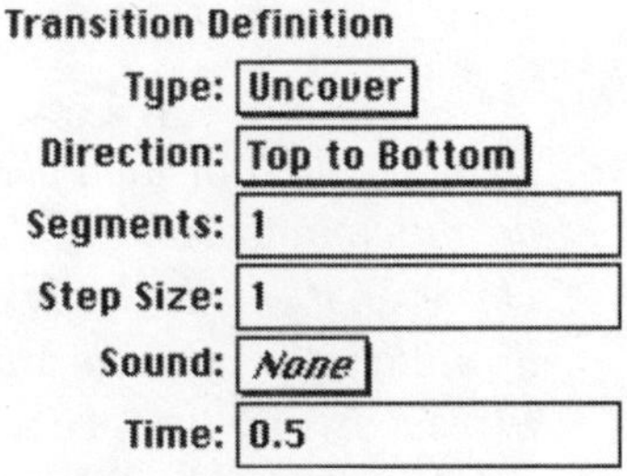

Transition Definition

Type:	Uncover
Direction:	Top to Bottom
Segments:	1
Step Size:	1
Sound:	None
Time:	0.5

Figure 6-33: Uncover settings.

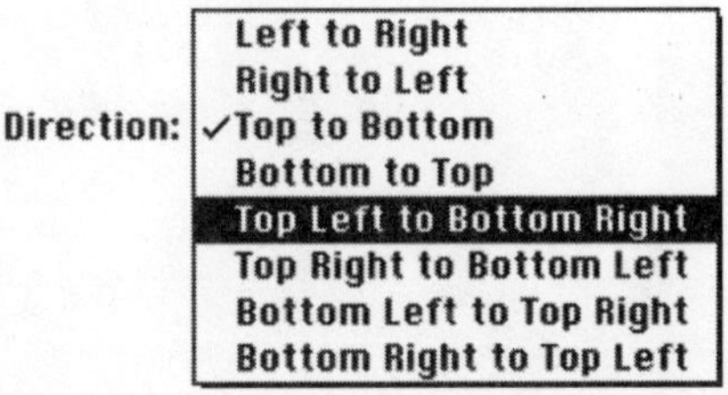

Direction:
Left to Right
Right to Left
✓Top to Bottom
Bottom to Top
Top Left to Bottom Right
Top Right to Bottom Left
Bottom Left to Top Right
Bottom Right to Top Left

Figure 6-34: From what direction should the new page be uncovered?

■ Venetian—This transition may or may not be set to resemble Venetian blinds in your installation of Immedia. A number of horizontal bands displaying the new page widen from both edges until they join, resembling the appearance of Venetian blinds as they're closed. The number of segments can be changed, and the bands made vertical (Figure 6-35). (In some shipped versions, the settings for Venetian are set to use only one vertical segment, like the Curtain transition.)

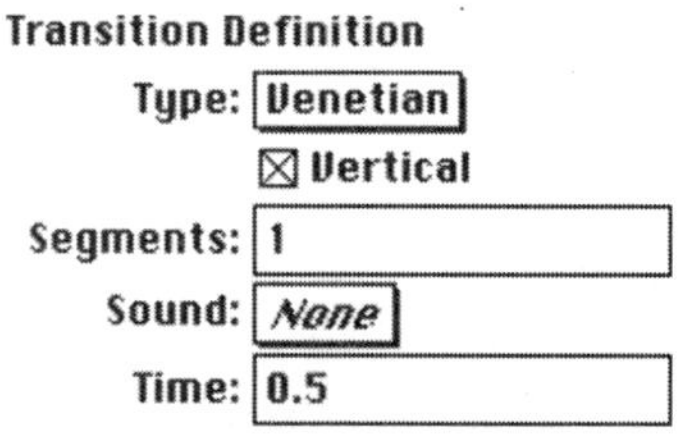

Transition Definition

Type: [Venetian]

☒ Vertical

Segments: [1   ]

Sound: [*None*]

Time: [0.5   ]

Figure 6-35: Venetian settings.

TIP

To make any transition play as rapidly as possible, adjust its definition in Custom Transitions by setting the time to 0. However, if you do this and also add a sound as part of the definition, the transition will take as long as the sound takes to play. Setting the time to 0.01 makes the transition play as rapidly as possible with a sound.

Exercise 6-1

Describing multimedia effects is an exercise in futility. To understand just how these transitions work, you really have to see them.

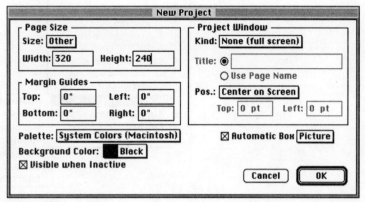

Figure 6-36: Begin a new project, using these settings.

1. Begin a new project (Figure 6-36). Set the page size to 320 points wide and 240 points tall. The starting values in this dialog box reflect whatever you entered the last time you were here. Check the Automatic Picture Box.

   Leave the other values as they are: Palette set to System Colors (Macintosh), Background Color Black, Kind None (full screen), Position Center on Screen, Visible when Inactive checked.

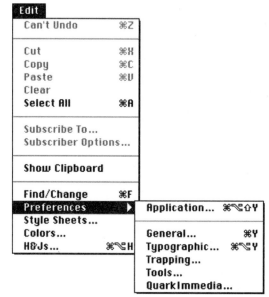

Figure 6-37: Call up QuarkImmedia Preferences.

2. Set the Edit | Preferences | QuarkImmedia command (Figure 6-37) to call up QuarkImmedia Preferences. Check Auto Advance and set the time to 30 seconds. Check Page Wraparound, so that the first and last pages are connected (Figure 6-38).

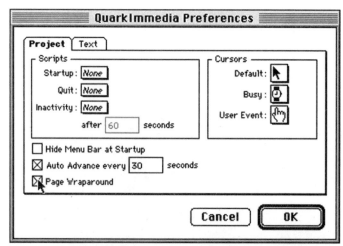

Figure 6-38: Set Auto Advance and Page Wraparound.

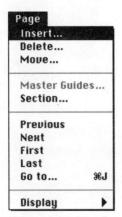

Figure 6-39: Use Page | Insert to add pages to the project.

3. Use the Page | Insert command (Figure 6-39) to add five pages to the end of the project (Figure 6-40). Now would be a good time to save your project. Call it something like Effects.qxd.

Insert Pages

Insert: `5`   page(s)   ○ before page:
                         ● after page: `1`
                         ○ at end of document

☐ Link to Current Text Chain

Master Page: `A-Master A`

[OK]   [Cancel]

Figure 6-40: Insert five pages.

---

4. Use the View | Show Colors command (Figure 6-41) to display the Colors Palette. Make certain the background-color icon—the gray box directly below the word "Colors" in the title bar—is highlighted (Figure 6-42).

View

Fit in Window	⌘0
50%	
75%	
✓Actual Size	⌘1
200%	
Thumbnails	
Windows	▶
Show Guides	
Show Baseline Grid	
✓Snap to Guides	
Hide Rulers	⌘R
Show Invisibles	⌘I
Hide Tools	
Hide Measurements	
Show Document Layout	
Show Style Sheets	
Show Colors	
Show Trap Information	
Hide QuarkImmedia Palette	

Figure 6-41: Show the Colors palette.

Figure 6-42: Change the background color of each page.

Click on the picture box on page 1. Drag the patch of blue from the Colors palette on top of the picture box on page 1 to give it a blue background.

5. Color the background of the boxes on the subsequent pages. Follow the same sequence as in the Colors palette: blue, cyan, green, magenta, red, and yellow.

6. Use the line tool to draw a single vertical line 10 points wide down the middle of page 1. Make it yellow (Figure 6-43).

Figure 6-43: What page 1 should look like—a vertical yellow bar centered on a blue page.

7. Add a 10-point horizontal line to page 2 (Figure 6-44), a diagonal line to page 3 (Figure 6-45), and the opposite diagonal on page 4 (Figure 6-46). Use a contrasting color to the background of these page for these lines. (Hint: depress the Shift key when creating the lines to constrain them to the horizontal, vertical, or 45-degree axes.)

Figure 6-44: What page 2 should look like—a horizontal magenta bar on a cyan page.

Figure 6-45: What page 3 should look like—a diagonal red bar on a green page.

Figure 6-46: What page 4 should look like—a diagonal green bar on a magenta page.

Be sure to save your project after every few steps.

8. On page 5, add a large circular picture box—Figure 6-47 illustrates how using the Shift key constrains the box creation so that the width equals the height. Use the Item | Frame command (Figure 6-48) to add a 10-point white border to the picture box (Figure 6-49).

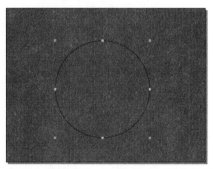

Figure 6-47: What page 5 should look like—a white circle on a red page.

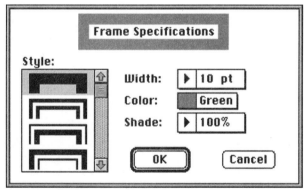

Figure 6-48: Use Item | Frame to add borders to a box.

Figure 6-49: Give the circle on page 5 a 10-point white border.

Use the Colors palette to change the background of the circle to None, so that it is transparent.

9. On page 6, use similar steps to add a large square with a 10-point red border and transparent background to the page (Figures 6-50 and 6-51).

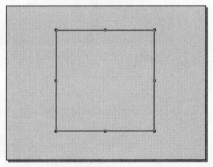

Figure 6-50: What page 6 should look like—a blue square on a yellow page.

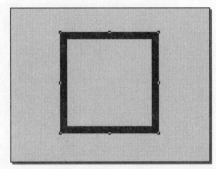

Figure 6-51: Give the box on page 6 a 10-point red border.

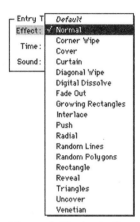

Figure 6-52: Apply the Normal transition to page 1.

We've set up these shapes and differently colored pages so that the full effects of the transitions are clearly illustrated. Now let's specify the transitions and see what they look like.

10. In the Page tab, click on page 1 in the scroll list and choose Normal from the Effect pop-up menu in the Entry Transition area (Figure 6-52).

11. Set the transition for page 2 to the next transition: Corner Wipe (Figure 6-53).

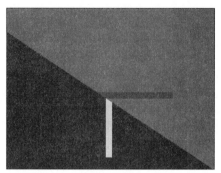

Figure 6-53: Halfway through the Corner Wipe transition to page 2.

12. Set the transitions for the subsequent pages to the next four choices: Cover, Curtain, Diagonal Wipe, and Digital Dissolve. (These transitions are pictured in Figures 6-54, 6-55, 6-56, and 6-57.)
    Save when you're done.

Figure 6-54: Halfway through the Cover transition to page 3.

Figure 6-55: Partway through the Curtain transition to page 4.

Figure 6-56: Halfway through the Diagonal Wipe transition to page 5.

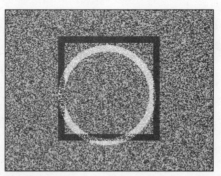

Figure 6-57: Partway through the Digital Dissolve transition to page 6.

Figure 6-58: Use
QuarkImmedia | Engage to
test the project.

Figure 6-59: The Entry
Transition area lets you adjust
the duration of the transition.

Figure 6-60: Duplicate a
custom transition to make
your own variation.

We'll only look at the first six transitions now. We'll
come back after seeing them and try out other transitions,
change the speed of the transition, and customize other
aspects.

13. Choose QuarkImmedia | Engage (Figure 6-58) or
    press function key F15 to engage the project. After
    you've seen all the transitions, press function key
    F15 again or Command-Q to disengage.

14. Slow down the transition speed on some pages by
    making the transition last 1 or 2 seconds (Figure 6-59).

15. If you want to explore how you can alter these ef-
    fects, Choose QuarkImmedia | Custom Transitions to
    change the definition of an effect. Changes that you
    make to these transition definitions affect only this
    project. However, to compare the original with your
    variation, you'll want to alter copies of the defini-
    tions and not the original.

To copy a transition, highlight a transition in the scroll
list, then click on the Duplicate button, located below the
scroll list (Figure 6-60). Now you can change the direction
of the effect in Cover copy so that it occurs from Left to
Right, and uncheck the Outward box for Curtain copy.

16. Remember to apply the new "copy" transition in the
    Page tab. Then engage the project again to see how
    the transitions look this time.

17. Choose the next set of six transitions—Fade Out,
    Growing Rectangles, Interlace, Push, Radial, and
    Random Lines—and apply them to your pages.
    Note that the duration time resets to the value in
    the transition definition.

18. Engage the project yet again to see what these transi-
    tions look like, as the next six figures show.

Figure 6-61: Partway through the Fade Out transition to page 1.

Figure 6-62: Partway through the Growing Rectangles transition to page 2.

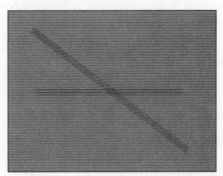

Figure 6-63: Partway through the Interlace transition to page 3.

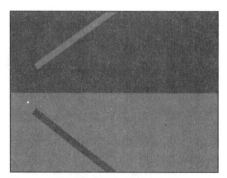

Figure 6-64: Halfway through the Push transition to page 4.

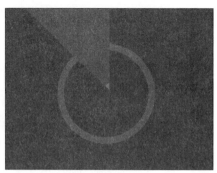

Figure 6-65: Halfway through the Radial transition to page 5.

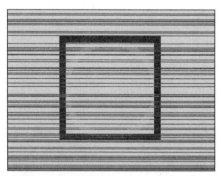

Figure 6-66: Partway through the Random Lines transition to page 6.

19. Explore how these six transitions can be altered using the QuarkImmedia | Custom Transitions command. Make copies of Radial, Push, and Random Lines. Change the effect in Radial copy from clockwise to fan or bow tie; choose a new direction for Push copy and use three segments, and uncheck Vertical for Random Lines copy.

20. Choose the next set of six transitions—Random Polygons, Rectangle, Reveal, Triangles, Uncover, and Venetian—and apply them to your pages.

21. Engage the project again to see what these transitions look like. The following six figures show examples of each transition.

Figure 6-67: Partway through the Random Polygons transition to page 1.

Figure 6-68: Partway through the Rectangle transition to page 2.

Figure 6-69: Partway through the Reveal transition to page 3.

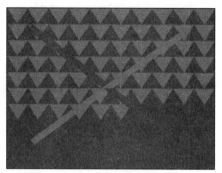

Figure 6-70: Partway through the Triangles transition to page 4.

Figure 6-71: Halfway through the Uncover transition to page 5.

Figure 6-72: Partway through the Venetian transition to page 6.

22. Explore how these six transitions can be altered using the QuarkImmedia I Custom Transitions command. Make copies of Reveal, Uncover, Venetian, and Rectangle. Try changing the direction of Reveal copy or Uncover copy, using fewer segments in Venetian copy and more in Uncover copy, and uncheck Outward in Rectangle copy.

23. When you're done exploring transitions, return to the Custom Transitions dialog and delete the "copy" transitions you created in this exercise.

Exercise 6-2

Now that you've experimented with all the transitions, let's use them in a project. We've put together a sequence of photographs taken during Carnevale in Venice. The atmosphere in Venice during Carnevale is anything but carnival-like. Europeans spend much of the year making elegant and ornate costumes based on medieval and eighteenth-century clothing as well as mythical and theatrical characters. During the week or two before Lent, they travel to Venice to stroll around the city, showing off their elaborate outfits.

We've added background music with a courtly classical theme to this sequence. Let's choose transitions that emphasize the stately, calm mood. Abrupt transitions such as Normal, which cuts from one page to the next, and Random Polygons, with its sharp and angular shapes, just won't do.

Open & View the Pages

1. Open the project file Exer06-2.imd and display it in its entirety using the View | Fit in Window command. We've placed the photos and named the pages for you in this document. We've also set the pages to automatically advance every 5 seconds. In this exercise, you'll specify the transitions between the pages. Before doing this, you'll want to look at each picture first.

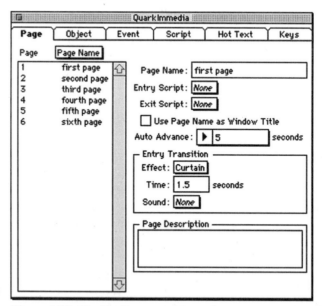

Figure 6-73: Use the Page panel to go from page to page quickly.

Click on the Page tab in the QuarkImmedia palette. Double-clicking on each page entry there will jump that page to the upper-left corner of your screen (Figure 6-73).

Select an Entry Transition for the Project

The atmosphere of Carnevale is rather dramatic, so let's open the curtain on the first act with a Curtain transition.

2. Make sure that you're displaying the first page of the document by double-clicking on page 1 in the scrollable list of the Page panel. In the Entry Transition area, change the transition in the Effect pop-up menu from Default to Curtain. This is the transition that is applied when page 1 is first displayed (Figure 6-75). The timing for this transition is 0.5 seconds, much too quick for the courtly measure of the music we're using. Change the time to 1.5 seconds by typing the number in the Time field (Figure 6-74).

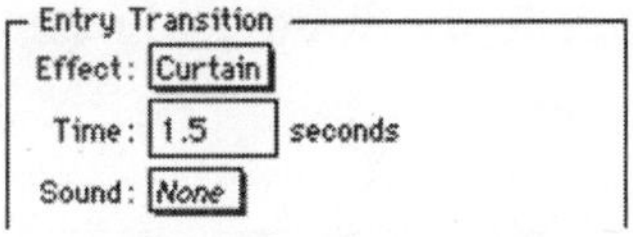

Figure 6-75: Here's what the transition looks like halfway through.

Figure 6-74: For the transition to page 1, choose the Curtain effect in the Entry Transition area.

Select Additional Transitions

Now let's take a look at the second page. The tonalities are different, warm versus cool colors, so we don't want a transition that would mix them too much. Diagonal Wipe sweeps from one corner to its opposite without mixing the images. So let's use that.

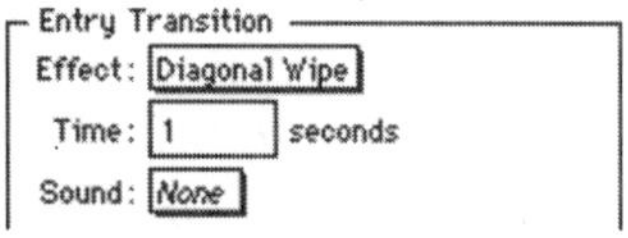

3. Double-click on page 2 in the scrollable list. Select Diagonal Wipe in the Effect pop-up menu and change the number of seconds in the Time field from 0.5 to 1 (Figures 6-76 and 6-77).

— Entry Transition —
Effect: [Diagonal Wipe]
Time: [1]   seconds
Sound: [None]

Figure 6-76: Use Diagonal Wipe as the transition to page 2.

Figure 6-77: Here's what the transition to page 2 looks like halfway through.

Now would be a good time to save your document. You could use a name like Carneval.qxd.

On the next page, let's try a transition that mixes the images. A dissolve in film actually does this, overlapping them as one fades and the other appears. A digital dissolve produces a similar effect by randomly changing pixels over the time of the transition.

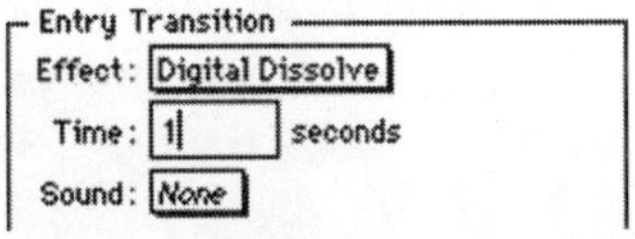

4. Select page 3 in the scrollable list. In the Effect pop-up menu of the Entry Transition area, choose Digital Dissolve. Type **1** into the Time field to make the transition longer (Figures 6-78 and 6-79).

Figure 6-78: Transition setting for page 3.

Figure 6-79: Here's what the transition to page 3 looks like partway through.

Remember to save your document frequently.

Making a Change From One Section to Another

At this point, the music changes, as do the character of the photographs. If this were a movie, we'd be on to another episode. In films, a common device for closing one scene completely and opening another is a fade. The first image fades to black and then the black fades into the second image (Figures 6-80 and 6-81). Let's try that for the next transition.

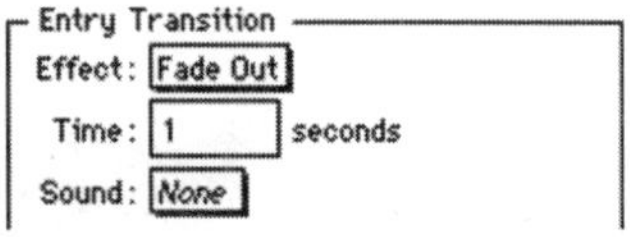

Figure 6-80: Use Fade Out to make a distinction between two distinct sections of the project.

5. Double-click on page 4 in the scrollable list and select Fade Out in the Effect pop-up menu. Give the transition 1 second in the Time field (Figures 6-80 and 6-81).

Figure 6-81: Here's what the transition to page 4 looks like partway through.

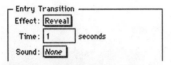

Figure 6-82: Reveal makes a strong transition between two different pages.

Now let's work with Reveal, a transition that mixes images. Although the images on pages 4 and 5 are both rather dark, you'll notice that the color differences produce a strong demarcation of change.

6. Make sure that you've got page 5 selected in the scrollable list. In the Effects pop-up menu select Reveal and change the time in the Time field to 1 second (Figures 6-82 and 6-83).

Figure 6-83: Here's what the Reveal transition to page 5 looks like partway through.

The last page is lighter than page 5. Rather than mix elements of the pages in a transition, we'll use a Push transition, which will move the previous frame right off the page and replace it with the last page.

Figure 6-84: Use a Push transition to move to the last page.

7. Double-click on page 6 in the scrollable list, then press on the Effects pop-up menu and select Push. Remember to change the transition time to 1 second (Figures 6-84 and 6-85).

Figure 6-85: Here's what the Push transition to page 6 looks like partway through.

Test the Document

Save your document. Then Engage from the Quark-Immedia menu and take a look.

Now that you've worked with the sequence once, you may want to try other transitions and see how they change the mood. Strong geometric transitions, such as Triangles and Growing Rectangles, will emphasize the transition much more than the ones used here.

Transitions & Objects

The variety of transitions we've seen so far can be applied to objects, too, when they are hidden or shown on your page.

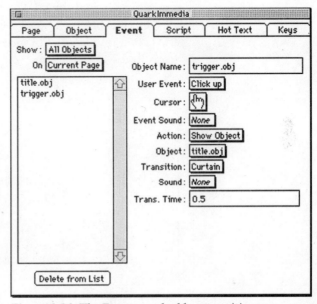

Figure 6-86: The Event panel adds a transition pop-up menu when the action is set to Show Object or Hide Object.

In the Event panel, when the Action pop-up menu is set to Show Object (Figure 6-86), another pop-up menu is added, letting you specify the transition to apply. Similarly, when the action is Hide Object, you can also specify any of these transitions.

Let's take a moment and see how this works.

■ Exercise 6-3

In the first exercise in Chapter 4, "Creating Multimedia: Making a Project," we had an object—the name of the lake—move onto the page when the mouse entered the area of the lake, and move back to the pasteboard when the mouse exited the lake.

. We'll modify that exercise now to show and then hide the lake name instead of moving it, and we'll apply transitions to these actions.

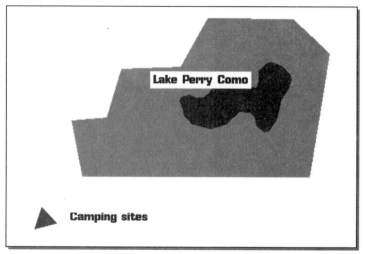

Figure 6-87: Page 1 of the exercise.

Open the Already Created Project

1. Open the Parkinfo.qxd project created in Exercise 4-1. If you did not complete that exercise (or didn't keep it), you can open Exer06-3.qxd in the Exercise folder on the Companion CD-ROM.

2. In the QuarkImmedia palette, click the Object tab.
Select Lake name.obj in the scrollable list.
    Change the Options pop-up menu to Initially
Hidden (from None). Change the Initially at pop-up
menu from Right to Home (Figure 6-88).

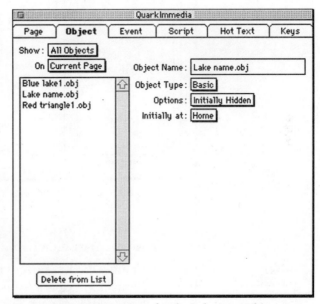

Figure 6-88: New settings for the Lake name.obj.

This latter change affects the location of this object.
When the page is displayed, however, you still won't see
the label, because the object remains hidden from sight
until we tell Immedia to show it.

3. Click on the Event tab and select Blue lake.obj in the
scrollable list. We'll need to choose new actions for
the Mouse enter and Mouse exit user events.
    Change the User Event pop-up menu to display
Mouse Exit. Change the Action pop-up menu selection to Show Object. The object remains identified as
Lake name.obj (Figure 6-89).

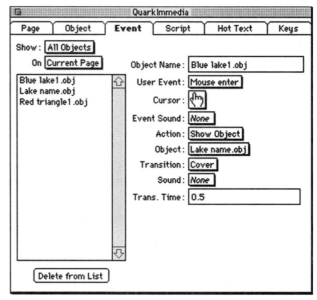

Figure 6-89: New action for Mouse enter.

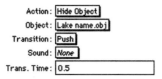

Figure 6-90: New action for Mouse exit.

4. Set the Transition pop-up menu to Cover.

5. Change the User Event pop-up menu to display Mouse exit. Change the Action pop-up menu selection to Hide Object. The object remains identified as Lake name.obj (Figure 6-90).

6. Set the Transition pop-up menu to Push.

7. Use the File | Save as command to save these changes to a new project. You can call the project Park2.qxd.

8. Engage and test the project by moving your mouse pointer over the blue lake. Note how the label now shows up on the page, and how it is removed.

9. To disengage the project, press function key F15 or Command-Q.

Moving On

In this chapter we've stepped back to look at a project from the page aspect. As a project becomes interactive, the amount of time a page displays and the manner with which one page changes to another gains importance. First we looked at interactive objects, how to make them and assign events. Next we looked at making pages interactive, how to name them, how to control the time they're displayed, and the transition from page to page.

Like objects, pages can be named in the Quark-Immedia palette. If events are linked to objects using Page Name, changing the order of pages does not break the links. This gives a flexibility to the creative process in Immedia that many other programs don't have. With Auto Advance, we can specify how long a page displays. There are preset times, but they can be changed to any duration in the Time field.

Transitions provide various ways of controlling what pages look like as they change. In the Entry Transition area of the Page panel, the Effects pop-up menu provides access to a number of different transitions. Immedia comes with a number of these already set, but through QuarkImmedia | Custom Transitions we can change them as we need.

In the next chapter, "Hot Text Links," we'll look at how text can become interactive. With hot text, words can create events just like objects and pages can.

chapter 7

Hot Text Links

Hypertext as a term has a longer history than any other Web concept—click on a hypertext word in the middle of text and it will take you someplace other than the next sentence.

Hot text, Immedia's execution of hypertext, is flexible and easy to execute. You highlight the word or words you want to make interactive, then treat it like an object. Give the text string a name and specify what actions happen with what user events. You get the full complement of user events—mouse enter and exit, double-click, and so on.

Creating Hot Text

Any text box can contain interactive text, not just boxes made into Immedia objects. The text can be formatted regularly—no extra restrictions apply. You should anticipate, however, giving the interactive text string a different appearance from non-hypertext. You set that up with the Edit | Preferences | QuarkImmedia command.

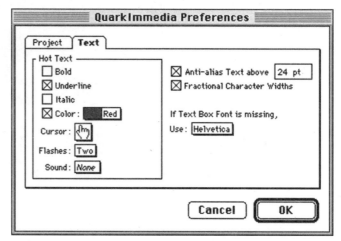

Figure 7-1: Set the "standard" appearance of interactive text in QuarkImmedia Preferences.

In the QuarkImmedia Preferences dialog box, click the Text tab for controls relating to hot text (Figure 7-1). You can make your text appear bold, underlined (this is checked as the default setting), and italic, or any combination of the three. You can additionally make the text colored.

Since users are accustomed to seeing hypertext colored and underlined in their Web browsers, you may want to give your project's hot text the same type of treatment. Be aware that a single visual cue, for instance, colored text, may not be enough to alert your users to the existence of the interactive text.

As you might expect, you can accompany hot text activation with a sound and change the cursor shape when it appears above the hot text. Quite usefully, you can make the text string flash once, twice, or three times after it's been clicked. Visual confirmation that the project recognizes the user interaction makes things go smoother for your users. Two flashes is the default setting. As with all preferences, changing this setting with no project open becomes the default value for all new projects.

Defining interactive text, as stated above, couldn't be easier:

1. Highlight the text using the I-beam pointer.
2. Click on the Hot Text tab in the QuarkImmedia palette.
3. Enter a name in the Name field in the Hot Text panel.

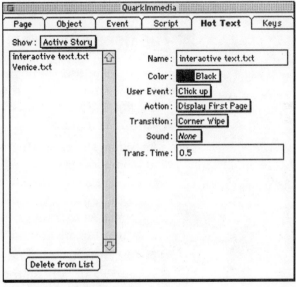

Figure 7-2: The Hot Text panel.

Look at Figure 7-2. You'll notice that the Hot Text panel resembles the Event panel. You set up events here, designating a user event—the same six as with objects: Click down, Click up, double-click, option click/right click, mouse enter, mouse exit—and action. All of the actions and transitions you can choose with an object are available here, and you can associate a sound with the event, as usual.

The one additional control is a Color pop-up menu, letting you override the default color set up in Quark-Immedia Preferences.

Above the scrollable list in the Hot Text panel is a pop-up menu that specifies what interactive text strings will display in the list. With objects, the choices are between the active page and all the pages, but the hot text Show pop-up menu makes more useful distinctions (Figure 7-3).

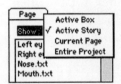

Figure 7-3: The Show pop-up menu determines whether the hot text scrollable list is more or less inclusive.

In addition to current page and entire project, Immedia restricts the listing to interactive text strings in just the currently active box or in the currently active story (which may span many boxes). We think you'll find yourself adjusting this Show pop-up menu more in the Hot Text panel than in the Object or Event panel because of the varying need to be more restrictive or more inclusive with this feature.

The Uses of Interactive Text

Since the execution of hot text so resembles that for an object, you might wonder when you should use it, and when not. We advise you to use interactive text in the following situations:

- **When the activating phrase is in running text.** If some information in your project's prose is going to trigger a user response—like the name of a product, company, or city—use hot text there, rather than add an object in the middle of text, or away from the triggering idea.

- **When you want a text equivalent of an object or button already on the page.** Redundancy makes for easy use. Make the object *and* the hot text that describes the graphic perform the same action. Then the user clicks the one that's in synch with the side of their brain that's in command at that moment.

- **For text-related actions.** If you have a glossary of terms used, biographies of the people in your company, addresses of the firms mentioned, or other reference material, it's all well and good to direct users to this information in your index or table of contents. But users will only want that information when they encounter the term or name in the middle of your presentation. Well, that's what hypertext is all about. Either jump them immediately to the right page or stick the information in a window and pop it up right next to the triggering word.

Enough about how to "use" interactive text. It's time for you to make your own.

Exercise 7-1

In this exercise you'll create several interactive text strings in separate boxes and use the text strings to hide and show objects. Everything will be created from scratch. No special files are needed.

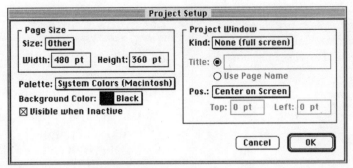

Figure 7-4: Use these values for starting the exercise.

Set Up the Project

1. Select the File | New | Project command to begin a new project (Figure 7-4).

   Set the page size to 480 points wide and 360 points high. The starting values in this dialog box reflect whatever you entered the last time you were here.

   Leave the other values as you usually find them: Palette set to System Colors (Macintosh), Background Color Black, Kind None (full screen), Position Center on Screen, and Visible When Inactive checked.

2. Select the Edit | Preferences | QuarkImmedia command. The QuarkImmedia Preferences dialog box appears.

   Click the Project tab and check the Page Wraparound check box (Figure 7-5).

   Click the Text tab.

   In the Hot Text area, make certain that Underline is checked. Check Color, and use the pop-up menu to select red.

Figure 7-5: Check the Page Wraparound check box.

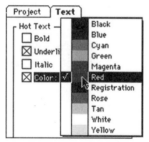

Figure 7-6: Also check the appearance of Hot Text in QuarkImmedia Preferences.

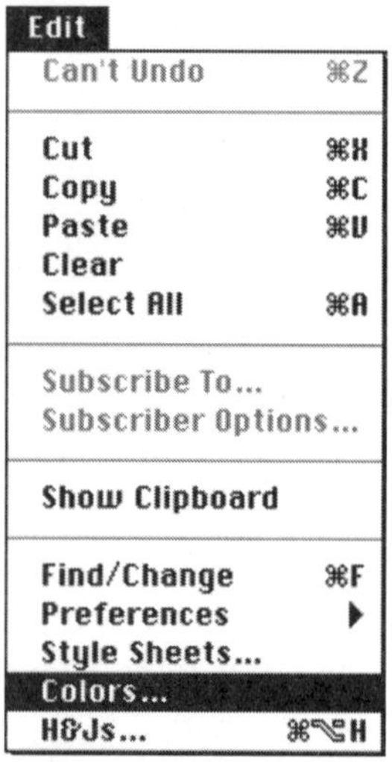

Figure 7-7: Add a new color using the Edit | Colors command.

When you make words or phrases interactive, they are formatted the same as the rest of the text and have these two attributes applied as well (Figure 7-6).

3. Use the Page | Insert command.

Now is a good time to save your project. Call it something like Hot-text.qxd.

Set Up the Content

Now we'll put all the objects and text needed on the first page and create the objects and hot text. The last step is to set up the actions for each of the interactive text strings.

4. Use the Edit | Colors command (Figure 7-7) to add two colors (Figures 7-8 and 7-9). After selecting New, use the RGB color model. First create the color Tan—100% red, 70% green, 45% blue—and then the color Rose—100% red, 20% green, 20% blue.

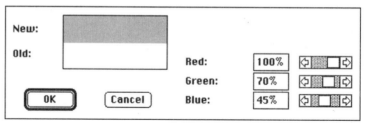

Figure 7-8: Create Tan with these settings...

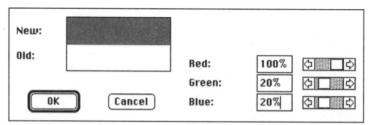

Figure 7-9: ...and Rose with these.

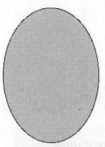

Figure 7-10: Add an oval—colored tan—for the face.

Figure 7-11: Two more ovals—tilted slightly—serve as eyes.

Figure 7-13: With a nose and mouth, the face is complete.

5. Next we need to make the simplified face using our item creation tools. Add an oval about 2 inches wide and 3 inches tall to the right side of the page. Apply Tan as the background color, and add a 1-point black border (Figure 7-10).

6. For eyes, draw an oval about ¼-inch wide and ¾-inch tall. Add a 1-point black border. Tilt the oval 10 degrees and position it as the left eye.

7. Use the Item | Duplicate command to make a copy of the left eye, and change the angle of rotation to -10 degrees. This will be the right eye (Figure 7-11). Position it appropriately, then use the Item | Space/Align command to align the bottoms of the two eyes.

8. Select each eye and create basic objects called "Left eye.obj" and "Right eye.obj" respectively. In each case, set the Options pop-up menu to read Initially Hidden (Figure 7-12).

9. Use the polygon picture box tool to draw a nose and mouth. Use the background color Rose for each (Figure 7-13).

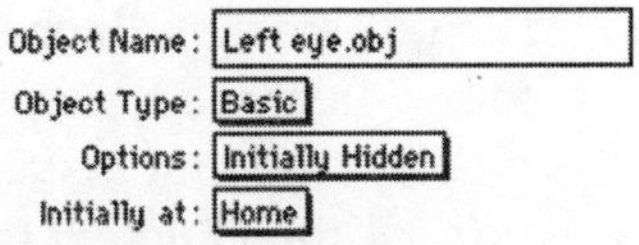

Object Name :	Left eye.obj
Object Type :	Basic
Options :	Initially Hidden
Initially at :	Home

Figure 7-12: The Object panel settings for one eye.

10. Create basic objects named "Nose.obj" and "Mouth.obj" from these items, each with Options set to Initially Hidden.

    Remember to save your work.

Left eye, right eye,
nose and mouth,

One by one
they all go out.
— Samuel Giotto

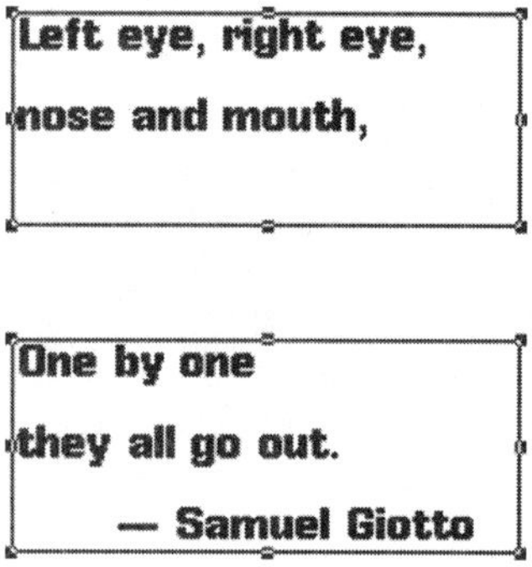

Figure 7-14: Add two text boxes, and enter the text.

Make Interactive Text Strings

We have more setup to perform—making our interactive text strings.

11. On the left side of the page, add two text boxes one above the other, and each about 1 inch tall and $2\frac{1}{2}$ inches wide (Figure 7-14).

12. In the upper box, enter this text, on two lines:

    Left eye, right eye,
    nose and mouth,

    In the lower box, enter this text, on three lines:

    One by one
    they all go out.
    — Samuel Giotto

13. Select the text in each box and make it 14-point bold. Set the leading to 28 points. In our examples we use Eurostile, a very legible, squarish face that reads well onscreen. Choose whatever font you prefer.

14. Now we will make nine interactive text strings from this brief text. Four pairs of two strings will first display and then hide the facial objects on our page. The last string will change the display to the next page where we'll put information about the author.

    Select the first instance of the word "eye."

    Click the Hot Text tab in the QuarkImmedia palette.

    In the Name field enter **Left eye.txt**.

    Reminder: save your work often.

You want the name here to clearly identify that this is a hot text string and to prevent confusion with the object that's also called "Left eye." Adding short extensions to your label names is a small but useful step you can take to keep things from becoming confusing—especially when you come back to the project weeks or months later and your memory of what does what is hazy.

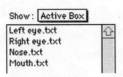

Figure 7-15: Four interactive text strings for the top box.

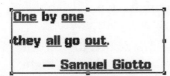

Figure 7-16: The text strings for the top box appear in the Active Box.

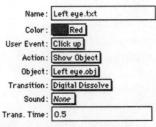

Figure 7-17: Five more interactive text strings in the lower box.

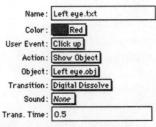

Figure 7-18: Use these Hot Text settings for making the facial features visible.

15. Make three more interactive text strings in the top box.

- The second instance of the word "eye." Call it **Right eye.txt**.
- The word "nose." Call it **nose.txt**.
- The word "mouth." Call it **mouth.txt** (Figures 7-15 and 7-16).

16. In the lower box, make five interactive text strings.

- The first instance of the word "one." Call it **Right eye out.txt**.
- The second instance of the word "one." Call it **Nose out.txt**.
- The word "all." Call it **Left eye out.txt**.
- The word "out." Call it **Mouth out.txt**.
- The last line: "—Samuel Giotto." Call it **Author.txt**.

Note that the features named—left eye, right eye, nose, and mouth—follow different sequences in the two boxes (Figure 7-17).

Define Events for the Hot Text

In the Hot Text scrollable list, you will see displayed only the interactive strings that appear in the active story (unless you linked the two boxes, you created separate stories for each box). You can have all nine strings displayed by changing the Show pop-up menu to Current Page. Strings in the more recently created text box appear above those in the older text box. Within each subgroup, the strings are listed in the order they were created.

17. Now we'll define the events. For all nine interactive text strings, we will define only the Click up user event.

As shown in Figure 7-18, the first four events follow similar steps to make the facial features visible.

- For "Left eye.txt" set the Action to Object | Show. In the Object pop-up menu, choose "Left eye.obj." Set the transition to Digital Dissolve.

- For "Right eye.txt" set the Action to Object | Show. In the Object pop-up menu, choose "Right eye.obj." Set the transition to Digital Dissolve.

- For "Nose.txt" set the Action to Object | Show. In the Object pop-up menu, choose "Nose.obj." Set the transition to Digital Dissolve.

- For "Mouth.txt" set the Action to Object | Show. In the Object pop-up menu, choose "Mouth.obj." Set the transition to Digital Dissolve.

18. The next four events will hide the features. We'll vary the effect for each, and use a different sequence to prevent things from becoming too predictable. Don't go too long without saving your work.

- For "Right eye out.txt" set the Action to Object | Hide. In the Object pop-up menu, choose "Right eye.obj." Set the transition to Cover (Figure 7-19).

- For "Nose out.txt" set the Action to Object | Hide. In the Object pop-up menu, choose "Nose.obj." Set the transition to Rectangle, and the Transition Time to 2 seconds.

- For "Left eye out.txt" set the Action to Object | Hide. In the Object pop-up menu, choose "Left eye.obj." Set the transition to Cover.

- For "Mouth out.txt" set the Action to Object | Hide. In the Object pop-up menu, choose "Mouth.obj." Set the transition to Digital Dissolve, and the Transition Time to 3 seconds.

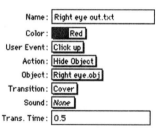

Figure 7-19: The second group of interactive text strings is used to hide the facial features.

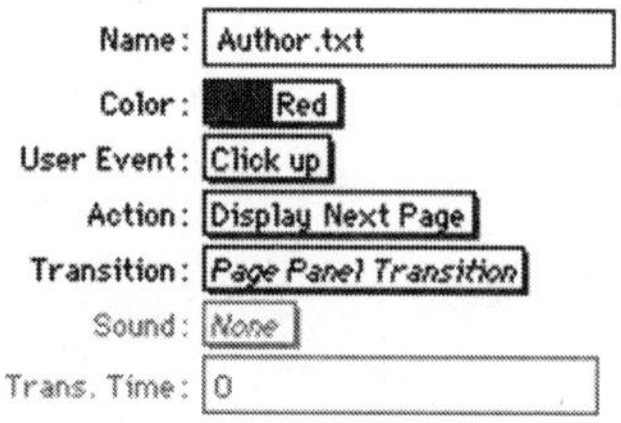

Switch to Page 2

The last steps relate to the display of the second page.

19. For "Author.txt" set the Action to Display Next Page (Figure 7-20).

Figure 7-20: The last string displays the next page.

20. On the second page, add a text box that contains something like the following: **Samuel Giotto is a distinguished, not to say esteemed, but eminently well-loved oral-doggerel-meister. He is available for parties and can usually be persuaded to perform balloon tricks** (Figure 7-21). Apply the same type specs as on the first page: 14-point bold, with 28-point leading.

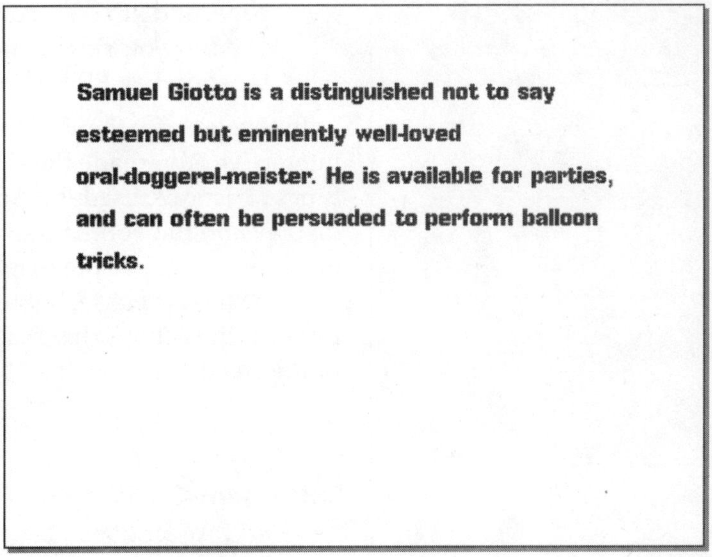

> **Samuel Giotto is a distinguished not to say**
>
> **esteemed but eminently well-loved**
>
> **oral-doggerel-meister. He is available for parties,**
>
> **and can often be persuaded to perform balloon**
>
> **tricks.**

Figure 7-21: The second page.

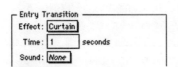

Figure 7-22: Page panel settings for page 1 entry transition...

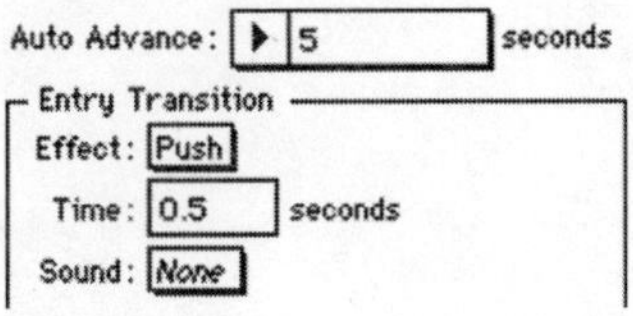

Figure 7-23: ...and for page 2 auto advance.

Choose Page Transitions

21. Click the Page tab. In the scrollable list, highlight page 1. Set the Entry Transition to Curtain and the Transition Time to 1 second (Figure 7-22).

    For page 2, set Auto Advance to 5 seconds. Set the Entry Transition to Push (Figure 7-23).

We've completed all the construction. Before engaging the project, save your work.

Test the Interactive Text

22. Return to page 1 and choose QuarkImmedia | Engage or press function key F15 to engage the project. Click on all the interactive text strings to make the facial features appear and disappear. Note how the transition effects applied to objects can be used to make certain types of emphasis. Clicking on the author's name sends the project to the second page, and after 5 seconds, it returns to page 1.

    After you've seen how everything works, press function key F15 again or Command-Q to disengage.

In this exercise you did more than just make words interactive. You made the interactive text perform different types of actions, used the Action | Object submenu to display and hide objects, and applied transitions not just to pages but also to the display and hiding of objects.

In the next exercise, hot text will again be exploited to perform the actions that make your project interactive and multidirectional.

Problems?

If your project doesn't seem to work right, try running the finished project located on the Companion CD-ROM. The finished project for this exercise is located in the Exercise folder, in the folder called Exer07-1.

In QuarkXPress, you simply open the project called Hot-text.qxd. You can engage the project to see exactly what is intended. And you can click on any object name or interactive text string name and study the settings in the Object and Hot Text panels to guide you in locating any place you may have gone astray.

Exercise 7-2

In this exercise, we'll build a project that's intended to be part of an interactive type catalog to be published both on CD-ROM and the Internet. The design specifies Helvetica, a font that is installed on most computers. If you discover that you don't have Helvetica, you may find that you have Arial, which will do nicely. You will need several other fonts to complete this exercise. We've provided them for you on the Companion CD-ROM with the files for this project.

Install Fonts From the Companion CD-ROM

To complete this exercise exactly as written, you need to use the same fonts that we've used. On the Companion CD-ROM, in the Exer07-2 folder (which is in the Exercise folder), you will find three freeware or shareware fonts: Village, Holstein, and Circle A. These are TrueType fonts. We have permission to distribute them, and you can use them for this and other exercises in this book. If you decide to use any of these fonts for commercial purposes, you may need to pay a modest license fee. Specifics on further use are also located in the Exer07-2 folder.

Before you proceed with this exercise, you need to install these fonts on your computer, or you may wish to substitute fonts that you already have installed.

Open the Project & View the Pages

1. Open the file Ex07-2.qxd and display the first page of the project completely using the View I Fit in Window command.

This document contains a series of linked text boxes. The text has already been placed on the pages. Your job is to add interactivity.

Before we get going, let's take a look at the Quark-Immedia preferences (Figure 7-24).

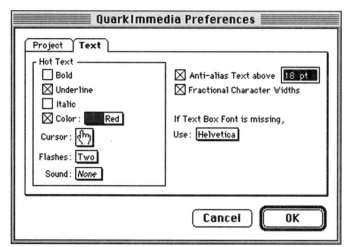

Figure 7-24: The choices you make in the Text panel affect the display of hot text in the project.

2. Click the Text tab to access the Text preferences panel.

    The design of our project calls for underlined Helvetica Bold to indicate interactive text. In the Hot Text area, make sure the Bold and Underline check boxes are checked. Set the hot text color, using the Color pop-up menu, to black.

    On the right-hand side of the Text preferences panel, make sure the If Text Box Font is Missing pop-up menu displays Helvetica.

As we have said before, using page names ensures that Immedia keeps track of events if the page order is changed. So let's give these pages names.

3. In the Page panel, highlight page 1 in the scrollable list. Name page 1 by entering **Front Page** in the Name field.

Next, as shown in Figure 7-25, select the subsequent pages and name them as follows:

■ Page 2, **Fonts intro.**

■ Page 3, **Holstein**

■ Page 4, **Village**

■ Page 5, **Circle A**

■ Page 6, **Order Form**

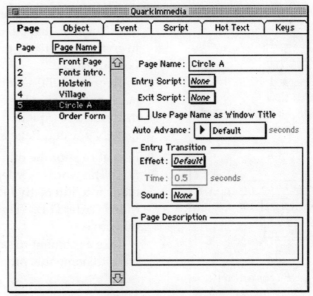

Figure 7-25: Name the pages in the Page panel.

Create Interactive Text

Because we want viewers to stay as long as they want on each page, we won't use Auto Advance to leave a page. Instead, interactive text will serve to trigger the movement from page to page (Figure 7-26).

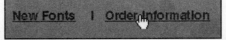

Figure 7-26: Using interactive text and pictures for navigation.

Figure 7-27: You can find the text for navigation in the library.

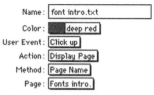

Figure 7-28: Setting the words New Fonts to display the Fonts intro page.

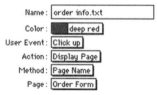

Figure 7-29: By clicking on the words Order Information, viewers will go to the Order Form page.

In the library for this exercise, there's a text box with the commands for navigating this project. Since they'll be the same on every page, we can place them on a master page.

4. Using the Page | Display | A-Master Page A command, go to the project's master page. Open Lib04-2.qxl and locate the text box labeled navigation (Figure 7-27). Drag the box onto the page and place it at the bottom of the page below the primary text box.

Now it's time to make the text interactive.

5. Highlight the word Fonts in the navigation text box. Click the Hot Text tab on the QuarkImmedia palette to go to the Hot Text panel. In the Name field enter **Font intro.txt**.

   To execute the action that displays the Fonts intro page, select Page | Display in the Action pop-up menu. In subsequent pop-up menus choose Method Page Name and Page Fonts intro (Figure 7-28).

6. Repeat this for the other page that we'll link to right now. The words "Order Information" need to be made into interactive text that will link to the page called Order Form (Figure 7-29), which is page 6 in this project.

   Take a moment to save this project. You might want to name this project Fonts.qxd.

Create Text Links to Display Windows

We now have a way to navigate through the document. Let's go work on the section that describes these fonts and make links from this page to the pages that describe each font.

7. Make sure that you're on page 2 of the document by double-clicking its name in the scrollable list of the Page panel. On the page, highlight the heading of the first section, Holstein (Figure 7-30). We'll make this interactive now.

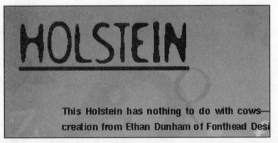

Figure 7-30: You can make text headings interactive text.

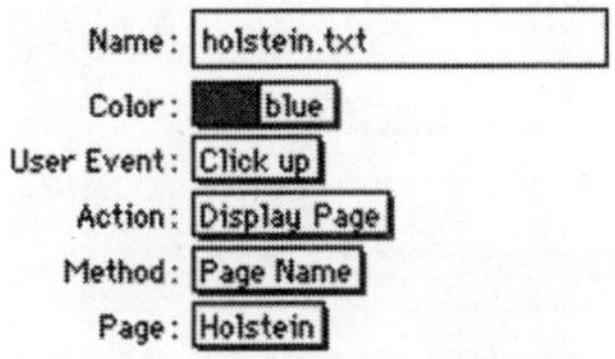

Name: holstein.txt
Color: blue
User Event: Click up
Action: Display Page
Method: Page Name
Page: Holstein

Figure 7-31: You can make a heading a link to another object.

8. Go to the Hot Text panel and give the text a name. Type **Holstein.txt** in the Name field. We want the heading to trigger the display of the page that describes this font (Figure 7-31). Set the action to Display Page, the method to Page Name, and the page to Holstein to make the trigger.

9. For the other two fonts, Village and Circle A, do the same thing: name the text **Village.txt** and **CircleA.txt,** and identify the Village and Circle A pages in the Page pop-up menu.

   Saving your project at this point would be a good idea.

Create the Windows

The user will want to see examples of these fonts, all of the letters, numbers, and punctuation. We'll create windows that open when the user clicks on the name of the font.

10. In the library, locate a text box with text for a display. Drag the text box onto the pasteboard. Make sure the text box is set in Holstein, not the Helvetica font with which it was created. Select all the text and, either in the measurements palette or with the Style | Font | Holstein command, change the font (Figure 7-32).

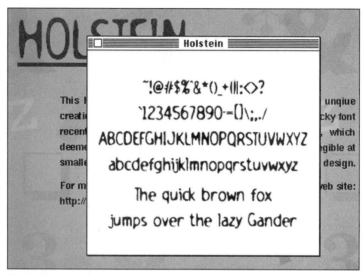

Figure 7-32: When the viewer clicks the hot text, a window appears.

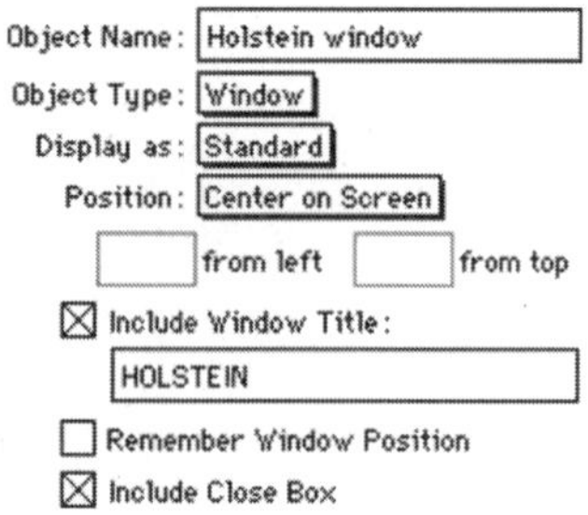

Object Name: [Holstein window]
Object Type: [Window]
Display as: [Standard]
Position: [Center on Screen]
[   ] from left [   ] from top
☒ Include Window Title:
[HOLSTEIN]
☐ Remember Window Position
☒ Include Close Box

Figure 7-33: Create a window object to display examples of the fonts.

11. To define this as a window object, type **Holstein.wdw** in the Name field of the Object panel. In the Object Type pop-up menu select Window. In the Display as pop-up menu choose Standard. For Position select Center on Screen. Be sure to check Include Close Box. Users will want to close one box and view another (Figure 7-33).

12. On the next two pages (pages 4 and 5), repeat the above procedure. Take the text box from the library and put it on the pasteboard next to page 3. Change the font to Village and to Circle A. Define the box as a window object with the same actions you just performed to create a window object.

13. The heading on each page opens these windows. Make the heading interactive in the Hot Text panel. Use the action Open Window for Click up, then select the text window you've created in the Window pop-up menu.

Test the Project

You now have the major elements of the project document. You still have one page to complete, but we'll save that for Chapter 16, "Text Box Objects." Save the project. Then use the QuarkImmedia | Engage command to take a look at how things work.

Moving On

Immedia's implementation of interactive text, whose antecedents date back to Ted Nelson and Vannevar Bush, gives the designer and the viewer lots to chew on. Hot text, as it's called here, extends the notion of multimedia properties beyond the items in a layout, extends them, in fact, all the way to any word or character in any story in the project.

The same user events—mouse enter and exit, click down and up, option click/right mouse and double-click—and the same long list of actions can all be connected to an interactive text string identically to how they are associated with a basic Immedia object in the Event panel.

Visual cues, of course, have to be provided for hot text, which can always be formatted using the same commands as any text in XPress or Immedia. The standard appearance for hot text in your project is set in QuarkImmedia preferences, as are such details as how many flashes you want to occur when the user clicks on a live link.

We turn our attention next to sound, whether it be incidental music or a major incident. While many transitions and events in general can have specific sounds associated with them, designing a document with sound is more than just utilizing that Sound pop-up menu that we've left alone so far. It's time now to tune in to the audio spectrum of Immedia that is discussed in detail in Chapter 8, "Sound."

Sound

Up to now, we've dealt only with the visual capabilities of QuarkImmedia, but multimedia is capable of communicating with much more—motion and sound as well as static images and text.

Sound is often comprehended faster than written words or text, which makes it an important and effective way of communicating. Think about how quickly you know that you've made an error when you hear a system beep. A text message wouldn't communicate to you as fast.

Sounds are useful for setting mood and providing atmosphere. Would a horror flick be as scary without the creepy music or a love scene as romantic without the violins? But sound does more than just dress up pictures. Appropriate sounds combined with strong visuals will produce a greater impact than either the sound or graphics would alone.

There are two basic types of sound to use in multimedia—sound effects and music tracks. Sound effects are the short sounds that punctuate or clarify events—button clicks, whooshes, thuds. Clicks can let users know that the computer registers their click on a button, or that what they tried to do won't work. Music tracks, rhythm grooves, and melodic pieces are longer sounds, often looped, that play in the background of a project. Although they are called background music, the interaction of music tracks with the visuals can be a strong element of a project, supporting or contradicting the mood or message of the graphics.

Music tracks aren't the only kind of longer sounds you're able to play. Narration is also sound. Spoken words often have a greater impact in conjunction with graphics than text. Studies have shown that people retain more when information is presented to multiple senses. Users will listen to someone talking for longer than they will sit reading explanations, so don't ignore ways to utilize narration.

Immedia has two ways of incorporating sound: event and page transition sounds and sound actions. These correspond in many ways to sound effects and music tracks.

Event Sounds

Every user event has an Event Sound pop-up menu (Figure 8-1). If you select a sound in the pop-up menu, it will play with that user event. This doesn't use the Action pop-up menu, so you don't have to sacrifice an action to play a sound. Every action can have a corresponding sound.

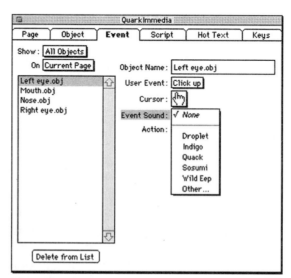

Figure 8-1: Every user event can have a corresponding sound.

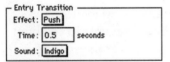

Figure 8-2: Add a sound to a page transition with the Sound pop-up menu.

Page transitions can have sounds, too. There's a Sound pop-up menu in the Entry Transition area of the Page panel, as you can see in Figure 8-2. Sounds with entry transitions serve to link or separate the elements of successive pages.

Neither event sounds nor sounds used with page transitions can be looped. They can only be played once, so they won't be useful as background music.

Sound Actions

There are also actions that will play sounds. You can use user events to start, stop, pause, and resume the play of longer sounds. Take a look at the Sound submenu of the Action pop-up menu and you'll see several ways to control sounds.

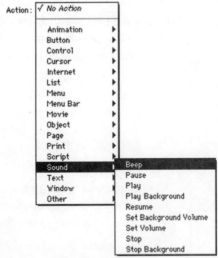

Figure 8-3: Beep is the simplest of sound actions.

■ Beep—This is the most basic use of sound, the system beep. It's used in most computer systems to indicate that an error has occurred. When you select Beep in the Action pop-up menu of the Event panel, you'll notice that there's no pop-up menu to select a sound. Beep plays the currently selected Alert

Sound. On computers running the Macintosh OS, the user can choose alert sounds, even add custom ones, so you don't have control over the specific sound file that plays with this action.

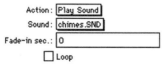

Figure 8-4: Play any sound with Play Sound action.

- Play Sound—If you want an action to play a sound, select Sound | Play in the Action pop-up menu. A Sound pop-up menu will prompt you to choose a sound (Figure 8-4). If the one you want isn't listed in the pop-up menu, click Other to open the Select a Sound File dialog box and locate the sound file. There's another field added with this action, the Fade-in sec. field. Enter the time to fade a sound into the project.

  Play Sound plays a chosen sound from start to finish. The sound will continue playing even if you go to another page.

Figure 8-5: Stop any sound that's currently playing with Stop Sound.

- Stop Sound—Use Sound | Stop in the Action pop-up menu to stop a sound that's playing (Figure 8-5). Like Play Sound, you'll be given a pop-up menu to select which sound and a Fade-out sec. box, in which you can specify the time in seconds for a fade.

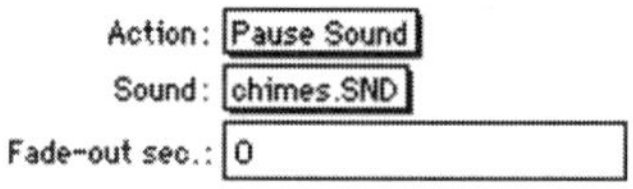

Figure 8-6: Use Pause Sound to halt a sound.

- Pause Sound—Sound | Pause halts the playing of a sound (Figure 8-6). You can specify which sound to pause in the Sound pop-up menu. If you want the sound to fade into the pause, enter a duration for the fade in the Fade-out sec. field.

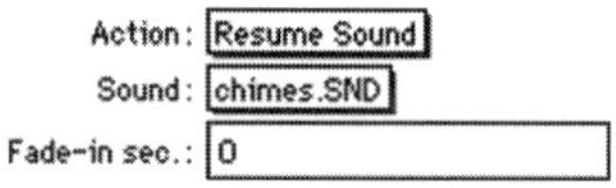

Figure 8-7: Resume Sound will start playing where the sound was paused.

- Resume Sound—This will start playing a sound that's been paused, from the place where it stopped. Specify which sound in the Sound pop-up menu and enter a time for a fade in the Fade-in sec. field (Figure 8-7).

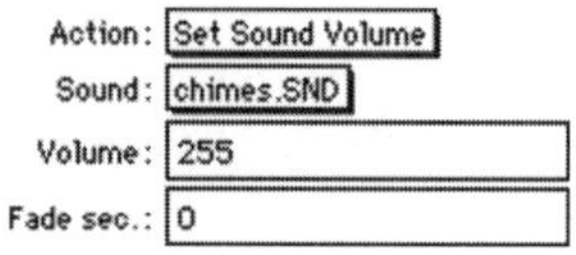

Figure 8-8: Change the level of a sound with Set Sound Volume.

- Set Sound Volume—If the sound has been recorded too loudly, you can set the volume to another level with this action. Select Sound | Set Volume in the Action pop-up menu and choose which sound in the Sound pop-up menu (Figure 8-8). Enter the level you want, from 1 (the lowest) to 255 (the loudest) in the Volume field. As with most of the other sound actions, there's a Fade sec. field to enter the length of time for a transition to the new level.

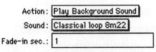

Figure 8-9: Only one sound at a time can be played as background sound.

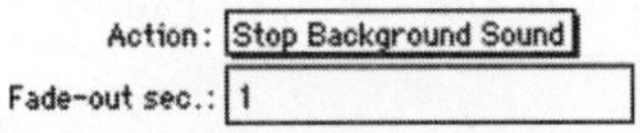

Action: Stop Background Sound
Fade-out sec.: 1

Figure 8-10: Stop any background sound with Stop Background sound.

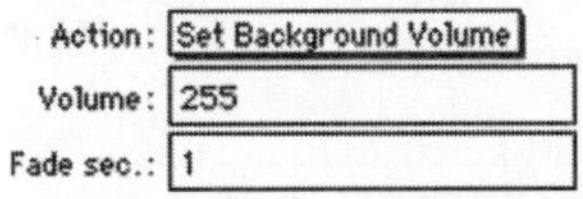

Action: Set Background Volume
Volume: 255
Fade sec.: 1

Figure 8-11: Adjust the level of Background sound with Set Background Volume.

■ Play Background Sound—Use Sound | Play Background to assign a sound that plays continuously in the background of a project (Figure 8-9). The sound will loop for the length of the project or until the Stop Background Sound command stops it. Only one background sound can play at any time, but you can play as many overlapping sounds as you'd like using the Play Sound action.

■ Stop Background Sound—Use Sound | Stop Background to stop whatever sound is playing in the background. In the Fade-out sec. field, fill in how long you want the sound to take to fade out.

■ Set Background Volume—Use this action to set the volume level from 1 to 255 of a designated background sound (Figure 8-11). Like the Set Sound Volume command, there's a field to enter the time for a fade.

Synching Music & Action

If the timing of your presentation or project fits with the rhythm and pacing of the music, the project will feel complete. You can use changes in music to underscore events in the project.

How do you synchronize music and pacing of the project? Using Auto Advance, you have control over how long each page displays. Listen to the music for breaks and strong musical interludes. With a metronome or stop watch, you can time sequences and transitions. Timing music is harder if you don't have any timing devices, but there's always counting—and trial and error! When you do synchronize the pacing of your project with the musical accompaniment, you'll be pleased with the difference.

Right now our capabilities are limited to one sound action per user event. But don't forget that you can also use an event sound with an action and thereby play multiple sounds—one as a special effect, the other as musical accompaniment or narration. In Chapter 12, "Scripts," you'll learn how to create scripts that can associate a number of actions with one user event. Then you'll be able to play a number of sounds with one mouse click, or play sounds as a project opens.

Working With Digital Sound Files

Graphic files have a number of formats—JPEG, EPS, PICT, TIFF—to name a few. So do sounds. Immedia can incorporate any sounds saved in the following formats:

- AIFF—(Audio Interchange File Format) A cross-platform format, AIFF can provide high fidelity, but at the cost of large file sizes. This is the sound format usually used by sound editors.

- AU or mLaw—A UNIX audio format playable on Mac and Windows. A compact format, it doesn't have the high fidelity of AIFF but can provide a good dynamic range. This format is commonly used on the Internet.

- WAV—The Windows sound format. Some sound players will play WAV on Macs.

- SND—The Mac sound format for System 7 and beyond. It's usually used for beeps and alerts, but can be used for larger files.

- MIDI—(Musical Instrument Digital Interface) A sound format that can deliver sound in small files. MIDI data is performance data, not digitized sound. Instead, MIDI sound files tell MIDI-compliant devices how to recreate sounds.

    MIDI is a different type of sound format. It's not sampled. Instead, the musical information is transmitted as code, actual text files that tell a MIDI player what to do. MIDI files are considerably smaller than sampled sound files, so they're useful for the Internet. But to play MIDI tracks, a user must have a MIDI player.

The process of turning analog sound into digital files is called sampling and is much like scanning images. Sound files, like graphics files, can be sampled at different "resolutions." High-resolution sounds are usually sampled at 44.1 kHz, with a bit depth of 16 bits.

For multimedia, sound is often downsampled to 22.05 kHz and 8 bits. This is adequate for music on most computer speakers and fine for voice. Sound files can also be compressed to as low as 5.5 kHz and 4 bits. You have control over sound compression levels when you export a project; we'll go over this in Chapter 19, "Exporting a Project." Converting from stereo to mono will also decrease the size of a file. Remember that smaller sound files generally have lower audio quality. It's always a good idea to test sounds at different sampling resolution, bit depth, and compression settings.

TIP

Sounds are buffered when played in the QuarkImmedia Viewer. One second of sound is held in a section of memory until it's ready to be played. When a sound is handed to the system to be played, another second of sound is transferred to the buffer. Each sound that is played has its own buffer. Consequently, playing a number of sounds can use a lot of RAM, which may require a higher memory allocation for Macintosh Viewers. Test your projects if you're using a number of sounds.

If you're not embedding the Viewer in the project, you may want to suggest to users that they add to the memory allocation for their Viewers. Do this by selecting the Viewer and choosing File | Get Info. Increase the number in the Preferred Size field in the Memory Requirements area.

Single-speed CD-ROMs may have problems playing high-resolution sounds, pausing and skipping in playback. This is why many multimedia authors require at least double-speed CD-ROM players for their projects. This problem can be more pronounced on the Internet, especially when delivered over modems. In these situations you're limited to short event sounds and short looping musical segments for adequate playback.

Alternatively, users using a more recent version of Macintosh System 7 can use their QuickTime Musical Instruments extension to listen to a MIDI file. If you save MIDI tracks as QuickTime movies, you can play them through Immedia on any Mac that has this extension.

TIP

There are two MIDI file formats. Standard MIDI assigns sounds to different instruments for playback by a MIDI synthesizer. Instrument assignments in the General MIDI format never change. Program 1 is always acoustic piano, program 57 is always trumpet. General MIDI format files can be played on any General MIDI-compliant synthesizer, of which the QuickTime Musical Instruments Extension is one, and will always sound the same.

Cross-Platform Sound

Sounds are exported in a compact Quark proprietary format, so you don't have to worry about whether a sound will play on one platform or another. As long as the user has a computer with sound capability, the project sound will play.

Almost every Mac has built-in sound—it's now an integral part of the Macintosh system. Even in newer Windows machines, however, sound capability isn't always a built-in option. Windows machines designed for multimedia typically have 16-bit sound cards. Machines with 8-bit sound cards will probably be able to handle 16-bit, but will play them with the lower resolution and sound quality of 8-bit.

TIP

If you're distributing a project to Windows users who may not have computers with sound capability, give them a way to turn the sound off. A machine without a sound card might play a continuous beep for a sound action. This can be extremely annoying and will probably prevent users from getting through your project! So include a message to Windows users, perhaps in a window at the beginning of the project, with an action to turn the sound off.

Exercise 8-1

In this exercise, we'll add sound to the user events in the first project we created in the last chapter. If you didn't complete that exercise, or had problems with it, you can use a completed version of it located in the Exer08-1 folder on the Companion CD-ROM.

You'll need sound files for this exercise, which you'll find in your System file (Figure 8-12). So before you open any projects or programs, open the System Folder and locate the System file—it looks like a suitcase, as Figure 8-13 shows. You can make copies of the sounds by selecting them, holding down the Option key, and dragging them out of the System file on to the desktop. Copy the following sounds: Droplet, Indigo, Quack, Sosumi, and Wild Eep.

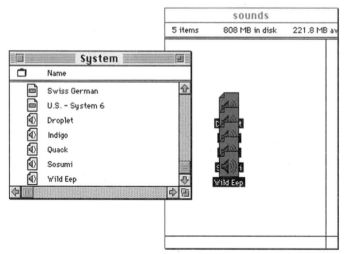

Figure 8-12: Copy the sounds from your System file for this exercise.

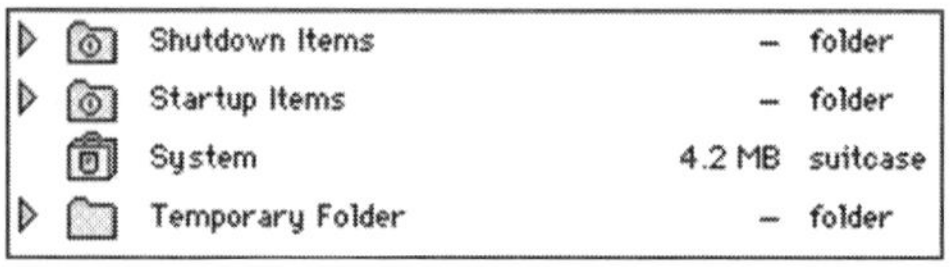

▷	🔲	Shutdown Items	—	folder
▷	🔲	Startup Items	—	folder
	🔲	System	4.2 MB	suitcase
▷	🔲	Temporary Folder	—	folder

Figure 8-13: The System file looks like a suitcase.

1. Open the project you created in Exer07-1 and save a duplicate file to use for this exercise using File | Save As. Name it Samsound.qxd.

2. In the Hot Text panel, select the first interactive text string, Left eye.txt. If you don't see any text strings in the scrollable list, make sure that one of them is highlighted in the text box on the project page.

Figure 8-14: Select Droplet in the Sound pop-up menu to add a sound to the first interactive text string.

3. In the Sound pop-up menu on the right-hand side, select Droplet (Figure 8-14). You probably won't see the sound in the list, so click Other to open the Select a Sound File dialog box and locate it.

4. Highlight the next text string, Right eye.txt, and select a sound file—this time Wild Eep.

5. For the third text string, Nose.txt, choose Sosumi in the Sound pop-up menu.

6. For the fourth in this group, Mouth.txt, choose Quack.

7. You've now selected sounds for all the text strings in the first text box. Let's save the file and take a look (and a listen). Use QuarkImmedia | Engage or the F15 function key to preview your file and try out the sounds.

Now that you've provided sounds for the hot text in one of the text boxes, let's do the same for the other.

1. Click on the second text box and highlight the first text string in the scrollable list, Right eye out.txt.

2. Go to the Sound pop-up menu and find Indigo. Since we haven't used it yet, you'll have to choose Other to get the dialog box to locate the sound.

3. For the next text string, Nose out.txt, try one of the sounds we've already used, Wild Eep.

4. For Left eye out.txt, select Droplet.

5. For the last in this group, Mouth out.txt, choose Quack.

Each interactive text string now has a sound that will play along with the action. In this exercise, we have selected sounds using the Sound pop-up menu on the Hot Text panel. Other types of objects, basic objects, windows, movies, and animations (which we'll look at in later chapters) can use the Event Sound pop-up menu on the Event panel, which functions in the same manner.

There's one text string left, Author.txt. Take a look at the Hot Text panel. The action you used in the last chapter, Display Next Page, doesn't have a Sound pop-up menu. How can you get a sound to play?

1. Go back to the Page panel and click on Page 2.

2. If you look at the lower right of the panel, you'll notice a Sound pop-up menu in the Entry Transition area. Choose a sound here—let's use Indigo—to play when the page opens (Figure 8-15).

3. Save your project and take a look.

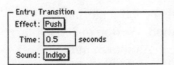

Figure 8-15: Assign a sound to the Entry Transition for the second page.

Exercise 8-2

Now we'll go back to another exercise we created previously. This time we'll use sounds to underscore the changes in character from one page to another in the Venice project we made in Chapter 6, "Transitions & Pages." The sounds we're using are from the Ventana Audio Labs section of their Web site (www.vmedia.com) and from the Quark Clip Media CD. There are also high-resolution versions of the Quark sounds on their CD if you want to use them.

1. Open the project you created for Exer06-2 and save a duplicate copy to work with. Give it an appropriate name, such as Venice sounds.

2. Using QuarkImmedia | Engage, play this project and observe how the pacing of the pages and sounds match up. We did this by adjusting the settings in the Auto Advance pop-up menu on each page.

Take a look at the first page and you'll see that this project begins with a 1.5-second curtain transition. The background sound, however, doesn't start until the page is fully displayed. That's 1.5 seconds of quiet while the image is unfolding. To fill in the dead air space we used a gong, which announces the entry of the background music.

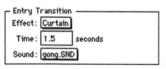

Figure 8-16: Select a sound for the entry to the project on the first page.

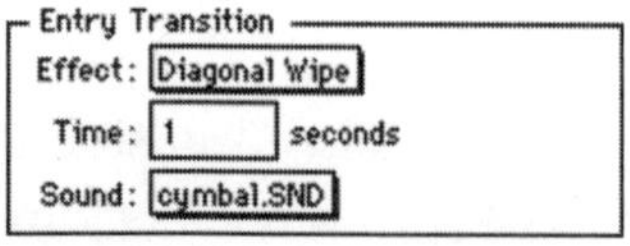

3. Go to the Page panel of the QuarkImmedia palette and click on page 1 in the scrollable list to display the settings for that page.

4. Use the Sound pop-up menu in the Entry Transition area to select the first sound, gong.SND, which you'll find in the Sound folder for this exercise (Figure 8-16).

Figure 8-17: Use a shorter and quieter sound for the transition to page 2.

5. The entry transition for the second page, Digital Dissolve, is a gentle transition. We don't need a loud or long noise to punctuate it. As shown in Figure 8-17, we've used a short cymbal sound, cymbal.SND, to accent the beat where the transition to page 2 starts. In the Sound pop-up menu, select cymbal.SND from the sounds in the sound folder.

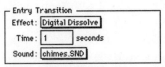

Figure 8-18: Accentuate a change in character from one group of pictures to another with a sound.

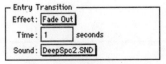

Figure 8-19: Use a strong sound to signal a new section of the project.

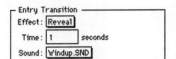

Figure 8-20: Choose a sound that goes with the character of the transition.

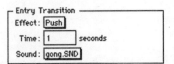

Figure 8-21: A gong-like sound goes with the oriental mood of the next image.

6. The third page, however, has a different character. The sound we use will influence the user's take on the next picture. We'll use a light chime sound to go with the friendly smile of the young woman. Make sure that page 3 is selected in the scrollable list.

7. Then find the Sound pop-up menu in the Entry Transition area and select the sound we'll use for this transition, chimes.SND (Figure 8-18).

8. Time to stop and listen to how this sounds. Save your project and, using QuarkImmedia | Engage, preview the additions so far.

The fourth page is the start of a new section. The character changes from a rather open to a more subdued air. We've used a Fade Out transition to separate the two parts and timed it so that the transition coincides with a change in the music.

1. Select page 4 in the scrollable list.

2. DeepSpc2.SND is a percussive sound that will emphasize the section change. Select it in the Sound pop-up menu (Figure 8-19).

3. Reveal is the transition to the fifth page. We have a windup sound that goes with the Venetian-blind like change. Select Page 5 in the scrollable list and select Windup.SND in the Sound pop-up menu (Figure 8-20).

4. The final image is also of a different character than the fifth. A gong sound, like we used in the beginning, goes with the oriental character of the costume on the last page and fills the time that it takes to move the last picture onto the page. So select gong.SND in the Sound pop-up menu (Figure 8-21).

You're finished! Take a look at the whole project, watching and listening to the way the sounds interplay with the transitions.

Exercise 8-3

We started out the exercises in this chapter using sounds to emphasize events. We moved into using sounds to accentuate the character of transitions. In this exercise, we'll focus on the sounds themselves. The exercise is a sound sampler. We'll play several sounds and set up a suite of objects to use as volume control.

1. Open the third exercise in the folder for this chapter, Exer08-3.

2. Using View | Fit in Window, take a look at the project window (Figure 8-22).

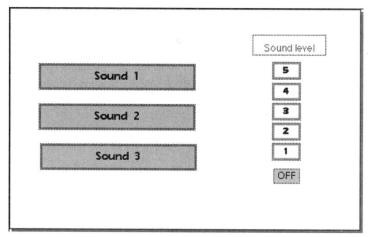

Figure 8-22: This project has objects that will turn on sounds and adjust volume levels.

The left side of the page has three objects which we'll make into buttons for sounds. Right now, we can only tie one action to an object with the user event Click up. We'd like to use a single object to turn a sound on and turn it off again. In Chapter 10, you'll learn how to work with Immedia's buttons, which have more than one state and can trigger more than one user event. Until then, we'll just use Click up to turn the music on and Option-click to turn it off.

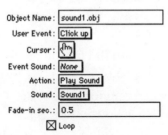

Figure 8-23: Assign a user event to play the music track.

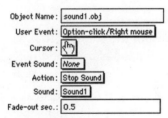

Figure 8-24: To turn the sound off with the mouse, use Option-click.

3. Select the first of the three sound objects on the project page. Define it as a basic object and name it Sound1.obj.

4. In the Event panel, select Click up in the User Event pop-up menu (Figure 8-23).

5. Instead of using Event Sound, which will play a sound only once, we'll use a sound action, Play Sound, which we can loop so it will play as long as you like. Select Play in the Sound submenu of the Action pop-up menu. In the Sound pop-up menu underneath the Action, find Sound1 in the folder of music tracks for this exercise.

6. With the Fade-in sec. pop-up menu you can fade in this sound and make a more gentle introduction to it. The default is 0.5 sec; let's stick with that. Check Loop to play the sound continuously.

7. To turn the sound for this object off, use the user event Option-click (Figure 8-24).

8. In the Action pop-up menu, choose Sound | Stop.

9. Select the same sound, Sound1, and use the default setting in the Fade-out sec. field. Use a gentle, not abrupt, end to this sound.

10. Using the same procedure, make the other two boxes into objects and assign Play Sound and Stop Sound actions to them. The second object uses Sound2 and the third one Sound3. Pretty easy, isn't it?

11. Time to save your project, engage it, and try it out.

Setting the Volume

Making the volume level control looks like it could be hard. If you use a sound action for one object, what do you do for the others? But it's not as hard as it might seem.

1. Select the sound level button on the right of the page. We'll make a button that puts the sound level on one setting, then copy it to make buttons for the other settings. When you duplicate an object, all of

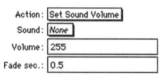

Figure 8-25: Use Set Sound Volume to change volume levels.

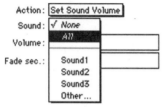

Figure 8-26: Assigning the action to all sounds in the Sound pop-up menu.

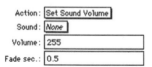

Figure 8-27: Enter a number from 1 to 255 in the Volume field.

the user events and actions associated with it are duplicated too. Rather than having to set each option for each copy, you'll only have to change the number in the Volume field to have different settings for each object.

2. Make this into a basic object as you did for the previous items, calling it sound button5.obj.

3. This time, we'll only need one event for each object. So, for the user event select the action Sound | Set Volume (Figure 8-25).

4. Then take a look at the list in the Sound pop-up menu under the Action pop-up menu (Figure 8-26). The second choice in the list is *All*. This will set the sound level for all sounds in the project. We won't have to make separate volume buttons for each sound.

5. Leave the number in the Volume field at 255 (Figure 8-27). This will be the loudest of the sounds. To be kind to the user we could leave the half-second fade.

6. Use Item | Step and Repeat to copy this button four times. The button is 20 points tall, so use a vertical repeat setting of 25 points. You want all buttons to line up vertically, so use 0 for the horizontal repeat setting.

7. All you have to do to make these buttons adjust the sound to different levels is change the number in the Volume field for each one. For the button labeled "4" use a setting of 200. For button 3, use 150. Set button 2 at 100 and button 1 at 50.

8. Save your project and test it out. Try changing one sound to all the different sound levels.

Moving On

As special effects or as music and narration, sound can greatly affect the perception and retention of the information in your project.

Studies have shown that people learn faster and retain information longer when they are presented information in more than one way, using multiple media. They might be daunted by what looks like a lot of information on a screen, yet listen comfortably to someone telling them the same material, without ever being aware of how much longer it takes orally. That's a real plus for spoken narration.

Sound is the first of the temporal elements in multimedia that we've worked with. Other kinds of events can happen over time. In the next chapter we'll look at simple ways to make objects move. Subsequent chapters will cover the use of video and animation. With these capabilities, QuarkImmedia moves us far from the printed page.

chapter 9

Movement

Movement attracts attention, creating excitement and interest. In the real world, things move and get our attention. In multimedia, one of the quickest ways to draw attention to information is to create activity, make something move, give it a noise.

In the previous chapter, we worked with ways to make projects interactive. You can now hide and show objects, move from one page to another, and open and close windows. With auto advance and transitions you have control over pacing. Music adds even more of a temporal nature. Yet the objects themselves are not active.

In traditional animation, you must create movement frame by frame. Because of how our brains perceive images, when individual frames are projected fast enough we see movement, not individual images. Movies and animation generally use 18 to 30 frames per second, which can add up to a lot of information.

There are several simple ways to create motion in Immedia that don't require you to draw individual frames for motion. You can give an object instructions to move from one spot to another or along a path. Immedia draws the different frames of the movement right on the screen. While this can't create sophisticated imagery such as cartoons or scientific visualization, it is an effective way of bringing motion and interest to your project. Giving your project screen a dynamic feel goes a long way towards differentiating it from the static, paper-based document on which it may have been based.

Sliding an Object Between Two Points

Perhaps the simplest way to add motion is to slide an object—to move it from one spot to another. You might bring a title from outside the page, move an object on top of another, or send a picture to the side. All it takes is an action, Object | Slide, tied to a user event. In fact, sliding a crucial design element such as a headline to a particular spot on every page can tie all of the page designs together while giving a focal event to the page entry.

A sliding action most often involves two objects: one that moves and one that triggers the motion. The moving object can be a basic, animation, movie, or text box object. It cannot be a window or pop-up menu object.

The object that initiates the motion can be any type of object or interactive text. In Chapter 12, "Scripts," you'll learn how to make scripts that will trigger events, also.

Let's look at how to slide an object from one spot to another.

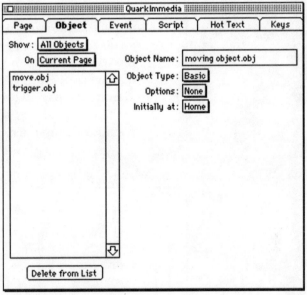

Figure 9-1: Define an object to move.

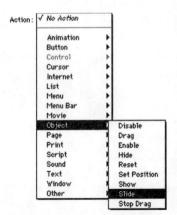

Figure 9-2: Use the action Object | Slide to move the object.

Figure 9-3: Identify the object that will slide as a result of the action.

1. First create an object to slide. The example in Figure 9-1 shows a basic object, moving object.obj. When you create a basic object, the Initially at pop-up menu defaults to Home in the Object panel. Every object has a Home, the spot where it is placed on the project page. Our example in Figure 9-1 shows an object, move.obj, in the Home position.

2. Next, create a trigger object. Assign a user event in the Event panel and select the action, Object | Slide (Figure 9-2). Usually, you set this user event for a different object than the one that will slide.

3. When you choose the action Object | Slide, several additional pop-up menus appear. The first is an Object pop-up menu. Since the object that slides may not be the one that the user clicks on, it's important to indicate here which object slides. Figure 9-3 shows a trigger object with an action to slide a moving object.

4. The Object pop-up menu indicates all slideable objects on the current page. But, if you want to bring an object from another page, you can select Other in the Object pop-up menu to open the Choose Object dialog box (Figure 9-4). In this dialog box you can identify the page whose objects you want to display in the left-hand scrollable list and the object you want to slide in the right.

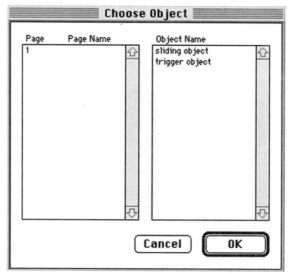

Figure 9-4: Selecting Other in a pop-up menu opens the Choose Object dialog box.

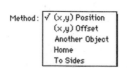

Figure 9-5: Methods for sliding objects.

Method: [(x,y) Position]
x Position: 100
y Position: 150

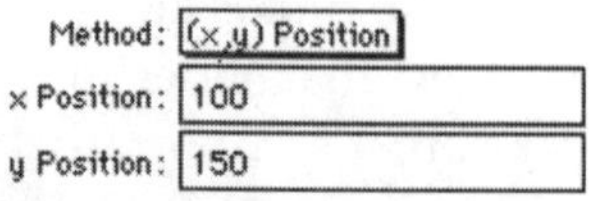

Figure 9-6: Define coordinates for the ending point of movement.

You've chosen the action and object to slide. Now it's time to select a method for sliding the object. In the Method pop-up menu, as shown in Figure 9-5, you have a number of choices.

■ **(x,y) Position.** You specify the x and y coordinates of the spot where the motion will stop (Figure 9-6). Remember that both QuarkXPress and Quark-Immedia measure the coordinates of an item at the upper-left corner of the box. Although picture boxes may look like ovals or polygons, they are all considered to be the rectangle in which they are inscribed (as indicated by the selection handles).

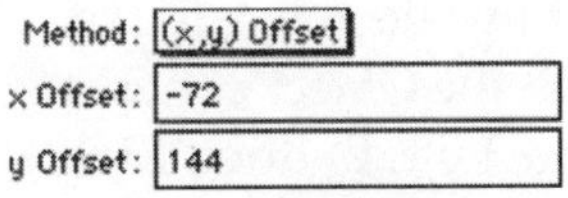

Method: (x,y) Offset

x Offset: -72

y Offset: 144

Figure 9-7: Specify the distance an object will move.

■ **(x,y) Offset.** If you want an object to move a certain distance, use this method. (x,y) offset refers to the distance (in points) you want the object to move; x points horizontally and y points vertically (Figure 9-7). (Remember that points are the equivalent of pixels.) Positive numbers move the object to the right and up, negative numbers to the left and down. If you want the object to move only in a horizontal or vertical direction, use 0 for the other offset distance. To move the object 2 inches up and 1 inch to the left, you would enter -72 for x Offset (to the left) and 144 for y Offset (up).

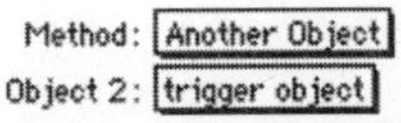

Method: Another Object

Object 2: trigger object

Figure 9-8: Send one object on top or behind another.

■ **Another Object.** This method sends an object to the same place as any object you indicate in the Object 2 pop-up menu (Figure 9-8). In this case, the same place means that the x,y coordinates of the two objects' upper-left corners are the same. With ovals, lines, and polygons, the left-most parts and topmost parts will line up. Remember that QuarkXPress and Immedia layer items in the order they were created, the newest on top. If you slide an object to one that was created before it, the object you slide ends up on top of the other. You can always change the layering of objects in the Item menu.

TIP

QuarkXPress items are layered in the order they are created, with newer items on top of older ones. In the Item menu you can choose to move an item to the back or front layer using the Send to Back or Bring to Front commands. If you hold down the Option key before selecting the Item menu, the menu commands read Send Backward and Bring Forward. The item moves only one layer in that direction.

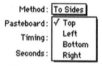

Figure 9-9: Slide an object from the pasteboard to Home.

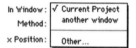

Figure 9-10: Slide an object to the pasteboard.

In Window: ✓ Current Project
Method: another window
x Position: Other...

Figure 9-11: Choose whether the object will slide on the page or in a window of the project.

■ **Home.** This is for objects that have been located in the Initially at pop-up menu on the Object panel at one side of the pasteboard (Top, Left, Bottom, Right) (Figure 9-9). The Slide Object action moves the object from the pasteboard to the object's Home position. Although you can see the object in Home position when you're working with the Quark document, it won't be visible when you engage or export the project until the slide action has been initiated.

■ **To Sides.** Slides the object from Home to one of the sides of the pasteboard. Specify which side in the Pasteboard pop-up menu: Top, Left, Bottom, or Right (Figure 9-10).

We skipped over one option for the Slide Object action, the In Window pop-up menu (Figure 9-11). You will not need to change anything in this pop-up for most Slide Object actions.

This option may seem curious. The default choice is Current Project. Does this mean you can bring in objects from other projects? Not quite. For this event at least, Immedia considers project pages to be separate from windows. Click on the In Window pop-up menu and you'll see the names of the other windows on the page, if any, plus Other. Just like in the Object pop-up menu, clicking Other opens a dialog box to locate windows on other pages. If the object you want to slide is already in a window and you select that window here, the object will only move in the window. If you leave the choice at Current Project, the object will move on the page, but not in the window.

Right now we're using mouse clicks and rollovers as user events to trigger sliding objects. In Chapter 12, "Scripts," you'll learn to write scripts to make objects slide when the viewer enters a new page or as a part of a series of events.

■ Movement on a Path

It doesn't take much to go from a straight-line movement
to more complicated motion. In fact, any line, text, or
picture box can become a path which an item can travel
along. The traveling object moves along the line or along
the perimeter of the box. Using the Polygon Picture Box
tool, you can create complicated paths and even approximate curves.

To move an object along a path, we make three objects:
one that moves, one that triggers the move, and one that
supplies the path for the movement. Later we'll see other
ways of triggering this action.

Define the Path of Motion

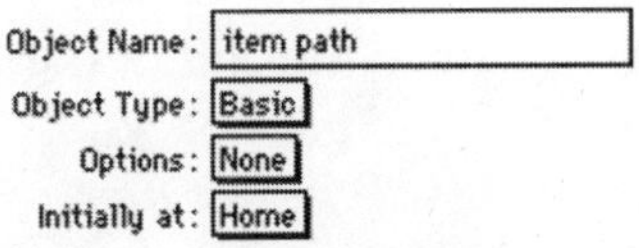

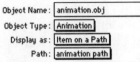

Object Name: `item path`
Object Type: `Basic`
Options: `None`
Initially at: `Home`

*Figure 9-12: The path on
which an item or animation
travels must be a basic object.*

First set up the path for the motion. This must be a basic
object (Figure 9-12). In the Object panel, name the object
and leave the settings at the defaults: Object type Basic,
Options None, and Initially at Home.

Define the Animated Object

Next, create the item to animate by moving along this
path. Right now, this can be a simple picture or text box. In
Chapter 14, "Making Animations," you'll learn how to
create sequences that can also be animated while moving
along a path.

Object Name: `animation.obj`
Object Type: `Animation`
Display as: `Item on a Path`
Path: `animation path`

*Figure 9-13: Choose Anima-
tion as the Object Type for
the moving object.*

In the Object panel, name the item you want to move and
define it as an animation object in the Object Type pop-up
menu (see Figure 9-13). Since it's a static box, it may not
seem like an animation, but when exported it will be the
basis for an animation that will be drawn frame by frame
on the viewer's screen. Immedia will prompt you with pop-
up menus for the other choices you'll need to make.

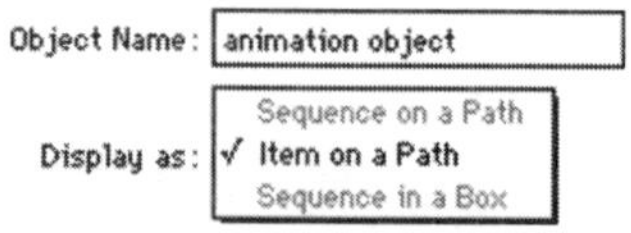

Object Name: animation object

Display as: | Sequence on a Path / Item on a Path / Sequence in a Box |

Figure 9-14: For Item on a Path there is only one choice available in the Display as pop-up.

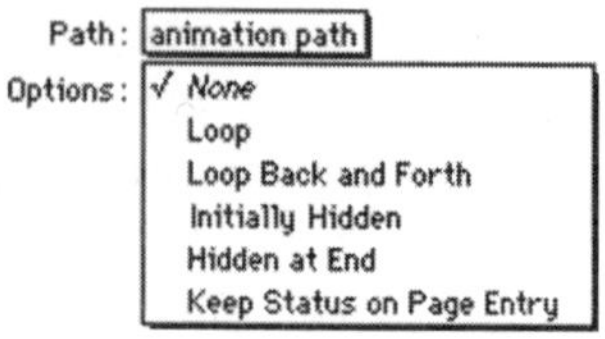

Path: animation path

Options: | √ *None* / Loop / Loop Back and Forth / Initially Hidden / Hidden at End / Keep Status on Page Entry |

Figure 9-15: Define the type of movement in the Options pop-up menu.

Speed: 50 | √ pixels/sec. / inches/sec. / cm/sec. / sec./path traversal |

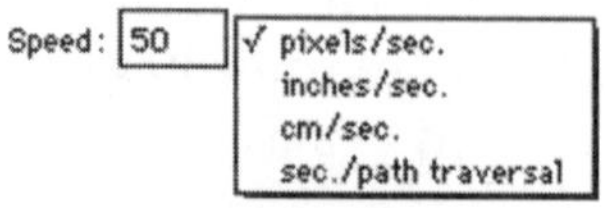

Figure 9-16: The item can travel at any speed you indicate.

Then select the type of movement, Item on a Path, on the next pop-up menu, Display as (Figure 9-14). Note the other choices: Sequence on a Path and Sequence in a Box. We're working with an item—it's just one frame, not a sequence of frames. When we progress to moving animated sequences on paths in Chapter 13, "Playing Animations," you'll select one of the sequence choices.

Identify the path on which the item will travel using the Path pop-up menu. Locate the path you created earlier.

You may also select an option for the movement in the Options pop-up menu, as shown in Figure 9-15. Choose one of the following options:

- **Loop.** When the item finishes traversing the path, it will start again at the beginning and continue around in the same direction until the action is stopped.

- **Loop Back and Forth.** When it gets to the end of the path, the object reverses direction and goes back along the path to the beginning. It will repeat this until the action is stopped.

- **Initially Hidden.** If you want this item not to be seen until a user event triggers the action, choose this option.

- **Hidden at End.** The item will disappear when it gets to the end of the action.

- **Keep Status on Page Entry.** Since the motion requires a user event to get started, the item will not be moving when a viewer first comes to this page. If the item is moving when the viewer exits the page, and you want it to be moving should the viewer return to this page, choose this option.

How fast do you want the item to travel? In the Speed field you indicate how many pixels or inches or centimeters the object should traverse each second (Figure 9-16). The last option in the Speed pop-up menu—Sec./path traversal—specifies how long it will take for the object to complete the full length of the path. The number you put in the field is not a rate but the length of time for the action.

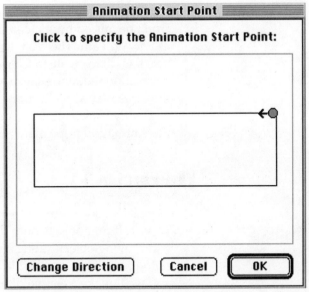

Figure 9-17: Indicate the start and direction of movement for the moving item.

You can actually choose where on the path you want the motion to start and in what direction the object will move. Use the Point and Direction: Specify button under the Speed pop-up menu to open the Animation Start Point dialog box (Figure 9-17). Here you can indicate the point on the path where the motion will start, just by clicking it. An arrow indicates the direction in which the item will travel. You can easily reverse it by clicking the Change Direction button in the lower-left corner of the window.

Define the User Event

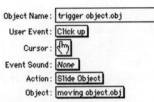

Figure 9-18: The action that initiates an Item on Path movement in Play | Animation.

After defining the properties of the moving object, you initiate the motion using the Action pop-up menu (Figure 9-18). Keep in mind that the user event that triggers the action won't usually be associated with the object that's going to move, but another object.

In the Action pop-up menu, select Animation | Play. Don't be misled by such other choices in the Play submenu as Play on Path. These are reserved for animations, which you'll learn to create in Chapter 14, "Making Animations." Animation sequences can also be played on paths in much the same way as we've done here.

Finally, make sure you identify the animation object in the Animation pop-up menu.

Exercise 9-1

Now let's take a minute to make a new project that involves sliding objects onto the page from the pasteboard and moving objects along a path.

In this exercise we'll slide a series of boxes onto a page, and we'll make a couple different paths for objects to follow. Everything we do will be constructed as we go along. You will need the Page-control palette you created in the first exercise of Chapter 5. If you didn't do that exercise, there is a completed palette in the folder for this exercise.

Set Up the Project

1. Use the File | New | Project command to begin a new project, making the page size 480 points wide and 320 points high.

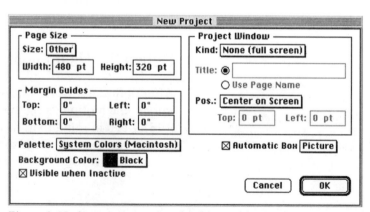

Figure 9-19: Start a new project for this exercise.

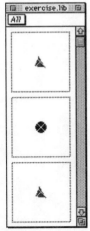

Figure 9-20: Exercise 9-2 (Exer9-2.qxl) has library objects that you can use in this exercise.

Figure 9-21: The Next and Previous buttons can be found in the Exercises library.

2. Check automatic picture box. You can leave the other settings as they are usually found: margins zero for all, palette set to Macintosh system colors, background color of black, the project window kind set to None, the position to center on screen (Figure 9-19).

3. In QuarkImmedia Preferences, check Page Wraparound.

4. Save this project using the name Movement.qxd.

5. Once you have the project page displayed, insert a second page, following page 1. Give the picture box on page 1 a 100% yellow background, and 30% magenta on page 2.

6. We'll use the navigation controls constructed in Chapter 5, "Window Objects." Open the library you created in that exercise, Exercise.qxl. If you skipped that exercise or don't have it available, open the library Exer09.qxl on the Companion CD-ROM.

7. Drag the palette that has the Next and Previous buttons from the library (Figure 9-21) onto the pasteboard and place it to the side of the first page of the new project.

   In the Immedia palette, you'll see that the palette has already been created as an Immedia window object. (If you don't have access to the Exer09.qxl library, the instructions for creating this palette window object are in Exercise 1 of Chapter 5.)

8. Drag the "Click here for Control Panel" box from the library onto page 1, in the lower left. It, too, brings its object properties with it.

Lay Out Page 1

9. On page 1, add a large green circle, about 3.75 inches in diameter, as shown in Figure 9-22. Position the circle just above the center of the page. You don't want to overlap the box that was just added to the page. Adjust its position if necessary.

10. For this exercise, use the green circle to trigger the sliding movements. Create a basic object from the circle, and call it "Green circle trigger.obj."

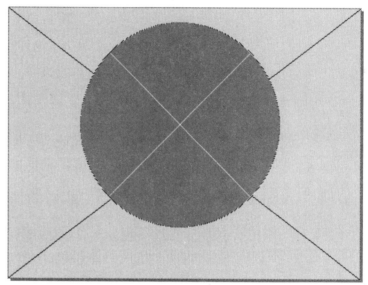

Figure 9-22: Add a large circle and a text box.

11. Add a text box on top of the circle that is .5" tall and 3.5" wide, positioned .75" from the top of the page. Make the box red.

12. Enter **Movement adds interest** in the text box. In the Text Box Specifications dialog box (Command-M), set Vertical Alignment to Centered, and the Text Inset to 6 pt.

   In our example, we are using 18-pt Eurostile Bold for the text. Use a similar bold sans serif font for your project. Make the type color white.

13. Duplicate the text box, positioning the new box on page 1. Change the text in this box to read **Color catches the eye**.

14. Make another duplicate, another inch down the page. Change the text to read **So does the unexpected**. Change the background color of this box to blue.

15. Use the Space/Align command to align the left sides of the three boxes and to make the space between them even (Figure 9-23).

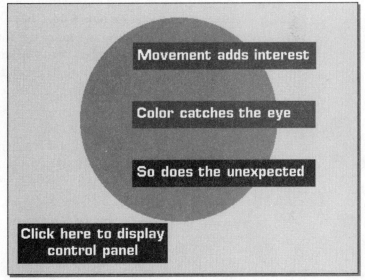

Figure 9-23: After styling type and duplicating the boxes.

Don't forget to save your project periodically as you go through these steps.

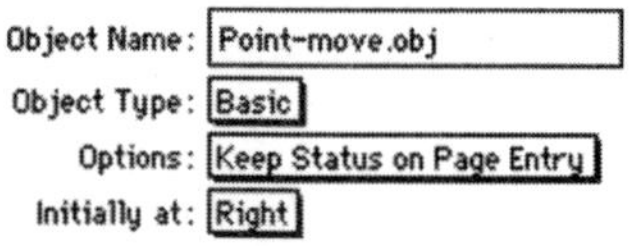

Object Name: Point-move.obj
Object Type: Basic
Options: Keep Status on Page Entry
Initially at: Right

Figure 9-24: Use these settings to create objects from the red text boxes.

Create the Objects That Will Move

Next we'll slide the three boxes onto the page, like bullet points in a presentation. Follow the steps below to create the boxes as objects and plan their movements:

16. Select the top box. In the Object panel, enter the name **Point-move.obj** and make it a basic object.

    We want this box to slide in from the right, so set Initially at pop-up menu to Right. To keep the box visible after visiting page 2, choose the Keep Status on Page Entry option (Figure 9-24).

17. Select the middle box, enter the name **Point-color.obj** in the Object Name field of the Object panel, and make it a basic object.

    This box, too, will slide in from the right. Set Initially at to Right and Options to Keep Status on Page Entry.

18. Select the bottom box, and give the name **Point-unexpected.obj**.

    This box will enter the page from the top, so set the Initially at pop-up menu to Top. Again, choose the Keep Status on Page Entry option.

Trigger the Movement

Next you need to arrange the action of sliding each of these boxes onto the page. For now, we will use three specific user events to trigger the sliding. Later, in Chapter 12, "Scripts," you'll learn how to slide them onto the page automatically.

19. In the Event panel, select the Green circle trigger.obj. We will set three user events for this circle, each one triggering one of the boxes to slide onto the page.

Object Name:	Green circle trigger.obj
User Event:	Mouse enter
Cursor:	
Event Sound:	None
Action:	Slide Object
Object:	Point-move.obj
In Window:	Current Project
Method:	Home
Timing:	Duration
Seconds:	2.5

Figure 9-25: Use these settings for each user event for the trigger object.

20. First, we'll bring the top box onto the page using the Mouse enter user event (Figure 9-25).

    In the Action pop-up menu, choose Object | Slide.

    In the Object pop-up menu you need to identify which object will slide onto the page. Choose Point-move.obj. Set the method to Home—the spot where you positioned this box on the page. Set Duration to 2.5 seconds.

21. Next we'll set up the middle box. In the Event panel scrollable list, Green circle trigger.obj should still be selected. For the middle box, use the Click up user event. Again, choose Object | Slide in the Action pop-up.

    In the Object pop-up menu, choose Point-color.obj. Again, set the method to Home and the duration to 2.5 seconds.

22. For the last box, use the Option-click/Right mouse user event. Set the action to Object | Slide.

    In the Object pop-up menu, choose Point-unexpected.obj. Once again, set the method to Home. Since this object is initially at the top of the page, the movement to home will come down the page, and not in from the right like the other two boxes. Set the duration for this action to 1 second.

Preliminary Testing

For our first page, we've established three boxes that are initially located on the pasteboards, and set up three user events to trigger the sliding movement of the boxes onto the page. Before proceeding to page 2, let's test out what we've done so far.

23. Save your project. Then Choose QuarkImmedia | Engage, or press F15 to begin the test. If the page-controls palette is in the way, move or close it.

24. Move the pointer over the green circle. The first bullet-point box slides in from the right side.
    Click to bring the second bullet-point box onscreen.
    Option-click to bring the last bullet-point box sliding down from the top.

25. Press Command-Q or F15 to disengage.
    Make certain that these events are all functioning properly before proceeding to the next part of the exercise.

Spot-Checking the Controls

The second part of this exercise illustrates movement along a path. So that you can move easily between pages 1 and 2 of the project, you want to double-check that all the settings for our Page-control palette are in order.

In Step 2 we went to QuarkImmedia Preferences and checked the Page Wraparound check box. That means that in the exported project, the Next Page button will move you from the last page of a project to the first page, and the Previous Page button will move you from the first page to the last.

26. You need to position the Page-control palette, a window object created in Chapter 5, "Window Objects" (Figure 9-26), on the pasteboard and not on the page. If you didn't put it there in Step 2, Immedia will alert you to this error and refuse to engage the project.

27. When the palette first appears in an exported project, you can place it in the center of the page or at any specific location. Since the project size in this exercise is smaller than the standard monitor size, you can specify in the Object panel that when the Page-control palette shows up, it should be positioned at a specific location outside the boundary of the page. To do this, set the Position pop-up menu for this object to Absolute. For instance, you can set X to 180 pt (2.5 inches from the left side of the page) and Y to -72 pt (1 inch above the top), as shown in Figure 9-27.

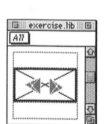

Figure 9-26: The Page-control palette, from the Exercises library.

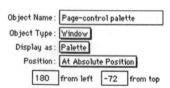

Figure 9-27: Position the palette above the page.

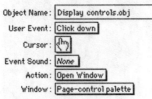

Figure 9-28: Set the user events for the palette trigger to display the palette and to hide the trigger.

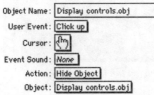

Figure 9-29: The palette trigger should be set to display the palette and hide the trigger.

28. Select the buttons in the palette and check that they have Click up user event set to display the previous or the next page of the project.

29. For now, we are using a trigger object to bring the palette onscreen (in Chapter 12, we'll encounter a more graceful way to do this). Of course, once the palette is onscreen, this trigger's not needed, so we can hide it.

    First, make sure that, in the Object panel, Options is set to Keep Status on Page Entry. That means this trigger won't reappear in an exported project if you leave page 1 and then come back.

30. In the Event panel, set two user events: Click down to activate the palette and Click up to hide the trigger.

    For Click down, choose Window | Open in the Action pop-up menu and specify the Page-control palette as the window you want to open (Figure 9-28).

    For Click up, choose Object | Hide in the Action pop-up menu. Specify the trigger itself, Display controls.obj, as the object you want to hide (Figure 9-29).

Laying Out Page 2

For the second page and the second part of this hands-on examination of movement, we'll move items on a path, making a simplified screen version of dueling model trains, with overlapping paths.

First we'll make tracks for the trains to run on.

31. On page 2, add two polygon picture boxes. Make the first one resemble a figure 8 on its side. Then draw a looping kidney shape, with twists and turns, that crosses over the first polygon in as many places as possible. Set the background color for both boxes to None; Add 4-point borders, one blue and the other black, to the boxes as shown in Figure 9-30. These will be the shapes whose perimeters your moving items will trace.

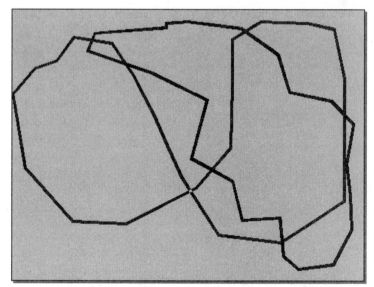

Figure 9-30: Add two polygon picture boxes for their outlines.

32. Create basic objects from the boxes, called 8-track.obj and Kidney-track.obj. Set the Options pop-up menu to None and the Initially at pop-up menu to Home.

Now we'll make trains to run on these tracks.

33. Make a circle picture box .25" in diameter on one part of the 8-track.obj, with a background color of red.

Duplicate this box, change the color of the duplicate to yellow, and move it to another part of the 8-track.obj.

Make a 2" square picture box on part of the Kidney-track.obj and color it green (see Figure 9-31).

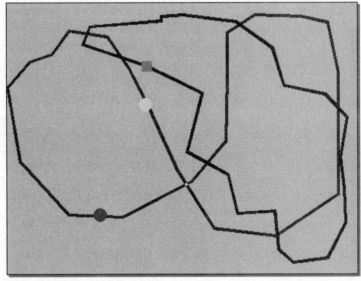

Figure 9-31: Add the "trains."

Creating Animation Objects

The boxes you just created will be your moving "trains," so the setup for them is a bit more complex. You not only have to create animation objects, but you also need to specify the paths these objects will trace, their speed, and other settings.

Figure 9-32: Specify path and speed with an animation object.

34. Select the red box and create an animation object from it called Train-red.ano (Figure 9-32). In the Display as pop-up menu choose Item on a Path.

35. All of the objects on this page are listed in the Path pop-up menu. Choose the 8-track.obj as the path for this animation.

    In the Options pop-up menu, choose Loop, so that your train will continue on its way after it's completed one circuit.

36. Then choose Keep Status on Page Entry from the same pop-up menu. This means the train will keep running even if you go back to page 1 for a while. When you press the mouse on the pop-up menu, it will display check marks next to both options that have been turned on; otherwise you see the legend "Multiple Options."

    Set the speed to 1 and select inches/sec. as the units.

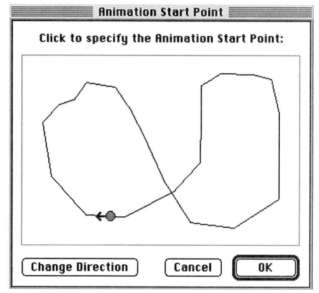

Figure 9-33: Make sure the starting location is where you've positioned the object.

37. Next click the Specify button to open the Start Point and Direction dialog box. The starting point for this animation should be indicated as the location where you drew the box, as shown in Figure 9-33. Choose one direction.

38. Select the yellow box and create an animation object from it called Train-yellow.ano. Set the path and options the same as for Train-red.ano.

    Set the speed to 1.5 inches/sec.

    Make certain the starting point is the location where the box is currently located. Choose the same direction as for Train-red.ano.

39. Select the green box and create an animation object from it called Train-green.ano. In Path pop-up menu choose Kidney-track.obj.

    In Options pop-up choose both Loop Back and Forth and Keep Status on Page Entry. To make things more interesting, this train will reverse directions as it completes each circuit.

    Set the speed to 1 inches/sec, and make certain that the starting point is the same spot as where the box is currently located.

    If you haven't been saving after creating each object, be sure to save now.

Making Hot Text Triggers

In addition to creating the moving objects and their paths, we need to create triggers to start—and stop—the movement. We use hot text for this.

40. Add a text box that's 1.25" wide and .5" tall. Enter the word **Go**. To align the next word with the right margin, press option-tab, then enter **Stop**. Highlight the type and style: we used 18-point Eurostile Bold (Figure 9-34).

41. In Text Box Specifications (Command-M), set the text inset to 6 points, vertical alignment to Centered, and the background color to black.

Figure 9-34: Designing interactive text controls.

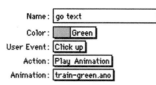

Figure 9-35: Set the color, user event, action, and animation in the Hot Text panel.

42. Select the word "Go," and click on the Hot Text tab in the QuarkImmedia palette. Create an instance of interactive text called "Go text." Set the color in the Color pop-up to green.

    We want the train to start when this word is clicked, so for the user event Click up, set the action to Play Animation, and specify the Train-green.ano as the animation (see Figure 9-35).

43. Now for "Stop." Highlight the word "Stop" and create an instance of interactive text called "Stop text." Set the color to red.

    We want this to stop the train, so for the user event Click up, set the action to Stop Animation and specify the Train-red.ano as the animation.

44. Typically, interactive text is underlined as a visual cue to the user. But here the words themselves serve as the cue and don't need to be underlined. In the Text panel of the QuarkImmedia Preferences, uncheck the Underline check box.

    To set up start and stop hot text for the other two trains, duplicate this box, and use the duplicates to control the other trains.

45. Select the box with the hot text and choose Item I Duplicate. The hot text in the duplicated box is called "Go text copy" and "Stop text copy." Change the animation affected by these two hot text instances to Train-yellow.ano.

    Duplicate the box again, changing the animation this time to Train-green.ano.

46. Position the three sets of controls on your page so that it's clear which controls affect which train, as shown in Figure 9-36.

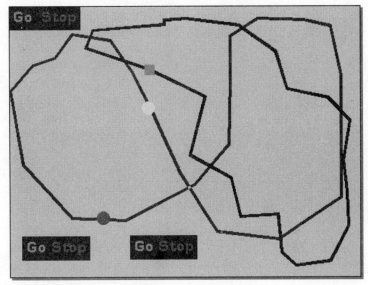

Figure 9-36: The finished page.

Testing the Project

Now you can test the entire project.

47. Press the Option key and choose QuarkImmedia | Engage or press Option-F15. (Depressing the Option key tells Immedia to start the project not from the currently active page but from the project's first page.)

48. Page 1 should work as before. Click on the box labeled "Click here to display control panel." It should do just that, and make the box disappear. The Page-control palette displays above the page.

   Click on either button to go to the second page.

   Click on each instance of hot text to start and stop the trains.

Note how starting an animation always starts it from its beginning, not from where it was halted. The Action pop-up menu gives you sufficient options—you'll want to use pause and resume—but you either have to add more buttons or figure out how to tell Immedia "Start the animation from the beginning if it's stopped, but if it's been paused, resume it from the point where it was paused." That's a little beyond the scope of this exercise. We won't cover that until Chapter 22, "Advanced Features." Multi-state buttons, in the next chapter, provide another way to handle this type of situation.

TIP

All of the objects you've created so far have been made from text and picture boxes. Click on the box and make it an object. It's easy to forget that you have to highlight text to make hot text. If you go to the Hot Text panel and everything is grayed out, check to see that your text is highlighted in the text box on the project page.

Figure 9-37: Use picture box items to make the interactive objects.

Exercise 9-2

Let's go back to Venice again. This time, instead of watching the parade in the Piazza San Marco, we'll go to the water and watch the boats.

This exercise will use both methods of movement, sliding an object and motion on a path. We'll start with the sliding object, a fish, and the first and most fanciful of the boats. Then we'll use motion on a path to move two other boats around. Hot text will trigger their motion.

Open the Project

1. Open Exer09-2.qxd in the folder for this exercise. The images you'll use are in the library Exer09-2.qxl, so open that too (see Figure 9-37).

Create a Sliding Object

The first object is a fish (one we really did see during Carnevale, this photograph proves it). The boat is resting in the water but will slowly move forward when the user triggers a sliding action. The trigger also creates a user event that will send the fish further along when anyone clicks.

Figure 9-38: Place the fish picture on the water near the right side of the page.

2. The object for this is labeled fish and you'll find it in the library. Drag it onto the page about one third of the way from the right side, as shown in Figure 9-38.

3. To slide anything, you need a basic object, nothing fancy. So in the Object panel name this "fishboat.obj" and select Basic in the Object Type pop-up menu. Leave the other pop-up menus in the Object panel at their default settings.

Figure 9-39: Interactive text triggers the motion of these objects.

We'll need a user event to start the movement of this as well as the others. We could simply put text in three separate objects to trigger the motion of each boat. But if all of the text is in one text box, it's much easier to make sure that the type is properly spaced and aligned.

   4. In the upper-left of the picture, make a text box object large enough to enter the following (see Figure 9-39):

   ■ **Transportation in Venice**

   ■ **Vaporetto**

   ■ **Gondola**

   ■ **Fish**

You may color the text if you wish; we used a blue-gray color that's prevalent in the photo.

Before you make any interactive text, it would be a good idea to check the QuarkImmedia preferences to make sure that they're set appropriately.

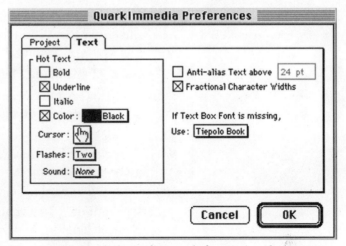

Figure 9-40: Check the preferences before setting the hot text.

5. Using the Edit | Preferences | QuarkImmedia command, go to the Text panel of the QuarkImmedia preferences.

   Make sure that Underline is selected—it should be, it's the default. You'll want to leave Bold and Italic unchecked, the underline will be enough to make the hot text stand out.

   Check to see that Fractional Character Widths is checked. You'll also want to set the font you've chosen in the If Text Box Font is Missing Use pop-up menu (see Figure 9-40).

6. Now, with the preferences set, go to the Hot Text panel, select the word "Fish," and name this text fish trigger.txt (Figure 9-41).

   The Color pop-up menu will show the color of your text. You can leave it as it is; the underline will distinguish the hot text from the title.

   When you click on the hot text word, the fish will start moving, travel a distance, and come to a stop.

7. In the User Events pop-up menu select Click up.

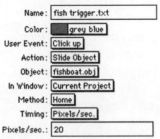

Figure 9-41: The hot text will be the trigger for the sliding object.

8. In the Action pop-up menu choose Object | Slide. Then find the sliding object, fishboat.obj, in the Object pop-up menu. It's in the Current Window.

9. Select Home in the Method pop-up menu.

10. Give this boat the languid speed of 20 pixels per second by typing **20** into the Speed field and selecting pixels/sec. in the pop-up menu.

11. To make the fish move again when it's clicked, let's go back to the Object panel and select fishboat.obj in the scrollable list.

12. We want the user event Click up and the action Object | Slide.

13. This time make the Method (x,y) Offset for a distance of -100 pixels. The negative distance assures that the fish will continue in the direction it was moving; a positive direction would take it to the right. For the timing, choose 20 pixels/second again (see Figure 9-41).

14. You've done quite a lot, so it's definitely time to save this file, naming it something appropriate—Boats.qxd, perhaps.

The First Item on a Path

The next object is another boat, a vaporetto, the bus of Venice. This will be the first of your objects that move along paths. We've created the paths for you already in the document. The one for the vaporetto is the large rectangle that covers the bottom third of the page and extends out into the pasteboard. We've extended it far enough so that the boat disappears off the screen, travels down and back under the page, then reappears later at its starting point.

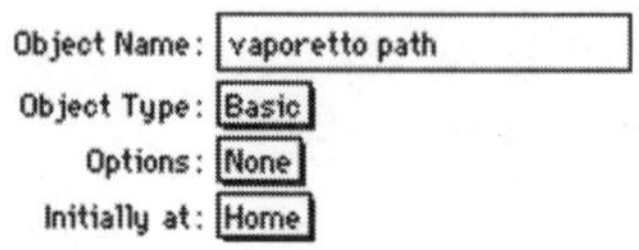

15. Select the large rectangular picture box item to be the vaporetto's path. In the Object panel, name it vaporetto path.

16. Make this item a basic object, leaving the Options menu set at None and the Initially at pop-up set to Home, as shown in Figure 9-42.

Object Name: vaporetto path
Object Type: Basic
Options: None
Initially at: Home

Figure 9-42: Create a path for the vaporetto animation.

17. To make the boat animation, get the vaporetto picture from the library. An item doesn't have to be placed on top of a path in order to travel on it, so put this picture box on the pasteboard (Figure 9-43).

Figure 9-43: Place the picture box with the vaporetto on the pasteboard.

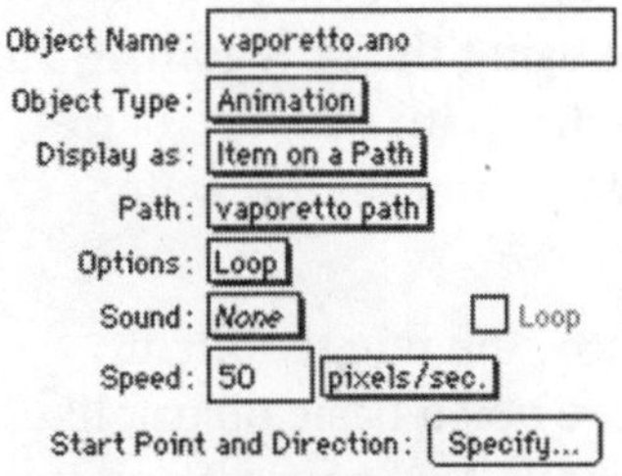

Object Name : vaporetto.ano
Object Type : Animation
Display as : Item on a Path
Path : vaporetto path
Options : Loop
Sound : *None*   ☐ Loop
Speed : 50   pixels/sec.
Start Point and Direction : Specify...

Figure 9-44: Use the Object panel to define the movement for an item on a path.

18. Now make this picture box into an animation object in the Object panel and name it vaporetto.ano (Figure 9-44).

19. Once it's defined as an animation object, there are other choices you're prompted to make. What kind of display? For Display as, choose Item on a Path and select vaporetto path in the Path pop-up menu (see Figure 9-44).

    Check Loop so that the boat will continue on its circle around Venice.

20. This boat needs to go faster than the first, these are business travelers as well as tourists, and they must get where they're going in a hurry. So type **50** in the Speed field, keeping the units pixels/sec.

21. To indicate a starting point for this animation, click Specify in the Start Point and Direction field to open the Start Point and Direction dialog box. The boat is facing left, so you'll want to click a point on the right side of the path and make sure the direction arrow is pointing left.

22. And now we need to make the trigger for this action. Select the word Vaporetto in the box with the text. Go to the Hot Text panel and make the text interactive. You'll use the same procedure as you did with the fish text, naming this vaporetto trigger.txt.

23. To assign an action, choose Animation | Play in the Action pop-up menu and select the animation object you just made, vaporetto.ano.

24. You've finished the first animation. Don't forget to save your project!

The Second Item on a Path

Our final boat is a gondola, Venice's taxi service. Gondolas are light, so they bob a bit on the water, especially in the wake of a larger boat. To suggest this, we've made a polygon picture box with wiggles in it using the Polygon Picture Box tool. We've also made the path smaller than the screen, so the gondola can turn around in the water and go back to where it started.

25. Select the polygon picture box, the wiggly one in Figure 9-45. Make this picture box a basic object, like you did with the vaporetto path, and name it gondola path.

Figure 9-45: Use the polygon picture box item to make the path for a bobbing boat.

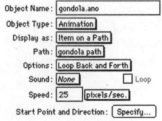

Figure 9-46: Define the gondola picture box item as an animation object.

26. Next let's get the gondola from the library and place it on the pasteboard.

27. To make the gondola picture box an animation object, give it the name gondola.ano in the Object panel (Figure 9-46).

28. The Object Type is Animation, which brings a number of new choices. Like the vaporetto, make Display as Item on a Path, but this time select the path you just made, gondola path.

29. Select Loop Back and Forth in the Options pop-up and give this boat the speed of 25 pixels/sec.

30. This boat can go in either direction. Let's start it on the left side and have it travel toward the right using the Start Point and Direction dialog box.

31. You need something to set the boat in motion. So, as you did with both the fish and the vaporetto, highlight the text "Gondola" in the upper-left text box.

32. In the Hot Text panel, name the trigger gondola trigger.txt and select the user event Click up. Select the action Play Animation, identifying gondola.ano as the animation object.

Testing the Project

Now that you've made the water traffic, let's save the project. Engage it and watch the boats go by.

Moving On

Sliding objects and moving them on paths is a great way to get action from interactivity. But by this point defining all the parameters can get complicated.

For sliding objects, you need an object to slide and an object to trigger the motion. The movement is part of the event for the object that starts the motion.

For the movement of objects on paths, our first type of animation, it's necessary to define one object as a path for the motion, another object to move, and a third object to trigger the motion. Remember that you define the start point, speed, direction of motion, and path all as part of the object, not as the user event that triggers the movement.

In the next chapter we'll take a look at buttons—multi-state objects that provide a way to give users feedback about their activities.

chapter 10

Buttons

Up to now, you've used interactive objects and hot text to initiate actions. They've certainly helped you open windows and get from page to page.

But what do you do when you want to give the user some feedback? *Yes, you did click on that object. No, you can't get anything if you click here now.*

Buttons on appliances and electronic equipment move to different positions to let a user know that an action has been initiated. Immedia buttons can display different graphics to represent different states of activity and to represent when a button is pressed or an action is functioning. There are even button states to display whether a button can be used or not.

Buttons have more capabilities than other interactive objects. Every button is made of several images which you can associate with user events to display different states of the button's activity.

People who spend time playing CD-ROM games or surfing the Web are used to clicking on any image to see if it's interactive. Still, many users prefer easily recognizable buttons to tell them where to click. There are standard symbols for start, stop, and pause, which we all recognize. If the goal of your site is direct communication, not play, you may want to create buttons that look like buttons.

Using Buttons & Button Libraries

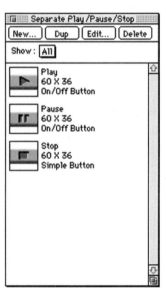

Figure 10-1: The Button Library palette.

Like QuarkXPress items that you save to use in other projects, buttons are stored in libraries that behave much like QuarkXPress libraries. Figure 10-1 shows the Button Library palette.

Here's how to place a button in a QuarkImmedia project:

1. Open a button library using the File | Open command and locate the button library in the Open dialog box. This brings you to the Button Library palette, in which you'll see one or more buttons.

2. Simply select the button you want to use and drag it onto your page. It's already a QuarkImmedia object so it has a name, but you can rename it if you wish (Figure 10-2). Now all you have to do is assign actions to its user events in the Event panel. It's that easy.

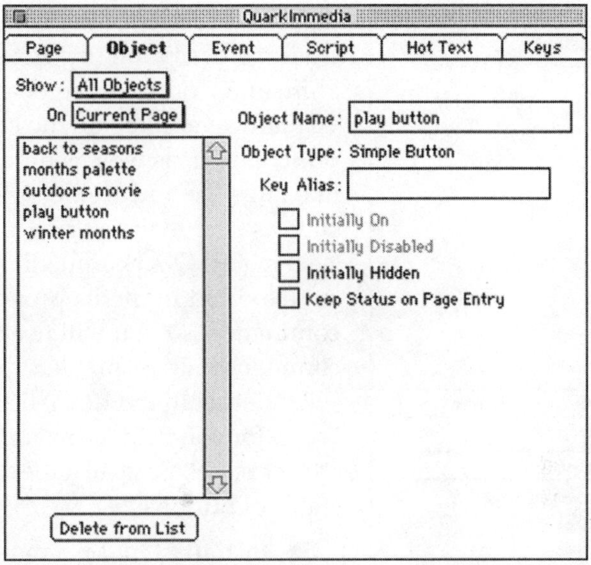

Figure 10-2: The Object panel for button objects.

You don't have to use the name a button had in the library. Once you've brought a button into a project, you can change its name in the Object Name field of the Object panel.

You'll notice that with a button object, there's no pop-up menu for Object Type. You cannot convert buttons into basic objects, windows, text boxes, or any other Immedia objects. You can't even change them to other button types except in the editing window of the button library, as you'll see later.

Keyboard equivalents come in handy, not only for frequently used buttons, such as one to move to the next page or to quit a project, but also because some users will naturally prefer using their keyboard to using the mouse. You assign a key command to a button in the Key Alias field simply by pressing the key or combination of keys

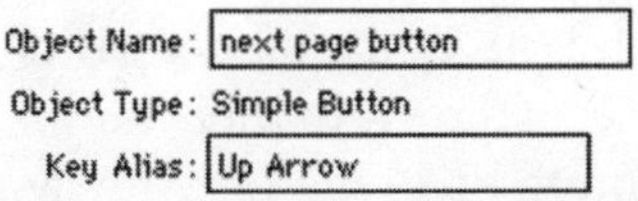

Figure 10-3: Assign keyboard commands in the Key Alias field.

you want to use for the equivalent. All the shifting keys—Command, Option (the Alt key on Windows computers), Shift, and Control—can be used as modifier keys with virtually every key on the keyboard—letters, numbers, punctuation, as well as function keys and navigation keys like Page Up and Home. A few select key combinations, such as Command-period, are reserved for Macintosh system and QuarkImmedia functions, and are unavailable. An exported Immedia project does not display keyboard commands, so you will need to tell your users when key commands are available.

Underneath the Key Alias field there are four check boxes for controlling the initial display of buttons on the Object panel. Basically, they change the default initial states of buttons.

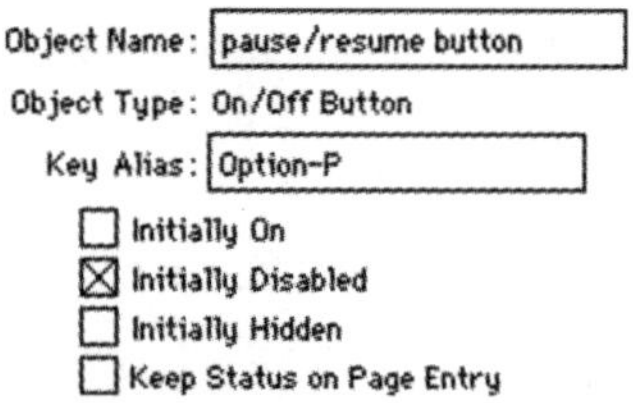

Object Name: | pause/resume button |

Object Type: On/Off Button

Key Alias: | Option-P |

☐ Initially On
☒ Initially Disabled
☐ Initially Hidden
☐ Keep Status on Page Entry

Figure 10-4: Check boxes for changing initial display of buttons.

- **Initially On.** Like most appliance buttons, Quark-Immedia buttons are initially in the Off state. A User Event turns them on. Select this option if you want the button to be on when you start a page.

- **Initially Disabled.** Buttons are initially enabled, meaning they do what they are supposed to when clicked. There may be times when you don't want a button to be functional until a specific action or event has occurred. Selecting Initially Disabled will prevent the button from functioning.

- **Initially Hidden.** This works like it does for other objects and hides the object when the page starts.

- **Keep Status on Page Entry.** This too works like it does for other objects. When you return to a page you've visited, all of the objects return to their initial states. If you want the button to be in the state it was when you left the page, choose this option.

While that may not make much sense now, when we've gone through how to create buttons, you'll be thinking in terms of Up/Down, On/Off, Enabled/Disabled—all the button states.

Different Button States

Think about your VCR, or any appliance that works with buttons. You need to know if it's on or off, if a tape is playing or paused. When you push in a button, it remains pushed in or turns on a display to tell you that it's working. It provides you feedback.

Unlike the other interactive items we've worked with, buttons have several states: Up/Down, On/Off, and Enabled/Disabled. Each of the states looks different and can have a separate user event attached to it. This way the user can tell what state the button is in.

Simple Buttons

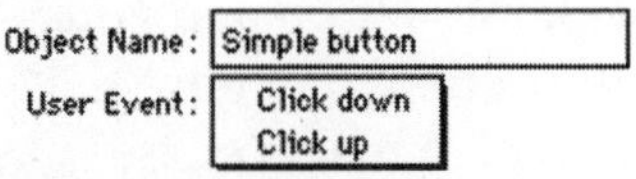

Simple buttons have only two states: up and down (Figure 10-5). Up and down refer to the position of the mouse button. If you look at the User Event pop-up menu for a Simple button, you'll see the familiar Click down and Click up.

A button at rest is in the up state. To initiate an action, the user clicks. While the mouse button is depressed (user event Click down), it's in the down state. The look of the button changes to show that it's being activated (Figure 10-6).

Take your finger off the mouse (Click up), and the button returns to the up state and looks the way it did before we started. And with the Click up user event, an action can be initiated. A movie plays, the project displays a new page. Two states and two images to show whether a button is in use or not.

This is how the buttons on a VCR work. You push on one to activate it. Once you take your finger off the button it pops back up and the VCR starts playing. The button remains in the up state until you push it again to start another action.

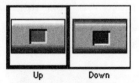

Figure 10-5: Up and down are the two states of Simple buttons.

Figure 10-6: Different states for Simple buttons.

On/Off Buttons

But what if you want more than one action for a button? When you pause a VCR you don't go to a Resume button to start it up again, you hit the Pause button again.

We can't do this with a Simple button. Well, we could if the user event Click down paused a movie and Click up resumed playing. But the user wouldn't have a chance to change his mind after "Click down." So we need to create additional states.

The power button on the VCR works in a different manner from pause (and all the other buttons). It's important that you know whether the machine is on or not. So, a VCR is designed so that you push the power button in and it stays in until you turn the power off. When you see that the power button's pushed in, you know it's on and you can play tapes. And when the button's up, you know you've got to turn the machine on to play that exercise video.

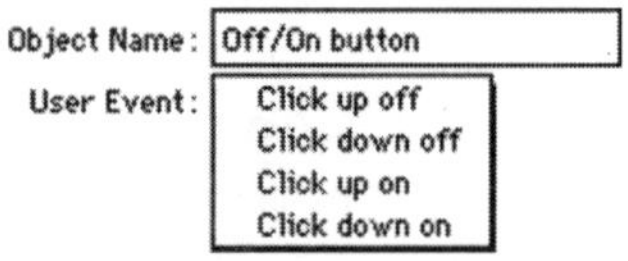

In QuarkImmedia, On/Off buttons work in a similar manner. A button to pause a movie, for example, has four user events: Click up off, Click down off, Click up on, Click down on, as you can see in Figure 10-7. At rest, this button is in the up and off states. Up because it hasn't been touched or pushed down and off because nothing's happening (Figure 10-8).

Object Name : Off/On button

User Event :
Click up off
Click down off
Click up on
Click down on

Figure 10-7: User events for On/Off buttons.

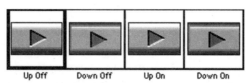

Up Off   Down Off   Up On   Down On

Figure 10-8: The different states for On/Off buttons.

- Press the mouse (Click down off), and the image changes to show that you've touched the button, but nothing happens to the movie. There's no action to this user event.

- Releasing the mouse (Click up on) turns the Pause button on, the action "movie pause" is initiated, and the button displays a third image to show that it's on.

- Press the mouse again (Click down on) and we've got another image to show that the button (in the on state) is being pushed. The movie is still paused.

- Release the mouse button (Click up off) to turn the Pause button off and initiate the action "movie resume."

There will be times when you want to make a button that doesn't function until some action occurs. To use the analogy of a tape recorder, you may have to push Record and then Play to start taping. Both Simple and On/Off buttons have a Disabled state to show that they won't work until an action activates them (Figure 10-9).

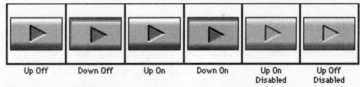

| Up Off | Down Off | Up On | Down On | Up On Disabled | Up Off Disabled |

Figure 10-9: Different states for buttons with Disable.

TIP

Button states can be confusing. If you remember that Up and Down refer to mouse position and On and Off refer to the actions controlled by the button, you may find it easier to master these concepts.

Making Custom Buttons

You get buttons from a button library in much the same way that you do from a standard QuarkXPress library. There's one major way that Immedia library objects, however, differ from QuarkXPress library items. Button objects must be created and changed within the library's editing window.

The first step in making a button is to have a button library open. You can do this two ways. Either open an existing library using File | Open and locate the library through the Open dialog box, or create a new one using File | New | Button Library and give the library a name in the New Library dialog box.

Next, in the library's palette, click the New button, as shown in Figure 10-10. The New Button dialog box will appear. Here you'll define the size and type of button with which you're going to work (Figure 10-11). There are four button types:

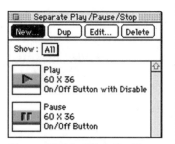

Figure 10-10: Click the New button in the Button Library palette to create new buttons.

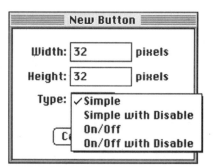

Figure 10-11: Choose button types and sizes in the New Button dialog box.

- Simple—A button with two parts: Up and Down.
- Simple with Disable—A button with three parts: Up, Down, and Up Disabled.

- On/Off—A button with four parts: On Up, Off Up, On Down, and Off Down.

- On/Off with Disable—A button with six parts: On Up, Off Up, On Down, Off Down, On Up Disabled, and Off Up Disabled.

Once you've OK'd your choice, it's off to the button editing window.

Button Editing Window

Quark's button editing window is actually a small paint program. If you've used any paint programs, working in this window will be familiar.

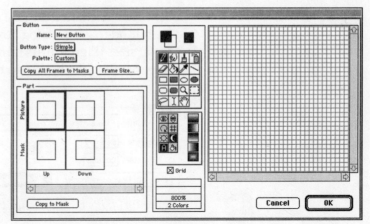

Figure 10-12: Create the looks for different button states in the button editing window.

As you can see in Figure 10-12, there are several sections to the editing window. In the Button area you can name the button and choose or change its type, palette, and size. The Part area displays a picture and mask for each of the different button states. In the Drawing area you'll find all the tools you'll need to create the looks for each state.

In the Button area are fields and pop-up menus to control the attributes of a button. To change the name of a button, type a new name in the Name field (Figure 10-13). If you want to change a button from Simple to On/Off or any other type, you can do this with the Button Type pop-up menu.

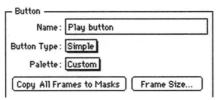

Figure 10-13: Name button objects in the Button area.

It's easy to change the size of a button. Click the Frame Size button to get a dialog box where you can enter new button sizes (Figure 10-14). You have the choice of cropping or scaling the button to the new size (Figure 10-15).

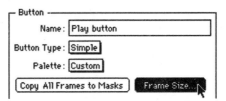

Figure 10-14: It's easy to change the size of any button.

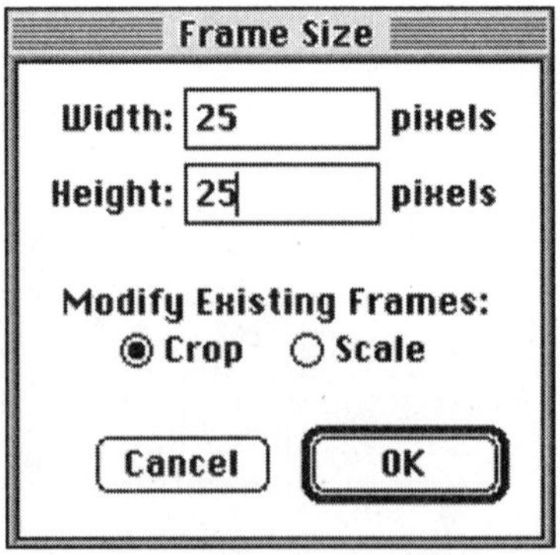

Frame Size
Width: 25   pixels
Height: 25   pixels
Modify Existing Frames:
● Crop   ○ Scale
Cancel   OK

Figure 10-15: Enter new dimensions in the Frame Size dialog box.

Use the Color Palette pop-up menu to assign a new color palette (Figure 10-16). Select one from the pop-up menu in the same way you selected the project's color palette. Even though a button is assigned a color palette here, it will use the palette of any project in which it's been placed.

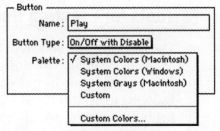

Figure 10-16: It's easy to assign another color palette to a button.

The Part area contains a scrollable window which displays two squares, a picture and corresponding mask, for each of the button looks (Figure 10-17). To select which button look to work on in the scrollable drawing area, click one of the squares in the Part area. The active frame is outlined with a heavy black line.

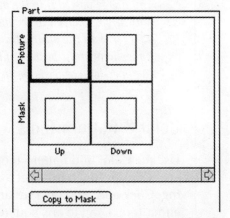

Figure 10-17: Select which part of the button to work on in the Part area of the button editing window.

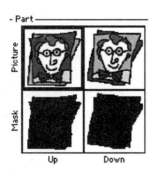

Figure 10-18: Each picture has a corresponding mask.

Figure 10-19: The tools for creating a button image are in the Drawing area.

Figure 10-20: The Color and Pattern tools.

All of the pixels in the drawing area are opaque. To make an area transparent, the Picture part must be masked. In Figure 10-18 you'll see that Immedia has a square in the Mask row for each square in the Picture row. Use the Copy to Mask button to create a mask for a selected picture.

Tools for Creating Buttons

The Drawing area shown in Figure 10-19 contains the tools to create the images for different states of a button. The following tools are included: Color and Pattern tools, Drawing tools, Blend and Effect buttons, informational fields, and a scrollable drawing area.

Use the scrollable drawing area on the right of the editing window to work on whichever picture or mask is selected in the Part area.

If you're a button maven and want to use the more sophisticated tools of Adobe Photoshop and Fractal Painter, you can. Just copy from your paint program and paste into the scrollable drawing area.

TIP

Any image pasted into the button editing window is automatically remapped to the button's color palette. If the image is larger than the button frame size, it is resized to the dimensions of the button. If it's smaller, it is pasted so that its upper-left corner is in the upper-left corner of the frame.

Color & Pattern Tools

Use the Color and Pattern tools at the top of the drawing area (Figure 10-20) to select a color and pattern for painting. Click and hold on a square to display the palette for either tool. Drag to any square to select a particular color or pattern (Figure 10-21).

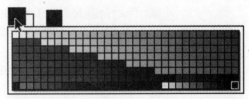

Figure 10-21: Click on the Color tool to access the color palette.

Drawing Tools

The Drawing tools shown in Figure 10-22 probably look familiar. These tools have appeared in various Macintosh image-editing programs and, with a few exceptions, they work much the same here.

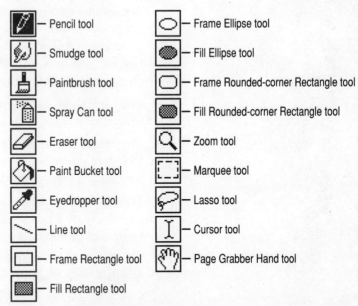

Figure 10-22: The Drawing tools. (The tools have been separated to more clearly illustrate them.)

■ The Pencil tool—is used to draw lines and fill in color. Hold the Shift key to constrain to horizontal and vertical lines.

- The Smudge tool—"pushes" pixels around to soften edges of lines or shapes.

- The Paintbrush tool—creates free-form lines. If you drag fast enough it will draw broken lines.

- The Spray Can tool—fills in areas using the current foreground color. Pixels to the outside of the stroke are lighter than those in the center.

- The Paint Bucket tool—fills all contiguous pixels of the same color or pattern with the foreground color and selected pattern.

- The Eraser tool—changes all pixels in its path to white. Double-click on the tool to erase an image or fill it with white.

- The Eyedropper tool—changes the foreground color to the color of a pixel in the drawing area on which it's been clicked. Option-click to change the background color. The Command key (not the Option key, as used by a number of paint programs) changes any other tool to the Eyedropper tool.

- The Line tool—draws straight lines in the current foreground color and pattern.

- The Frame Rectangle, Rounded-rectangle, and Ellipse tools—make one-pixel-wide outlines in the current foreground color and pattern.

- The Fill Rectangle, Rounded-rectangle, and Ellipse tools—create filled shapes in the current foreground color and pattern.

- The Zoom tool—will be familiar to anyone who works with a Macintosh—click to zoom in or increase magnification. Option-click to zoom out.

- The Marquee tool—selects a rectangular area that you can then use with the Effect and Blend tools and the Copy, Cut, and Paste commands. Double-click on this tool to select the contents of the scrollable drawing area.

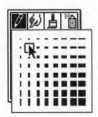

Figure 10-23: Click a tool to select a line width.

■ The Lasso tool—is for selecting irregular or freeform shapes to use with the Effect and Blend tools and the Copy, Cut, and Paste commands. Double-click on this tool to select all of the image.

■ The Cursor tool—is used to create text. Choose Font, Size, and Type Style with the QuarkXPress Style menu.

■ The Page Grabber Hand tool—moves oversized images around in the scrollable drawing area.

You can change the width on any of the above tools except the Eyedropper and Paint Bucket tools—click and hold on the tool's icon to get a selection of stroke widths (Figure 10-23).

Effect Buttons

Use the Effect buttons, as shown in Figure 10-24, to make changes to areas you've selected with either the Marquee or Lasso tools.

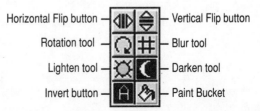

Figure 10-24: The Effects buttons will change the orientation and tones of an image.

■ The Horizontal Flip button—flips a selection from left-to-right and right-to-left.

■ The Vertical Flip button—flips top-to-bottom.

■ The Rotation tool—rotates a selection ninety degrees clockwise.

■ The Blur tool—softens or blurs pixels in a selection.

- The Lighten tool—lightens pixels in a selection, changing them to the next lighter color in the color palette used in the project.

- The Darken tool—changes pixels in a selection to the next darker pixel in the project's color palette.

- The Invert button—inverts the color light to dark, dark to light. It also changes a color to the opposite color in the color palette.

- The Paint Bucket—fills a selection with the current foreground and pattern.

Blend Tools

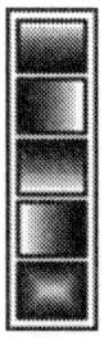

The Blend buttons, shown in Figure 10-25, fill pixels with gradients using the foreground and background colors. Each button displays the direction of the blend it will create. You can change the direction simply by clicking another Effect button.

You may want to know precisely where your tool is located in the scrollable drawing area or how large the shape you're drawing is (Figure 10-26). The informational fields display X and Y location when you're using the painting tools, or height and width as you draw shapes. If you want to know how big the image is in relation to its actual size, the magnification is displayed under the X,Y fields.

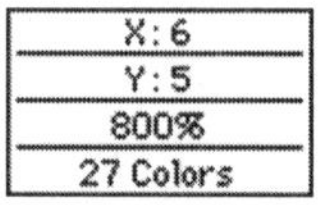

There is also a field that shows the number of colors in the image. This can be quite useful if you need to work with a restricted palette or reduced number of colors.

The light blue grid in the scrollable drawing area is useful for finding the location of pixels in the image. It can get in the way of the image, though, especially at low magnification. Turn it off by unchecking the grid check box (Figure 10-27).

Figure 10-25: Individual Blend tools show direction of gradient blends.

| X : 6 |
| Y : 5 |
| 800% |
| 27 Colors |

Figure 10-26: The informational fields display location, size, and magnification of objects.

Figure 10-27: Turn off the grid by deselecting the grid check box.

Using the Tools to Make Button Looks

With these tools you're able to draw and paint in the scrollable drawing area on the right side of the editing window.

Once you've drawn a button look in the scrollable drawing area, go back to the Part area of the editing window, and select another frame to work with by clicking on the Picture square for that state.

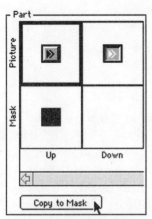

Figure 10-28: Copy individual Picture frames to Mask frames.

> **TIP**
>
> *Forgetting to select another square in the Part area when making another button look is one of the most common mistakes made in the editing windows. If you don't, you work on the image you've just completed.*

To use the image you've just created as a basis for another look, you must copy it from the scrollable drawing area, then click on the Picture square in the Part area for the state that you want to work on, and paste. The image will be pasted into a new frame in the scrollable drawing area.

Masking Button Looks

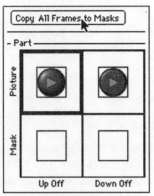

Figure 10-29: Make masks for all button looks with the Copy All Frames to Masks button.

Unless they're masked, all of the pixels in the drawing area will be visible in your button. To make round buttons, oval buttons, or any shape other than the rectangle of the drawing area, you need to create a mask for each picture, as shown in Figure 10-28.

There are two ways to make masks. Create them for each picture individually using the Copy to Mask button in the Part area, or make them all at once using the Copy All Frames to Masks button in the Button area (Figure 10-29). Immedia makes an image in the Mask row with the same shape as the one above it, a black pixel in the mask for every nonwhite pixel in the image. The white areas in the mask will be transparent in the button.

> **TIP**
>
> *Remember that Immedia creates masks for all nonwhite areas of a button picture. To mask any white area of a button, you'll have to paint the mask in the scrollable drawing area. Simply click the mask frame in the Part area and paint the graphic of the mask in the drawing area. To select all of an image, double-click the Lasso tool. Then click the Paint Bucket effect button (not the drawing tool) to fill the selected area with black.*

Editing Buttons

We've been talking about creating buttons in the editing window. You can edit any button here also. Simply click the Edit button in the Button Library palette to get to the button editing window (Figure 10-12). If you want to work on a duplicate of an existing button, just click the Dup button in the Button Library palette. Use the different fields, pop-up menus, and tools to change any part of the button. The Delete button will remove a button from a button library.

There's no requirement that you make buttons look like real-world buttons. A button is a sequence of images representing different button states. You can use any group of images in a button. And, as we'll see in the next chapters, movies and animation can be buttons. Your job as a designer is to determine what appearance best expresses what the button does.

Exercise 10-1

There are so many tools and controls in the button editing window, that all of our description might obscure a key fact about Immedia—making buttons here is about as easy as it gets in the multimedia world. So let's focus on that aspect in a hands-on look at buttons.

In this exercise, we'll make a variety of buttons from scratch and use them with an existing exercise called Movement.qxd. You created this exercise earlier in Chapter 9, "Movement." If you skipped that exercise or if it's not available to you now, use the file called Exer10-1.qxd, located in the Exer10-1 folder on the Companion CD-ROM.

1. Open the project created in the first exercise in Chapter 9, or use Exer10-1.qxd on the Companion CD-ROM. Our first step is to make simple buttons for the Page-control palette, located on the right pasteboard of Page 1.

2. Create a new button library, using the File | New | Button Library command (Figure 10-30). Call the button library something straightforward, like Buttons.qxl.

Figure 10-30: Create a new button library.

Make the Next Button

3. Click the New button in the button library to call up the New Button dialog box (Figure 10-31).

   At this point you need to specify the size of the button—we'll make this 25 pixels wide and 25 pixels tall—and the type—Simple, to start with (Figure 10-32).

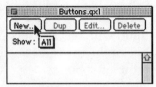

Figure 10-31: The library New button gets you to the button editing window...

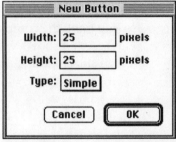

Figure 10-32: ...via this New Button dialog, where you set the size and kind of button you want.

4. We'll make a right-pointing triangular-shaped button first, with a black outline. This will be for the "Next page" button.

   Select the pencil tool, and black as the color. In the scrollable drawing area, in the upper-left corner, fill in the corner pixel, and then the one to its right.

   Drop down one row and fill in two pixels—the second row, the third and fourth columns. Drop down another row and fill in two more columns' pixels.

   Keep doing this until you've reached the thirteenth row, where there's room for only a single pixel (Figure 10-33).

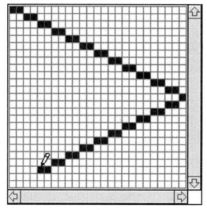

Figure 10-33: Fill in pixels along a diagonal.

5. Now fill in pixels in a mirror fashion heading back to the left and continuing down the page. When you're finished, fill the entire first column with black pixels so you have the complete outline of the triangle. Figure 10-34 shows what the completed button image should look like.

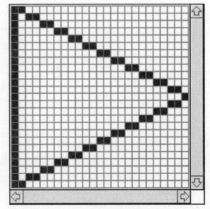

Figure 10-34: The complete triangle outline.

6. To color in the button, choose a light turquoise color. We used the turquoise that is in the 5th row and the 17th column in the Color pop-up menu, as shown in Figure 10-35. Use the Paint Bucket tool to fill the inside of the button. This is the Up state of the button, what the button looks like before it's been clicked.

Figure 10-35: Select a color for the button.

7. To make the clicked or Down state, it's simplest to copy what we have in the Up frame in the part area to the Down frame. Use the Marquee tool to select all of the pixels in the drawing area and copy this selection to the clipboard.

   Then make the Down frame in the Part area active, and paste in the arrow from the clipboard.

8. At the moment, the two frames are identical. While the Down frame still shows the selection marquee around the colored pixels, click twice on the Darken tool. That provides a dark turquoise fill for this frame.

Changing the color of the button when it's clicked will provide feedback to the user that the click has been registered. Physically changing the button also helps.

9. Change the color of the black outline pixels to white. Now, when the user clicks on the button, it will change colors and seem to compress in on itself.

10. Click the Copy All Frames to Mask button. Name the button "Next.btn" and click OK.

Make the Previous Button

Making the companion button is far simpler because we can use the first button as a starting point.

11. Highlight "Next.btn" in the button library and click the Dup button to duplicate it.

12. With "Next.btn copy" highlighted, click the Edit button to bring up the button editing window (Figure 10-36).

13. The back-pointing triangle button should be a mirror image of the Next button. All you have to do is point these frames in the opposite direction. With the Up frame active, click twice on the Rotation tool to rotate the image 180 degrees, as shown in Figure 10-37.

Make the Down frame active and again, click twice on the Rotation tool.

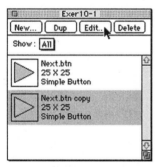

Figure 10-36: Create a duplicate button, then edit it.

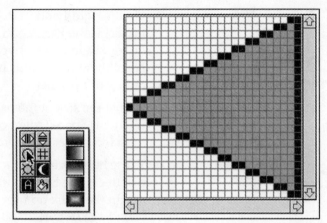

Figure 10-37: Rotate the image once to point down, twice to point to the left.

14. Click the Copy All Frames to Masks button.

```
┌ Button ─────────────────────────────────────┐
│        Name : │Previous.btn                │ │
│ Button Type : │Simple│                        │
```

Figure 10-38: Name this button Previous.btn.

15. Change the name of the button to "Previous.btn" in the Name field and click OK (Figure 10-38).

Using the Buttons in a Palette

Let's try these two new buttons out.

16. Open the project Movement.qxd, if you haven't done so already.

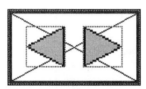

Figure 10-39: Put the new buttons in the palette and adjust its size.

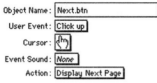

Figure 10-40: When the Next button is clicked, have it display the next page.

17. On the right-hand pasteboard of Page 1 of our project is the Page-control palette, with two triangles on top. Delete these two triangles and drag the Next.btn and Previous.btn from the button library on top of the palette.

18. Adjust the size of the palette (Figure 10-39), and use the Item | Space / Align command to align the buttons and center them on the palette.

19. These buttons already show up in the Immedia palette. In the Event panel, highlight Next.btn and assign the Click up user event the action Display Next Page (Figure 10-40).

    Similarly, for the Previous button, set the action to Display Previous Page.

20. Save the project, then choose QuarkImmedia | Engage or press the function key F15 to test. Remember that the palette appears only after clicking the Display Page Control Palette box. When you're finished, disengage by pressing the F15 key or Command-Q.

When you click on the palette's new buttons, note how they darken and "compress" when the mouse button is depressed, then re-expand on Click up. The simple button is useful and good-looking, but it's when you get into the various states of the buttons that you really appreciate the power you have at your fingertips.

Play, Stop & Pause Buttons

For the second page of the project, we'll replace the hot text controls that start and stop our "trains" with three buttons: Play, Stop, and Pause. The different states of the Pause button will allow us to specify different actions.

21. In the button library, make a new button, 32 pixels tall and 32 pixels wide. Make the type Simple.

22. Fill the scrollable drawing area with a medium gray using the Paint Bucket tool. Make the bottom two

rows and the right-hand two columns black. Then make the top two rows and the left-hand two columns light gray.

This will be a rough approximation of a three-dimensional button with a light source above and to the left. Where the light-gray and black intersect, give the black precedence in one corner and the light-gray in the opposite. Figure 10-41 shows what the button should look like at this state.

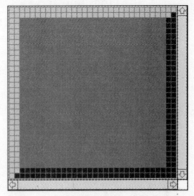

Figure 10-41: A simple 3D button in gray.

23. Using the Fill Rectangle tool, create a red square 16 pixels wide by 16 pixels high in the middle of the scrollable drawing area (Figure 10-42). This will be our Stop button.

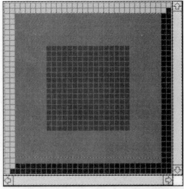

Figure 10-42: A red square will indicate "Stop."

To provide responsiveness to the button, and to imitate a physical button's being pushed in:

24. Copy the contents of the Up frame into the drawing area for the Down frame.

25. Select everything except the top row and the left column of pixels. Depress the Option key and drag the selection up one pixel and to the left one pixel.

    This leaves you with one row and column of light pixels and three of black. If you click alternately on the Up frame and Down frame, you'll see the movement of the button when it's depressed (Figure 10-43).

    Adjust the corners' appearance so that the black and light-gray alternately predominate.

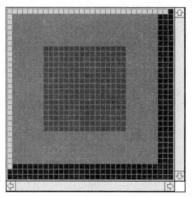

Figure 10-43: Shift the image up and to the left, to imitate movement.

26. Copy all frames to masks, and name this button "Stop.btn." Click OK when you're finished.

Make the Play Button

To make the Play button, copy and alter the Stop button:

27. In the button library, duplicate Stop.btn. Click the Edit button to open the button editing window and work on the copy that is made. We'll keep the button the same, but you'll need to transform the Stop square into a Play triangle.

Use the same red as before, and with the Pencil tool, color in the two pixels on the row above the leftmost two columns of the red square. Then color in the two pixels on the row below the red square, in the same two columns as shown in Figure 10-44.

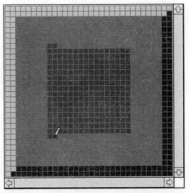

Figure 10-44: Make the triangle a little taller than the square.

Add a 2 pt X 2 pt red square just to the right of the middle two rows and rightmost column of the large square, as shown in Figure 10-45. The point of the triangle we make extends the square farther to the right. The visual center will be the same.

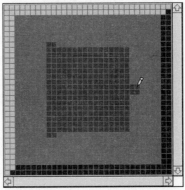

Figure 10-45: And make the point extend to the right.

28. Command-click on the medium gray background to switch the foreground color from red to gray.

Now go down the diagonal from the upper left to the small red square, two columns at a time, one row at a time, changing the red pixels to medium gray (see Figures 10-46 and 10-47).

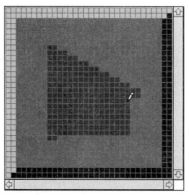

Figure 10-46: Transform the square...

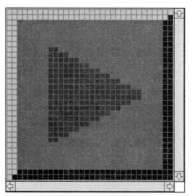

Figure 10-47: ...until it's a triangle.

29. Copy the inner portion of this frame into the Down frame. Use the keyboard up arrow and left arrow to position the triangle in the same position on the medium-gray square as it is in frame 1.

Check that the triangle moves with the rest of the top of the button by clicking alternately on the Up and Down frames.

30. Change the name of this button to "Play.btn." and click OK to close the Button editing window.

Make the Pause Button

The Pause button has to be more complex than the Play or Stop buttons, but we can use one of them as your starting point to expedite the Pause button construction.

31. To make our Pause button, duplicate the Stop button in the button library. Highlight the duplicate, Stop btn. copy, and click the Edit button to open the button editing window.

32. In the Button area of the button editing window, change the name to Pause.btn and the Button Type from Simple to On/Off (Figure 10-48).

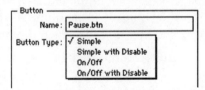

Figure 10-48: Make the Pause button type On/Off.

33. Note that the Down image from our Stop button now occupies the Up off frame, and the Up image the Up on frame. This isn't quite what we want.

Select the image from the Up off frame by double-clicking the Marquee tool. Cut and paste it into the Down off frame. Then select and cut the Up on frame image and paste it into the Up off frame. The two images from the Stop button now occupy the first two frames of the On/Off Pause button.

34. To change the Stop icon to a Pause icon, select the red color already being used, and with the Pencil tool make the red area wider by adding a column of red pixels on the left and on the right.

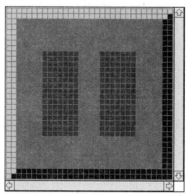

Figure 10-49: Make the square into two bars.

35. Now change the foreground color to medium gray and split the red area into two bars by filling in the middle four columns with gray, as shown in Figure 10-49. Copy the red bars into the Down off frame.

36. Double-click on the Marquee tool to select the whole image in the scrollable drawing area. Copy the image from the Up off frame into the Up on frame, that is from the first frame into the third frame.

37. Choose a bright green color, such as the eighth row, second column in the Color pop-up menu. Use the Paint Bucket tool to replace the red in the bars with green (Figure 10-50).

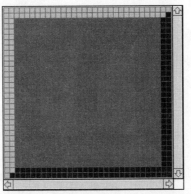

Figure 10-50: The two bars should be green in the Up on and Down on frames.

38. Follow similar steps for the Down frames: Copy the whole drawing area from the Down off frame into the Down on frame, that is from the second frame into the fourth frame. Replace red with green in the Down on frame, too.

Now we have four frames: the two Off frames (1 & 2) have red bars, the two On frames (3 & 4) have green bars. The two Up frames (1 & 3) have the same appearance, one with red bars and one with green. The two Down frames (2 & 4) have the same relation to each other (Figure 10-51).

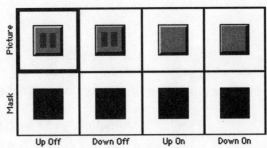

Figure 10-51: The Pause button's frames.

39. To finish the button, copy all frames to masks and click OK.

Using the Buttons

To use these new buttons with your trains, we'll need to add them to our project's second page and associate actions with user events for each button. And of course, we'll have to do that for each train.

Let's start by hooking up one set of controls and pretesting them to see how these new controls work.

40. Go to page 2 of the document. Drag the Stop, Pause, and Play buttons from the Buttons.qxl library onto an empty area of the page.

     In the QuarkImmedia palette, note that the Object panel scrollable list now includes the three buttons. Remember, creating a button in a button library already confers object status on the button.

41. For each of the three buttons, change the name by adding the word "red" and check the box labeled Keep Status on Page Entry (Figure 10-52).

Figure 10-52: The Object panel already shows the buttons, so all you need to do is change their names.

42. Click the Event tab and highlight the Play button in the Event panel scrollable list. Set the action for the Click up user event to Play Animation, and the animation to train-red.ano.

     For the Stop button, set the Click up action to Stop Animation, and the animation to train-red.ano.

43. Because it's an On/off button, the Pause button has four user events. For the Click up on user event, set the action to Pause Animation. Again, you need to specify the animation, train-red.ano (Figure 10-53).

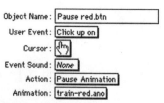

Figure 10-53: For the Click up on user event, set the action to Pause Animation.

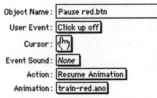

Object Name: Pause red.btn
User Event: Click up off
Cursor: 🖑
Event Sound: None
Action: Resume Animation
Animation: train-red.ano

Figure 10-54: For the Click up off user event, set the action to Resume Animation.

44. For Click up off, set the action to Resume animation, specifying train-red.ano, as shown in Figure 10-54.

What did we just arrange? When the train is moving, the user clicks on the Pause button. The button changes state so the red bars change to green. When the button is in this state, Click up on, the action taken is to pause the animation.

Clicking again on the button changes it to the Click up off state, which causes the animation to resume.

Test the Buttons

45. Choose QuarkImmedia | Engage or press function key F15 to try out our new buttons.

Since page 2 is the currently active page, the Engage command begins operation on this page. Disengage when finished by pressing Command-Q or function key F15.

Note the operation of the three buttons. Starting and stopping work as before, while clicking on Pause halts the train and changes the button appearance. A second click resumes motion, reverting the button.

What happens if you click on Start with the train already going? Nothing. The Play Animation command is ignored. But if you click on Start with the train paused, the animation will begin from the beginning, and the Pause button will be left in its Click up on state, green bars showing, even though the train is running and not paused.

We'll need to adjust this.

Turning the Pause Button Off

46. In the Event panel scrollable list, highlight the Play-red.btn. We'll take advantage of the fact that each click has two parts and use the Click down user event to turn our Pause button off.

Object Name: | Play-red.btn
User Event: | Click down
Cursor: | 🖑
Event Sound: | None
Action: | Set Button Off
Button: | Pause red.btn

Figure 10-55: For the Click down user event, turn the Pause-red.btn off.

47. Choose the Click down user event. Now in the Action menu, choose the Off command in the Button submenu. The action will now read "Set Button Off." For the button desired, specify "Pause-red.btn" (Figure 10-55).

    Do the same thing with the Stop button.

48. Save and engage. Note that pressing the Start or Stop buttons while the Pause button is on will turn that button off.

49. We'll want to add three buttons for the yellow train and three more for the green train. Instead of dragging the buttons from the button library, duplicate the three buttons that have already been set up to control the red train. You'll have to adjust the names, and identify different animation, but you will save steps by not having to specify the action for each user event. And since the Go–Stop hot text strings are no longer needed, you can delete them from the project.

50. Copy the revised Page-control palette into your Exercise library. You may even want to copy the set of three buttons.

Final Test

51. When you have all nine buttons in place and connected, engage the project again.

If two trains are about to collide, click the Pause button for one or the other train to prevent the collision, then resume progress.

To make things more interesting, you can add more trains and tracks, with the appropriate controls.

Exercise 10-2

In this exercise, we'll create a remote control unit. We'll learn about movies and animation in the next three chapters. The remote will be handy for viewing them.

This is a rather simple remote. We won't need channel selectors or volume controls—only three buttons: Play, Pause, and Stop.

We'll make the buttons and then add them to a graphic of a remote control unit which we'll make into a palette window object. Because it's a palette, it will stay on the top level of the project. It can be moved around from page to page, allowing the viewer to use any of the other objects on the page.

Access the Button Images

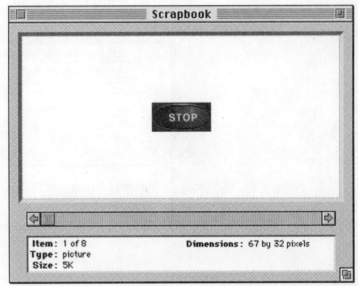

Figure 10-56: Copy the different button looks from the Scrapbook file into the button editing window.

1. The images for the buttons are in a Scrapbook file in this exercise on the Companion CD-ROM. Double-click on the Scrapbook file to open it and find the first picture. This will be the Up state—look for the button shown in Figure 10-56.

2. Using the Edit I Copy command, copy this image to the clipboard. From the clipboard, we'll be able to paste it into the drawing area for our button.

Create a New Button Library

3. To create a button we'll need a button library. If you did Exercise 10-1, you can use the Buttons.qxl library created for that exercise. Otherwise, use the File I New I Button Library command to open the New Button Library dialog box. Let's call this 3Dbuttons.qxl in the Button Library field (Figure 10-57).
   Click OK to create the library.

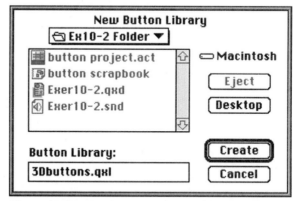

Figure 10-57: Naming a new button library.

Make the Stop Button

We're going to make the Stop button first. This will be a Simple button with only two states—Up and Down.

4. Click the New button in the upper left of the palette to open the New Button dialog box.

5. Enter the dimensions of the button in the width and height fields: 67 pixels wide and 32 pixels high.
   In the Button Type pop-up menu select Simple (Figure 10-58).
   Click OK. This will open the button editing window.

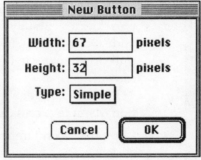

Figure 10-58: Enter the width and height for the button in the New Button dialog box.

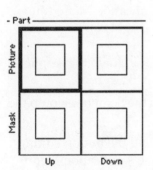

Figure 10-59: Click on the first Picture square in the Part area of the button editing window to start.

Figure 10-60: The pasted image appears in the scrollable drawing area.

6. In the Name field of the Button area, give this button the name "3Dstop.btn."

7. In the Part area of the button editing window, click on the frame for the Up state (Figure 10-59). By doing this, whatever we draw or paste in the scrollable drawing area will become part of the look for this state.

8. You copied the Up state for the Stop button to the clipboard in Step 1. Selecting Paste from the Edit menu puts the image into the drawing area, as shown in Figure 10-60.

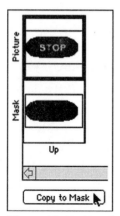

Figure 10-61: Use the Copy to Mask button to create a mask.

Right now, if we took this button into a project, all you would see is white. We need to mask the image in order to see it.

9. To make a mask for this button look, use the Copy to Mask button in the Part area (Figure 10-61). You'll notice that the Mask square under the picture now has a black image with the same size and shape as the Picture square. If you click on the Mask square, the image it contains will show up in the drawing area.

We now need a Down state. The image for this state is the second of the images in the Scrapbook.

10. To get this image, click on any of the Macintosh Desktop that is visible outside of the Quark document window. You may find it useful to hide QuarkXPress first by selecting the first command, Hide QuarkXPress, in the Application Menu (the pull-down menu in the upper-right corner of your screen).

    From the Finder, you can pull down the Application Menu to access the button Scrapbook.

11. Copy the second image from the Scrapbook onto the clipboard.

12. To return to QuarkImmedia and the button editing window, simply pull down the Application Menu and select QuarkXPress.

If you have trouble with the process, you will find a library of images in the folder for this exercise. You can copy the images from the picture boxes and paste them into the editing window. To return to the project page that contains your picture boxes from the button editing window, use the View | Windows command.

13. Click on the Down frame to make it active in the Drawing area, then paste the image from the clipboard.

You'll notice that the shadow color on the button has changed. Its appearance provides the visual cue that the button is being pushed in.

14. This button will need a mask. Click on the Copy to Mask button to do this.

This completes the first button.

15. Click OK to close the editing window and return to the button palette and take a look.

What, you ask, you haven't saved anything yet? Like QuarkXPress libraries, QuarkImmedia button libraries automatically save what's in them.

Make the Play Button

The Play button is more complex. There are Up and Down states, to indicate when the button is being pressed. But how do we let the viewer know with the button that our movie or animation is playing? The answer is to use a button with more than one state, indicating both Off and On conditions, each with its own Up and Down positions.

16. For the Play button we'll use the next four frames in the Scrapbook, Items 3, 4, 5, and 6, for the four states of the Play button. Copy the first of these images, item 3, into the clipboard; we'll use it for the Up Off state (Figure 10-62).

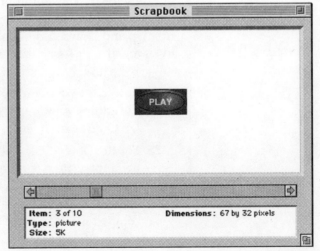

Figure 10-62: The Up Off state for the Play button is the third selection in the Scrapbook.

17. Once again, go to the Button Library palette and click the New button to create a new button.

    As before, set the size to 67 pixels wide and 32 pixels high. This time however, select On/Off in the Type pop-up menu. Click OK to open the button editing window.

18. In the Button area, name this button "3D Play.btn."

19. Now click the first Picture square, the Up Off state, in the Part area.

20. Paste the image that you just put in the clipboard into the Drawing area as the first button look, the Up Off state.

21. Repeat the actions of steps 1 through 6 for the next image, which is used for the Down Off state.

22. Return to the Scrapbook and copy the next image, Item 4, into the clipboard. You'll notice that, like the Stop button Off state, this button looks pushed in.

    Be sure to click on the Down Off frame.

23. Then paste the image from the clipboard into the scrollable drawing area.

So far what we've done resembles what we did with the Stop button. We've created both Up and Down positions, but only for the Off condition and we also need looks for On. The next two images from the library resemble the first Up and Down positions, except their letters are green to let the viewer know that the action is on.

24. Repeat the actions again, closing the editing window, copying Item 5 into the clipboard, returning to the editing window, and pasting the image into the Up On frame.

25. For the Down On position, use the next image from the library, Item 6, following the same steps as before. Be sure that you click on the Down On frame before pasting in the image.

26. With all the images in place, click on Copy All Frames to Masks.

Click OK to complete the button creation.

Create the Pause Button

This button will function much like the Play button. The procedure for making it is identical.

27. To make this button, go to the Scrapbook file and copy the first image of this sequence, Item 7, into the clipboard.

28. Click the New button in the Button Library palette. Just like you did in the first two buttons, make this button 67 pixels wide and 32 pixels tall. Select the On/Off in the Type pop-up menu. Click OK to open the button editing window.

29. Name this button "3D Pause.btn."

30. With the Up Off frame active, paste the clipboard image into the drawing area (Figure 10-63).

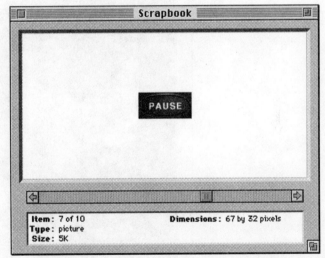

Figure 10-63: The Up Off state for the Pause button.

31. Repeat the steps above and copy the next image into the button's Down Off frame.

32. Now repeat the steps for the Up On frame and Down On.

33. Click on Copy All Frames to Masks to mask the picture parts. Click OK to complete the button.

This finishes all of the buttons.

Make a Window Object for the Buttons

Now that we've got a set of buttons, we want to put them into a remote. Once again, we'll use an existing illustration, paste it into a picture box as a background, and create a palette window object from it. On top of this, we'll place the buttons we just made. Then we'll use the remote to play, pause, resume, and halt music, as we did in Chapter 8, "Sound."

Figure 10-64A: The remote starts out as an illustration in a QuarkXPress picture box item.

Figure 10-64B: Drag the 3D buttons from the button library into the window.

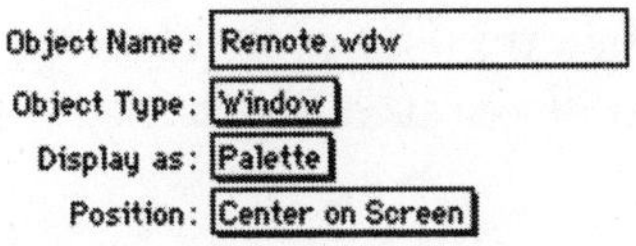

Object Name: `Remote.wdw`
Object Type: `Window`
Display as: `Palette`
Position: `Center on Screen`

Figure 10-65: Make the QuarkXPress item a Quark-Immedia window object.

Object Name: `Play/Pause group`
Object Type: Button Group

Key Alias: [   ]

☐ Initially On
☐ Initially Disabled
☐ Initially Hidden
☐ Keep Status on Page Entry

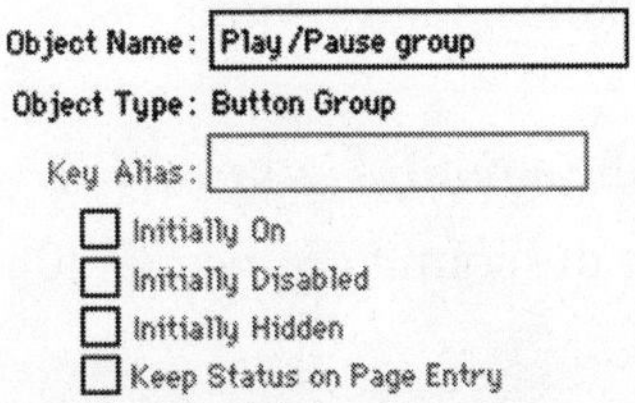

Figure 10-66: Select and group the buttons to make a button group.

34. Open the file Ex10-02.qxd. On the pasteboard you'll find a picture box with the image of a remote in it, as shown in Figure 10-64A.

35. You need to make the picture box into a window object. In the Object Name field of the Object panel type **Remote.wdw** (Figure 10-65).

    In the Object Type pop-up menu select Window. Choose Palette in the Display as pop-up menu. Leave the Position at Center on Screen. You can change it later if you wish.

36. From your button library, drag the Play, Stop, and Pause buttons into the Remote window and place them on the image of the remote, as shown in Figure 10-64B. Their object type has already been assigned—we did this when we created them in the button editing window. We don't need to change any of the other settings right now.

    In the previous exercise we used the Set Button Off action to turn an On/Off button off when another button that controlled the same object was turned on. By grouping the buttons we can accomplish the same thing. In a group of On/Off buttons, turning one button on automatically turns the others off.

37. Go to the Object panel. To group the buttons, select the two On/Off buttons, Play and Pause. Use the Item | Group command to group them.

38. You'll notice that the Object Name field has been activated and the Object Type field now says Button Group. To name the group, just type a name—we'll use Play/Pause group for these—in the Object Name field (Figure 10-66).

39. Drag the window and buttons into the library, so it will be available for other projects.

Assign User Events to the Buttons

40. In the Event panel, highlight 3D Play.btn. Assign the Play Sound action to the Click up user event (Figure 10-67). Specify Exer10-2.snd, the sound file in the Exer10-2 folder.

41. For the 3D Stop.btn, assign the Stop Sound action to Click up. As before, specify Exer10-2.snd (Figure 10-68).

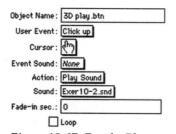

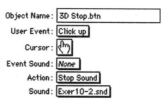

Figure 10-67: For the Play button's Click up user event, choose the Play Sound action.

Figure 10-68: For the Stop button's Click up user event, choose the Stop Sound action.

42. For the Click down user event, choose the Set Button Off action and specify the Play button.

When the user clicks on the Stop button, pressing down on the mouse button turns off the Play button, and releasing the mouse button stops the music.

43. The Pause button has four states, with actions assigned to each state.

- For Click up on, pause the sound (Figure 10-69).

- For Click up off, resume the sound (Figure 10-70).

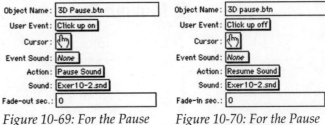

Figure 10-69: For the Pause button's Click up on user event, choose the Pause Sound action.

Figure 10-70: For the Pause button's Click up off user event, choose the Resume Sound action.

■ Use the Down actions to turn the Play button off while the music is paused and back on again when the music resumes.

■ For Click down off, choose Set Button Off, specifying the Play button (Figure 10-71).

■ For Click down on, choose Set Button On, specifying the Play button (Figure 10-72).

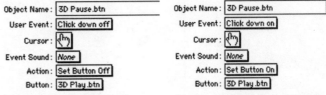

Figure 10-71: For the Pause button's Click down off user event, choose the Set Button Off action.

Figure 10-72: For the Pause button's Click down on user event, specify the Play button.

44. Save and engage the project.

Play, stop, pause, and resume work the way you would expect from your experience with CD players and VCRs. However, if you press stop after pause, the pause button stays on. That's because you don't yet know how to turn off both the Play and Pause buttons from a single user event (that will be covered in Chapter 12, "Scripts"). You can use the remote control unit with any project. Copying the palette and buttons into a library makes it easily accessible. All you have to do is specify the user events for each button.

Moving On

In this chapter, we've looked at how buttons differ from other interactive objects. Because a button can have different looks for different states, it's able to provide feedback to a user about what the button's doing.

Creating buttons is relatively simple—certainly simpler than in other multimedia programs—but you must create your buttons in the button editing window of a button library. The tools provided work like the tools in many simple paint and drawing programs. In fact, the button editing window is a simple paint program. A lot of the ease with which you'll work with Immedia buttons stems from the compact way in which you can create the different looks the button has in different situations, and associate actions with them.

In the next chapter, we'll look at how Immedia plays QuickTime movies. After that, we'll try playing and then making animation. Buttons will make it much easier to play, pause, stop, and control other actions in these objects.

chapter 11

Playing Movies

The movement we've made in Immedia so far has been pretty simple, sliding objects around the screen and moving images on a path. Objects do move, but the movement is not very complex. We can show an object moving along, but we don't have any way to make the object look like it's moving. We can't show different phases of motion, such as a ball rotating as it bounces or one leg moving in front of the other as a person walks.

QuarkImmedia does have a way to show motion using movies, video, and animations recorded in Apple's QuickTime format. If you can record motion on video or simulate it with animation, it can be transferred to QuickTime and played in Immedia.

Movies Can Make Multimedia Vivid

Nothing matches the capabilities of video: synchronized sound and a detailed image. Video can be used to report on events, demonstrate the capabilities of products, provide how-to's for procedures, and to entertain. Complex

3D animation and special effects can be created and re-corded on video. If you want lots of activity on the screen, video is certainly the way to do it.

Apple's QuickTime format is an excellent way to bring video and motion graphics into a project. But QuickTime isn't just for playing video—it also has tracks for audio, closed captioning, MIDI sound, and JPEG files—just about any kind of temporal data. QuickTime also plays cross-platform, on both Windows and Mac.

Movies Can Make Internet Projects Unplayable

QuickTime displays individual frames ten to thirty images per second. That's a lot of information. Consequently, file sizes for QuickTime movies can be very large. One minute of uncompressed video can be as large as 180 megabytes!

On the Internet, you can count on a viewer's attention wandering after 20 or 30 seconds of nothing happening on the screen while files are downloading. Who wants to spend time looking at a screen that doesn't change and a moving red bar on the status area of the controller? The general rule of thumb for download time on the Web, assuming a 14400 baud modem, is that 1K of information takes 1 second to download. At this rate, a megabyte, which is roughly 1,000 kilobytes, takes more than 15 minutes to download.

Are you still sure you want to play that movie?

You may also have problems playing QuickTime mov-ies on older, slower machines. A computer will drop frames if it can't process and play a movie fast enough, causing jerky playback. It's a good idea to test your project on a range of machines and make sure your movie looks good before you accept a final version of your project.

CD-ROMs and intranets can handle much more infor-mation at once, so you don't have the same speed issue. For these projects, QuickTime movies are useful and quite effective.

◼ Making QuickTime Movies

We can't give you the details of creating digital video—that's enough information to fill another book. In this chapter, we assume that you will have movies in QuickTime format, or have access to a program like Adobe Premiere to convert video to QuickTime.

Once you have your QuickTime movie, it's easy to play it in an Immedia project. The movie is played by the Macintosh or Windows system, not the Immedia project, so the display is not restricted to 256 colors, as the rest of the project is. Do remember, however, that the more colors in an image or movie, the larger the file size will be. If file size is an issue, you can convert to 256 colors in the Export Settings dialog box when exporting your project, which we'll go over in Chapter 19, "Exporting a Project."

Making QuickTime Movies Cross-Platform

Although most designers use Macs, there are many more people who use Windows machines. One of the great things about QuickTime is that it's cross-platform.

Macintosh files have two parts, data and resource. Windows files have only one of those. For QuickTime movies to play in Windows, they have to be "flattened" so that all of the video and audio data is contained in one file, not in two parts, as on the Mac. This can be done in MoviePlayer, an application from Apple. Simply save the movie using the File|Save As command, and in the resulting dialog box select the Make Movie Self-Contained radio button. To make sure the movies are cross-platform, check Playable on non-Apple computers.

Flattened movies play fine on Apple computers, so make sure your movies are flat if you want them to play on both platforms.

Movie Objects

As you might expect, movies are placed in picture boxes.
The first thing you must do to put a QuickTime movie in
your project is make a picture box. Of course, you'll name
it and define it as an object, choosing Movie from the
Object Type pop-up menu (Figure 11-1).

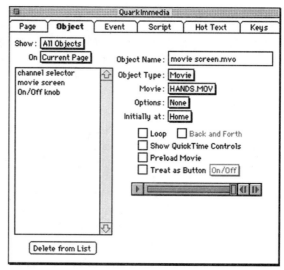

*Figure 11-1: Define a movie object and the movie it contains in the
Object panel.*

TIP

*Here's a fast way to make a movie object and place a
QuickTime movie in it. Make a picture box, and use
File | Get Picture to import the movie. Immedia defines the
picture box as a movie object and puts your QuickTime
movie in the Movie pop-up menu. Immedia even gives the
object a name—the name of your movie!*

Next you'll have to tell Immedia what movie to play in
the object. Just select it from the Movie pop-up menu. If

the movie hasn't been used in your project yet, it won't be displayed in the list. To import your movie into the project, select Other in the Movie pop-up, which will open the Select a Movie File dialog box. Find your movie using the dialog box, then click Open to import your movie.

The contents of the Options pop-up menu will probably look familiar: None, Initially Hidden, Initially Disabled, and Keep Status on Page Exit. You've certainly seen these before. They work in movie objects the same as they have in other objects.

In the Initially at pop-up menu, select Home or the side of the pasteboard where you want the movie object to be when the page opens. Are you thinking that you might be able to slide a movie object? Yes, indeed.

There are some new commands in the check boxes underneath these pop-up menus (Figure 11-2).

Object Name: movie screen.mvo
Object Type: Movie
Movie: None
Options: Initially Hidden
Initially at: Home
☐ Loop   ☐ Back and Forth
☐ Show QuickTime Controls
☐ Preload Movie
☐ Treat as Button On/Off

Figure 11-2: The Object panel for movie objects has several new options.

Figure 11-3: The QuickTime Controller can play, pause, and stop a movie, as well as adjust sound levels.

■ Loop—When you get to the end of the movie, the movie starts again at the beginning. If you select Loop, the Back and Forth check box, which is currently grayed out, becomes active. With Back and Forth selected, your movie will play from start to finish, and then play backwards to start.

■ Show QuickTime Controls (Figure 11-3)—QuickTime movies have a control bar that you can display underneath a movie object. The buttons on the bar are, from left to right, a sound volume control button, play, progress bar, rewind, and fast forward. If you display the QuickTime Controller with your movie object, the viewer can play movies without buttons or any other kind of control.

■ Preload Movie—Loads the movie in RAM before playing. This can make your movie play faster, although it won't necessarily make it start faster.

■ Treat as Button—Movies can be used as buttons, which we'll discuss later in this chapter.

User Events to Control Movie Objects

After creating the movie object, it's time to choose the user events.

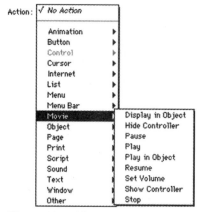

Figure 11-4: The Action pop-up menu for movie objects.

As with animation and sound, you'll probably have another object, a button or basic object, that controls the movie. There are a number of choices in the Action pop-up menu for movies (Figure 11-4).

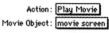

Figure 11-5: The Play Movie command requires that you select a movie object in which to play the movie.

Figure 11-6: Use Stop Movie to stop playing a movie in one object or in all of the movies in your project.

- Play Movie (Figure 11-5)—To play the movie in an object, select Movie | Play in the Action pop-up menu for the object that triggers the movie. Another pop-up will appear, asking you to identify the movie object in which the movie is playing.

- Stop Movie (Figure 11-6)—Stopping a movie is simple to do, it's the same procedure. In the Event panel for the object that controls the movie, a button, basic object, or another movie object, select a user event (usually Click up) and the Action | Movie | Stop command.

  In the Movie pop-up menu that follows you can select One Movie and identify which movie object that movie is playing in, or choose All Movies and stop all of the movies that are currently playing.

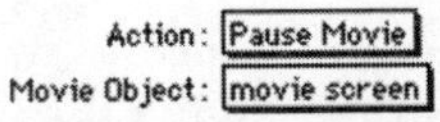

Action: | Pause Movie |
Movie Object: | movie screen |

Figure 11-7: Halt the playing of a movie with the Pause Movie action.

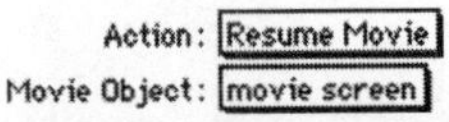

Action: | Resume Movie |
Movie Object: | movie screen |

Figure 11-8: There's also a command to resume play of a movie at the point it was paused.

Action: | Play Movie in Object |
Movie Object: | movie screen |
Movie: | HANDS.MOV |
☐ Loop

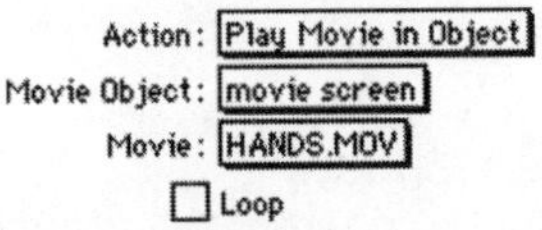

Figure 11-9: Use Play Movie in Object to play another movie in a movie object.

■ Pause Movie (Figure 11-7)—What if you just want to pause a movie to look at something else? There are pause and resume commands in the Movie submenu of the Action pop-up menu. Just like Play, when you select the Pause action, you'll be given a pop-up menu to select which movie object the movie you want to pause is playing in.

■ Resume Movie (Figure 11-8)—And, if you've paused a movie and want to start up again, there's resume, which works the same way. But why resume, why not just use Start again? Start always plays from the beginning of a movie, no matter where the movie was when it stopped. Resume will play the movie at the point at which it was paused.

TIP

Movies are a great place to use the multi-state capabilities of buttons. Start, Stop, Pause, Resume—if each button controls only one action this can lead to a lot of buttons. Remember that On/Off buttons give you several states, On to set an action and Off to stop it, plus Up and Down to indicate whether the mouse is being pressed or not. These are useful for paired sets of actions such as start/stop or pause/resume.

■ Play Movie in Object (Figure 11-9)—You don't have to make separate movie objects for every movie. Just like a TV or movie screen, movie objects can play more than one movie.

In the Action pop-up menu of the object that controls the movie object, choose Movie | Play in Object. Next, specify which movie object, locating it using the Movie Object pop-up menu.

Once you've chosen the object that will display the movie, you must designate which movie to play. Use the Movie pop-up menu to do that. And, if you want this movie to loop while playing in the object, check the Loop check box underneath.

Action: [Display Movie in Object]
Movie Object: [movie screen]
Movie: [HANDS.MOV]

Figure 11-10: Use Display Movie in Object to show a still frame of a movie when the movie is not playing.

Action: [Set Movie Volume]
Method: [Movie File Name]
Movie: [HANDS.MOV]
Volume: [126]

Figure 11-11: Set the volume level of a QuickTime movie playback.

Action: [Show Movie Controller]
Movie Object: [movie screen]

Figure 11-12: You can show and hide the QuickTime movie controller.

⊠ Treat as Button [✓ Simple] [On/Off]

Figure 11-13: Movie objects can function as buttons.

■ Display Movie in Object (Figure 11-10)—You can show the first frame of a movie without playing the movie. Perhaps you want to provide a preview to give the viewer an idea of what the movie is like. The Display in Object action will do this. The pop-up menus in the Event panel for this action are the same as for Play in Object: specify the movie object and then the movie.

■ Set Movie Volume (Figure 11-11)—You can even set the volume on a movie. As you might guess, the Set Volume command on the Movie submenu will do this. When you choose this action, you can then select a movie by filename or movie object. The volume level can be set from 1 to 255, with 1 being the lowest volume.

■ Show/Hide Movie Controller (Figure 11-12)—Show and Hide Controller refers to the display of the controller in movie objects, not the QuickTime movie itself. If at some time you want to hide the controller during the movie, or show a hidden controller, you can use this command.

■ Treat as Button (Figure 11-13)—Movie objects can be used as buttons. When you check the Treat as Button check box, you'll get a pop-up menu to choose the type of button, Simple or On/Off. The number of states your button will have depends on which kind you choose.

If you choose Simple, the movie will run as long as the mouse is pressed on it. Then it will rewind itself, back to the beginning of the movie.

If you choose On/Off, the movie will run until you click the Up Off state. Then it, too, will rewind to the beginning. With both, you'll see the movie running backwards at normal speed while it rewinds.

You may have noticed that we quite often make a distinction between movies and the objects in which they play. One key thing to understand is that a movie object is not the same as a QuickTime movie. Movie objects are like the screen in a theater or the TV attached to your VCR—you can play a number of movies on one.

Most of the properties defined in the Object panel and actions defined in the Event panel refer to the object that the movie is in, not the QuickTime movie itself. For example, the Play Movie action plays whatever movie is currently displayed in an object. If you play a second movie in the object, using the Play in Object command, and then click the Play button that controls that movie object, you'll start the movie you just played, not the one that was originally defined as part of the movie object.

Movie objects are made from QuarkXPress picture boxes. Like picture boxes, they can be resized and reshaped. You can turn a rectangular movie object into a polygon just as you can a rectangular picture box. You cannot, however, rotate or skew movie objects.

Playing Movies With MIDI Sound

MIDI sound is a format that has very small file sizes compared to other sound formats. An interesting application of QuickTime movies is playing MIDI sounds. If you have MIDI sound files, you can convert them to QuickTime using SimpleText. Open the sound file in SimpleText. You should see a button labeled Convert. Click on it and you'll make a movie from the sound.

You can use a QuickTime movie with no video to play sound on the Web. Put the movie on a window object if you want the sound to play throughout the project.

Exercise 11-1

In this exercise we will simply create a movie object and use the standard controls to play, pause, and resume a QuickTime movie. If you have worked your way through the exercises for the previous chapters, you may have realized that the first exercise in each chapter is intended to be created from scratch, so that it can be completed even if you don't have access to the Companion CD-ROM. However, to use a movie object, you must have a QuickTime movie, which can't be created from scratch using QuarkXPress or QuarkImmedia. To complete this exercise, you will need to access the QuickTime movie [MOVIE1] from the Exer11 folder on the Companion CD-ROM.

If you don't have access to the Companion CD-ROM, you can substitute any QuickTime movie that you do have.

If you installed the tutorial files with QuarkImmedia, you can use any of the five movies in the Preview to QuarkImmedia Files folder. The installation CD also includes two QuickTime movies in the Made in Quark-Immedia Logo Files folder. The clip media CD that accompanies Immedia contains five QuickTime movies in the FourPalms folder. You may also find QuickTime samples in the Avid Video Studio digital video editing application folder that comes on many Macintoshes. To locate a QuickTime movie installed somewhere else on your computer, use the Find command and look for files with the file type MooV. On a PC, you would look for a file with an extension .mov. If all this fails, QuickTime movies are readily accessible from many Internet sources, commercial online services such as America Online and CompuServe, and electronic bulletin boards.

Set Up the Project

1. Begin a new project. Set the page size to 480 points wide and 320 points high. (The starting values in this dialog box reflect whatever you entered the last time you were here.)

2. Check the Automatic Box and choose Picture. Set the Background Color to White. Leave the other values as you will usually find them: Palette set to System Colors (Macintosh), Kind: None (full screen), Position: Center on Screen, and Visible when Inactive checked (Figure 11-14).

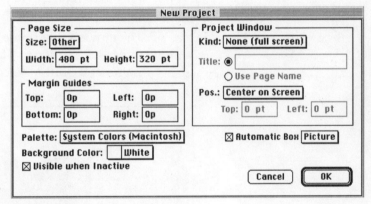

Figure 11-14: Set up a new project.

3. In the Project panel of the QuarkImmedia Preferences, check Hide Menu Bar at Startup (Figure 11-15).

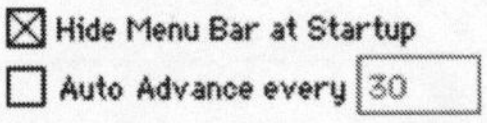

☒ Hide Menu Bar at Startup
☐ Auto Advance every [30]

Figure 11-15: Hide the menu bar.

Object Name: `Playbox.mvo`
Object Type: `Movie`
Movie: `Movie1`
Options: `None`
Initially at: `Home`
☒ Loop ☐ Back and Forth
☐ Show QuickTime Controls
☒ Preload Movie

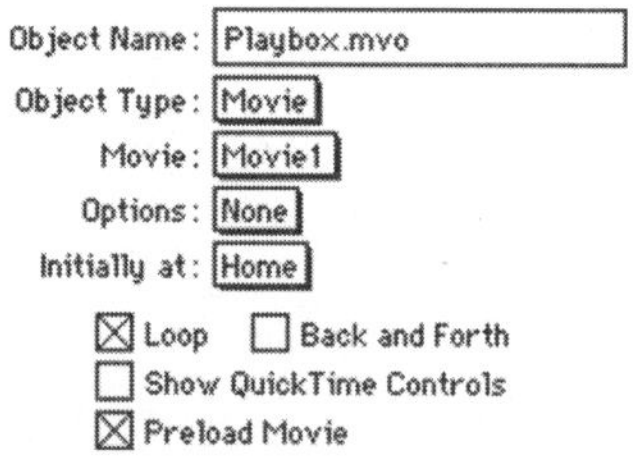

Figure 11-16: Make a movie object for the QuickTime movie.

Create the Movie Object & Set It Up

4. On the first page, select the picture box and create a movie object. In the Object Name field of the Object panel name the Object "Playbox.mvo." (We use "mvo" to indicate a *movie object*.) Select Movie in the Object Type pop-up menu.

5. Check both Loop, so that the movie will play in a continuous loop, and Preload Movie. Leave the other settings at their defaults (Figure 11-16).

6. In the Movie pop-up menu, choose Other to open the Select a Movie File dialog box and locate [MOVIE1] or the QuickTime movie you are using for this project. Click Open to import the movie into your project.

7. The movie's first frame poster is now located in the upper-left portion of the picture box on Page 1. Use Command-Shift-M to center the movie in the object.

Figure 11-17: Center the movie and resize the picture box to the size of the poster.

8. Use the middle box handle on each side to adjust the

picture box until it is the size of the poster (Figure 11-17).

Display the QuickTime Controls

As you will see in the next exercise, we can use our own buttons to control a movie, or we can use the QuickTime controls. In the Object panel, we could have checked a box to automatically show QuickTime controls for our movie. Instead, we'll wait to display the controls.

9. In the Event panel scrollable list, highlight Playbox.mvo. Set the user event pop-up menu to Double-click.

10. In the Action pop-up menu, choose Movie | Show Controller, and in the Movie Object pop-up menu, choose Playbox.mvo (Figure 11-18).

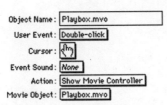

Figure 11-18: Set the Double-click user event to display the movie controller.

Test the Project

11. Save your project as Showtime.qxd and use Quark-Immedia | Engage or press function key F15 to test it. Note how the mouse pointer changes to the pointing finger when it passes over our movie box. Double-click to display the QuickTime controls, and play the movie, pausing and resuming as you like.

    Press function key F15 or Command-Q to disengage.

Change the Box Shape & Size

To further illustrate the possibilities when working with a
movie object, let's change the shape and the size of our
picture box.

> 12. Click on the picture box on page 1. Use Item | Box
> Shape command to convert the rectangular picture
> box to a polygon picture box (Figure 11-19).

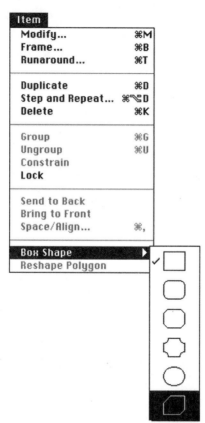

Figure 11-19: Convert the rectangular movie object to a polygon.

Item	
Modify...	⌘M
Frame...	⌘B
Runaround...	⌘T
Duplicate	⌘D
Step and Repeat...	⌘⌥D
Delete	⌘K
Group	⌘G
Ungroup	⌘U
Constrain	
Lock	
Send to Back	
Bring to Front	
Space/Align...	⌘,
Box Shape	▶
✓Reshape Polygon	

Figure 11-20: Check Item | Reshape Polygon to edit the shape of the polygon picture box.

13. Check Item | Reshape Polygon (Figure 11-20). Press the Command key and click on the "vertex" or handle in the upper-left corner to remove it.

14. Shift the vertex in the upper-right corner to the middle, so that the box is now a triangle (Figure 11-21).

Figure 11-21: Alter the shape to a triangle.

Note how changes made to the box shape and size crop the movie image, so parts of it are not displayed.

15. Uncheck Item | Reshape Polygon. Press the Command, Shift, and Option keys simultaneously and drag any of the box handles towards the center of the box to make it smaller (Figure 11-22).

Note that the box and picture are both changing size. You can scale the movie to any size you wish. The movie will become pixelated when you make it larger.

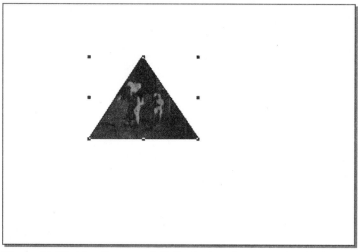

Figure 11-22: Use Command-Shift-Option-drag to resize the box and contents simultaneously.

16. Save and engage the project to see how it plays now.

Exercise 11-2

CD-ROM

Open the Exer11-2.qxd project in the Exer11-2 folder on the Companion CD-ROM. This folder also contains two QuickTime movies. In this exercise we'll play two movies in a single "TV screen," utilizing a single set of controls. To do this, we use the Movie | Play in Object action.

Create a Movie Object

Figure 11-23: Create a movie object from the rounded rectangle picture box.

To create a movie object, follow the steps below:

1. Open Exer11-2.qxd. A one-page project containing the image of a TV appears. The screen area is a rounded rectangle picture box that you'll use for the movie object.

2. Select this picture box and name it "TVscreen.mvo" in the Object panel (Figure 11-23). Define the picture box as a movie object in the Object Type pop-up menu.

3. When you define the picture box as a movie item, Immedia will prompt you to select a movie for this object. Select the file Movie1.mov. Since it hasn't been used yet in the project, you'll have to go to Other in the Movie pop-up menu and use the Select a Movie File dialog box in the Exercise folder.

Having defined a movie object and the movie to play in it, let's look at the other choices on this panel.

4. You can leave the Options pop-up menu setting at None and the Initially at pop-up setting as Home.

5. In the check boxes below these fields, select Loop and Show QuickTime controls, so the user can play the movie without any buttons or user events.

Test the Project

It's a good idea to save a project as often as you can. So take the time now to save your project and let's take a look.

6. Save the project. Use QuarkImmedia | Engage or the function key F15 to engage and preview the project.

   Try out the QuickTime controller to play and rewind the movie (Figure 11-24). You can even adjust the sound using the sound pop-up on the left of the controller.

   Use F15 to disengage and return to your project page.

Make an On/Off Button for the TV

The QuickTime controller is rather obtrusive, so you'll make a button that will play and stop the movie.

7. Make sure that TVscreen.mov is highlighted in the scrollable list of the Object panel. Uncheck the Use QuickTime Controller check box.

Figure 11-24: Use the QuickTime controller to play your movie.

Figure 11-25: Use a button to make an on/off switch.

Object Name: Off-in.btn
User Event: Click up on
Cursor:
Event Sound: None
Action: Play Movie
Movie Object: TVscreen.mvo

Figure 11-26: The action Play Movie will start the movie.

Object Name: Off-in.btn
User Event: Click up off
Cursor:
Event Sound: None
Action: Stop Movie
Select: One Movie
Movie Object: TVscreen.mvo

Figure 11-27: The action Stop Movie will stop playing the movie.

We've put a button in the button library for this exercise. This you'll make into an On/Off button for the TV. This button will start and stop the movie. Since it's an On/Off button, it has the necessary states to do this.

8. Drag the button from the library and place it on the side of the screen under the words Off and On (Figure 11-25). Name the button "Off-on.btn" in the Object panel.

9. Then go to the Event panel and select the Click up on in the User Event pop-up menu. This event controls the action that starts the movie, so for the Action choose Movie | Play (Figure 11-26). Immedia needs to know which movie object, so you need to select TVscreen.mvo in the Movie Object pop-up menu.

10. To stop the movie, select the Click up off user event (Figure 11-27). Choose the action Movie | Stop. In the Movie Object pop-up menu, select TVscreen.mvo again.

Save & Preview Your Project

Now is a good time to save your project; call it "TV-show1.qxd." Then engage the project and take a look. Use the Off-on button to start and stop the project several times. Observe what happens to the movie.

Create a Command to Play Another Movie

In the previous step, you chose a movie object to start and stop, not a movie itself. Your buttons will start and stop whatever movie is playing in that object.

We've set this up with only one movie and, as you know, objects can play more than one movie. How do we do that? A TV has different channels to pick up different broadcasts. Perhaps we could do something similar on our TV.

Figure 11-28: Place a button on the TV to control which movie plays in the movie object.

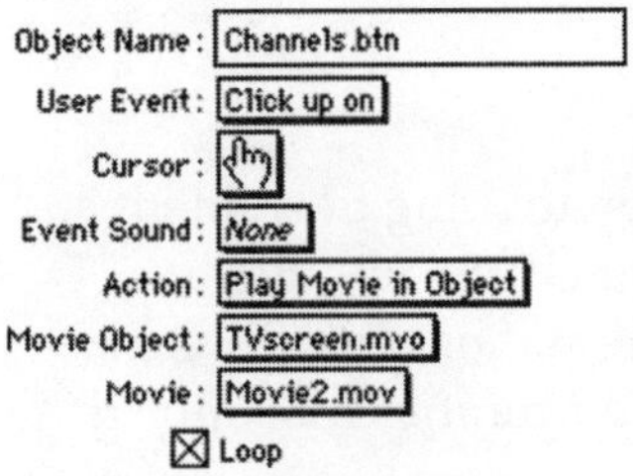

Object Name : | Channels.btn |
User Event : | Click up on |
Cursor : | 🖑 |
Event Sound : | *None* |
Action : | Play Movie in Object |
Movie Object : | TVscreen.mvo |
Movie : | Movie2.mov |
☒ Loop

Figure 11-29: Select Play Movie in Object for the Click up on state of the button.

11. Drag the button from the library onto the project page once more. Place the button under the numbers 1 & 2 (Figure 11-28). In the Object panel name this Channels.btn.

12. The first state we'll define is the On state, so go to the User Event pop-up menu in the Event panel and select Click up on (Figure 11-29).

13. For the action, select Action | Movie | Play in Object. This action assumes that you will play more than one movie in an object, so it prompts you with a pop-up menu that asks you to identify a movie object and one that asks for a movie.

    In the Movie Object pop-up menu select the movie object that we've been using, TVscreen.mvo. We'll select another movie for this object in the Movie pop-up menu. Select Other in the list and find the movie Movie2.mov in the folder for this exercise.

Save & Preview the Project

14. Once again, save the project and use Quark-Immedia | Engage to preview it.

    After starting the movie with the Off-on button, use the Channel button to change to channel 2. Movie 1 will stop and Movie 2 will start playing.

    Next, try the Off-on button and see what happens.

Play the First Movie in the Object

Now that you've got the second movie playing, how do you play the first? You can try clicking the Off-on button, but that just stops and starts the second movie, the one that's currently playing in the TV screen movie object.

You've only assigned an action to one button state for the channel selection knob, so select the Click up off user event for this button. If you make the action for this state Play Movie in Object and select Movie 1, it will play whenever you click the button. The setting moves to 1.

Object Name: Channels.btn
User Event: Click up off
Cursor: 🖑
Event Sound: None
Action: Play Movie in Object
Movie Object: TVscreen.mvo
Movie: Movie1.mov
☒ Loop

Figure 11-30: Select the action Play Movie in Object to play the first movie in the object.

15. Make sure that the Channel Selection button is highlighted in the Event panel. In the User Event pop-up menu, select Click up off (Figure 11-30).

    Next, in the Action pop-up menu, select the action Movie | Play in Object. For the object, select the one we've been using for this exercise, TVscreen.mvo. When Immedia prompts you to choose a movie, find Movie1, the original movie playing in this object.

16. This project is complete. So save it and use QuarkImmedia | Engage to preview.

Moving On

Movies are the most complex way to bring movement and motion into a project. Because QuickTime movies can contain video, audio, complex animation, and JPEG picture files, they provide many opportunities for sophisticated movement and activity.

Video made into QuickTime movies results in large file sizes, so they're not playable on most Internet Web sites. Intranets, however, and CD-ROMs are able to handle them well. QuickTime can be a very effective way of making your projects active and exciting.

Movies are played in movie objects. While an object is initially defined with a particular movie, other movies can be played in movie objects. But what if you want to play more movies than you have user events for or perform a sequence of actions in response to a user event?

Right now, we don't have the tools to initiate more than one action with a user event. Nor do we have a way to use an action or page change to initiate other actions. But QuarkImmedia does have a way to do this, scripts, which we'll examine in the next chapter.

chapter 12

Scripts

Sometimes you want more than one thing to happen when the user clicks the mouse button. You want two objects to slide around the page. You want an object to appear, display for ten seconds, then disappear. You want a movie box to slide onto the page and wait for the entry music to finish before the movie starts playing.

That's what scripts are about—doing a series of things.

The idea of scripts is easy to grasp. When you want to perform more than one action, you make a list of actions in the Script panel and give the list a name. Essentially, a script is just a list of actions. Then in the Event panel's Action pop-up menu you identify the script as the "action" you want to take, using Run Script.

Combining Events Into Scripts

Basic scripting simply uses a batch file approach to actions. As you begin using scripts you might think of this operation as "perform this list" instead of "run this program." Later, in Chapter 22, "Advanced Features," we'll see how the Action|Control submenu allows for a limited number of programming-like actions.

You make your list in the Script panel (Figure 12-1). Like the other panels, this one has a Name field and a scrollable list. The controls here let you make a new script by clicking the New button or by using the Delete button to delete an existing one. As a shortcut for making similar scripts, you can also begin by duplicating an existing script. This is different from the way we've worked with objects: you create the script with a button, and then name it.

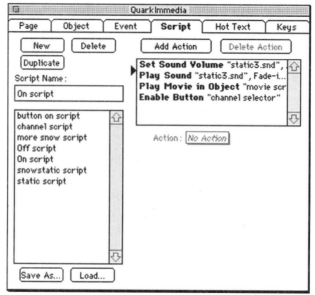

Figure 12-1: The Script panel.

When you make a new script or highlight an existing script in the scrollable list, each line of the script is displayed in the Action scrollable list, on the panel's right-hand side. When you make a new script, the only action showing is the action place holder, "No Action." Below the scrollable list is an Action pop-up menu, like the one in the Event panel.

Figure 12-2: Clicking Add Action puts a No Action *place holder in the script.*

Figure 12-3: Move this insertion triangle to the position in the script where you want a new action inserted.

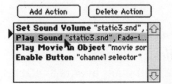

Figure 12-4: Dragging a script action to a new location is all that's required for reordering the sequence of actions.

The basic procedure is simple: you click the New button, and give a name to your new script. For each action, you add a line to your script, using the Add Action button. This adds a line reading *"No Action"* (Figure 12-2). You highlight a line reading *No Action* and then choose an action from the Action pop-up menu, setting any of the appropriate options that appear with your choice. The *No Action* line in the Action scrollable list is replaced by a short description of the action you set (of which you can see only the beginning).

You can add one line at a time and change it or you can add several. If you make a mistake and add too many *No Action* lines, you simply highlight the extra(s) and hit the Delete Action button. Any line can be changed into another action by simply choosing a different action from the pop-up menu.

You can add an action later on, anywhere in your sequence, very simply. The left side of the Action scrollable list has a small triangle you can move to the spot where you want the next action added—at the end of the list, at the beginning, or between two lines (Figure 12-3).

To move an action around the list, simply highlight a script action and drag it to the spot you want (Figure 12-4). You can even make a copy of an action by holding down the Option key while you're dragging.

Loading Scripts

If the scripts you make in one project might be useful to you in another, click the Save As button to save the scripts as an independent file (Figure 12-5). In the new project, the Load button calls up a dialog box in which you identify the script file you saved previously. All of the scripts are then loaded into the scrollable list of this second project, where they can be edited and renamed (or deleted) as necessary.

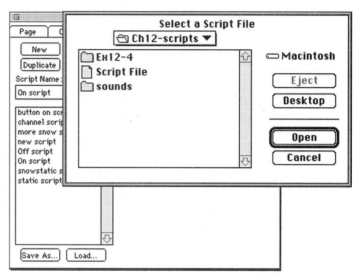

Figure 12-5: Saving scripts allows you to load them into other projects.

◼ Page Entry Scripts

Tying a user event to an action lies at the heart of how Immedia operates. But often you will want events to start up without waiting for a mouse click. For instance, when you enter a new page, you will often want a series of actions to take place—certain animation, movements, or even movies should begin right away and not depend on user interaction. (From the user's standpoint, these actions may logically be seen as an extension of whatever action they took—such as a mouse click—that led them to this page, and further clicking might seem superfluous.)

The Page panel, in fact, lets you specify actions to take place when a page is first entered, but these actions must be listed in a script—even if you only want to take a single action. The Entry Script pop-up menu lets you identify which script you want performed (Figure 12-6).

Similarly, exiting any page offers you an opportunity to run a script, using the Exit Script pop-up menu.

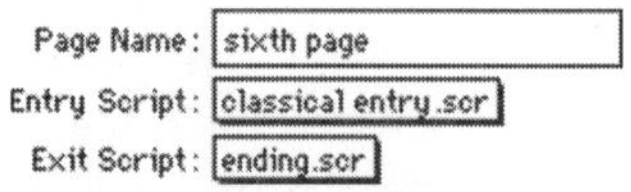

Page Name: sixth page
Entry Script: classical entry.scr
Exit Script: ending.scr

Figure 12-6: Use the Entry Script and Exit Script pop-up menus in the Page panel for any action(s) that should occur when a page is entered or exited.

Naming Extensions

We are firm believers in keeping things straight when constructing a project. Despite earnest exhortations, you're likely to begin your project without having mapped out absolutely every step and every possibility, and, as you go along, you'll find yourself adding pages, objects, and events, and adjusting things as needed.

Though it may seem like overkill to you now, we suggest ending each script name with something that identifies it as a script—the word "script" or maybe just "scr" or simply an uppercase "S." This way you minimize the potential for confusion between the pages, objects, buttons, and scripts all associated with one particular aspect of your project and which might all seem to need the same name like Order form, Company background, or some such.

Later on, as you become familiar with the program and aren't easily confused by all the details, you may think you don't need this over-obvious kind of identification. But we say, take pity on the person who has to revise this project six months or a year from now and who has no idea how things tie in to each other—that person is liable to be you.

Immedia accounts for several other occasions when you may want to specify certain actions independent of mouse activity. These are:

- When the project starts up.
- When the project quits.
- When there has been no activity for some period of time (whose duration you specify).
- When you want to initiate an action from a menu.

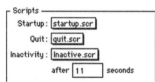

Figure 12-7: Scripts for starting up, quitting, and taking action when things have been too quiet are specified in QuarkImmedia Preferences.

As Figure 12-7 shows, you specify the scripts that you want to run in the first three of these circumstances in the QuarkImmedia Preferences dialog box. The startup script could differ from the entry script to page 1 in a variety of ways. For instance, you would want to include an Open Window action to open the palette with navigation controls when you initially enter the first page. That action, however, is superfluous when the user is simply returning to the first page after looking at some other page. Likewise, you may want to reset certain options on handing control over to another project; you can't assume that this will happen from the last page or from any specific page at all, so you can't put these actions in the Page exit script.

And, by definition, user inactivity excludes the possibility of triggering an action or script by some user event.

We'll see scripts used in menus—pop-up menus in the middle of a project page and menus dropping down from the menu bar—in Chapter 17, "Menus & Keys."

Focusing on One Task

Page entry and exit scripts offer marvelous opportunities for confusion to you as a novice Immedia user. In the process of setting up a page in the Page panel and thinking you should specify everything right then including the Page entry script, you'll find yourself jumping to the Script panel, creating a new script, adding and defining actions, then jumping back to the Page panel and accessing that script. Immedia's structure leads to this grasshopper behavior, because, of course, you can't reference a script until you've created it.

The script might involve elements on the page that you haven't yet made into objects. You interrupt the scriptmaking to create and name objects on the page. This itself might take you out of the Immedia palette altogether. You finish in the Object panel; go back to the Script panel, finish there; go back to the Page panel, finish there; and then go to the next page and start grasshoppering all over again.

Before things get out of hand, stop interrupting yourself and analyze what you want to do on all your pages. Get the design finished, with all objects in place and named, before you set about making scripts. Break your page work into two parts—naming the page and setting up the transition early on in the process, and specifying the entry and exit scripts at a later stage.

By keeping your focus on one step at a time, you won't let the interdependency of the different aspects of Immedia throw things into a muddle.

Exercise 12-1

In the exercises up to this point, we've restricted every user event to a single action and triggered every action with some form of interaction with the mouse. (Well, to be completely up-front about this, we've used Auto Advance to sidestep the issue a few times, too.)

With scripts, we can now initiate actions on page entry, specify a series of actions and delays between actions, as well as trigger multiple actions from a single user event.

A Multiple Action

In Chapter 10, "Buttons," we connected a series of buttons to actions that would play, pause and resume, and stop a musical selection. At that time, we found we couldn't have the Stop button turn off the Pause button if we paused before stopping the music. Now we can handle that set of events.

1. Open Musicpla.qxd. This is the project created in Exercise 10-2 (Figure 12-8). (If you skipped that exercise or if it's not available to you now, open Exer12-1.qxd in the Exer12-1 folder on the Companion CD-ROM.)

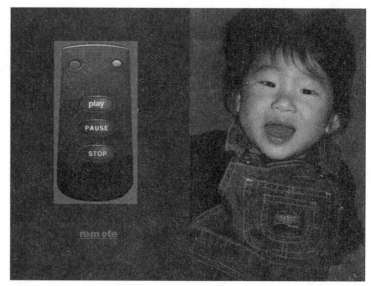

Figure 12-8: Begin by opening the Musicpla.qxd project from Exercise 10-2.

Figure 12-9: In the Script panel, add a new script called "Turn buttons off.scr" with two actions.

Figure 12-10: Set the action to Button | Off, specifying the Play button.

2. In the Script panel, create a new script called "Turn buttons off.scr."

3. Click Add Action (Figure 12-9).

4. Replace one *No Action* line with the Set Button Off action, specifying the Play button (Figure 12-10).

5. Replace the other *No Action* line with Set Button Off, this time specifying the Pause button (Figure 12-11).

Figure 12-11: Set the second action to Button | Off also, this time specifying the Pause button.

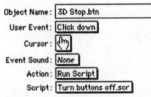

Figure 12-12: In the Event panel, highlight 3D Stop.btn, and set the Click down action to run the "Turn buttons off.scr" script.

6. In the Event panel, highlight 3D Stop.btn. For the Click down user event, change the action to Script | Run. Specify "Turn buttons off.scr" (Figure 12-12).

7. Save the project and test it.

Note how the Stop button now turns off both the Play button and the Pause button when it is clicked. After disengaging, close the project.

■ Exercise 12-2

In Chapter 9, "Movement," we learned about sliding objects onto a page, and we used a palette to move from page to page. Scripts provide a more elegant solution to bringing these objects onscreen. Let's go back to our exercise project, which we called Movement.qxd, and use scripts to effect a smoother operation.

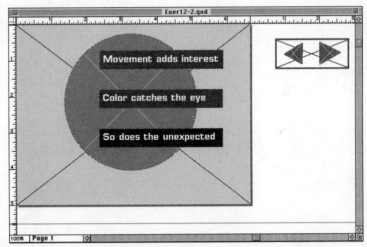

Figure 12-13: Begin by opening the Movement.qxd project from Exercise 9-1.

Figure 12-14: Set all the user events for Green circle trigger.obj to No Action.

Figure 12-15: In the Script panel, add a new script called "startup.scr" to open the Page-control palette.

Figure 12-17: Add another action choosing Other | Delay to give some breathing space before the bullet points start sliding in.

1. Open Movement.qxd, the project created in Exercise 9-1 (Figure 12-13). (If you skipped that exercise or if it's not available to you now, open Exer12-2.qxd in the Exer12-2 folder on the Companion CD-ROM.)

2. Remove the unnecessary triggers. Delete the Control Panel trigger.obj from page 1. When the user clicked on this box, the Page-control palette appeared. We can effect this now with a simple startup script.

3. Highlight Green circle trigger.obj and set all of its user events to *No Action* (Figure 12-14). We'll slide all three objects onto the page using a single script.

Make a Script for the Project Startup

4. In the Script panel, make a new script and call it "startup.scr" (Figure 12-15).

5. In the Action scrollable list, highlight the single *No Action* line. In the Action pop-up menu choose Window | Open, and specify Page-control palette (Figure 12-16).

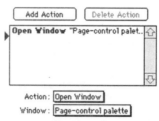

Figure 12-16: Make the first action open the Page-control palette.

6. Add an action place holder, highlight it, and choose Other | Delay from the Action pop-up menu. Leave the Type set to Time, and set duration to 1 second, to allow breathing room before the bullet points start sliding in (Figure 12-17).

Figure 12-18: In QuarkImmedia Preferences, choose "startup.scr" from the Startup pop-up menu.

New   Delete
Duplicate
Script Name:
Slide-bullet.scr
Script2
startup.scr

Figure 12-19: In the Script panel, add a new script called "Slide-bullet.scr" for use as the Page entry script for page 1.

Add Action   Delete Action
Slide Object "Point-movement.ob..
Slide Object "Point-color.obj", C..
▶ *No Action*

Action: Slide Object
Object: Point-color.obj
In Window: Current Project
Method: Home
Timing: Duration
Seconds: 2

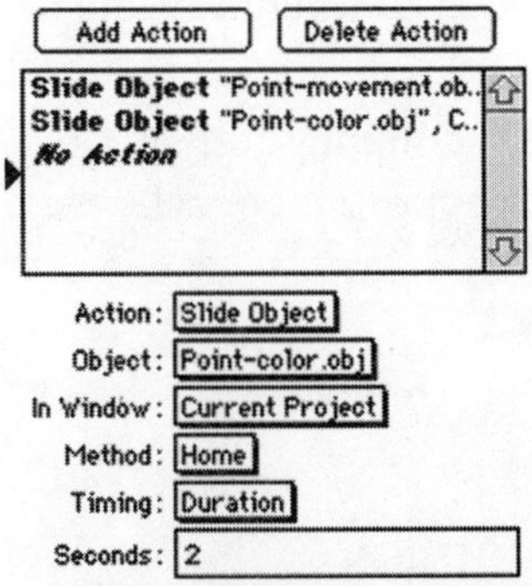

Figure 12-21: Set the second action to Object | Slide and specify Point-color.obj.

7. In Edit | Preferences | QuarkImmedia, click on the Project tab. Set the Startup pop-up menu to read "startup.scr." Now when you begin the project, this script will run (Figure 12-18).

Make a Script to Slide the Bullet Points

8. In the Script panel, make a new script and call it "Slide-bullet.scr" (Figure 12-19). It will have three actions.

    This script slides all three bullet points onto page 1 and is triggered by the entry to page 1. For each action described here, you will need to first click the Add Action button to add a *No Action* place holder.

9. For the first action, choose Slide Object, and specify Point-movement.obj. Set Method to Home, and Duration to 2 seconds (Figure 12-20).

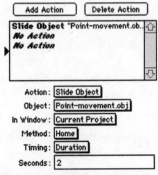

Figure 12-20: Set the first action to Object | Slide and specify Point-movement.obj.

10. For the second action, choose Slide Object, and specify Point-color.obj. Set Method to Home, and Duration to 2 seconds (Figure 12-21).

11. For the third action, choose Slide Object, and specify

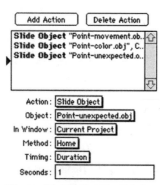

Figure 12-22: Set the third action to Object | Slide and specify Point-unexpected.obj.

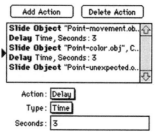

Figure 12-24: Insert a new action between the last two slides, setting it to Other | Delay.

Point-unexpected.obj. Set Method to Home, and Duration to 1 second (Figure 12-22).

12. Position the triangular insertion marker between the first two actions and insert a new action.

    Change the place holder between the first two slides to the action Other | Delay, setting the Time to 3 seconds (Figure 12-23).

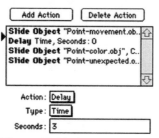

Figure 12-23: Insert a new action between the first two slides, setting it to Other | Delay.

13. Position the triangular insertion marker between the last two actions and insert a new action.

    Change the place holder between the last two slides to the action Other | Delay, setting the Time to 3 seconds (Figure 12-24).

14. In the Page panel scrollable list, highlight the first page, and in the Entry script pop-up menu, choose Slide-bullet.scr (Figure 12-25).

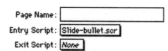

Figure 12-25: In the Page panel, set the Entry script for page 1 to "Slide-bullet.scr."

Test the Scripts

15. Choose QuarkImmedia | Engage or press function key F15 to test the project.

    Note how the Page-control palette appears by itself, followed by the three bullet points sliding serially onscreen.

■ Exercise 12-3

In addition to executing specific scripts on startup and quitting, Immedia can execute a script if there's a period of inactivity, for which you can specify the duration. Let's see how we might use this feature.

This exercise uses a Button library located in the Exercises folder on the Companion CD-ROM.

1. Open the Button library called Buttons2.qxl in the Exer12-3 folder (Figure 12-26).

2. Open the Musicpla.qxd project created in Exercise 10-2 and used in Exercise 12-1 (Figure 12-27). (If you skipped this exercise, or don't have access to it now, use the file Exer12-3.qxd, located in the Exer12-3 folder.) This exercise created a remote control and used the buttons to play a music file.

    We'll add a dialog box that appears if the project is idle for 30 seconds, asking the user if he or she wants to quit. We'll set up the dialog box first.

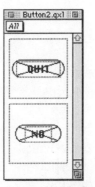

Figure 12-26: Open the Buttons2.qxl library.

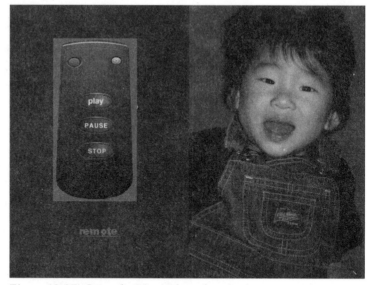

Figure 12-27: Open the Musicpla.qxd project.

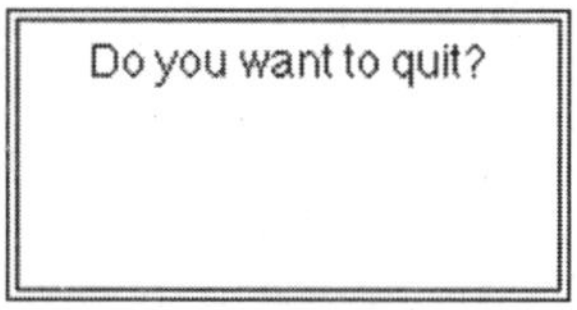

Do you want to quit?

Figure 12-28: Add a box with a border on the pasteboard. Make it 2.5 inches by 1.25 inches. Inside it, add another box with the text, "Do you want to quit?"

3. On the pasteboard off to the side of page 1, add a box that's 2.5 inches wide and 1.25 inches tall. Add a double border that's 4 points wide. Inside this box, add a text box in the top half with the words "Do you want to quit?" (Figure 12-28).

4. From the larger box, create a window object called Quit.wdw. Choose Dialog Box from the Display as pop-up menu, and Center on Screen from the Position pop-up menu.

5. From the Buttons2.qxl button library, drag the Quit and No buttons onto the bottom of the Quit window (Figure 12-29).

Figure 12-29: Drag the Quit and No buttons from the button library onto the Quit window.

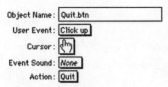

Figure 12-30: Set the Click up user event action for the Quit button to Other | Quit.

6. In the Event panel, highlight Quit.btn in the scrollable list. For the Click up user event choose Other | Quit in the Action pop-up menu (Figure 12-30).

7. Next, highlight No.btn. For the Click up user event choose Window | Close in the Action pop-up menu and specify Quit.wdw (Figure 12-31).

    When the dialog appears, click on the No button to remove it or click on Quit to quit the project.

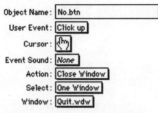

Figure 12-31: Set the Click up user event action for the No button to Window | Close, specifying Quit.wdw.

Make an Inactivity Script

Figure 12-32: In the Script panel, add a new script called "Inactivity.scr" to call up our dialog box.

8. In the Script panel, make a new script called "Inactivity.scr."

The sole action of this script is to open the Quit.wdw window (Figure 12-32).

9. In the Action pop-up menu, choose Window | Open and specify Quit.wdw.

10. In QuarkImmedia Preferences, choose Inactivity.scr in the Inactivity pop-up menu. Set this script to run after 30 seconds of inactivity (Figure 12-33).

11. Save and test this project. Note that Immedia defines inactivity as no mouse movement, no scripts running, and no actions taking place. The Quit dialog box won't come up while music (other than background music) is playing.

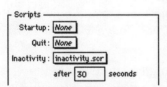

Figure 12-33: In Quark-Immedia Preferences, choose "Inactivity.scr" from the Inactivity pop-up menu, setting the trigger at 30 seconds.

Having Problems?
Some extensions in your System folder continuously monitor activity on your computer and may prevent an Inactivity script from being triggered. Try running with only standard extensions if nothing happens when nothing is happening.

Exercise 12-4

Open & View the File

1. Open the file for this exercise, Exer. 12-4.qxd, and display it completely using View | Fit in Window. This is the same TV that we used in the previous chapter. We're going to do some different things to it. This time, the On/Off button will turn the TV on, but to a screen full of static or snow.

Define the Movie Object

You may have noticed that the TV screen in Exercise 11-2 was never dark or empty, even when it was supposed to be off. We defined the movie object with a movie in it and its poster or first frame was displayed until the movie started. If we want the movie object we created now to remain dark until a movie plays, we'll have to define this movie object without a movie.

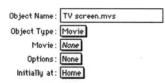

Figure 12-34: Define the rounded rectangle as a movie object with no movie.

2. Click on the rounded rectangle picture box in the middle of the TV. Define this box as a movie object in the Object panel by entering the following settings—Object Name as TV screen.mvo, Object Type as Movie Object, Movie as *None* (nothing displays in this object before a movie starts playing), Options as None, and Initially at as Home (Figure 12-34).

New   Delete
Duplicate
Script Name:
TVon.scr

Figure 12-35: Create a script to play a movie in the movie object.

Play Movie in Object "TV screen
Play Sound "static.snd", Fade-in ...

Action: Play Sound
Sound: static.snd
Fade-in sec.: 0
☒ Loop

Figure 12-36: Add an action to play a sound with the QuickTime movie.

Create the Off & On Scripts

3. Go to the Script panel and click the New button to create our first script. In the Script Name field, type the name of this script, TV-on.scr (Figure 12-35). Press Return or Enter to enter the name and start the script.

4. For the first action in this script, go to the Action pop-up menu. Since there's no movie in this movie object, we'll need to select an action that specifies both a movie object and a movie to play in it. Play Movie won't do that, so we'll use Play in Object in the Movie submenu of the Action pop-up menu.

    You'll need to select a movie to play in this movie object. Try Static.Mov, a QuickTime movie made from a sequence of Photoshop images. It hasn't been used in the project yet, so you'll have to click on Other in the pop-up list and locate the movie in the folder for this exercise on the Companion CD-ROM.

    We don't want the movie to stop before a user switches to one of the channels, so be sure to check the Loop check box.

The QuickTime movie we're using has no audio track. To have any noise with it, we'll have to play a sound. We can do that by adding another action to the script.

5. Click on the New Action button to add an action to the script. In the Action scrollable list, select Sound | Play (Figure 12-36). You'll need to locate the sound as it hasn't been used in the project. Use Other in the Sound pop-up menu and find the sound static.snd.

    Leave the Fade In field at 0 and check Loop so that the sound will play as long as the movie does.

Loud noise can be irritating, especially TV static! Let's be nice to viewers and set the sound to a low level. We'll need another action in the script to do this, but we can add as many as we want.

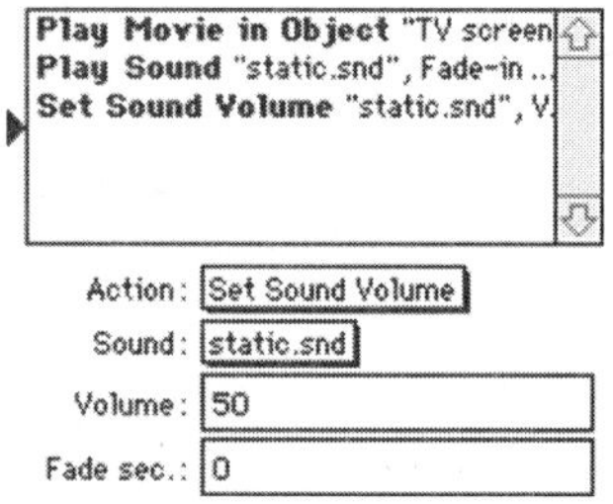

```
Play Movie in Object "TV screen
Play Sound "static.snd", Fade-in ..
Set Sound Volume "static.snd", V.
```

Action: Set Sound Volume
Sound: static.snd
Volume: 50
Fade sec.: 0

Figure 12-37: Set the volume level for the sound with another action in the script.

```
Stop Movie All Movies
Reset Object "TV screen.mvo"
```

Action: Reset Object
Object: TV screen.mvo

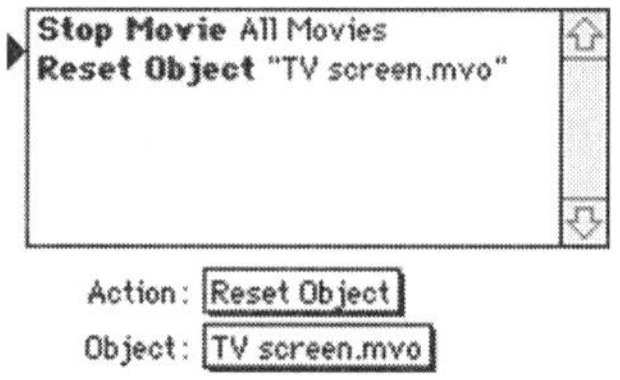

Figure 12-38: A new script to stop all movies and reset the movie object to its original state.

Object Name: Off-on.btn
User Event: Click up on
Cursor:
Event Sound: None
Action: Run Script
Script: TV-on.scr

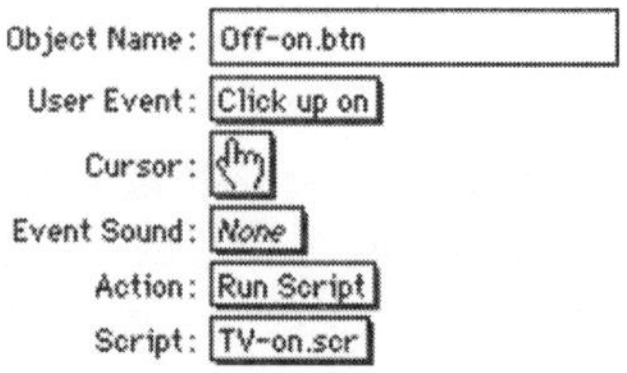

Figure 12-39: Assign the TV-on.scr to Click up on for the On/Off button.

6. Once again, click the New Action button to add another action to the script. With *No Action* highlighted in the Action scrollable list, select Set Sound Volume in the Action pop-up menu and choose the sound that's playing, static.snd (Figure 12-37).

Volume levels range from 1 to 255. To get a relatively low but still audible sound level type **50** into the Volume field. We want an abrupt change from silence to noise, so leave the Fade sec. field set to zero.

If the Set Sound Volume is executed after Play Sound, the noise will be pretty loud until the volume is adjusted. To prevent a loud burst of sound, drag the Set Sound Volume action above Play Sound in the Action scrollable list.

We can turn the TV on, we now need a way to turn it off. We'll need to write a script that will stop whatever movie is playing in the movie object. To make the TV screen dark again, we'll add an action that sets the TV screen object back to the state it was in before the project started.

7. In the Script panel, click the New button to create a new script. Name this one TVoff.scr. For the first action, select Stop Movie in the Action pop-up menu. We want to stop every movie that might be playing, so select All Movies and not One Movie in the Select pop-up menu.

8. Add an action to the script by clicking the New Action button (Figure 12-38).

Now we want to set the movie object to its original state. There's an action to do this, Reset Object. Pull down the Action menu to Object | Reset and specify the movie object, TV screen.mvo.

These scripts need something to activate and deactivate them. We'll use an On/Off button to do this. The first user event, Click up on, will run the On script and the second, Click up off, will run the Off script.

9. Go to the Event panel and select Off-on.btn in the Object scrollable list. For Click up on choose Run Script in the Action menu and select the script we just made, TV-on.scr (Figure 12-39).

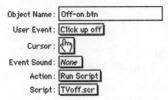

Figure 12-40: Use TV-off.scr for Click up off.

10. Next, select the Click up off user event and choose the TV-off.scr from the Action pop-up menu (Figure 12-40). This will stop any and all movies that are playing and set the movie object to its original setting, with no movie showing.

Test Your Project

11. Save your project and preview it using Quark-Immedia | Engage or the F15 function key. Try the On/Off button and check to see that the QuickTime movie and associated sound play together.

Assign Actions to the Channel Selection Button

The TV now works, but we can't get any picture. We'll have to use the channel selection button for that. In Exercise 11-2 we used the action Play Movie in Object to play the different movies, and you'll do the same here.

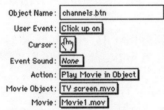

Figure 12-41: Use Play Movie in Object to play Movie1 in the movie object.

12. In the Object scrollable list of the Event panel, select the channel selection button. Then, select Click up on in the User Event pop-up menu. This event will play the first movie channel, so in the Action pop-up menu choose Play Movie in Object. Identify which movie object, TV screen.mvo, and which movie, Movie1, in the pop-up menus (Figure 12-41).

13. Now, select Click up off in the User Event pop-up menu. We want to play the other movie in this object, so once again choose Play Movie in Object in the Action pop-up menu. Specify the movie object, TV screen.mvo again, and movie, this time Movie2 (Figure 12-42).

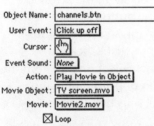

Figure 12-42: Play a second movie with Play Movie in Object.

Test the Project

14. Save your project and engage it to preview. Turn the TV on and then try out the channel selection. Turn the TV off when you're playing channel 2 and observe what happens to the channel selection button. Next try to select a channel when the TV is off. What happens?

Use Disabled State for the Channel Selection Button

We don't want anyone to play either of the movies when the TV isn't on, so we'll have to disable this button. Because it was created with disabled states, we can easily do that in the Object panel. So that channel 1 is the first channel to play a movie, we'll make the button initially on (the on state points to channel 2).

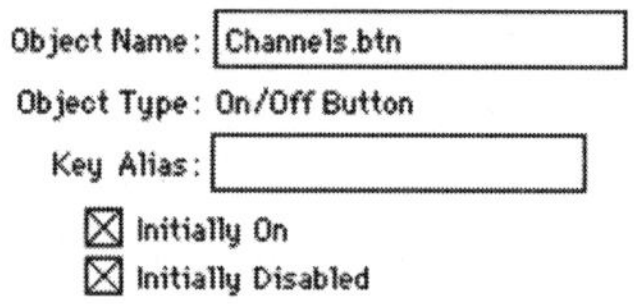

15. In the Object panel, make sure that the channel selection button is highlighted in the scrollable list. Check the Initially On check box to start this page with the button in the On state. Then check the Initially Disabled check box (Figure 12-43). This will disable any user events for the button.

Now we need a way to get the button to work when the TV's turned on.

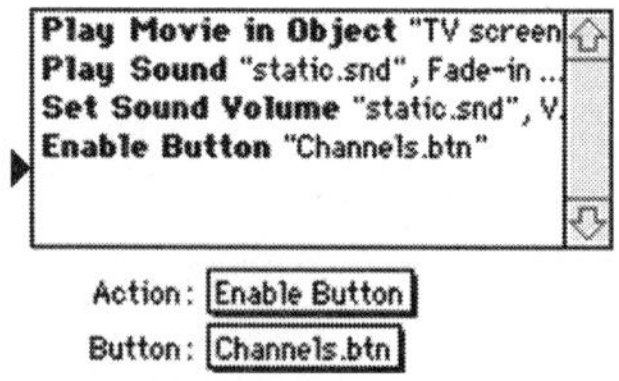

16. In the Script panel, select TV-on.scr in the scrollable list. The action that enables the button should be last in the list of actions for the script, so move the Insertion triangle to the bottom of the list. Click New Action to create another action. Select Enable from the Button submenu of the Action pop-up menu and specify which button channel selection (Figure 12-44).

The channel selection button shouldn't be able to work when the TV's turned off. We could use the Reset Object action, but that would set the channel button back to its original position. If we use Disable Button, the button will stay in position when the TV's turned off.

Object Name: Channels.btn
Object Type: On/Off Button
Key Alias:
☒ Initially On
☒ Initially Disabled

Figure 12-43: Disable the channel selection button at the beginning of the project by checking Initially Disabled.

Play Movie in Object "TV screen
Play Sound "static.snd", Fade-in ...
Set Sound Volume "static.snd", V
▶ Enable Button "Channels.btn"

Action: Enable Button
Button: Channels.btn

Figure 12-44: Add an action to TV-on.scr that enables the channel selection button.

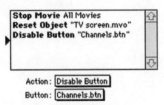

Figure 12-45: Add an action to disable the channel selection button.

17. Highlight the TV-off script in the Script scrollable list. Add an action to the list by clicking the New Action button and choosing Button | Disable. Identify the channel selection button in the Action pop-up menu (Figure 12-45).

Once again, save your project. Use QuarkImmedia | Engage or the F15 function key to preview the project. Check to make sure the buttons work at the right times.

Moving On

To keep things simple, Immedia assigns a single action per user event. However, you can put multiple actions into a script and run the script you specify as the "single" action.

Scripts also supply the only method for specifying actions on entering or exiting a page, when beginning or ending a project, as well as when no activity has occurred for a set period of time, and for commands used in a custom menu.

In a later chapter, we'll see how scripts can be assigned actions only when certain conditions are met, giving this powerful tool even more flexibility in making the multimedia project more interactive and responsive to the user. The very richness of scripts comes at a price of potential confusion, though: planning the logic of a project's flow and the scripts in it becomes critical, lest the welter of details become overwhelming.

Next, in Chapter 13, "Playing Animations," we turn our attention to what often proves to be the central feature of multimedia—the animation. Because of its combination of movement, liveliness, and compactness of size, especially in relation to video, using animation well can provide you with a sure route to multimedia success.

Playing Animations

Roughly defined, animations are homemade movies. Just playing an animation scarcely differs from playing a movie. But unlike QuickTime movies, we can get in there and edit the contents of any and every frame.

We could say animations are homemade cartoons, although the objects, characters, and backgrounds of our animations don't have to be drawings. They can be any kind of image, even photographs. You'll learn how to create your own animations in the next chapter.

What's wonderful about animation in Immedia is how efficiently the program handles it. Immedia doesn't even blink at moving an animation around the screen, so we really treat animations as two activities—playing the animation in a box like we did QuickTime movies, and zipping that box around the page, even with an animation playing in it.

Animation in Immedia is unlike anything you've ever seen before on a desktop computer—you can keep adding and moving those animations around until everything on your screen is spinning. Compare Immedia's results to any other program's, from Macromedia Director on down, and without argument this is the top. You can have more happening onscreen at one time using Immedia's animations than in any other program. Period.

When we look at Immedia's basic flip-book method of animation in Chapter 14, "Making Animations," however, it will be time to acknowledge advantages in the other direction. Immedia's capability for making animation is not the most sophisticated. But who says you can't use each program you have for what it does best? Like XPress, Immedia's strength lies in its ability to assemble elements created in other programs.

Creating Animation Objects

Animation objects are created just like any other type of Immedia object. Just name the object in the Object Name field of the Object panel and identify which type of object in the Object Type pop-up menu.

When you select Animation in the Object Type pop-up menu, Immedia presents you with several new pop-ups. The first, Display as, determines the type of animation. There are three choices: Sequence on a Path, Item on a Path, and Sequence in a Box (Figure 13-1).

We looked at Item on a Path, the simplest of Quark-Immedia's animation features, in Chapter 9, "Movement." While the item itself moves in Item on a Path animation, the image in it doesn't. A person's legs don't move back and forth to indicate that she is walking or a bird's wings flap up and down to look like it's flying.

With animation sequences, you can create frames that represent individual phases of motion so that objects really do look like they're in motion—you'll learn how to do this in Chapter 14, "Making Animations." In this chapter, we'll work with animations that have already been created.

As you go through this chapter, you'll see that playing animations is a lot like playing movies. Just as movie objects can be thought of as screens to display QuickTime

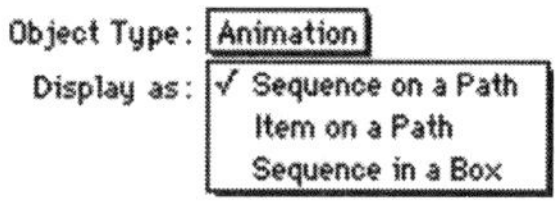

Figure 13-1: When you make an animation object, you have a choice of three types.

movies, animation objects act as screens to display animation sequences. And, just like movie objects, the actions that control individual animations are applied to the animation objects, not the animations themselves.

Sequence in a Box Animation

Let's look at Sequence in a Box animation. In many ways it's a lot like a movie. A Sequence in a Box animation object is a static box to which a moving sequence is assigned.

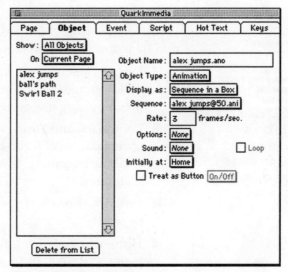

Figure 13-2: For a Sequence in a Box animation you must identify a sequence and a frame rate.

To make a Sequence in a Box animation, define an object as Animation in the Object Type pop-up menu. Immedia will then add a Sequence pop-up menu to the Object panel (Figure 13-2). Which sequence do you want to display in your object? You can select any of the animation sequences in your project. If the one you want isn't displayed in the pop-up menu list, choose Other and open the Select an Animation File dialog box to locate it.

The Rate field is added to the Object panel when you make a Sequence in a Box animation object. This shows you the frame rate, the number of frames displayed per second, which is determined when the animation sequence is created. You can easily change it if you want—just type a new number in the Rate field.

Fast-paced animations will require a higher frame rate than animations, with little change from frame to frame. The frame rate also has an impact on how smooth or jerky the animation will look. Generally a higher rate will be smoother, but slower machines may not be able to process and display frames fast enough, especially if the picture is large or visually busy, causing jerky playback.

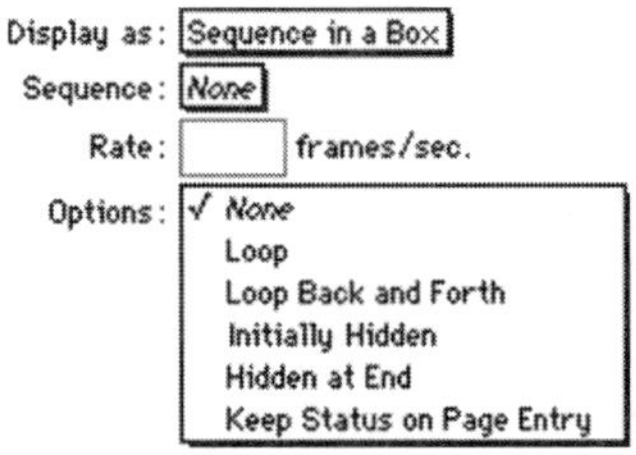

The Options pop-up menu that follows the Rate field gives you the same choices as it does with movie objects and Item on a Path animation sequences (Figure 13-3):

Figure 13-3: The choices in the Options menu are the same as they are for movie objects and other animation sequences.

- **Loop.** When the sequence reaches the end of play, it will start again at the beginning and continue playing, repeating this cycle until the action is stopped.

- **Loop Back and Forth.** When it gets to the end of the sequence, it will reverse itself and play backward until the beginning. It will repeat this until the action is stopped.

- **Initially Hidden.** If you don't want this sequence to be seen until a specific event, choose this option.

- **Hidden at End.** The animation will disappear when it gets to the end of the action.

- **Keep Status on Page Entry.** When you return to a page, the events are the same as they were on first entry. If the sequence is playing when the viewer exits the page and you want it to be playing if the viewer returns to this page, choose this option.

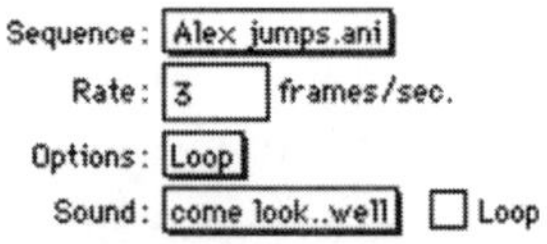

Figure 13-4: Use the Sound pop-up menu to select a sound that will play with the animation.

Unlike QuickTime movies, animations don't have sound tracks. However, you can play a sound with an animation. Use the Sound pop-up menu to select one (Figure 13-4). If you want the sound to play continuously while the sequence is playing, check the Loop check box next to the Sound pop-up.

☒ Treat as Button | √ On/Off |
| Simple |

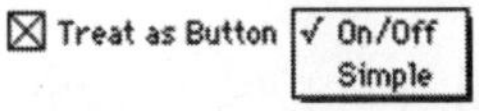

Figure 13-5: Sequence in a Box animation objects can be used as Simple or On/Off buttons.

You've also seen the settings for the Initially at pop-up menu before. Select Home to play an animation object at the spot where you've placed it on the project page. Select a side of the pasteboard—Top, Left, Bottom, or Right—if you want to display the object after page entry.

Like movie objects, Sequence in a Box animation objects can be used as buttons. The entire sequence will play for each user event. Select this option by checking the Treat as Button check box. As you see in Figure 13-5, you can choose to make an animation either a Simple or On/Off button. Of course, you can use animation objects—or any other type of object, for that matter—to trigger actions just by assigning user events and actions in the Event panel. Unlike an animation treated as a button, an animation will stop playing when its user event is activated.

Don't be alarmed if the Sound pop-up menu disappears when you select Treat as Button. Sounds can't be associated with buttons in the Object panel. This must be done in the Event panel. If you want a sound to play with an animation object button, use the Event Sound pop-up menu in the Event panel.

Sequence on a Path Animation

Sequence on a Path animation is created almost the same way as Item on a Path animation, which we discussed in Chapter 9, "Movement." Start with a QuarkXPress item—any line, picture, or text box will do—to make a path for the animation. Name the path in the Object panel and make it an object. You can usually leave the other options in the Object panel at the default settings—Options set at None, Initially at set at Home.

Having created a path for the animation, you're ready to make the animation object itself. As you might expect, to do this you select a text or picture box item, name it in the Object panel, and choose Animation in the Object Type pop-up menu. You can identify the object as a Sequence on a Path in the Display as pop-up menu. There are several other new pop-up menus and fields that accompany this choice.

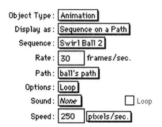

Object Type: Animation
Display as: Sequence on a Path
Sequence: Swirl Ball 2
Rate: 30 frames/sec.
Path: ball's path
Options: Loop
Sound: None ☐ Loop
Speed: 250 pixels/sec.

Figure 13-6: For Sequence on a Path animation you must specify a path and speed.

Choose which animation to play in the Sequence pop-up menu (Figure 13-6). The frame rate of a Sequence on a Path animation is determined when the animation is created. It can easily be changed, just as it can for a Sequence in a Box animation, by entering a new number in the Rate field.

The Path pop-up menu under the Rate field displays all of the objects on the page. Select one to be the path for your animation. The Options and Sound pop-up menus for Sequence on a Path animation are the same as those for Sequence in a Box. For Sequence on a Path animation you must also set a speed at which animation will travel on the path. This, too, is usually done when the animation sequence is created and is displayed in the Speed field. You can change it the same way you change the setting in the Rate field, by entering a new number into the field.

Figure 13-7: Set the Start Point and Direction dialog box for the animation.

When making an Item on a Path animation, you must indicate a starting point and direction for the animation to travel. Sequence on a Path animations work the same way.

Open the Animation Start Point dialog box using the Specify button in the Start Point and Direction field (Figure 13-7). Click on the path displayed in the dialog box to indicate the spot where the animation should start. The Change Direction button in the lower left will change the direction in which the object moves.

Playing Animation Sequences

Once you've created an animation object, you've defined most of what the object will do. But how do you start the animation? As you would expect, the Event panel has ways to do that. The actions you'll use with animation sequences are:

Action: [Play Animation]
Animation: [alex jumps]

Figure 13-8: Use Play Animation to start playing an animation in an animation object.

- **Play Animation.** Most of the time you'll use the simple choice Action | Animation | Play, shown in Figure 13-8. Select which animation to play in the Animation pop-up menu. Almost everything else involved with the animation—its speed, rate, and path if it is a Sequence on a Path animation—is defined in the Object panel.

Action: [Pause Animation]
Animation: [alex dances]

Figure 13-9: Use Pause Animation to halt the play of an animation in an animation object.

- **Pause Animation.** Just as with movies and sound, you can halt the playing of an animation until the Resume action starts it up again. Use the Pause Animation action to do this, then select which animation to pause in the Animation pop-up menu below the Action pop-up (Figure 13-9).

Action: [Stop Animation]
Select: [√ One Animation]
Animation: [All Animations]

Figure 13-10: Stop Animation can halt the play of one animation or all animations.

- **Stop Animation.** Like movies and sound, there is an action that will stop the play of the animation sequence in an animation object. Figure 13-10 shows that you have a choice of stopping just one animation or all of the animations playing in the project. If you choose to stop only one animation, you must identify which one in the Animation pop-up menu that accompanies this pop-up.

Figure 13-11: Play Animation in Object converts Sequence on a Path animation to Sequence in a Box.

Figure 13-12: Play Animation on Path converts a Sequence in a Box animation object to Sequence on a Path.

■ **Play Animation in Object.** This might seem strange. Don't we define the animation to play in an animation object in the Object panel? Like Play Movie in Object, this action will override any settings for the animation object in the Object panel. This way, you can convert a Sequence on a Path animation to a Sequence in a Box (Figure 3-11). You'll need to identify which object and sequence in the subsequent pop-up menus and enter a number in the Frame Rate field.

■ **Play Animation on Path.** The Play Animation on Path action also overrides settings in the Object panel. With this action you can play a Sequence in a Box on a path. As with the Play Animation in Object action, you must identify the object and sequence to change as well as the frame rate and speed (Figure 13-12).

You can also use this action to play multiple animations on a path. Each animation will need a separate user event or action in a script to trigger the motion.

In QuarkXPress, you can reshape and resize as well as skew and rotate picture boxes. This is not always the case for animation objects, even though they are made from QuarkXPress picture boxes. Animation objects can be resized and reshaped. However, if you change the size of an animation object, the size of the animation doesn't change. If the box gets smaller, the animation will be cropped. If the animation object gets larger, the animation stays the same size with its top left corner located in the upper left of the object. You cannot skew or rotate animation objects. If you try, Immedia will display an error message and refuse to engage or export your project until you rectify your error.

■ Exercise 13-1

In this exercise, we're going to construct a project from photo animations, a simpler version of the stop motion animation technique that's used in films and ads.

1. Open the file Exer13-1.qxd, which can be found in the folder for this exercise on the Companion CD-ROM.

   The background images for this project are illustrations on top of which we'll run several animations. Right now there are picture boxes on these pages. You'll turn them into animation objects by importing animation sequences.

Figure 13-13: The project is created from animated sequences of photographs placed on an illustrated background.

Create the Animations on the First Page

We've created two animations for this page. The first is a sequence made from photographs of our favorite 4-year-old jumping off of a pedestal. The second is a rotating ball that travels onto the page from the right side and falls off the bottom of the page and onto page 2.

2. Select the rectangular picture box on the left side of the page. Turn this into an animation object the way you import pictures in QuarkXPress using the File | Get Picture command. Import the animation sequence "Alex jumps.ani."

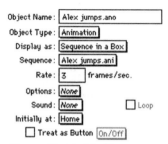

Figure 13-14: The first animation is a Sequence in a Box animation object.

3. You won't have to define this object as an animation object. When you bring an animation sequence into a picture box, Immedia automatically transforms the picture box into an animation object, giving it the name of the animation sequence. The object is defined as Animation in the Object Type pop-up menu and Sequence in a Box in the Display as pop-up menu (Figure 13-14).

    Let's change the extension on the name of the animation object from .ani, which we use to indicate animation sequences, to .ano, so we know it's an animation object.

You'll notice that the Rate field is already filled in (Figure 13-14)—the rate was determined when the animation sequence was created. We'll leave it at 3 frames/second.

4. To make the next animation, select the small picture box on the right pasteboard and, using File | Get Picture, import the next animation sequence, Ball.ani.

    This will turn the picture box into an animation object and define it as a Sequence in a Box. In the Display as pop-up menu, change this to Sequence on a Path. Change the name to rotating ball.ano (Figure 13-15).

Figure 13-15: The second animation is a Sequence on a Path.

5. On the right side of the page is a large picture box you can use as a path for this animation. Name it "ball path" and define it as a basic object. If you select Initially Hidden in the Option pop-up menu, the path won't be visible when the sequence plays.

6. Select the previous animation, rotating ball.ano, in the scrollable list of the Object panel again. In the Path pop-up menu for this object, select the path you just made, ball path.

   The frame rate should be entered in the Rate field; check to see that it's 20 frames per second. Since this is a Sequence on a Path animation, it will need a speed to travel. Enter 200 in the Speed field and select the units pixel/sec. in the Speed pop-up.

7. Finally, you'll need to indicate a spot where the animation will start. Click the Specify button in the Start Point and Direction field. In the Start Point and Direction dialog box click a point in the upper right of the path for the start. Make sure that the direction arrow points onto the page, as shown in Figure 13-16.

Figure 13-16: Specify a start point for the rotating ball animation.

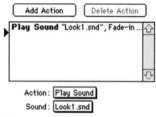

Figure 13-17: Play Sound is the first action in the script.

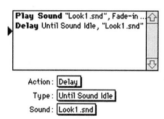

Figure 13-18: The Delay action will prevent the script from performing any other actions until the sound has finished playing.

Create a Script to Play the Sound & Animations

We'll use this animation to trigger several events. When the user clicks on Alexandra, she'll cry, "Look at me!" An animation of Alexandra jumping will start when the sound has finished playing. Then an animation of a ball will fly through the scene and down to the next page, serving to tie the two pages together. We'll write a script to do this all with one mouse click.

8. First, let's create the script. In the Script panel, click the New button to create a new script, which you'll name "Jump.scr."

9. The first action in the script plays a sound, so select Play Sound in the Action pop-up menu under the Action scrollable list (Figure 13-17). Then, in the Sound pop-up menu under the Action pop-up, choose the sound "Look1.snd." It's in the folder for this exercise.

10. We don't want anything else to happen until the sound is over. A Delay action, which can be found in the Other submenu of the Action pop-up menu, will do this. In the Type pop-up that accompanies this action, choose Until Sound Idle and then select the sound used in the first action "Look1.snd" in the Sound pop-up just below (Figure 13-18). The QuarkImmedia Viewer will read this as "Delay doing anything else until Look1.snd has stopped playing and is idle."

TIP

The Delay action tends to confuse people. Thinking of scripts as a list of instructions for the QuarkImmedia Viewer might help. The Delay action is short for "Delay doing anything else on this list until...." The Immedia Viewer waits the amount of time specified in the Type pop-up menu before it takes on the next task in the list.

Alexandra is now ready to show us how well she can jump. You'll start this animation by adding another action to the script.

11. Click the Add Action button to add another action to the script. In the Action pop-up menu under the scrollable list, choose Play Animation. In the accompanying Animation pop-up menu, select the animation object we want to play—Alex jumps.ano.

12. To prevent any other actions from occurring until the animation of Alex finishes, add another Delay action to the script. In the Type pop-up menu for the Delay action, select Until Animation Idle. Make sure you identify Alex jumps.ano in the Animation pop-up just below the Type pop-up menu.

13. Now it's time to add an action to play the ball animation. Create another action for the script by clicking the Add Action button. Once again, select Play Animation and identify the animation to play, rotating ball.ano.

Figure 13-19: Another Delay action will give the ball time to move across the page.

14. We'll use a Delay action again to give the ball time to make it across the page. This time we want to delay the action for a specific time, 3.5 seconds. Select Time instead of Until Sound Idle in the Type pop-up menu, and enter 3.5 in the Seconds field, as shown in Figure 13-19.

15. Time to send the user to the next page, so add one more action. Select Display Next Page in the Action pop-up menu. Use a Digital Dissolve transition with a time of 1 second to move to the next page.

We've got the script, now how do we play it? We'll need a user event.

16. Go to the Event panel and select the first animation object you made, Alex jumps.ano. For the Click up user event, choose Script | Run in the Action pop-up menu (Figure 13-20). What script? The one you just made—Jump.scr.

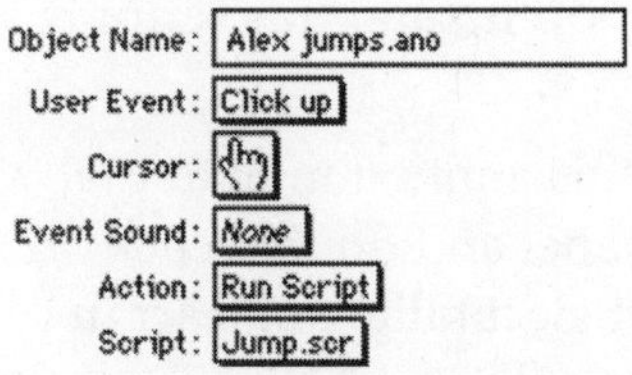

Object Name: Alex jumps.ano
User Event: Click up
Cursor:
Event Sound: None
Action: Run Script
Script: Jump.scr

Figure 13-20: The script will run when the animation object is clicked.

Now that we've completed one page, let's take a look.

17. Save your project, calling it AlexAbby.qxd and preview it using the QuarkImmedia | Engage command. Start the action by clicking on the picture of Alexandra and see what happens.

Make the First Animation for Page 2

18. The ball animation, rotating ball.ano, is the first animation to play on page 2. It will need a path to travel on, so go to page 2 and make a vertical line on a slight angle to accommodate the ball's direction of motion. If you want to make the ball bounce a bit, you can use a polygon picture box as we did. Name the line or box "ball path2.obj." Define it as a basic object and select Initially Hidden in the Option pop-up.

19. Duplicate the ball animation on the first page, drag the copy down to the second page, and name it rotating ball2.ano. The original animation object was defined as Sequence on a Path in the Display as pop-up menu and you'll notice that this one is too. Make sure that it's assigned to the correct path, ball path2.obj.

How do we get the animation to play when the page opens? An entry script will work perfectly.

20. Go to the Script panel and click the New button to create a new script. Name this one falling ball.scr.

21. Next choose Play Animation in the Action pop-up menu. Select the animation we just named rotating ball2.ano in the Animation pop-up and this script is ready.

22. To synchronize the start of this animation with the page entry, go to the Page panel and double-click on page 2 in the scrollable list. Select falling ball.scr in the Entry Script pop-up menu (Figure 13-21).

Page Name: | second page

Entry Script: | falling ball script |

Figure 13-21: An entry script will play the animation when the page opens.

Add Another Animation to the Page

Alexandra has been taking dance lessons and can't wait to show us her fancy footwork. We'll import an animation sequence into a picture box once again to make the animation object in which she'll dance.

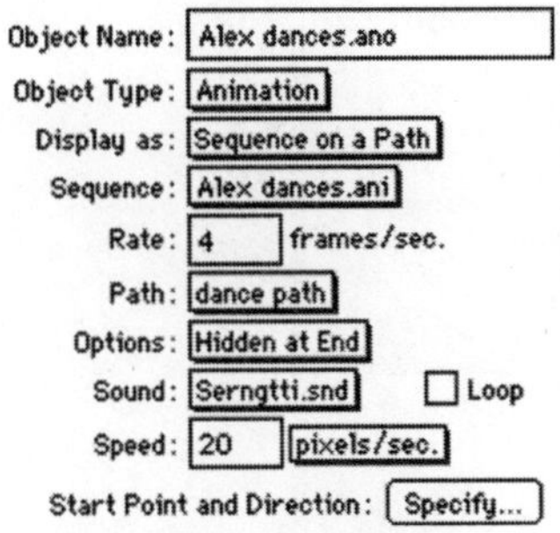

Object Name: [Alex dances.ano]
Object Type: [Animation]
Display as: [Sequence on a Path]
Sequence: [Alex dances.ani]
Rate: [4] frames/sec.
Path: [dance path]
Options: [Hidden at End]
Sound: [Serngtti.snd] ☐ Loop
Speed: [20] [pixels/sec.]
Start Point and Direction: [Specify...]

Figure 13-22: Define the animation as a Sequence on a Path.

23. Select the rectangular picture box on the left side of the page. Import an animation into this box using the File | Get Picture command. The "picture" to get is Alex dances.ani. Name the animation object Alex dances.ano (Figure 13-22).

24. Check the animation type in the Display as pop-up menu. It should be Sequence on a Path. If not, change it.

25. Of course, the animation needs a path on which to travel. We've made one for you—it's the horizontal line about one third of the way up the page from the bottom. Make this line a basic object named dance path.

    The rate for the animation should automatically be inserted into the Rate field in the Object panel. Check to make sure it's 4 frames per second.

26. If you want Alex to dance across the page only once, you can choose Hidden at End in the Options pop-up menu.

27. One can't dance without music—using the Event Sound pop-up menu we can play music along with the animation. Select Serngtti.snd. Check the Loop check box so that the sound will play continuously along with the animation.

28. The animation needs a number besides 0 in the Speed pop-up menu in order to move. Type in **20**.

29. Then click on the Specify button in the Start Point and Direction field to set the starting point for the dance. Alexandra was dancing from left to right when these photos were taken, so click on the leftmost point of the line to start the animation.

Make sure that the arrow is also pointing to the right. If not, use the Change Direction button shown in Figure 13-23 to reverse it.

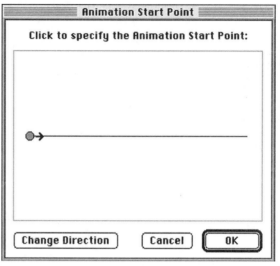

Figure 13-23: Use the Start Point and Direction dialog box to set the start of the animation.

Figure 13-24: Use a Click up user event to play this animation when the object is clicked.

30. We'll need a way to start this animation. Go to the Event panel and make sure that this object, Alex dances.ano, is highlighted. For the Click up user event choose the action Play Animation as shown in Figure 13-24, and select this animation object, Alex dances.ano.

31. Don't forget to save your project as you go along. This also might be a good time to preview the second page and check out how it works.

The Third & Final Animation for This Page

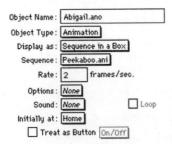

Object Name:	Abigail.ano
Object Type:	Animation
Display as:	Sequence in a Box
Sequence:	Peekaboo.ani
Rate:	2 frames/sec.
Options:	None
Sound:	None □ Loop
Initially at:	Home

□ Treat as Button On/Off

Figure 13-25: The third animation is also a Sequence in a Box.

Play Animation "Abigail.ano"
Delay Time, Seconds: 1.5
Play Sound "Peekaboo.snd", Fade...

Action: Play Sound
Sound: Peekaboo.snd
Fade-in sec.: 0
□ Loop

Figure 13-26: Use a script, not an event sound, to control when a sound plays.

We still have one more animation for this page. Alexandra's sister Abigail is waiting to play peekaboo with you.

32. Select the picture box in the lower-right corner of page 2. Use the File | Get Picture command to import the animation sequence Peekaboo.ani. This will change the picture box into an animation object. Let's name it Abigail.ano (Figure 13-25).

33. Check the Display as pop-up menu to make sure that it reads Sequence in a Box. The frame rate, 2 frames/second, should already be inserted in the Rate field. Keep the Options and Sound pop-up menus set at *None* and the Initially at pop-up menu at Home.

We have a sound that will play with this animation. We could select it in the Event Sound pop-up menu and let it start with the animation. But we'd like to time it to appear toward the end of the animation sequence. This can only be done with a script.

34. Go to the Script panel and click on the New button again to create another script. Name it Peekaboo.scr. In the Script panel's Action pop-up select Play Animation. In the accompanying Animation pop-up menu find Peekaboo.ano (Figure 13-26).

35. Once again we'll use a Delay action to play the sound after the animation starts. Click the Add Action button, then select Other | Delay in the Action pop-up menu. We've timed this delay for 1.5 seconds. You might want to try other times to synch the sound with different motions. After the Delay action, make an action to play the sound, which is Peekaboo.snd.

Figure 13-27: This animation will also play with the object's Click up user event.

36. Of course, the animation needs a user event to play it. In the Event panel, select this object, Abigail.ano. For the Click up user event choose Run Script and select the script you just wrote, Peekaboo.scr in the Script pop-up menu (Figure 13-27).

37. Try it out—save your project and preview. Click on the two animations to see how they work together.

Moving On

Having been introduced to animations with Items on Paths in Chapter 9, "Movement," we've finally looked at Immedia's different animation types. We've learned how to create animation objects and to play them on paths and in boxes. This is not much different than playing movies and Item on a Path animations.

In planning for animation, think small. You don't have to animate everything in a picture. One or two moving objects on a still background is an effective way of making interesting action on the screen.

Animations such as Item on a Path and short Sequences in a Box or Path are efficient ways of adding movement. Unlike movies, which are memory intensive, animations are more feasible for use on the Internet.

In the next chapter, we'll look at how to create the animations which you've just learned to play.

chapter 14

Making Animations

Now that you know how to make animation objects and play animation sequences in them, it's time to learn how to create the sequences themselves. Animations can be as complex as feature cartoons and 3D imaging or as simple as two or three looping frames. QuarkImmedia's capabilities for making animation sequences are best for short, somewhat simple animations. Small animations can be an efficient and effective way to introduce motion and activity to a Web project.

Flip books are a simple kind of animation and demonstrate well how they work—a sequence of individual frames played fast enough that the viewer perceives a moving, not still, image.

Making animation sequences in QuarkImmedia is much like making flip books. You create individual frames in the animation editing window or in another program and assemble them in the animation editing window to make a sequence that can be played in any animation object.

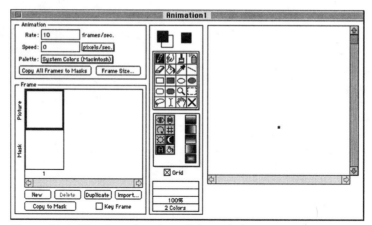

Figure 14-1: Use the animation editing window to create animation sequences.

The Animation Editing Window

Like buttons—and, as you'll see in Chapter 15, like cursors—animations are made in an editing window. Figure 14-1 shows the animation editing window, which looks and functions much like the button editing window we saw in Chapter 10, "Buttons."

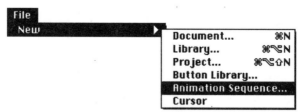

Figure 14-2: Use File | New | Animation Sequence to create an animation.

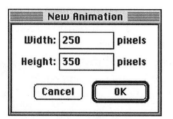

Figure 14-3: Define the size of your animation in the New Animation dialog box.

To create a new animation sequence, use the File | New | Animation Sequence command (Figure 14-2). This will open the New Animation dialog box (Figure 14-3). Here you can enter the dimensions, in pixels, of your animation sequence, any size up to 1024 X 1024 pixels. Click OK to move on to the animation editing window.

The animation editing window looks like the button editing window, and works like it, too. The Animation area in the upper left has pop-up menus and fields to set the rate, speed, and color palette for an animation, as well as to change the frame size of an animation sequence after it's been created (Figure 14-4).

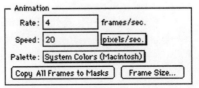

Figure 14-4: Specify rate, speed, and color palette in the Animation area of the animation editing window.

The rate is how fast the animation will play, in frames per second, which you can set in the Rate field. The number you enter here will be the default rate for the animation, but as we saw in the last chapter, you can easily change it later when you define an animation object.

Use the Speed field to specify the speed at which a Sequence on a Path animation object will travel. The Speed pop-up menu next to it gives you a choice of units in pixels per second, inches per second, centimeters per second, or "sec/path traversal." (That's a mouthful; it really means how many seconds it will take for the animation to go over the path.) Like the Rate setting, the Speed setting will be the default for the animation sequence, but you can change it in the animation object.

Use the Palette pop-up menu to assign another color palette to the animation, as you've done for buttons in the button editing window and for projects in the New Project Setup dialog box. Be reminded, however, that an animation will be remapped to the palette of the project in which it's used—it's a good idea to check out the colors of an animation in the editing window and make adjustments as needed before proceeding with your project.

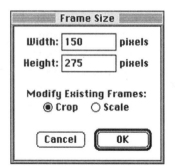

Figure 14-5: Crop or scale an image by changing the frame size.

It's easy to change the image size of an animation—click on the Frame Size button in the Animation area to open the Frame Size dialog box (Figure 14-5). Enter a new width and height in the appropriate fields. As in the button editing window's Frame Size dialog box, you have a choice of cropping (the image will be cropped on the bottom and right edges) or scaling an animation sequence to a new size.

Creating individual frames of an animation is much like creating button looks. In the scrollable window of the Frame area, shown in Figure 14-6, click the picture or mask part on which you want to work. Make new images, or modify existing ones, in the scrollable drawing area on the right side of the editing window.

Figure 14-6: Select a part of the sequence to work on in the scrollable window of the Frame area.

Unlike buttons, animations don't have a fixed number of frames. You can make them as long or short as you want. To add another frame to a sequence, just click the New button at the bottom of the Frame area (Figure 14-7). A new frame will be inserted after the one that's currently active. To delete a frame, select it in the Frame area and click the Delete button next to the New button.

Figure 14-7: The Frame area has buttons to import, duplicate, delete, and create new frames for a sequence.

You can easily duplicate and modify frames to create other ones. Use the Duplicate button, next to the Delete and New buttons to do this. Sections of animations are often built on one image, making small changes from frame to frame. Duplicating images will be an important part of creating animation sequences.

Importing Sequences From Other Programs

There's another new button next to Duplicate—the Import button (Figure 14-7). With this, you can import PICS files, sequences of images you've created in other programs or converted to PICS in a program like DeBabelizer. Use the Import button to open the Select a Graphic File dialog box and locate the PICS file you want to import. It will be automatically scaled to the size of the animation. It's a good idea to know the size you want it to be before you import it.

QuarkImmedia can't import images in other file formats into the animation editing window. It is possible, however, to cut and paste from other graphics programs. Just select the image you want and copy it. Then return to the animation editing window, select or create the frame part you want to work with, and paste the image into it. The pasted image will show up in both the Frame area and the scrollable drawing window.

Imported PICS sequences and images pasted into the editing window will be automatically scaled to the size of the window. If too small, they'll be pasted, actual size, in the frame with the upper-left pixel of the copied images in the upper-left corner of the animation frame. You can't actually scale individual images in the animation editing window. But you can change the frame size—use the Frame Size dialog box to scale and crop all frames of an animation.

You can also select frames or parts of frames in the drawing area, using the Marquee or Lasso tool, and copy them to other programs. This makes it possible to use Photoshop tools and filters to manipulate animation frames or clean up mask parts.

Figure 14-8: The drawing tools in the animation editing window have one more tool than those in the button editing window.

Figure 14-9: The picture or mask part of the sequence displays in the scrollable drawing area.

| Duplicate | Import... |
⊠ Key Frame

Figure 14-10: Indicate which frames must be displayed with the Key Frame check box.

TIP

Anti-aliased graphics often leave a halo around an image that isn't completely masked in the animation editing window. To correct this, copy the mask part and paste it into an image-editing program such as Photoshop. Select the white background and enlarge it one pixel using Select | Modify | Expand. Fill the selected area with white. Then invert the selection using Select | Inverse, copy the image, and paste it back into the mask part of the animation editing window.

You'll recognize the drawing tools—they're the same ones that are in the button editing window (Figure 14-8). There is one new tool, though, the X tool. With this tool you can change the hot spot—the pixel that follows an animation path. A single click on a pixel in the drawing area moves the hot spot for all frames of a sequence to that point. Shift-click to move the hot spot for individual frames.

The scrollable drawing area looks and functions like its counterpart in the button editing window. And, like you did in the button editing window, you'll use the drawing tools to create and modify individual frames and masks (Figure 14-9). When you copy and paste images from other programs they'll show up here.

If a computer doesn't have the processing capability to display images at the rate set for the animation, it won't be able to keep up and will drop frames. Check the Key Frame check box to identify frames that must be played (Figure 14-10). If the computer still can't display frames at the indicated speed, it plays the animation at a slower rate.

Exercise 14-1

In this exercise, we'll make an animation of a spinning electron, then place multiple copies circling an atomic nucleus. We'll make everything we need, so no special files are necessary to complete this exercise.

Set Up

1. Start a new project, 480 points wide and 480 points high. Make sure the Automatic Box check box is not checked. All of the other options can be left to their default settings (Figure 14-11).

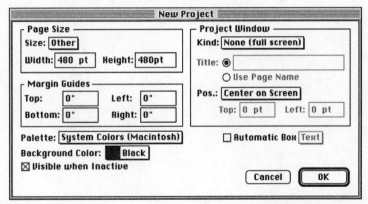

Figure 14-11: Start a new project 480 points wide and high.

2. Add an oval picture box 220 points wide and 440 points high. Make the box transparent and give it a 2-point black border. Then duplicate it twice. Rotate one oval box 60°, and the other -60° (Figure 14-12).

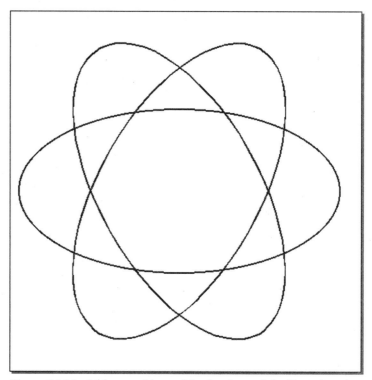

Figure 14-12: Add an oval box with a border and duplicate it twice, then rotate the new boxes.

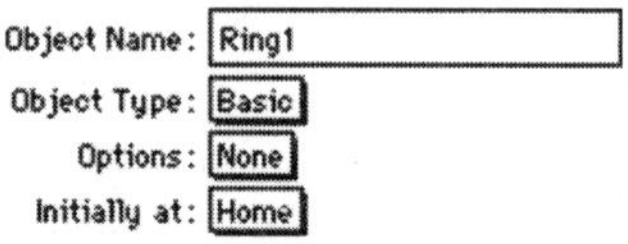

Object Name:	Ring1
Object Type:	Basic
Options:	None
Initially at:	Home

Figure 14-13: Define the ovals as basic objects.

3. Now you have three oval boxes. Define all three as basic objects, called Ring1, Ring2, and Ring3 (Figure 14-13). We'll use these as paths for the animation.

4. Add a circular box with a blue background in the middle of these ovals. This will be the "nucleus" of the atom. Use Item | Space/Align to line up the centers of all four boxes, as shown in Figure 14-14.

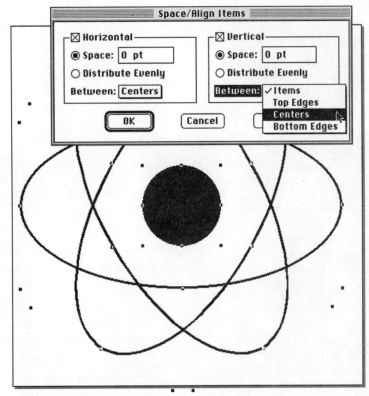

Figure 14-14: Add a "nucleus" and center all the boxes.

Make the Animation

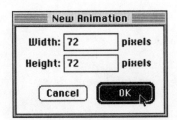

Figure 14-15: Make a new animation sequence 72 pixels wide and high.

5. With the File I New I Animation Sequence command, create a new animation sequence. In the New Animation dialog box, enter 72 pixels for width and 72 pixels for height (Figure 14-15). Click OK to open the animation editing window.

6. There isn't a Name field in the Animation area or anywhere in the animation editing window, so how are you going to name this animation? Do this like you'd name any file or document. Use the File I Save command to open the Save as dialog box, in which you can name and save this animation sequence. Name it Electron.ani.

Figure 14-16: Add a filled circle to the frame.

Figure 14-17: Remove a quarter of the circle.

7. Set the foreground color to dark gray. With the Fill Ellipse tool make a dark gray circle in the scrollable drawing area as shown in Figure 14-16.

8. Click the Copy to Mask button to make a mask for this picture. Then click the Duplicate button to make a copy of the complete frame, both the picture and mask parts. Since we want a full circle masking the pixels of our frames, even though some of them won't be full circles, duplicating the frame saves us from having to add a full circle for each mask. Note that the first frame stays active when you duplicate it.

9. Click on Frame 2. Change the foreground color to white and use the Spray Can tool to erase the left-hand quarter of the circle, as smoothly as you can. Figure 14-17 shows you what the partially-erased circle should look like.

10. Duplicate Frame 2, and—making sure you click on the new frame, Frame 3, and not the original—use the Horizontal Flip button to flip the contents so that the right quarter is now missing, as shown in Figure 14-18.

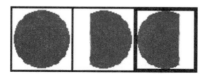

Figure 14-18: Duplicate Frame 2 and flip it horizontally.

What we have so far are the first, second, and last frames of the rotating electron sequence. The rotation of the electron will be indicated by a white stripe moving vertically across the front, from left to right. Now to make the inner frames.

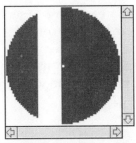

Figure 14-19: The third frame has an inner quarter removed.

Figure 14-20: Duplicate and flip the frame.

Figure 14-21: The middle frame has a stripe down the center.

11. Make Frame 2 active and use the Duplicate button to add a new frame, which appears to the right.

12. Next, make Frame 1 the active frame. Double-click the Marquee tool to select Frame, Copy it, and paste it into Frame 3, the new, empty frame.

13. Use the Spray Can tool to remove another quarter of the circle, as shown in Figure 14-19. You may need to zoom in to the drawing area or use the Pencil tool to finish this cleanly.

14. Duplicate this frame—you now have five frames. Make the new frame, Frame 4, active and flip its contents horizontally, as shown in Figure 14-20.

We'll add one last frame, in the middle.

15. Add a new frame following Frame 3. Remember to make Frame 3 active before clicking the Duplicate button or the new frame will be placed after Frame 4!

16. Make Frame 1 active. Double-click the Marquee tool to select the image. Copy the picture part of Frame 1 into the picture part of the new Frame 4.

17. Next click on the mask part of Frame 1 to make it active. Double-click the Marquee tool to select the mask part. Copy it and paste it into the mask part of the new frame.

18. Use the Spray Can tool to make a stripe down the center of this circle, broad at the middle and narrowing toward the top and bottom, as shown in Figure 14-21.

19. Mark Frames 1, 3, and 5 as key frames by checking Key Frame under the buttons in the Frame area.

20. In the Rate field of the Animation area, enter 6 to set the rate for this animation to 6 frames per second. In the Speed field enter 100 and select pixels/sec. in the Speed pop-up menu to set the speed for this animation to 100 pixels per second, or just under an inch and a half per second (Figure 14-22).

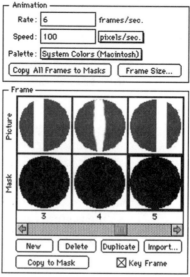

Figure 14-22: Set the rate to 6 frames per second and the speed to 100 pixels per second.

There are now six frames in this animation sequence. Each should have a mask that's a filled circle. The roughness of this rotating ball can be mitigated somewhat by reducing the size of the animation.

21. Click the Frame Size button to open the Frame Size dialog box (Figure 14-23). Enter 24 in both the Width and Height fields to scale the animation sequence to 24 pixels wide and high. This makes the edge of the image much softer.

22. Save and close the animation sequence.

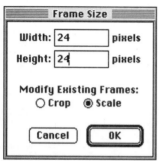

Figure 14-23: Scale the whole image down to one third of the size.

Sequences on a Path

Now we'll set up the spinning electron animation sequence to play while traveling around the paths we created earlier. We'll use multiple instances of the animation playing at different speeds and traveling in different directions.

Object Name: Spin.obj
Object Type: Animation
Display as: Sequence on a Path
Sequence: Electron.seq
Rate: 6 frames/sec.
Path: Ring1
Options: Loop
Sound: None ☐ Loop
Speed: 100 pixels/sec.
Start Point and Direction: Specify...

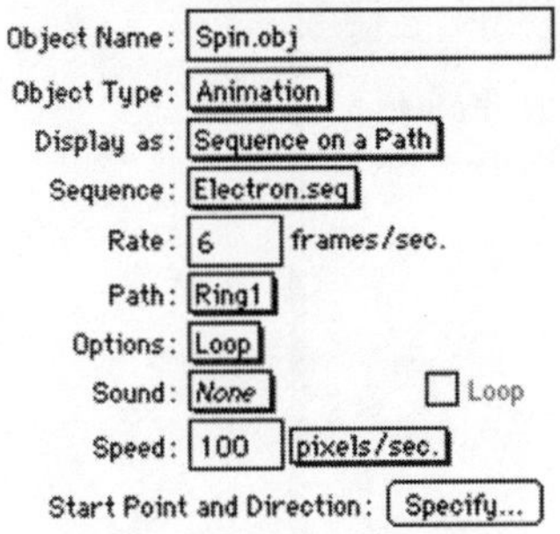

Figure 14-24: The settings for Spin.obj.

23. On the pasteboard of the QuarkImmedia project you made in steps 1 through 4, make a picture box 24 points wide and 24 points high (that's .333" square).

24. In the Object panel, define this item as an animation object, naming it Spin.obj (Figure 14-24).

25. Next, in the Display as pop-up menu below the Object Type pop-up, select Sequence on a Path. This will bring up several more pop-up menus. In the first, the Sequence pop-up, select the animation we've just made, Electron.ani.

26. You'll notice that the Rate field displays the rate we set for this animation sequence when we created it. The Speed field at the bottom of the Object panel displays the speed entered in the animation editing window also. We'll leave both settings as they are.

27. In the Path pop-up menu underneath the Rate field, select the first path you made, Ring1.

28. We want the electrons to move continuously around the nucleus of the atom, so specify Loop in the Options pop-up menu.

29. Duplicate this object seven times. To do this use Item | Step and Repeat with Horizontal Offset of 0 pt and Vertical Offset of 30 pt (Figure 14-25).

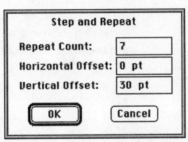

Step and Repeat

Repeat Count: 7

Horizontal Offset: 0 pt

Vertical Offset: 30 pt

OK   Cancel

Figure 14-25: Make seven duplicates of the animation object.

30. Specify the start point and direction of these objects in this fashion (Figure 14-26):

   - Spin.obj, 12 o'clock clockwise (CW)
   - Spin.obj copy, 3 o'clock counterclockwise (CCW)
   - Spin.obj copy 2, 6 o'clock (CW)
   - Spin.obj copy 3, 9 o'clock (CCW)

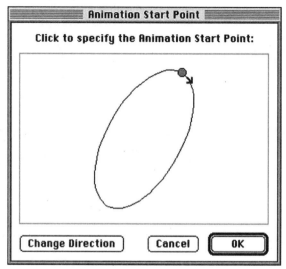

Figure 14-26: Start Spin.obj at 12 o'clock, heading clockwise.

For copies 4, 5, 6, and 7 use the same locations and directions as above. In the Object panel, change the speed of these four copies to 500 pixels per second.

31. Select all eight boxes, and use Item | Step and Repeat to make a single duplicate (of all eight boxes), with a horizontal offset of 18 pt and vertical offset of 0 pt.

For each of these new eight boxes, change the path to Ring2. No other settings need to be changed.

32. Repeat step 31, making duplicates of these eight boxes. Change the path to Ring3 for each (Figure 14-27).

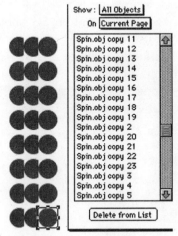

Figure 14-27: 24 boxes in all.

Triggering the Animations

We'll use a script to trigger these animations.

33. In the Script panel, make a new script called Starting.scr.

    Add 24 *No Action* place holders, replacing each one with the Animation | Play action, and specifying the 24 different animation objects created in steps 29-32 (Figure 14-28).

34. In QuarkImmedia Preferences, set the Startup script pop-up menu to Starting.scr and check Hide Menu Bar at Startup.

35. Save and test the project.

    You will note a hesitation at the beginning while the animation information is being loaded, and then an awesome display of movement dispersed across your screen.

Figure 14-28: The script Starting.scr has 24 almost-identical actions.

Exercise 14-2

We're going to add another animation to the project you created in the last chapter. When we've finished, we'll put this animation in the project, alternating it with the peekaboo animation. So Abby will play peekaboo with one user event and jump up and down with the other.

Like the other animations in Exercise 13-1, this animation is created from a sequence of photos that were scanned and silhouetted in Photoshop. You'll copy them one by one into the animation editing window to build an animation sequence.

Construct the Animation Sequence

If you have enough RAM, you can open the images in Photoshop and copy them into the editing window. You'll have to switch back and forth between the two programs using the Application Menu in the Finder.

The instructions we provide below will show you how to copy the images without opening Photoshop or another image editing program. You'll import them into a picture box in QuarkImmedia, then copy and paste the images into the animation editing window.

1. Use File | New Project to create a new project. In the New Project Setup dialog box, enter 200 pt in the Width field and 335 pt in the Height field. Make sure that the Automatic Box check box is checked and select Picture in the pop-up menu beside it.

   Since we're only using this project to get images into the animation editing window, the rest of the settings can be left however they appear.

2. Select the picture box that covers the project page. Using File | Get Picture, import the first frame, jump1.pict, as shown in Figure 14-29. Since you want to copy the contents of this picture box, not the box itself, make sure you're in the Content tool and then copy this image.

Figure 14-29: Bring the images for the sequence into Quark by placing them in a picture box.

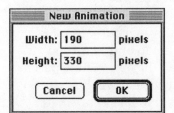

Figure 14-30: Enter the frame size in the New Animation dialog box.

3. Open the New Animation dialog box using the command File | New | Animation Sequence. Determine the size of the animation by entering 190 in the Width field and 330 in the Height field (Figure 14-30). Click OK to close this dialog box and move on to the animation editing window.

4. The animation editing window is ready for you to make the first frame of the animation sequence—the first picture part is selected. Paste the image from the clipboard using Edit | Paste. It will appear in both the scrollable drawing window and the Frame area. It's too big to fit in the window at 100%, but you can use the scroll bars to move the image around the scrollable drawing area.

If you click anywhere on the project page outside the animation editing window, you'll return to the main project window. The Windows submenu of the View menu will do the same thing (Figure 14-31).

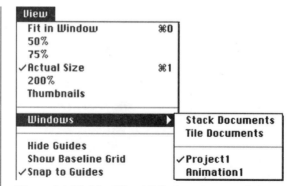

Figure 14-31: Use View | Windows to move between the main project window and the animation editing window.

5. Use Get Picture to import the next image in the sequence, jump2.pict, into the picture box. Copy the image to the clipboard (make sure that you're in the Content tool when you do). To return to the animation editing window, use the command View | Windows | Animation1.

6. With the New button at the bottom of the Frame area you can create a new frame for this image, as shown in Figure 14-32. But watch out—you don't want to paste this image on top of the one you've just done! Unless you select the new picture part in the scrollable window, that's what will happen. So click on the new picture part to make sure that it's selected—it will be outlined with a heavy black line as shown in Figure 14-33. Then you'll be ready to paste the image you just copied into that frame.

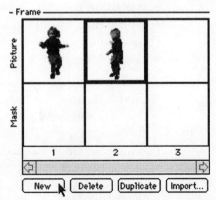

Figure 14-32: Create a new frame with the New button.

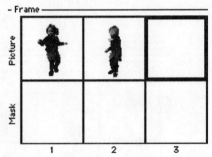

Figure 14-33: Be sure the frame is active before you paste in the image.

To get back to the project window you can use View | Windows and locate the project window or just click on it outside the editing window.

7. Use the same procedure for the third, fourth, and fifth frames of the sequence, using the images jump3.pict, jump4.pict, and jump5.pict, respectively. When you've got all five frames copied into the animation editing window, save the animation and call it "Abby jumps.ani."

If you try to use this sequence in a project as it is right now, you'll find a pure white image. You can try using keyboard commands to center the image or fit it to the size of the picture box, but you still won't be able to see an image.

8. To make sure that the images show when the animation is used, you'll need to make masks for each frame. You can do that for each individual frame using the Copy to Mask button on the bottom of the editing window. But it's much faster to make masks for each frame all at once.

    Click the Copy All Frames to Masks button in the Animation area at the top left of the editing window to do this (Figure 14-34).

Figure 14-34: Mask all of the frames at once with the Copy All Frames to Masks button.

This animation is designed to play as a Sequence on a Path. To line it up properly on the path, we'll have to move the hot spot from its default position at the middle of the frame and put it at the bottom of the image, on Abby's foot. Then, when the animation plays, she'll dance along the line.

9. Take the X tool and move into the scrollable drawing area. The current hot spot is the white square at Abby's waist. Scroll down the window until you can

see her feet, then Shift-click on the toe of her shoe (Figure 14-35). You'll see a white rectangle, the new hot spot, on her foot. By using the Shift key when you change the hot spot, you change it for all images in the sequence.

Figure 14-35: To make sure that Abby's foot runs on the path, click on her toe with the X tool.

We've created the animation parts, but still haven't done anything in the Animation area—no rate or speed—so the sequence won't play or move. Let's take care of this.

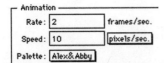

Figure 14-36: Enter the rate and speed, and assign the color palette in the Animation area.

10. Type **2** in the Rate field and **10** in the Speed field (Figure 14-36). This is a slow speed, but then little girls don't jump very fast.

11. The color palette is System Colors, not the palette that was created in DeBabelizer just for this exercise. In the Palette pop-up menu, find the color palette for this project, Alex & Abby (Figure 14-36).

12. Save the animation sequence, naming it Abby jumps.ani. You don't need to save the project created to import the pictures.

Add the Animation Sequence to the Project

Now you're ready to use this in the project we created for Exercise 13-2. There's already one animation of Abigail, playing peekaboo, which is a Sequence in a Box animation. We'll alternate the new animation with this one. By treating the animation object as a button, you can switch from one to the other with a mouse click.

13. Open Exer14-2 and go to page 2. Figure 14-37 shows you what the finished page 2 should look like.

Figure 14-37: Open the animation project from the previous chapter.

This is the finished version of the exercise you worked on in the last chapter. We've added a few elements to it which you'll need for this exercise. If you haven't done that exercise or didn't save it, you'll find a finished version in the folder for this exercise.

14. The animation we've just made is a moving animation, Sequence on a Path, so we'll need a path on
which to play it. There's a line under the Abigail
animation object (Figure 14-38). Select it and name it
"Abby's path," then make it a basic object. To prevent
the line from showing up before the animation plays,
set the Option pop-up menu to Initially Hidden.

*Figure 14-38: Select the line under the animation object and turn it
into a path for the animation.*

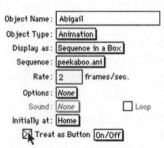

*Figure 14-39: Make the
animation object a button to
have two user events for
single mouse clicks.*

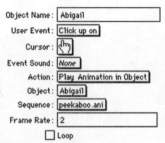

*Figure 14-40: Play the
peekaboo animation with
Click up on.*

We've started animations by clicking on the object,
assigning an action to the Click up user event to do this. It
would be nice to have a way to turn the animation off, or
switch animations, like you can do with On/Off buttons.
Animation objects can be treated as buttons. We can assign
one action, play an animation perhaps, to Click up on and
another play animation action to Click up off.

15. The first thing you'll do is check the Treat as Button
check box on the bottom of the Object panel and
make sure it's an On/Off button. This will give you,
as Figure 14-39 shows, Click ups and Click downs
for two states, On and Off. You can assign the action
to play an animation to each state. The animations
will switch each time the object is clicked.

16. Now, go to the Event panel. The first animation will
play with Click up on, so select it in the User Event
pop-up menu.

    Then, in the Action pop-up, select Play Animation
in Object (Figure 14-40). The animation object is
Abigail.ano, and the first sequence to play is
Peekaboo.ani. The frame rate 2 was assigned in the
animation editing window—make sure the number
shows up in the Frame Rate pop-up menu.

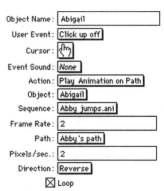

Object Name : Abigail
User Event : Click up off
Cursor :
Event Sound : None
Action : Play Animation on Path
Object : Abigail
Sequence : Abby jumps.ani
Frame Rate : 2
Path : Abby's path
Pixels/sec. : 2
Direction : Reverse
☒ Loop

Figure 14-41: Play the new Sequence on a Path animation for Click up off.

17. We'll use jumping animation for Click up off, so select it in the User Event pop-up menu. The next animation is a moving animation, so select Play Animation on Path in the Action pop-up menu (Figure 14-41). This will convert the animation object from a Sequence in a Box to a Sequence on a Path.

    Be sure that Abigail shows up in the Object pop-up menu, and the animation sequence is correct, Abby jumps.ani.

    The frame rate was determined when we created this sequence, check to see that the Frame Rate field reads "2." You'll need to make sure there's a path for this to run on. Use the one we recently created, Abby's path.

    Finally, check the Speed field and make sure it's 10.

18. There's no Start Point and Direction field with this action—that's because the object's a button—but you can determine the direction the animation will go, Forward or Reverse. Forward is to the right and Abby's facing to the left, so choose Reverse in the Direction pop-up menu.

19. The project is complete so save it and take a look using Engage. Click several times on the animation in the animation object Abigail and watch how it changes.

Moving On

In planning for animation, think small. You don't have to animate everything in a picture. One or two moving objects on a still background can be an effective way of making interesting action on the screen. Small animations are viable on the Internet, unlike QuickTime movies and complicated animations.

The animation editing window is almost identical to the button editing window, and, as you'll find in the next chapter, the cursor editing window. They all contain a small paint program you can use to create images for individual frames of sequences. You can also import images from paint programs, which give you more sophisticated image-making capabilities.

One type of animation that we haven't looked at is cursors. Animated cursors are made in a manner much like animation sequences. We'll take a look at making still-frame and animated cursors in the next chapter.

chapter 15

Cursors

We're so used to seeing cursors that they often go unnoticed—the arrow, the hand with the pointing finger that indicates that an object is clickable, the hand counting its fingers during a software installation, the watch with moving hands that says, "Wait, something's happening, you'll see in a minute."

Even though we don't usually pay attention to cursors, they convey a lot of information—a change in state, for example, or activity in the CPU when nothing's happening on the screen.

The default cursors for Immedia are set in the Quark-Immedia preferences (Figure 15-1). Out of the box they are: the arrow as default, the watch for busy, and a pointing finger to indicate a user event.

Cursors can be customized to the theme of the project. The kid's game *Winnie the Pooh* has a bee cursor. Pooh always has an eye out for bees because they lead to honey. In some games, a hand with all fingers extended means that you can pick up the object under the hand. A hand can even be made to look like it's carrying an object or have a small animation releasing the object when the user decides to drop it.

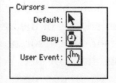

Figure 15-1: Assign default cursors for a project in the Quark-Immedia Preferences.

Cursors can communicate to the user a change in state, or unseen activity—like the watch cursor does. This is particularly useful if the viewer has to wait for long download or processing times. You can use a cursor with a small animation sequence to keep the user's attention as a page downloads on the Web, or at least let the viewer know that something actually is still happening.

Immedia has great capabilities for working with cursors, either as single frames or small animation sequences.

Changing Cursors

Every user event has a Cursor pop-up menu that displays the selection of cursors used in the project. Unlike the other objects we've worked with, you don't create an object to display a cursor and you don't name a cursor in the Object panel. They're made in the cursor editing window and are usually brought into projects using the Cursor pop-up menu.

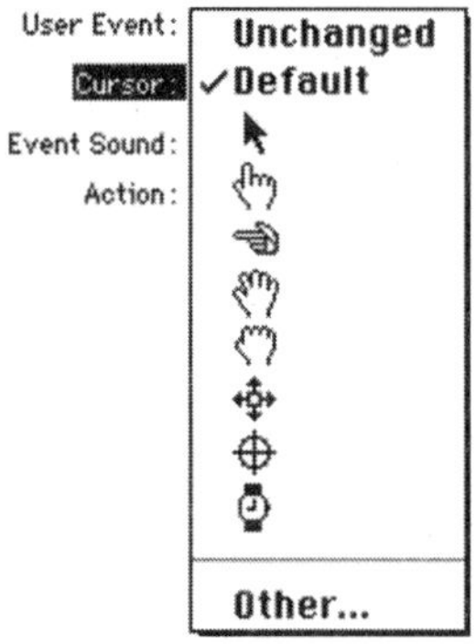

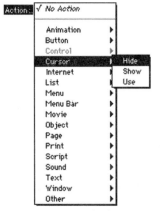

Figure 15-2: Cursors in a project are displayed by icon, not name.

The cursors used in a project are displayed in the pop-up menu by their icon or the first frame of the sequence, not by name (Figure 15-2). Click on the cursor you want to use to select it. If it's not displayed in the list, use Other at the bottom of the pop-up menu to open the Select a Cursor File dialog box and locate the cursor file.

There are only three actions that control the use of cursors—Hide Cursor, Show Cursor, and Use Cursor.

- **Hide Cursor.** If you want to indicate to the user that all user events have been disabled, one of the best ways to do it is to hide the cursor. No cursor, no way of getting an action by clicking on the mouse. When Hide Cursor is selected in the Action pop-up menu, you won't see another pop-up menu to select a cursor. You can only hide the cursor that's currently in use (Figure 15-3).

Figure 15-3: Hide the cursor to indicate no user interaction.

Figure 15-4: Display cursors to show user interactivity.

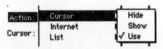

Figure 15-5: The Use Cursor action lets you change from one cursor to another.

■ **Show Cursor.** To indicate that user events have been enabled, display the cursor again. Once again, you won't find a pop-up menu in which to identify a cursor (Figure 15-4). The cursor displayed will be the one in use before the Hide Cursor action, or the one defined with the Use Cursor action.

■ **Use Cursor.** To change a cursor without a user event, at page entry perhaps, use this action. Unlike the two previous actions, you will find a Cursor pop-up menu to select a cursor from those used in the project (Figure 15-5). Use Other in the list to locate a cursor that hasn't been used in the project.

Making Cursors

Like buttons and animation sequences, cursors are made in an editing window. The cursor editing window works like the other two editing windows. The command File | New | Cursors takes you straight to it (Figure 15-6). There's only one type of cursor and it can be only one size, 16 X 16 pixels, so there's no need for a New Cursor dialog box.

Figure 15-6: Open the cursor editing window from the File menu.

If you've spent time in the button and animation editing windows, you'll understand how to use the cursor editing window (Figure 15-7). It has a number of the same elements—a Cursor area to set rate and color palette, a Frame area to select the frame used in the scrollable drawing area on the right, and drawing tools to create the look of cursors. For an extensive discussion of the editing window, see Chapter 10, "Buttons."

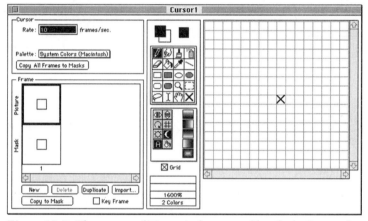

Figure 15-7: The cursor editing window resembles the button and animation editing windows.

The Cursor area in the upper left of the window corresponds to the Button area in the button editing window and the Animation area in the animation editing window. You'll notice that there's no Name field here. Cursors aren't like other objects in this respect. Once cursors have been brought into a project, they're identified by icons, not names.

You set the default rate for an animated cursor in the Rate field (Figure 15-8). There's no Speed field—the speed is determined by how the user moves the mouse. There's also no Frame Size button. Cursors can only be one size: 16 X 16 pixels.

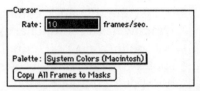

Figure 15-8: Set the frame rate of a cursor and choose a color palette in the Cursor area.

Cursor images that are smaller than 16 X 16 pixels or have nonrectangular shapes must be masked. The Copy All Frames to Masks button works like it does in the other editing windows. Click here to create masks for all frames in a sequence, or use the Copy to Mask button in the Frame area to create masks for individual frames.

You can select a color palette for a cursor in the Palette field. Like buttons and animation sequences, cursors remap to the palette of the project in which they're used.

The Frame area also works like the Part area of the button editing window and the Frame area of the animation editing window. Click on a picture or mask part in the scrollable window to activate it (Figure 15-9). Then use the drawing tools to create or modify an image or mask in the scrollable drawing area on the right of the editing window. The drawing tools are explained in detail in Chapter 10, "Buttons."

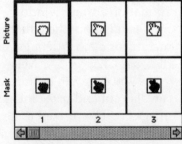

Figure 15-9: Select a part of the cursor sequence to create or edit in the scrollable window.

Like the animation editing window, the cursor editing window has an additional tool, the X tool, to change the hot spot in a cursor (Figure 15-10). Click to change the hot spot for all frames in a sequence. Shift-click to change the hot spot for individual frames of a cursor.

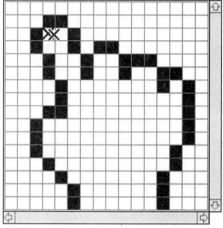

Figure 15-10: The X tool can change the hot spot in a cursor for all frames in a sequence or for individual ones.

Using the buttons at the bottom of the Frame area, you can create and duplicate frames as well as import PICS files, just as you do in the animation editing window. PICS files behave the same as they do when imported into the animation editing window—they are resized to fit the frame and adopt the palette set in the Palette pop-up menu. For a more detailed explanation of importing PICS files, see Chapter 14, "Making Animations."

As you can with buttons and animation sequences, you can also cut and paste images from paint programs. The images will be resized if they don't fit the frame.

When you're finished creating a cursor, either as a single frame or an animated sequence, save the file as you would any QuarkXPress file, using File | Save. While cursors themselves aren't represented in Immedia by name, the cursor file on your hard disk does have a name, just like every other file.

Exercise 15-1

Our first exercise takes the form of a quiz. The user will be given a short time to enter the answer to a question in the answer field. While the project is waiting for the answer, it will display a blinking question mark cursor. If the user gets the correct answer, the project displays a congratulatory page with a blinking exclamation point cursor.

Create the Quiz

1. This project will be small. Since the quiz has only one question, we won't need a large page. Use File | New | Project to open the New Project dialog box. Make a small page—320 points high and 160 wide will do. Leave the Background Color and Project Window settings at their defaults. Select Text for the Automatic Box (Figure 15-11).

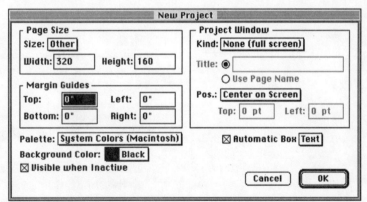

Figure 15-11: Create a small project page, only 320 X 160 points.

2. There are three pages in this project, so add two more using Page | Insert. All three of the pages will have the same settings in the text box—it's easiest to enter them into the master page. You can use Page | Display | A-Master Page A to access the master page.

3. Select a font for the type. We used 12-pt Helvetica. The few lines of text are centered both horizontally and vertically on the page. Set horizontal alignment in the Measurements palette and vertical alignment in the Text Box Specifications dialog box (Item | Modify will get you there).

4. You're ready to enter the text. Use Page | Display | Document to return to the first page, and enter the first line of text: "Who are the primary users of QuarkImmedia?" as shown in Figure 15-12. We gave the text some zip by making the first word a different color; we used magenta. We also used a serif font, Times, for the word Quark and a bold sans serif type, Helvetica Bold, for Immedia, like the Immedia logo.

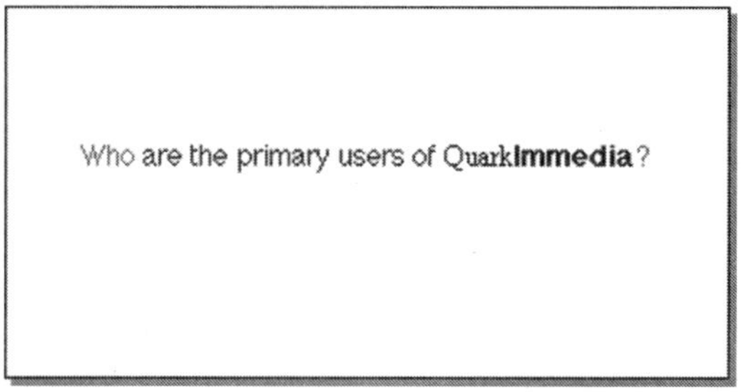

Who are the primary users of Quark**Immedia**?

Figure 15-12: The text on the first page is the essential question.

5. As you can see in Figure 15-13, page 2 gives two choices to answer this question: "Print designers" and "Multimedia designers" typed in two rows, one on top of the other. The correct answer will take the user to the congratulatory page. If you put these two lines of text in separate text boxes, then make them into separate objects, you can assign different user events to them. Make two basic objects and place them one over the other on the page. Name the box with the text Print designers "print.obj" and the box with Multimedia designers "multi.obj."

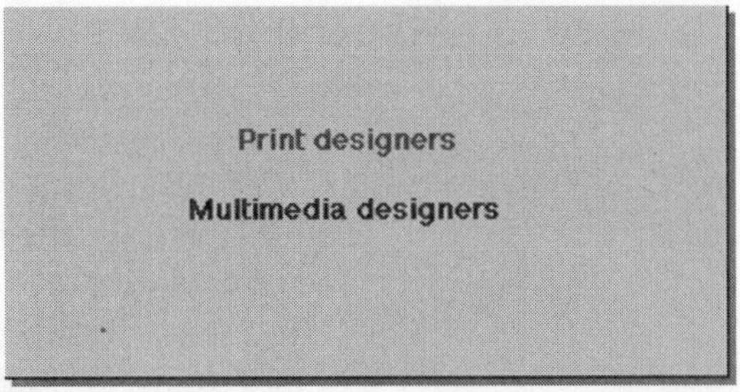

Figure 15-13: The two choices for the answer are on page 2.

> To further distinguish the two answers, color the type for the first answer, Print designers, red and the type for the second answer, Multimedia designers, blue. To make the page itself stand out from the others, we've changed the background to 20% blue.

6. Users who select the correct choice will be taken to page 3, which has the message "That's exactly right!" Let's go to page 3 and type that phrase in the text box. As you can see in Figure 15-14, we colored the text to make the page more exciting—we make the letters "ex" in the word "exactly" and the word "right" blue and the letters "act" in the word "exactly" magenta (Figure 15-14).

Figure 15-14: And the correct answer is on page 3.

> You might ask why there isn't a page for the wrong answer. Instead, the project will have a script to take the user back to the first page to answer the question again.

7. Save this document before going on to the next section, naming it Question.qxd.

Make the Cursors

8. You're ready to make the first cursor. Open the cursor editing window by selecting New | Cursor. The first frame of the scrollable window will be selected and you're ready to start.

   The cursors in this project will be made from letters, actually from punctuation marks—we'll use the text insertion Cursor tool in the bottom row of the drawing tools (Figure 15-15). Click near the lower-left corner of the scrollable drawing area with the Cursor X tool. You'll see an insertion point and blinking cursor.

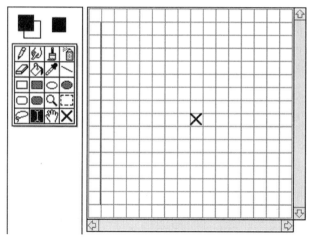

Figure 15-15: Use the Cursor tool to make a question mark.

9. To make this a big, fat cursor, we'll increase the font size and make the letter heavier. Although you use the Cursor tool in the scrollable drawing area to insert letters, you spec the type in the Font menu. Use Style | Font to select a heavier font. We used Helvetica Black. In the Size submenu, make the font larger than 12 points—we used 18 points (Figure 15-16).

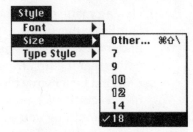

Figure 15-16: The Style menu has the commands to change font and type size.

You're now ready to type a question mark. To make it colorful, select a foreground color—press on the foreground color square and choose one from the palette. The Paint Bucket tool will fill the question mark with your chosen color (Figure 15-17).

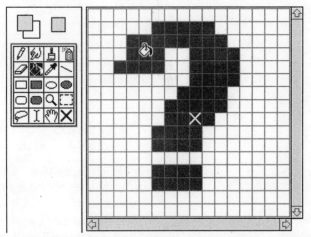

Figure 15-17: Click on the question mark with the Paint Bucket tool to change its color.

10. Having made one frame, it's easy to make others. Duplicate this frame using the Duplicate button under the scrollable window (Figure 15-18). You'll notice that the first frame is still active. It's surrounded by a heavy black line. To make the new frame active, click on it. If you don't select the new frame, anything you do to the image in the scrollable drawing area will by applied to the first, not the second, image.

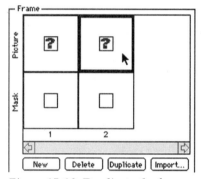

Figure 15-18: Duplicate the frame and make the new frame active by clicking on the picture part.

Choose a new foreground color and use the Paint Bucket tool to fill the second question mark.

11. Follow the same procedure for the next frame. Duplicate the second frame. Make sure the new frame is selected, then fill it with another color. When you've got all of your frames, mask them by clicking Copy All Frames to Masks in the Cursor area.

12. You're now ready to save the cursor. Use File I Save and name it "?". You'll need to locate the cursor by this name using Other in the Cursor pop-up menu the first time you use it in the project.

13. To make the exclamation point, you'll follow the same procedures, using a different letter, the exclamation point (Figure 15-19). Name the file "!".

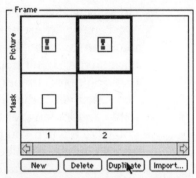

Figure 15-19: Make the exclamation point cursor in the same way.

When you've finished making the two cursors, return to the project by clicking on the project window outside the cursor editing window. You can also use the menu command View | Windows Question.qxd to return to the project window.

Incorporate the Cursors Into the Project

Now it's time to put the cursors in the project. But first we'll have to make the navigation from one page to the other.

14. Make sure you're on page 1 of the project by double-clicking on it in the Page scrollable list. Type the word **next** in the line after the questions, and line it up with the right margin. We'll use interactive text for navigation; highlight this text and go to the Hot Text panel. To make this hot text, name it in the Name field—we've labeled it next. Color it by selecting Magenta in the Color pop-up menu. Select the user event Click up to trigger the Display Next Page action, which will take the user to the page that has the answers (Figure 15-20).

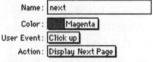

Figure 15-20: Use interactive text to navigate from page 1 to page 2.

The default cursor for this project is the arrow—that's what's displayed when there's no user event and the project's not busy computing an action or answer. We'd like another way to remind users that they must choose one of the two words on page 2 as the correct answer. Displaying a cursor when the mouse is over the words will do this nicely.

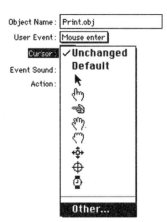

Figure 15-21: Display the cursor with the Mouse enter user event.

Figure 15-22: Make a script to change the cursor and display page 3.

Object Name: Print.obj
User Event: Click up
Cursor: 🖑
Event Sound: None
Action: Run Script
Script: answer

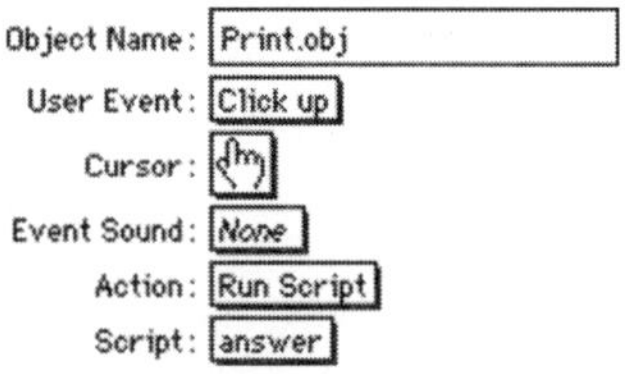

Figure 15-23: For the Click up user event, select both a cursor and the Run Script action.

15. Go to page 2 and select print.obj in the Event panel. You can use Mouse enter to display the question mark cursor when the mouse is over the object—click on the Cursor pop-up menu and select the question mark cursor (Figure 15-21). Since it hasn't been used yet in the project, you'll locate it using Other and looking for the file named "?"—the name you gave it when you first saved the cursor file. To go back to the default cursor when the mouse leaves the object, select default in the Cursor pop-up menu for the Mouse exit user event. Having set this for print.obj, do the same for multi.obj.

You might have noticed that we didn't choose any action with these user events. You don't need an action with a user event to display a cursor.

Now for the answer to the question. This is what will take users to page 3. And the answer is.... Well, we'll let you in on a secret—both print and multimedia designers are the primary users of QuarkImmedia, so both answers are correct. When the user clicks on either answer, the project will display a new cursor, the exclamation point, and display page 3.

16. To both take the user to page 3 and use a new cursor, we'll need a script. In the Script panel click the New button to create one, which we'll name "answer." Select Use Cursor in the Action pop-up menu and the "!" in the Cursor pop-up menu to change the cursor for this page from the project default to the exclamation point.

Follow the change of cursor action with Display Last Page action (Figure 15-22).

This script will be applied to the Click up user event for both objects on page 2, print.obj and multi.obj. Go to the Event panel and select them, one by one, and choose Run Script in the Action pop-up menu and answer in the Script pop-up menu (Figure 15-23).

The question mark cursor is the one in use when a user clicks on either of these objects. It won't change to !, the exclamation point, until the page changes.

How do we get the cursor to change to ! when the user clicks on the correct answer? The user event to click on each object, Click up, has a Cursor pop-up menu. If you set this to ! in each object, the cursor will change when the user clicks on the object, and maintain that change when the user goes to the next page.

17. We still need to provide a way for users to get back to the beginning of the project. Let's create a script that will send the users back to the first page 5 seconds after entering the third one. Go to the Script panel and create a new script, which we'll call "Back to page 1.scr."

18. This script will have three actions.

   First give the script instructions to wait 5 seconds before doing anything. Do this by selecting Delay in the Other pop-up menu and Time in the Type pop-up. Type **5** into the Seconds field (Figure 15-24).

   The next action will send the user back to the first page. Use Display First Page to do that. To give it an exciting transition back to that page, select Random Lines in the Transition pop-up menu.

   You don't want the exclamation point cursor to appear on the first page, so make a third action, Use Cursor, which will display the default cursor for this project.

19. The easiest and most reliable way to make sure that users run into this script and return to the first page is to apply it to the whole automatic text box object which covers the page.

   Turn the text box into a basic object by naming it "Right box.obj." In the Event panel, assign the script we just made, "Back to page 1.scr" to the Mouse enter user event by selecting Script | Run in the Action pop-up menu, and selecting "Back to page 1.scr" in the accompanying Script pop-up. Choose the exclamation point again in the Cursor pop-up menu.

   Time to save and try out your project.

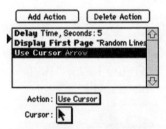

Figure 15-24: A script will take the users back to page one and change the cursor back to the default.

Exercise 15-2

In this exercise you'll take a group of images that have been exported as a PICS animation and create a cursor animation sequence with them. The files for this exercise can be found in the folder for Exercise 15-2 on the Companion CD-ROM.

Use a PICS File to Create an Animated Cursor

To start the process of creating the cursor, follow these steps to make a new cursor file:

1. Use File | New | Cursor, which will open the cursor editing window.

2. Click the Import button in the lower-right corner of the scrollable window. This will open the Select a Graphic File dialog box in which you can locate the PICS file named match.PICS (Figure 15-25). You'll find the file in the folder for this exercise.

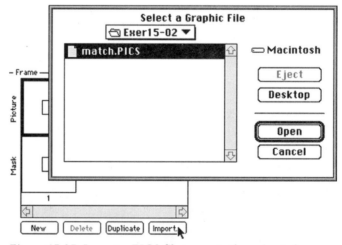

Figure 15-25: Import a PICS file to create the animated cursor.

3. The importing process creates a frame part for each frame of the PICS file. You'll notice that there's an empty frame at the beginning of the sequence. This generally happens when PICS animations are imported into either the cursor or animation editing window. You certainly don't want a white flash every time the animation completes a cycle, so select it and use the Delete button to remove it from the sequence.

4. The sequence will need masks for the individual frames since their outlines are not a 16 X 16 square. Click the Copy All Frames to Masks button in the Cursor area to do this (Figure 15-26). Check to see that there are no white spaces in the image.

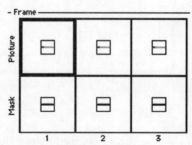

Figure 15-26: Mask all frames in the sequence.

5. While you can assign a frame rate when the cursor file is used in the project, you might as well do that here. Type **4** into the Rate field. When you engage the project you can check to see if this rate is the best one for the image.

6. This sequence was made for a specific image with its own color palette. You'll need to check the image with that palette to make sure you don't need to change any colors when the files remap to the custom color palette. Locate the palette fire.act in the folder for this exercise using the Palette pop-up menu (Figure 15-27).

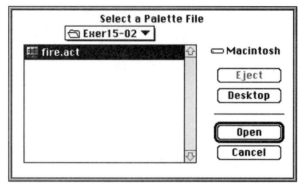

Figure 15-27: The Palette pop-up menu.

7. You're ready to save the sequence, naming it Lit Match, and bring it into the project.

Use the Cursor in a Project

A match is just what one needs to illuminate a dark room. You'll start this project using a plain match as a cursor. When you want to see what's there in the dark, you can strike the match, using a Click up user event, and display the page with the view of your surroundings.

8. Open the file Exer15-2.qxd, which you'll find in the folder for this exercise. This project has two pages. Page 1 represents a scene so dark it's almost black. Page 2 is the scene that will be revealed by the lighted match.

9. There's a file of an unlit match that we'll use for the default cursor for this page. You can set this in the QuarkImmedia preferences by selecting the match cursor in the Default pop-up menu in the Cursor area of the Project panel.

10. To strike the match we'll use a user event attached to the entire picture box covering page 1. Like we did in the last exercise, we'll make the background picture into an interactive object.

11. In the Event panel for this object, select the Click up user event. When the match lights, the project will display page 2, so select Display Next Page in the Action pop-up menu. Then change the cursor in the Cursor pop-up menu to Lit Match.

12. Save and engage the project.

Moving On

As we've seen, the process for creating cursors is like the process for creating buttons and animation sequences. The editing windows are almost identical, with identical tools.

Cursors are different from other objects in one way—they aren't displayed in objects that are defined in the Object panel. Instead, every user event has a Cursor pop-up menu. Cursors are identified by image, not by name. They are controlled by three actions—Hide Cursor, Show Cursor, and Use Cursor.

With cursors, we've pretty much finished our discussion of the basic graphic and animated capabilities of Immedia. There's still quite a bit that can be done with text to display and collect information. In the next chapter we'll go over how to do this with text box objects.

chapter 16

Text Box Objects

Text box objects are what lift Immedia out of the realm of merely a super presentation program. With them, your projects can truly take advantage of the "electronic" in electronic publishing:

- Publishing becomes two-way, since now you can capture user-entered text—so a name can be saved to a file or used later in the project.

- Text box objects save space and prevent you from having to wade through irrelevant text. Instead of ten pages of crucial reference material, your project can utilize a single, scrollable text box object, with user-initiated searches bringing the right material into the display.

- Up-to-the-minute information can be read into a text box object from an outside file, so price lists can be changed on the fly, or a weather report updated hourly, or stock prices posted as they come in from a stock-monitoring program.

If print publishing is "frozen" information and pictures, Immedia projects are the polar opposite. The kinetic properties of movement and sound catch the eye and ear, but unfreezing the content makes for a very hot interest indeed.

Differentiating Text Box Objects

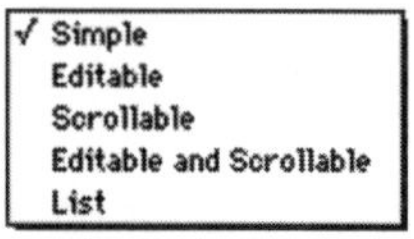

It's easy to confuse text box objects with text boxes that are basic objects. Their different forms—simple, editable, scrollable, editable and scrollable, and list (Figure 16-1)—with their different uses compound the identification problem.

If all you want is for the user to be able to search the contents of the box, then you want to use a basic object. But when you need to insert text into the box from a file or from some other box, that's the time to use a simple text box object.

Scrollable text box objects save space in your project. If the text doesn't fit inside the text box, the user simply scrolls the text up—and back down, as desired—to read it all (Figure 16-2). You can use this type of text box object when you don't know how long the text will be that's going into the box. Otherwise it might be trimmed to fit the box size. You'll want to make use of scrolling text conservatively, in our opinion, as it inhibits reading text.

Figure 16-1: Types of text box objects.

Figure 16-2: A scrollable text box object.

Formatting Text

You can style the text in a basic object using the full range of QuarkXPress's formatting commands. Not so with the text in text box objects. You can specify the font, size, style, and color, but other specs—such as leading, indenting, and space between paragraphs—don't show up in the exported project, *even though you may see them onscreen when you're constructing the page*.

With unchanged text boxes and text boxes made into basic objects, at the time the project is exported, the text itself is rasterized: a screen picture of it is made, and this image of the box is what the user reads and interacts with. (Which means of course, that you don't need to make objects from text boxes that your reader isn't going to interact with.) This is why you can control the appearance of type in your Immedia project, unlike pages written in HTML (HyperText Markup Language).

However, with text box objects, Immedia can't make an image of the text, which limits your control over its appearance. Even though you can specify the font for a text box, the font may not be available on the system playing the project. In this case, the Immedia Viewer will substitute the default font specified in the QuarkImmedia Preferences if possible. If that's not available either, you'll get whatever system font is deemed appropriate.

Editable text box objects are for those instances where the user should enter (or edit) text. This could be a form collecting information you want from the user, or a field used for initiating a search operation.

The editable and scrollable text box object allows the user to enter (or edit) text without a length restraint, and without having to provide a large space for this in the project. As you can tell from its name, it combines the features of being scrollable and of being editable.

List text box objects are discussed in Chapter 22, "Advanced Features." You use them with lists of text strings, or items, which you can alter dynamically.

When you choose Text Box in the Object Type pop-up menu (Figure 16-3), you can specify that the contents of the box are to be searchable (as you can with a text box that is a basic object). When the text box object is editable, you can specify "not empty" to require the user to fill it in before proceeding. Another option—protected—displays asterisks in lieu of regular text characters so what is entered can't be read onscreen. You would use this with passwords, for example.

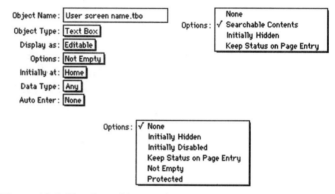

Figure 16-3: Text box object options.

Collecting Text

Figure 16-4: The Action | Text submenu.

An editable text box object can be filled in (or changed) by the user, and that information saved to an ASCII text file. The Text submenu of the Action pop-up (in the Event, Script, and Hot Text panels) has a variety of operations that relate to the movement of text from one location to another (Figure 16-4). Whatever text has been entered in an editable box can be written to a file that is located in the same folder as the project. You have to specify the exact name of the file—if it's not there, Immedia will create one

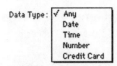

Figure 16-5: Data type helps prevent inappropriate information from being entered in an editable text box object.

Figure 16-6: Formatting a number in an editable text box object.

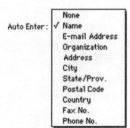

Figure 16-7: The date and time can be filled in automatically.

using that name. And you specify whether the text should come only from a single text box object or from all of them on the page.

For certain types of information that you want to collect, you can ferret out incorrectly entered data. That is, you can set up any editable text box object to accept only numbers, credit card information, dates, or the time (Figure 16-5). These types of data can then be formatted in the manner you desire. For instance, you can set things up so that you will only accept a number as an integer (or whole number), as a regular decimal number, or formatted as dollars and cents, indicating additionally whether negative numbers or zero are acceptable (Figure 16-6).

And the date and the time can be filled in automatically from the user's system (Figure 16-7).

More dramatically, a whole pile of information, including name, company or organization, address, e-mail address, and phone and fax numbers can be pulled from the user's preferences as entered in their copy of Viewer (Figure 16-8) and entered automatically into appropriate text box objects. As noted, this material can be written to a file; users can request the Viewer to notify them when a project submits a page to be sent over the Internet. If this happens unexpectedly, it may indicate that the project was capturing this information on the sly.

User Preferences	
Name:	Samuel Giotto
E-mail Address:	sgiotto@immediacy.com
Organization:	The Immediacy Group
Address:	75 Prospect Park West 1B
City:	Brooklyn
State/Prov.:	NY Postal Code: 11215
Country:	USA
Fax #:	212-572-4914
Phone #:	212-572-2252

[Cancel] [OK]

Figure 16-8: An editable field can be filled in automatically with information from the user's system and from the Viewer preferences.

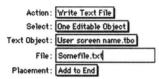

Figure 16-9: The Write Text File command specifies the text box objects that supply the information and the file where it will be stored.

The Action | Text | Write File command (Figure 16-9) will take whatever appears in a single editable text box object, or all the text box objects on one page, and save it in an ASCII text file. You can choose to append new information to the end of the file or to replace whatever information is there. When you collect the information from multiple text box objects, Immedia separates the information using tabs. The file in which the information is saved must be located in the same folder as the project.

Of course, Write Text File is the centerpiece of collecting information from forms. But it can also be used when you want to temporarily save some information that you will want later—like a user's first name—because Immedia can also read from this same file and put the information into any text box object.

As you would expect from its name, an editable and scrollable text box object shares the attributes of editable and of scrollable text box objects. If you want to let your users write back to you, the text box has to be editable, and if you want to let them write as much as they want, you had probably better make the box scrollable (Figure 16-10). As long-winded as some folks might be, you won't have to use more project space to accommodate them.

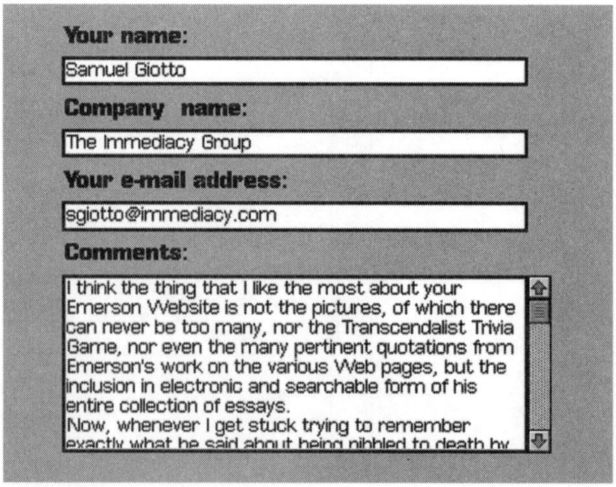

Your name:

Samuel Giotto

Company name:

The Immediacy Group

Your e-mail address:

sgiotto@immediacy.com

Comments:

I think the thing that I like the most about your Emerson Website is not the pictures, of which there can never be too many, nor the Transcendalist Trivia Game, nor even the many pertinent quotations from Emerson's work on the various Web pages, but the inclusion in electronic and searchable form of his entire collection of essays.
Now, whenever I get stuck trying to remember exactly what he said about being nibbled to death by

Figure 16-10: A forms page combining short editable text box objects and an editable and scrollable text box object for longer remarks.

You can format the text in scrollable boxes, but not completely. That is, you can specify such attributes as font, color, size, and type style, but leading, alignment, and indenting information, while displaying properly on your screen, is ignored in the exported version (see "Formatting Text" sidebar).

Text in an ASCII file can be put into text box objects, using Action | Text | Read file (Figure 16-11). Of course, being ASCII, this text carries no formatting information at all. If you apply a type spec to the empty box, the spec is applied globally to the text as it is read into the box—that is, font, color, size, and type style are applied, but not leading, alignment, or indenting information. And of course, all the paragraphs are formatted identically.

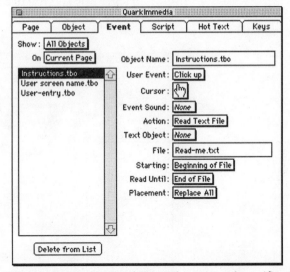

Figure 16-11: The Read Text File command specifies the source and what text box object in the project should display it.

Reading text files into text box objects means that the information in your project can change as often as the information in the ASCII text file is updated. Headlines, news articles, weather reports, traffic conditions, stock prices, booking information, transportation schedules, sales information, price lists, class registration, meeting calendars, the boss's schedule, the status of ongoing competitions—all of this and anything like it can be posted to your Immedia server and automatically reflected in your project. Each time the page displaying the information in question is displayed, it looks for the ASCII text file. Whatever the file contains at that time is then read into the text box object.

Searching Text

Immedia can search for specific text that appears in its basic objects, text box objects, page names, and the page description box for each page that is located in the Page panel. The search string can be specified in several ways, but you can easily let the user specify it by entering it in an editable text box object.

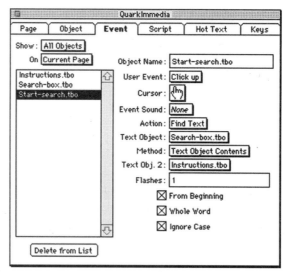

Figure 16-12: Immedia permits searches of any basic object and text box object defined as "searchable."

The Action | Text | Find command (Figure 16-12) lets you specify the following:

- What box you want to search.

- Whether you want to look for a specific string of characters (a "literal") that you specify at the time you are setting up your project or the contents of another text box object.

- If it's from another text box object, which text box object.

You might place twenty pages of reference material in a single scrollable text box object and use the search command to bring the pertinent information into view. If you didn't use an editable text box object, you could use buttons, hot text, or simply basic objects to be clicked, each hard-wired to bring up the pertinent spot in the text.

Exercise 16-1

In this exercise, we'll construct the first of two companion projects, one that collects and saves information from users. The second project, which we'll make in the next exercise, will display the frequently updated information. No special files are necessary to complete these projects.

Setting Up the Collection Project

The first half of our exercise pair will be a two-page project that collects scores from hundreds of observers participating in a national sports festival. Observers will enter scores on the first page and write that information to a file, and then indicate whether or not additional information needs to be entered on the second page. The time and date of login and the user's name will be automatically captured and written to the file on logoff.

1. Begin a new project, 480 points wide, 320 points high, automatic picture box checked, and the other settings as they are usually set (Figure 16-13).

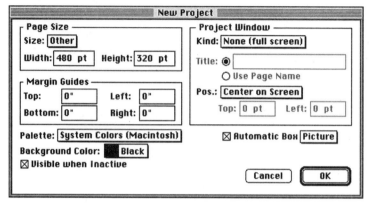

Figure 16-13: Start a new project with these specs.

2. On page 1, set the background color of the picture box to 30% blue. This will help set off the data-collection field as a user-entry box.

3. Add three text boxes at the top of the page, centered on the page (Figure 16-14). Set the background color of all three boxes to None. Put this information in the first box: "**National Sports Festival Score Recorder.**" Set this text in 14-point bold type; we use Eurostile in our examples, but you can choose any suitable type.

4. In the next, larger box, enter this text: **Enter the results of the competition you observed and click on the submit button.** Then type: **Then either enter additional results, or log out. Your name and the time you called in will be recorded automatically.** Make this text 14 points.

   In the third box, enter this text: **Enter results of competition here:** (Figure 16-14). Make this text 14-point bold.

   If you haven't already saved the project, do so now, using the name Scorkeep.qxd.

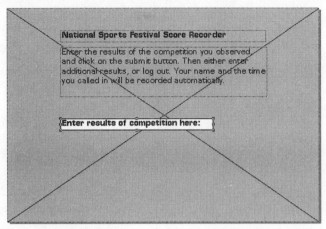

Figure 16-14: Color the background and add three text boxes at the page top.

Next you'll add a fourth text box to hold the competition results.

5. Add a text box and make this box one line tall (about .3 inches high) and 4 inches wide. Make the background of this box opaque white and add a 1-point black border (Figure 16-15).

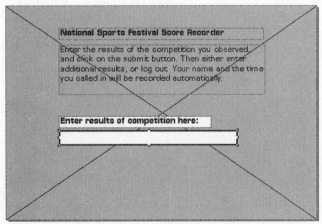

Figure 16-15: Add a text box for entering the results.

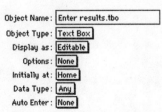

Figure 16-16: Define the box as an editable text box object.

6. Define this box as an editable text box object, called Enter results.tbo (Figure 16-16).

Adding a Button

Now add a button to the picture box:

7. Add one more box, to act as a button (we won't go through the process of making an actual button, as you would in a live project). Make the box 24 points or .333 inches high, and 65 points or .9 inches wide. Set the background color to 100% blue, with the text centered vertically and horizontally. Make the text 14-point bold, colored white. Enter **Submit** in this box (Figure 16-17), and define the box as a basic object with the object name of "Submit.obj."

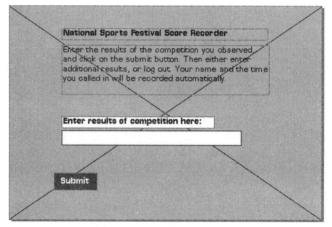

Figure 16-17: Add a text box to use as a button.

Clicking on the Submit box will save the data to an ASCII text file and move you to the next page.

Script

8. In the Script panel, add a new script, called Submit results.scr.

Click on the Add Action button so that there are two *No Action* placeholders. Replace the first one with Action | Text | Write File.

The controls now let you specify what information on your page is going to be written and to what file.

9. Set the Select pop-up menu to One Editable Object, and the Text Object pop-up menu to Enter results.tbo.

10. In the File field, enter **playoffs.txt** and choose Add to End in the Placement pop-up menu. Whatever text appears in the editable text box object will be added to the end of this ASCII text file; if the file is missing, Immedia will create a new file using this name, in the same folder as the project (Figure 16-18).

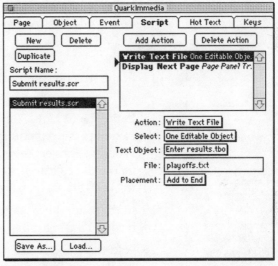

Figure 16-18: Create a script to write information to a text file.

Figure 16-19: Clicking on the Submit box will trigger the Submit script.

11. Replace the second *No Action* place holder with Action | Page | Display Next.

Now we'll associate the script with our Submit button.

12. In the Event panel, highlight Submit.obj. For the Click up user event, set the Action pop-up menu to Script | Run and specify Submit results.scr (Figure 16-19).

On the project's second page, create two basic objects that resemble the Submit button: 24 points or .333 inches high and 65 points or .9 inches wide, background color 100% blue, 14-point bold, white text centered vertically and horizontally (Figure 16-20).

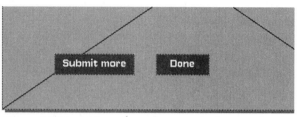

Figure 16-20: Add two boxes on page 2, formatted as buttons.

13. In the first box, enter the text: **Submit more** and define a basic object called More.obj.

14. In the Event panel, for the Click up user event, set the Action pop-up menu to Page | First (Figure 16-21). When the project returns to the first page, the entry field will be cleared, because we declined the option to "keep status on page entry."

15. In the second box, enter the text **Done**. Define this box as a basic Immedia object.

16. Add three text boxes on the page, each tall enough to display one line of type (refer to Figure 16-20). Each of these will become an editable text box object, in which the current time, date, and the user's name will be entered automatically, from the user's system and from the QuarkImmedia Viewer's user preferences.

17. Define an editable text box from the first box; call it Date.tbo. Set the Data Type pop-up menu to Date, the separator to a forward slash, and the format to MDY. Check the box to insert the date on page entry (Figure 16-22).

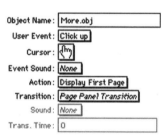

Figure 16-21: Clicking on the Submit More box returns the project to page 1.

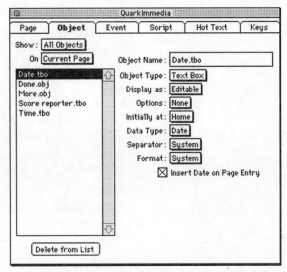

Figure 16-22: Set up an editable text box object that will contain an automatically entered date.

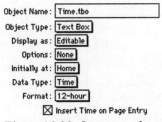

Figure 16-23: Set up another editable text box object for the automatically entered time.

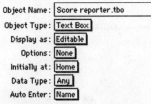

Figure 16-24: Set up the last editable text box object for the user's name to be entered automatically.

18. Define an editable text box from the next box; call it Time.tbo. Set the Data Type pop-up menu to Time and the format to 12-hour. Check the box to insert the time on page entry (Figure 16-23).

19. Define an editable text box from the third box; call it Score reporter.tbo. Set the Data Type pop-up menu to Any and the Auto Enter pop-up menu to Name (Figure 16-24).

20. Add text boxes with identifying labels for these three text box objects.

Capturing Information

Now that we have these three text box objects defined, we want to capture the information that will automatically be entered in them when the user recording the scores has finished. So our "Done" button will need to trigger two actions: writing the time, date, and name information to a file, and quitting. That calls for a script.

21. In the Script panel, add a new script, with two *No Action* place holders. Call this All done.scr.

For the first action, choose Action | Text | Write File. Set the Select pop-up menu to All Editable Objects on Current Page and enter **playoffs.txt** in the File field. This will gather what's in all three boxes on page 2 and add it to the file that contains the competition results (Figure 16-25). Note that a project can capture other information, such as address and phone number, from the Viewer's user preferences as well.

For the second action, choose Other | Quit. Save the project.

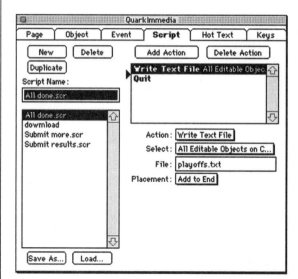

Figure 16-25: In the All done.scr script, capture information from all the editable text boxes on the current page.

22. You can test this project using the Engage command, but you won't see your name in the automatically entered name field since the Viewer isn't open. To really test it, we need to export the project and open it in the Viewer.

Exporting files is covered in more detail in Chapter 19 and using the Viewer in Chapter 20.

Choose QuarkImmedia | Export, and name the exported file Scorkeep.imd. Choose Standard (One File) in the Export format pop-up menu, and don't embed a Viewer (Figure 16-26).

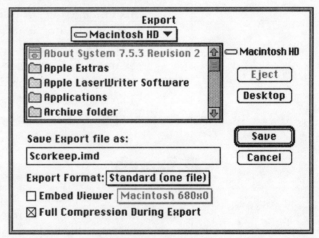

Figure 16-26: Export the project.

23. Launch the QuarkImmedia Viewer (found in the QuarkXPress folder). Check Edit | Preferences | User and be sure that your name, address, and other information is filled in (Figure 16-27).

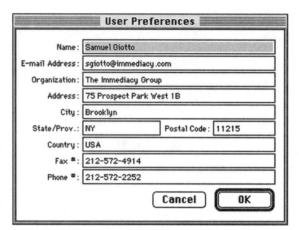

Figure 16-27: Fill in the user information in the Viewer Preferences.

24. Choose File | Open, specifying Scorkeep.imd, and go through the steps to enter a number of scores. (You need to have more than the height of that scrollable box on page one, or else you won't be able to see that the scrolling feature works.) Close and reopen the project at least once, so that, checking later, you'll see more than one date and time of entry recorded.

Close the project and quit the Viewer. Return to QuarkXPress and Immedia to complete the companion project, in the next exercise.

■ Exercise 16-2

This project views the information entered and saved using the Scorkeep.imd project, completed in the previous exercise. If you did not complete that project or had trouble with it, you can use the Exer16-1.imd project on the Companion CD-ROM to enter scores or simply use the playoffs.txt file from the exercise folder.

Set Up

1. Start a new project, with the same settings as the previous exercise: 480 points wide, 320 points high, Automatic Picture Box checked (Figure 16-28).

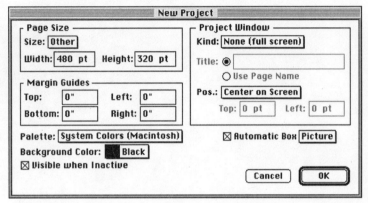

Figure 16-28: Start a new project with these specs.

This project will be only one page long, with a scrollable text box object to display the playoffs.txt file. Since users won't want to scroll through every result that's been submitted if they are looking for the results of just one event, we'll provide them with a search capability, as well.

2. Make the background of the automatic picture box 30% blue.

Using the same specs as used in the previous project, make a headline box that reads "Welcome to the National Sports Festival Scorecard" (we used 14-point Eurostile bold in our project) and a text box that reads simply: "Locate this competitor:" Set the background of both boxes to None (Figure 16-29).

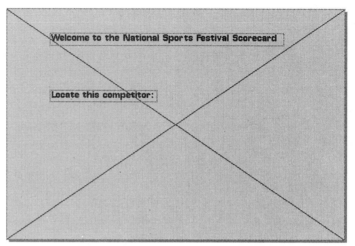

Figure 16-29: Color the background and add text to the page.

Searching

3. Add the box for searching: make the box tall enough to hold one line of type, with an opaque white background and a 1-point border (Figure 16-30). Define the box as an editable text box object, with the name Search for.obj (Figure 16-31). Enter as a default type spec 14-point Palatino bold, colored red. (This is what the type will look like when the user enters the team to search for.) Make the text inset 3 pt.

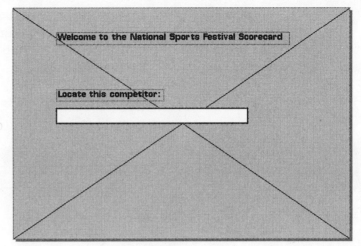

Figure 16-30: Add a search box.

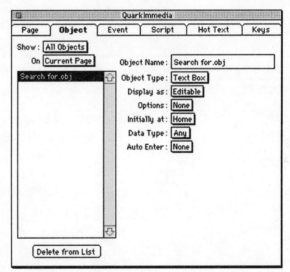

Figure 16-31: Define it as an editable text box object.

4. Below this we need a large box to hold the file containing the scores (Figure 16-32). Give the box an opaque white background and a default type spec of 14-point Palatino.

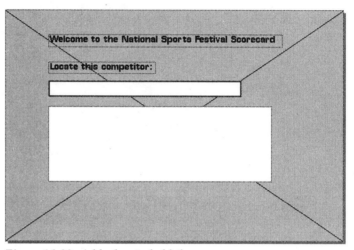

Figure 16-32: Add a box to hold the scores.

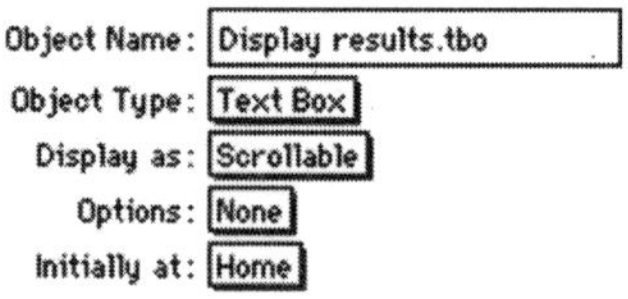

Object Name: Display results.tbo
Object Type: Text Box
Display as: Scrollable
Options: None
Initially at: Home

Figure 16-33: Define it as a scrollable text box object.

Use this box to create a scrollable text box object, called Display results.tbo (Figure 16-33).

The Buttons

5. We need two more boxes to act as buttons, one to initiate the search and a second to quit the project. Make two text boxes, each 24 points, or .333 inches, tall. Make one box 108 points, or 1.5 inches, wide and the other 54 points, or .75 inches wide. Color both boxes blue, with white 14-point bold type centered vertically and horizontally.

   In the wider box, enter the text **Initiate Search**. In the other box, enter **Quit** (Figure 16-34).

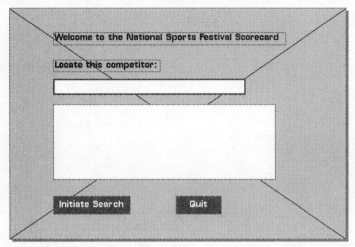

Figure 16-34: Add two boxes.

6. Make the first box a basic object, called Start searching.obj (Figure 16-35). Set the action for the Click up user event to Text | Find and specify Display results.tbo in the Text Object pop-up menu as the object that has the text that should be looked through.

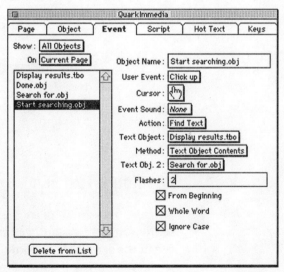

Figure 16-35: Make a basic object that searches the scrollable text box for the text contained in the Search for.obj text box object.

Set the Method pop-up menu to Text Box Contents and the Text Object2 pop-up menu to Search for.obj. This tells Immedia to use the contents of the text box object as the string to search for.

7. Make the other box a basic object called Quit.obj (Figure 16-36). Set the action for the Click up user event to Other | Quit.

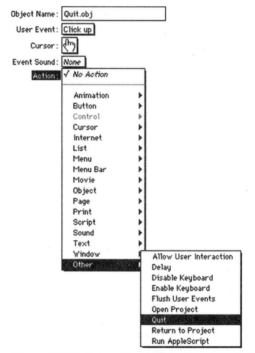

Figure 16-36: Set up the Quit button to quit the project.

Loading a Text File

All the boxes are in place, but since the file containing the scores will be constantly changing, you can't put the text file in the scrollable list now. That would freeze the information, ignoring the input from observers logging in to the score-recording project.

Instead, we will read the text file into the scrollable list every time a new user opens the project, thus ensuring the information is always up to date.

8. In the Script panel, make a new script called Load scores.scr (Figure 16-37). The single action of this script should be Text | Read File. In the Text Object pop-up menu, specify Display results.tbo as where the file should go, and identify playoffs.txt as the file.

   Choose Beginning of File in the Starting pop-up menu, and End of File in the Read Until pop-up menu. Set the Placement pop-up menu to Replace All.

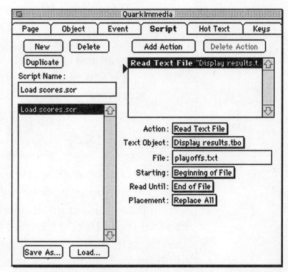

Figure 16-37: Create a script to put the text file with the scores into the scrollable text box object.

9. In QuarkImmedia Preferences, set the Startup pop-up menu to Load scores.scr.

Searching for Results

10. Save and test the project. You don't need to export the project to test it fully. Note how the results entered in the previous project are displayed in the scrollable list. As you scroll through the results, note how the file includes the automatically entered time, date, and scorekeeper's name. In this case, it's your name.

Use the search box to look for any particular result you entered before, noting how this result moves into view in the scrollable box. Disengage when finished.

If you don't have enough results to make the scrolling and searching behave reasonably, reopen the score-recording project in the QuarkImmedia Viewer and enter additional scores. These are added to the end of the playoffs.txt file. Re-engaging the scorecard project will now display these new scores.

Exercise 16-3

In this exercise, we'll work with a list of the Web addresses of 1,500 computer manufacturers and software publishers. We'll place this information in a scrollable text box object, so that the entire list, despite its length, occupies only a single page of the project. Scrolling to locate the desired URL in such a long list is impractical, so we will also make an editable text box object for use as a search field. The files necessary to complete this exercise are located on the Companion CD-ROM in the Exer16-3 folder.

CD-ROM

1. Open the Exer16-3.qxd project, and save it on your local hard drive as Websites.qxd.

2. Black picture boxes appear on the project page where you need to add items (Figure 16-38).

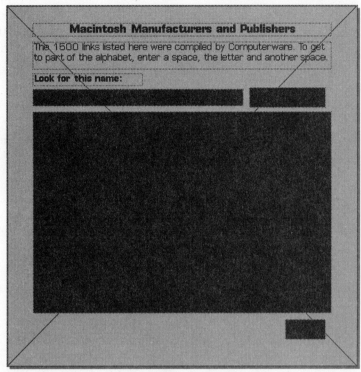

Figure 16-38: The project page with which to start.

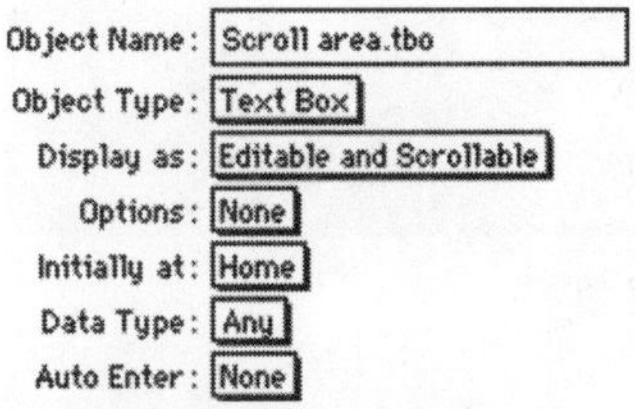

Object Name: Scroll area.tbo
Object Type: Text Box
Display as: Editable and Scrollable
Options: None
Initially at: Home
Data Type: Any
Auto Enter: None

Figure 16-39: Create an editable and scrollable text box object. Then get the Websites.doc file, being sure to check the Include Style Sheets box so that it comes in properly formatted.

3. Add a text box over the large black area and define it as an editable and scrollable text box object called Scroll area.tbo (Figure 16-39). Use File | Get Text to put the Websites.doc file into this box.

   Make sure you check the Include Style Sheets box so that the text is formatted appropriately. If not, delete and re-import. Each of the paragraphs in this list has a style sheet applied to it. You can change the appearance of the whole list by altering the style sheets' appearance. But the font you choose must be on a user's system or else a substitution will occur.

4. Add a text box over the short wide black area. This will be the box where users enter the name they want to locate. You can give it a 1-point black border to help set it off. Make the box background opaque white (Figure 16-40).

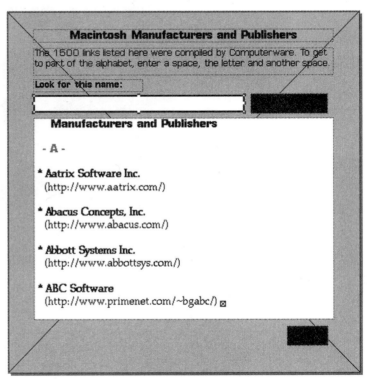

Figure 16-40: Add a box for the search field.

Object Name: Searching box.obj
Object Type: Text Box
Display as: Editable
Options: None
Initially at: Home
Data Type: Any
Auto Enter: None

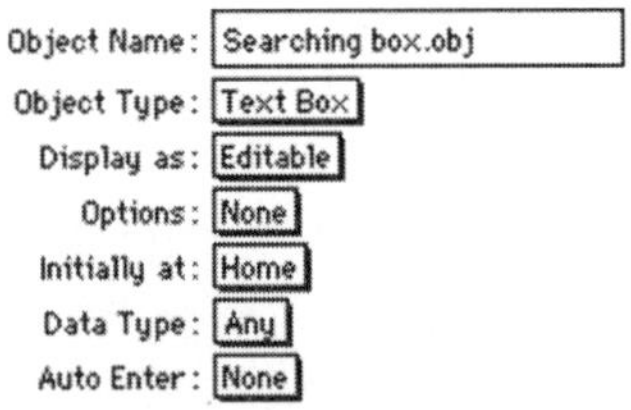

Figure 16-41: Define it as an editable text box object.

Define this box as an editable text box object called Searching box.obj (Figure 16-41). Although no text appears in this box now, set the default type spec to 14-point Palatino. That spec will be applied when the user completes this field.

Figure 16-42: Drag the Search and Quit buttons from the button library for this exercise.

5. Open the Ex16-3bl.qxl button library and drag the Search and Quit buttons onto the page (Figure 16-42). Position them where the small black boxes appear.

6. Select the Search button. Set the action for the Click up user event to Text | Find. Identify the box to be searched (Text object) as Scroll area.tbo in the Text Object pop-up menu.

   Set the method to Text Object Contents, and the Text Obj.2 pop-up menu to Searching box.obj. This tells Immedia that it should search for whatever has been entered in the search field (Figure 16-43).

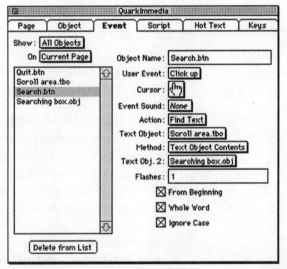

Figure 16-43: Set up the Search button so that clicking on it will trigger a search of the scroll area for whatever is entered in the search field.

7. Select the Quit button. Set the Click up user event to quit the project (Figure 16-44).

8. Save and test the project.

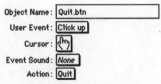

Figure 16-44: Set the Quit button to quit the project.

Search for both company names such as "Apple" and "Ventana" as well as for letters of the alphabet. Note that entering a space after a company name may make it easier to locate Apple, but not Quark (which is followed by a comma in the main listing: "Quark, Inc.").

This complete listing of Web sites was put together, in a different form, by Computerware and dates from December 1996.

Moving On

In terms of the Web, multimedia means so much more than just making things move. Think of changing a project's content daily—or hourly—without having to be a programmer, putting acres of information into postage-stamp pages, and collecting names, numbers, and whatever in forms. These are simple to set up using Immedia's text box objects. In prosaic terms, you can make text boxes scrollable, so long descriptions can fit into small boxes. You use them when you want to let users enter information—for forms or specifying a search. And you use text boxes to grab information from ASCII text files and display them on your project pages. All in all, text box objects make for a rich environment, not as easily set up in other programs as in Immedia.

Next we turn our attention to another feature that makes your project compact and Web-useful—making menus, the pop-up variety for your page and those that pull-down (and drop down) from the menu bar.

chapter 17

Menus & Keys

Interface design is a redundant term when you're talking print—what you see *IS* how you interface with print pages. It's another story entirely with multimedia. Your project pages may look wonderful completely independent of how well users understand how to get at things.

Menus are well-understood tools for navigation and access—users learn about menus simultaneously with mastering the mouse. In multimedia, menus are a vital part of interface design. They provide a compact way to put a lot of choices before the user. You can add menus to the menu bar, put them in dialog boxes, or plunk them down anywhere on a page or palette. In short, they are new/old aspects of the interface you will incorporate into your design.

But user access isn't limited to menus—don't forget keystrokes. In Immedia, it may seem no big deal that any item in any of your menus can be given a keyboard equivalent (which displays in the menu). In fact, you can assign a keystroke to any action whatsoever. Keystrokes provide shortcuts to actions that those who access your project regularly may welcome as a partial antidote to network, Internet, or slow-CPU doldrums. And that's interface design.

Using Menus

Immedia lets us add menus to the QuarkImmedia Viewer menu bar and put pop-up menus on our pages and in our windows, palettes, and dialog boxes. While we might think of menu bar items as "commands" and pop-up menu items as "choices," both types work the same. When we set up a menu, we designate for each item a script that Immedia runs when that item is activated. We might want only a single action, but unlike the Event panel, where we have a one-action choice, we can't choose between specifying an action or a script. Here it's always and only a script. So we make a single-action script in these cases.

Since we must identify scripts for each item in a menu, the first step in making a menu is making the scripts. Then we use the QuarkImmedia | MenuMaker command to construct the menus and identify what items we want (and in what order) on them. In the MenuMaker dialog box, we specify the script to run for each item, and any keyboard equivalent.

Then, depending on where the menu will show up, we either define a pop-up menu object and identify the menu that goes with it, or we use the Action | Menu Bar | Add Menu command to put the menu on the Viewer's menu bar.

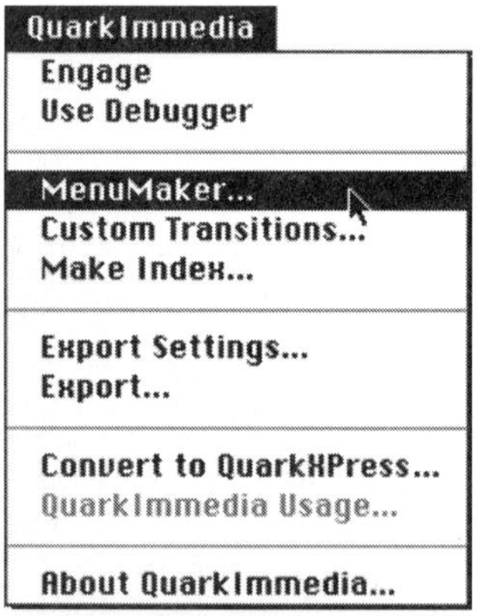

Using MenuMaker

Both types of menus are predefined using QuarkImmedia | MenuMaker (Figure 17-1). In the MenuMaker dialog (Figure 17-2), you create and delete what will be menus in the Menus area. As with several other features in Immedia, such as scripts, you click the New button to create and then name a new menu. Duplicate and Delete let you manage this list. You can alter a menu's name at any time in the Name field. What is entered here is what appears in the menu bar when the menu is used there.

Figure 17-1: Construct menus using Quark-Immedia | MenuMaker.

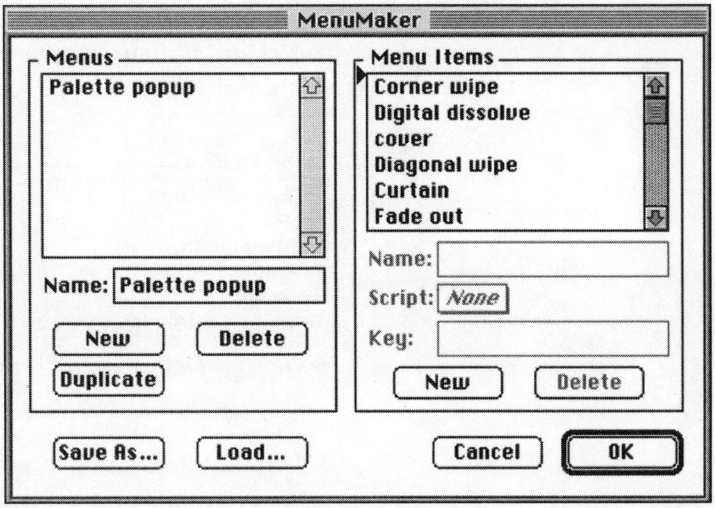

Figure 17-2: The MenuMaker dialog box.

The Load and Save As buttons let you transfer menus from one project to another.

We construct the actual menus in the Menu Items area. A New button adds a menu item, with a place holder name of Menu Item # (where an actual number appears in place of #). You enter the actual name you want, and then specify for that command or item what script should be run and what keyboard command will serve as its equivalent.

Key: Command-☐

Figure 17-3: Non-alphanu-
meric characters don't show
up in your custom menus.

Although you can set up virtually any combination of keys as a key command in an Immedia project, Immedia menus will only display those using the Command key and an alphabetic character, or the Command key and a number. So for instance you might set up the Home key to return your project to its first page, and, in the menu itself, only a non-defined character rectangle appears (Figure 17-3).

Once you've created the menu items you want, you can rearrange their sequence. To do this, simply drag any item to the spot you want (Figure 17-4). A rectangular outline representing the command and a locator triangle appear, indicating position. You can adjust the order, add new items, and delete superfluous items at will. Any changes you make to a menu will impact the menu only in that project and not any others in which you loaded the existing project's menus.

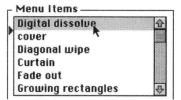

Figure 17-4: Drag a menu item to reposition it in the menu.

Although efficient procedures would dictate that you make the scripts before the menu, you can always construct your menu first, setting up the item names and order without specifying scripts. Then you can come back later and identify which script is used for each item.

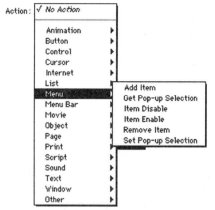

Figure 17-5: The Action | Menu submenu.

The Action | Menu submenu (Figure 17-5) includes actions to disable and enable specific menu items, which gray out and restore the item, as well as actions to add and remove items altogether (changes that disappear when the project is closed). You can also transfer information from a menu to a text box object.

Action: [Add Menu Item]
    √ Pop-up Menu Object
      Menu Bar

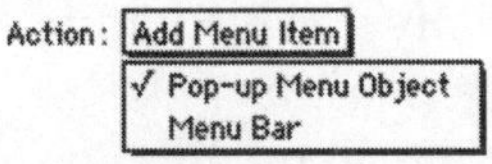

Figure 17-6: Add Menu is required to get your custom menu on the menu bar.

√**Corner wipe**
Digital dissolve
cover
Diagonal wipe
Curtain
Fade out
Growing rectangles
Interlace
Push
Radial
Random lines
Random polygons
Rectangle
Reveal
Triangles
Uncover
Venetian
Quit   ⌘Q

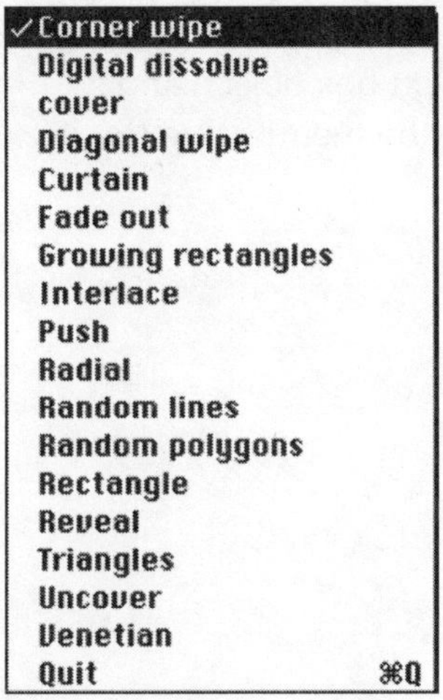

Figure 17-7: When your pop-up menu is fully displayed, a check mark appears next to the last-selected item.

[Grow... ▼]

Figure 17-8: If your menu isn't wide enough for long item names, they're shortened.

A Menu in the Menu Bar

Adding a menu to the Viewer menu bar requires use of the Action | Menu Bar | Add Menu command (Figure 17-6). If you want your menus to show up at the project launch, then you use that command, once for each menu, in the startup script. Or you could have a menu appear, triggered by some event in your project, such as entering the order form page.

In general, you want to use menu-bar menus for global actions, which might be taken from any page in your project. Use pop-up menus for actions specific to a page.

The Menu Bar submenu includes the commands to add and remove menus from the menu bar, to disable (or gray out) a menu and to enable (or restore) a menu, and to hide or show the menu bar itself. (In QuarkImmedia Preferences, an option appears where you can also choose to show or hide the Viewer menu bar.) Commands to add and to remove check marks next to any specific menu item also appear here. This applies only to a menu-bar menu. When you display all of a pop-up menu, a check mark indicates the last accessed item, so you can't put a check mark anywhere else in the pop-up menu (Figure 17-7).

Pop-Up Menu Objects

Text boxes and picture boxes can be defined as pop-up menu objects. They are primarily location indicators, and not containers. The upper-left corner of the box becomes the upper-left corner of the menu. The height of a pop-up menu is one line tall, no matter how tall or short you make your box. The width of the box should be longer than your longest menu item name, to allow for the check mark on the left and a pop-up menu triangle indicator on the right. If the box isn't quite wide enough, the menu item name is shortened and an ellipsis replaces the trailing letters (Figure 17-8).

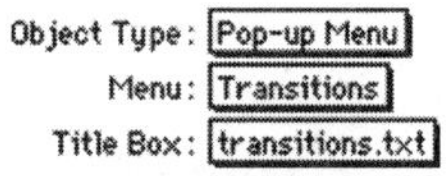

Object Type: [Pop-up Menu]
Menu: [Transitions]
Title Box: [transitions.txt]

Figure 17-9: Defining a pop-up menu object.

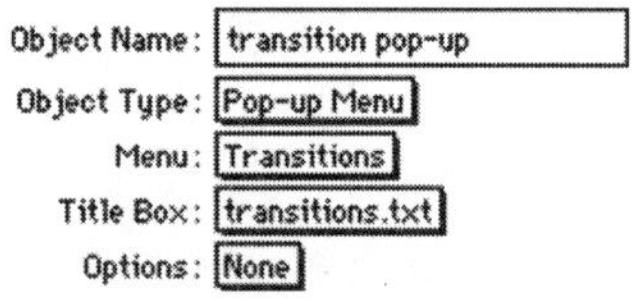

Object Name: [transition pop-up]
Object Type: [Pop-up Menu]
Menu: [Transitions]
Title Box: [transitions.txt]
Options: [None]

Figure 17-10: You can attach a title to a pop-up menu.

Of course, you define a pop-up menu object in the Object panel, as you do with every object, with the usual options of being initially hidden or initially disabled and of keeping changed status on page entry (Figure 17-9).

A pop-up menu object has to identify which menu pops up when you press on it. Only menus that have previously been defined in MenuMaker show up in the Menu pop-up.

The pop-up menu can have a title, which attaches itself to the left of the menu in the exported or engaged project. It also displays in white on black when you pop up the menu. For the title, you specify a text box object, and whatever's in that box displays as the menu's title (Figures 17-10 and 17-11).

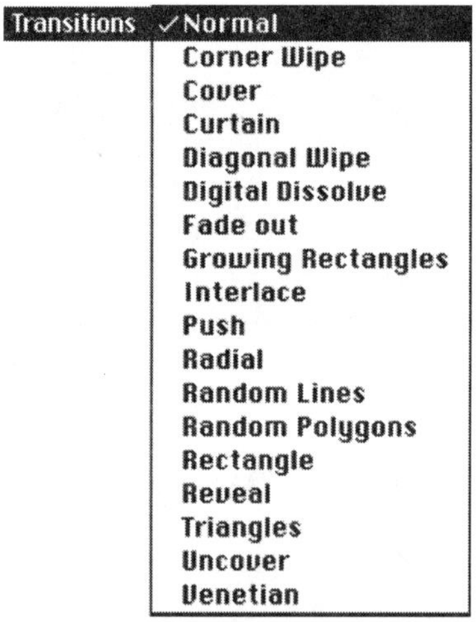

Transitions	✓ Normal
	Corner Wipe
	Cover
	Curtain
	Diagonal Wipe
	Digital Dissolve
	Fade out
	Growing Rectangles
	Interlace
	Push
	Radial
	Random Lines
	Random Polygons
	Rectangle
	Reveal
	Triangles
	Uncover
	Venetian

Figure 17-11: It displays white on black when the menu is accessed.

Key Commands

In the Keys panel (Figure 17-12), you identify keyboard commands that direct Immedia to run scripts, perform the operations associated with button states, or activate any commands in a menu. You can edit the key commands you set up in MenuMaker, but you can't create and delete them here.

In addition to setting up alternatives for your menu items, you might want a key command as an alternative to some standard user event with the mouse, or as a stand-alone event, such as using Shift-Home to jump to the project's first page.

Because you can make keyboard commands that work on only one page, on all pages, or with a master page (and consequently, all pages using that master page for their design), the Keys panel works a little differently than the other panels.

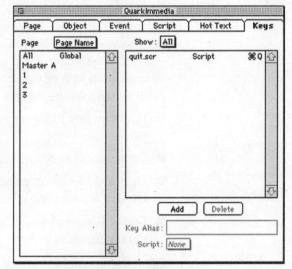

Figure 17-12: The Keys panel.

The scrollable list on the left side contains the different bounds possible for a keyboard command:

- Global, that is, all pages
- Each master page used in your project
- Each individual page of your project

When you highlight one of these categories on the left side, the right side scrollable list identifies all the existing applicable keyboard commands. A pop-up menu at the top of the scrollable list limits the display to key commands attached to scripts, to menus, and to buttons. To add a new key command, simply click on the Add button in the panel's lower right and depress the key or key combination you want. To display the combination, Immedia uses these symbols:

⇧ Shift   ⌥ Option
⌘ Command   ⌃ Control

You can specify any key on your keyboard except these:

- Power on
- Delete
- Escape
- Del

Use them singly or in any combination with any of the shifting keys—Shift, Command, Option, and Control. That is, you can use the letter z or Command-Option-Shift-z, the Page-Down key, or Control-Option-comma.

Additionally, Immedia reserves for its own use:

- Function key F15—for engaging and disengaging projects
- Command-Q—for quitting a project
- Option-F15—for engaging and disengaging with QuarkDispatch software
- Shift-F10—used for hiding and showing the QuarkImmedia palette

Of course, it wouldn't make sense to use standard keyboard commands—Command-period for Cancel, Command-Z for Undo, Command-P for Print, among others—for something other than what users already expect.

Having chosen an individual key or some combination of keys, you then specify the script that you want to run when that key or combination is pressed.

Exercise 17-1

In this exercise, we'll add a global menu—commands in the menu bar that can be accessed from any page. We'll use the five-page project created way back in Chapter 6, "Transitions & Pages," and add commands to change pages.

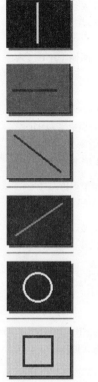

Figure 17-13: Use the Effects.qxd project, created in Chapter 6, "Transitions & Pages."

To make things compatible with user expectations, we'll add keyboard shortcuts and a Go To dialog box.

If you didn't finish the Effects.qxd exercise or don't have it available, you can use Exer17-1.qxd from the Companion CD-ROM, or any project you have on hand with four or more pages.

1. Open Effects.qxd, or Exer17-1.qxd (Figure 17-13) and use File | Save As to save a version under the name Addmenus.qxd.

First we need to make some alterations to the existing project, to use it to maximum effect. (Even if you're working with one of your own projects, you'll need to take these steps.)

2. In the QuarkImmedia Preferences Project panel, uncheck Auto Advance (Figure 17-14). That's how we got from page to page before we had access to the Page submenu. (In your own project, confirm that Auto Advance isn't active for any pages in the Page panel as well.) Make sure that you haven't checked Hide Menu Bar at Startup, and that the Action | Menu Bar | Hide command isn't used in your own project.

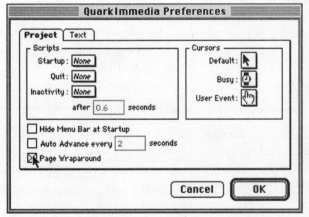

Figure 17-14: Uncheck the Auto Advance feature in QuarkImmedia Preferences, as well as Hide Menu Bar at Startup.

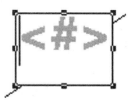

Figure 17-15: Use the command for inserting a page number: Command-3.

Figure 17-16: Make a script to display the first page of the project.

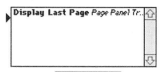

Figure 17-17: Make a script to display the last page of the project.

Figure 17-18: Make a script to display the next page of the project.

3. On the master page, add a text box in the lower-left corner; make it an inch or less in size, with a transparent background.

Set the type spec to 36-point bold, white type. (We use Eurostile in our exercises, but you may choose whatever font you deem appropriate.)

Add a page number. Enter Command-3 (Figure 17-15). Of course, on a master page, we see a code and not a page number; we won't see the number until we look at the document pages. Do that now.

Because we're going to jump from page to page, this page number will help us keep track of where we are.

Add Scripts

When we make our menu, we'll specify a script for each command in the menu. We'll make most of the scripts now.

4. In the Script panel, make a new script called "Go first.scr." Set the action to Page | Display First (Figure 17-16).

5. Add another script, called "Go last.scr." Set the action to Page | Display Last (Figure 17-17).

6. Add two more scripts, called "Go next.scr" and "Go prev.scr." Set the actions to Page | Display Next and Page | Display Previous, respectively (Figures 17-18 and 17-19).

Figure 17-19: Make a script to display the previous page of the project.

Make the Menu

All menus are created first in MenuMaker, then accessed by the project.

    7. Choose the QuarkImmedia | MenuMaker command.

        In the Menus area, make a new menu. Call it "Page," as shown in Figure 17-20. Whenever you want to work with the items of a menu, make sure it is highlighted in the Menus scrollable list.

        In the Menu Items area, add a new item, changing the name from Menu Item 1 to First (Figure 17-21).

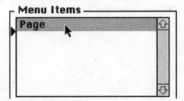

Figure 17-20: Make a Page menu.

Figure 17-21: Create a First item.

        Set the script pop-up menu to Go first.scr.

        Click in the keyboard field, and then press Command-F. The menu bar keyboard equivalents are restricted to the Command key plus alphanumeric keys.

8. Add a new command called Last.
   Set the script to Go last.scr and the keyboard to Command-L (Figure 17-22).

Figure 17-22: The next menu item is called Last.

9. Add a new command called Next.
   Set the script to Go next.scr and the keyboard to Command-N (Figure 17-23).

Figure 17-23: Set up a Next command.

10. Add a new command called Previous.
    Set the script to Go prev.scr and the keyboard to Command-P (Figure 17-24).

Figure 17-24: And set up a Previous command.

Activate the Menu

We need another script to access this menu's commands.

11. In the Script panel, add a new script, called "Starting.scr."

    For the sole action, choose Menu Bar | Add Menu. In the Menu pop-up, specify Page (Figure 17-25).

12. In QuarkImmedia Preferences, set the Startup pop-up menu to Starting.scr (Figure 17-26).

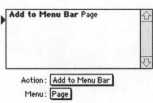

Figure 17-25: Make a script to run on startup.

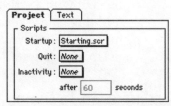

Figure 17-26: Trigger the Starting.scr script in QuarkImmedia Preferences.

13. Save the project and test it. Try out commands both from the menu and using the keyboard equivalents. Note how these are listed in the Page menu.

    Disengage, by pressing Command-Q or function key F15.

Figure 17-27: Add a global
key command to go to page 1.

Go prev.scr	Script	<pg up>
Go next.scr	Script	<pg dn>
Go last.scr	Script	<end>
Go first.scr	Script	<home>

Figure 17-28: Add additional
key commands for the other
display page options.

Go first.scr	Script	⇧ <home>
Go prev.scr	Script	<pg up>
Go next.scr	Script	<pg dn>
Go last.scr	Script	<end>
Go first.scr	Script	<home>

Figure 17-29: You can assign
a script to more than one key
combination.

Adding More Keyboard Equivalents

Most users won't expect to go to the next page by pressing
Command-N, even though that's what's identified in our
Page menu. Let's add some additional keyboard com-
mands, in spite of their not being listed in the menu.

14. In the Keys panel, click Global in the Page scrollable
    list. Click the Add button to add a new keyboard
    command. Set the script to Go first.scr and, with the
    Key Alias field highlighted, press the Home key
    (Figure 17-27).
    Make three more keyboard commands, using the
    End key with Go last.scr, Page Down with Go
    next.scr, and Page Up with Go prev.scr (Figure 17-28).

These are far more likely to be utilized for page navigation than any alphanumeric keys. However, really
experienced QuarkXPress users will instinctively press
Shift-Home to go to the first page, not just Home. So let's
accommodate them.

15. Add another key command, again choosing Go
    first.scr. In the Key Alias field, press Shift-Home. As
    you can see, you can use more than one keyboard
    equivalent with a script.
    Add three more key commands as before and
    include the Shift key with the End, Page Down, and
    Page Up keys (Figure 17-29).

Adding a Go To Dialog Box

To bring the project even more in line with user expectations, we can add a dialog box for specifying any page.
    We'll add another command to our menu, which will
open a Go To dialog box.
    The dialog will need an editable text box object so the
user can enter a page number, a cancel button, and an OK
button that jumps the document to the page specified and
closes the dialog box.

Object Name: Go to box.wdw

Object Type: Window

Figure 17-30: Add a box and define it as a dialog box window object.

16. On the pasteboard, add a picture box that's 3 inches wide and 1.5 inches tall. Define it as a window object, setting the object type to dialog box. Give it the name "Go to box.wdw" (Figure 17-30).

17. Add two text boxes. In the first, enter **Go to page:** and spec the type as 12-point Chicago. Position the second box next to this text. This box will hold the page number. Define it as an editable text box object called Page no.tbo (Figure 17-31).

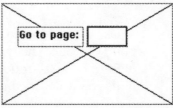

Figure 17-31: Add the dialog contents, making one box an editable text box object.

Add Buttons

We need two simple buttons, for Cancel and OK.

18. Open the button library created in Chapter 10 (or create a new button library, using File | New | Button Library).

19. To make a Cancel button, click on the New button in the button library.

    Make this button 64 pixels wide and 20 pixels tall. Keep type set to Simple (Figure 17-32).

    Name this Cancel.btn.

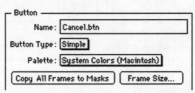

Figure 17-32: Make a new button called Cancel.btn.

With frame 1 active, use the rounded corner rectangle tool to make a black 1-pixel border for the button (Figure 17-33).

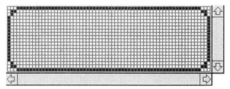

Figure 17-33: Add a rounded corner border for the Cancel button.

Use the text tool to enter the word Cancel in 12-point Chicago. The type specs are in the Style menu in the menu bar. You may need to reposition the text until you're satisfied with its position (Figure 17-34).

Figure 17-34: Add 12-point Chicago text.

Double-click on the rectangular selection tool to select the full frame and copy the contents to frame 2. In frame 2, click the Invert button to turn black pixels to white, and white to black (Figure 17-35).

Figure 17-35: Copy the frame and invert it.

Figure 17-36: This is what the OK button looks like.

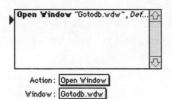

Figure 17-37: The Go to.scr script opens the dialog box.

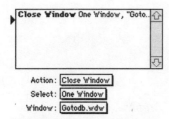

Figure 17-38: A cancel script removes the dialog box from the screen.

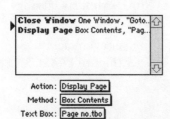

Figure 17-39: Display Page lets you specify a page number from the contents of a text box object.

Click on the button Copy All Frames to Masks, and then close the button editing window.

20. Follow the same steps to create an OK button. The only differences—make this button 76 pixels wide and 28 pixels tall, and use an Oxford rule around the button (indicating that it is the default button in the dialog box).

    You can paste your Cancel button into the first frame as a starting point, adding a heavier border on the outside of the 1-pixel border. And of course, this button says "OK" (Figure 17-36). Call this OK.btn.

21. Once you've completed making the OK button, drag both the Cancel and OK buttons onto the Go to box.

The Dialog Box

Now we're ready to set up the dialog box.

22. First we'll add scripts—to open the dialog box (for the menu's Go to command), to close the dialog box (for the Cancel button), and to close the dialog box and change the page (for the OK button).

23. In the Script panel, make a new script called Go to.scr. For the single action, choose Window | Open and specify Go to box.wdw (Figure 17-37).

24. Make a second script, called Cancel.scr. For the single action, choose Window | Close and specify Go to box.wdw (Figure 17-38).

25. Make one more script, called OK.scr, with two actions. For the first action, choose Window | Close and specify Go to box.wdw. For the second action, choose Page | Display. In the Method pop-up menu, choose Text Box Contents and specify Page no.tbo. This command will go to whatever page is identified in that text box object (Figure 17-39).

Assign the Scripts

With the scripts made, we need to assign them to their triggers—the first to a command in our Page menu, the others to the buttons in the dialog box.

26. Choose QuarkImmedia | MenuMaker, and in the Menus area highlight the Page menu. In the Menu Items area, add a new menu item at the bottom of the menu, giving it the name "Go to ..." (you get the ellipsis by pressing Option-semicolon). For the script, choose Go to.scr, and in the Key field enter Command-J (Figure 17-40).

Figure 17-40: Assign Go to.scr in the MenuMaker dialog box.

27. In the Event panel, highlight Cancel.btn. Set the Click up user event action as Run | Script, specifying the Cancel.scr.

28. For the OK.btn, set the Click up user event action as Run | Script, specifying the OK.scr (Figure 17-41).

Figure 17-41: Cancel and OK buttons use the Click up user event to trigger their scripts.

Test

29. Save and engage the project and test out its new methods of changing from page to page—the Home, End, Page Up, and Page Down navigation keys, and the Go to command in the Page menu.

Exercise 17-2

In this exercise, we'll take five Christmas carols—text in ASCII files and music in MIDI format in QuickTime movie files—and make a pop-up menu so the user can choose which carol to listen to, while the words display onscreen. You must have the QuickTime Musical Instruments extension installed on your Macintosh for this project to play properly.

As in the previous chapter, we'll work with a scrollable text box object. We'll also be reading in different text files to this box, depending on which carol is chosen.

Although the entire project includes 15 minutes of music and all the verses of each carol, we'll fit everything onto one page and into only 66K of space.

The files for this project are located in the Exer17-2 folder on the Companion CD-ROM.

Set Up

1. Copy all of the files for this exercise to your hard disk. When Immedia is looking for the files used in this project, it will expect them to be in the same folder as the project itself.

   Open Exer 17-2.qxd. It is one page long, with a graphic already placed.

Note how the background color in the graphic is dithered to approximate the shade used in the original on a computer with a monitor depth set to thousands of colors.

In programs like Photoshop, ScreenReady, and DeBabelizer, you can reduce the graphic to 256 colors and you can export the color palette containing those colors. This has already been done for the holly border.

2. Choose File | Project Setup. In the Palette pop-up menu, choose Other and load in the Carols.pal palette from the Companion CD-ROM (Figure 17-42).

Now Immedia will use just those colors the graphic needs. In this project, using the palette makes the exported file 10 percent smaller.

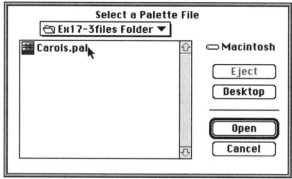

Figure 17-42: Use the custom color palette, in File | Project Setup.

Figure 17-43: Add a box to the page to hold the verses.

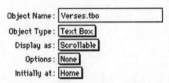

Object Name:	Verses.tbo
Object Type:	Text Box
Display as:	Scrollable
Options:	None
Initially at:	Home

Figure 17-44: Define the box as a scrollable text box object.

3. Place a text box in the open area of the page. Set the background to opaque white and add a 2-point black border (Figure 17-43). This box will hold the text of the carols. While the box is empty, set the default type spec to 14-point Palatino. Define this box as a scrollable text box object called "Verses.tbo" (Figure 17-44).

Each time you play a carol, the text will load in automatically. You can put the text to the first carol in the box now, so that it isn't empty when the project opens.

The five carols are in QuickTime format, so they can be played using the QuickTime Musical Instruments extension. MIDI-formatted music files are considerably smaller than other formats and thus make your project play more smoothly over the Web.

Instead of using the Sound | Play action, we'll use Movie | Play and use the QuickTime controller to set sound levels and allow us to play, pause, and resume. So we'll need a movie object in which to play our pictureless QuickTime movies.

Figure 17-45: Make a picture box into a place holder for the movie objects.

4. Add a picture box in the upper-right corner of the page, 3.25 inches wide and only 1 point tall (Figure 17-45). Later, we'll place this box directly below our menu, and the QuickTime controller will position itself where this box is. Give this box a transparent background.

Define this box as a movie object, called Music placeholder.mvo.

Now is a good time to save this project, calling it something like Carols.qxd.

Action:	Read Text File
Text Object:	Verses.tbo
File:	adeste.txt
Starting:	Beginning of File
Read Until:	End of File
Placement:	Replace All

Figure 17-46: Each script will display the text and play the movie/music.

The Scripts

We will set up one menu item for each movie. That means one script for each item.

5. In the Script panel, make a new script, calling it Adeste.scr, for the first carol "O Come All Ye Faithful" (or "Adeste Fideles") (Figure 17-46).

When an item is chosen in the menu, we will want to put the verses to the carol in the text box object on the page and begin playing the music. So the script needs two actions.

- Set the first action to Text | Read File, and specify Verses.tbo as the Text Object and Adeste.txt as the text file.

- For the second action, choose Movie | Play in Object, specifying "Music placeholder.mvo" as the movie object and "Adeste.mov" as the movie.

Each of the other four scripts not only follow similar steps, they also display the text and play the QuickTime movie in the same boxes. The fastest way to create these additional scripts is simply to duplicate this script and plug in the different names.

6. Duplicate this script and rename the copy to "Silent.scr." In the first action, substitute "Silent.txt" as the text file and in the second action "Silent.mov" as the movie file. This will be for the carol "Silent Night."

7. Follow the same duplicate, rename, and substitute steps for:

- Joy.scr, using Joy.txt and Joy.mov ("Joy to the World")

- Midnight.scr, using Midnight.txt and Midnight.mov ("It Came Upon a Midnight Clear")

- Holy.scr, using Holy.txt and Holy.mov ("O Holy Night")

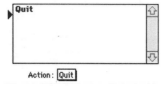

| Action: | Quit |

Figure 17-47: Make a quit script.

8. Make one more script, Quit.scr, with a single action: Other | Quit (Figure 17-47).

The Menu

Now we'll make our menu and pop-up menu object.

> 9. Choose QuarkImmedia | MenuMaker, and make a new menu called "Carols menu."
>
>> Add six menu items, one for each carol and one for quitting (Figure 17-48).

Figure 17-48: Set up menu items for each carol.

>> Rename each menu item using the Carol names, and specify the scripts just created:

O Come All Ye Faithful	Adeste.scr
Silent Night	Silent.scr
Joy to the World	Joy.scr
It Came Upon a Midnight Clear	Midnight.scr
O Holy Night	Holy.scr

>> Rename the last menu item "Quit," specifying Quit.scr.

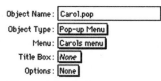

Figure 17-49: Create a pop-up menu object to locate the pop-up onscreen.

10. Add a picture box to the upper-right area of the page, exactly 3.25 inches wide and 15 points tall. Define this as a pop-up menu object, called "Carol.pop" and specify the Carols menu in the Menu pop-up (Figure 17-49). (We use a picture box as a reminder that we don't worry about the contents of this box, and a text box might confuse things.)

Position the Music placeholder.mvo box aligned with and directly below the Carol.pop pop-up menu object box.

11. Save and test this project.

Note how the appropriate text flows in when you choose different carols in the pop-up menu. The scroll bar attaches to the right side of the scrollable text box object, allowing the text of the longer carols to be scrolled and the volume to be adjusted with the QuickTime controller.

Moving On

Adding custom menus to our project's menu bar and pop-up menus on our pages and in our windows (and palettes and dialog boxes, too) makes for efficient and intuitive controls in our projects.

Immedia uses MenuMaker to construct menus, each item of which simply triggers a script. Thus a menu becomes just another way to get things done in Immedia. Pop-up menus attach to the page using a pop-up menu object. Menu-bar menus use a special command that adds them to the menu bar, where they are accessible at all times from all pages.

You can set up keyboard equivalents to our menu items in MenuMaker, or you can set up key commands that trigger other scripts, or buttons, in the Keys panel. Since keyboard access is faster than using a mouse, setting up key commands makes life easier for your frequent user. And isn't that what interface design is all about?

In all the hoopla about multimedia, we sometimes forget the basic medium of print. But not in our next chapter, where we pay our respects to the portable medium, print.

chapter 18

Printing

When the term multimedia is bandied about, we think of video, audio, and animation. Colorful screens with interactive features, and objects that move. Hypertext and Web links. And in the glorious rush of it all, we might overlook the newly humble medium of print because "it just sits there."

Print, we might need to be reminded, is one of the media in multimedia. And however we downplay print because it lacks flash and things don't move, it possesses portability and permanence in spades. Our project may dazzle viewers, but unless we give them something to stuff in their pockets with our name and address on it, it's all over when the show is over.

In your Immedia project, you can include standard printing activities as a record of what's onscreen, of what was entered during the user session, or of material you don't choose to display. You can also provide access to the occasionally necessary, standard Page Setup dialog box.

The Print Action

As you would expect, the Action pop-up menu's Print commands can be accessed from a script, triggered from interaction with any object, or made available from a custom menu. For the different print actions you can choose to display the Print dialog box before printing, or not. Here's what you can do:

- **Print the current page.** What you see onscreen is what you're going to get out of the printer. You as the project designer can decide whether or not you want the standard Print dialog box to be accessed by the user.

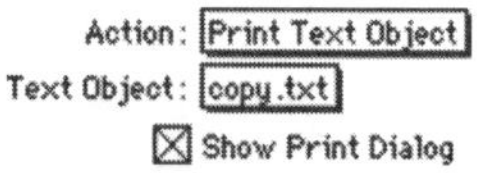

- **Print the contents of any text box (unformatted).** Instead of printing the whole page, Print Text Object limits the print action to the contents of any text box. This is printed as ASCII text, which lacks formatting. Displaying the Print dialog box is optional (Figure 18-1).

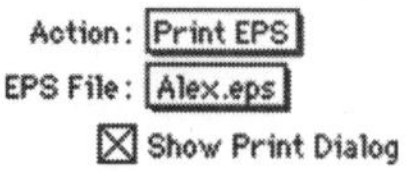

- **Print any EPS graphic in the project.** Encapsulated PostScript files can be printed individually. Displaying the Print dialog box is optional (Figure 18-2).

- **Display Page Setup dialog box.** This lets users specify certain settings for their printer. These settings remain in effect for subsequent print jobs (Figure 18-3).

Of course, when you're constructing your project, you have access to the QuarkXPress Print command, as you would with any QuarkXPress document.

Action: Print Text Object
Text Object: copy.txt
☒ Show Print Dialog

Figure 18-1: You can print the contents of any text box object.

Action: Print EPS
EPS File: Alex.eps
☒ Show Print Dialog

Figure 18-2: EPS files can be printed individually.

Action: Page Setup

Figure 18-3: Provide users with access to the Page Setup dialog box.

Using Print

You'll want to include printing capabilities in your projects when the information onscreen is something the user will want to study or refer to later. While Print Current Page will handle many instances, if the user has searched and collected information, you'll want to use Print Text Object to output that material.

For instance, in an interactive catalog, you'll want to allow users to print out the descriptions of products they have searched for, and perhaps images of those products.

Keep in mind that the resolution of an EPS graphic printed using the Print EPS action will be the same as the resolution of the printer. If your laser printer's 300 or 600 dots per inch (dpi), EPS graphics will print at that resolution. But EPS and other images printed as part of a project page appear at the resolution of 72 dpi, which is quite low for print.

And while Page Setup is not frequently accessed, you may want to include it as an option when providing print capabilities.

Exercise 18-1

In this exercise, we'll add printing and page setup capabilities to an existing project. We'll use a menu on the menu bar for these functions, but you could just as easily provide a button or pop-up menu.

1. Open the Movement.qxd project, which was created in Exercise 9-1. If you skipped that exercise or it's not currently available, you can use any project that has at least two pages, or you can open the Exer18-1.qxd project in the Exer18-1 folder on the Companion CD-ROM.

Create Scripts & the Menu

When you want to provide printing capabilities on every page, you'll need to provide either a button on a floating palette that is available at all times or use the menu bar.

Using the menu bar requires that you create scripts for each command that will appear on the menu, then use the MenuMaker to construct the menu, and finally create one final script to display the menu.

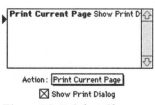

Action: Print Current Page
☒ Show Print Dialog

Figure 18-4: Select Show Print Dialog to display the print dialog box with the Print command.

Figure 18-6: Access the MenuMaker from the QuarkImmedia menu.

Figure 18-7: Add a menu called File in the Menus area.

2. In the Script panel, add a new script called "Print.scr." For its single action, choose Print | Current Page. For this exercise, check the box to show the Print dialog box (Figure 18-4).

3. Add another script, called "Page-setup.scr." Set the action to Print | Page Setup (Figure 18-5).

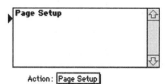

Action: Page Setup

Figure 18-5: Another script will display the Page Setup dialog box.

4. Choose the QuarkImmedia | MenuMaker command (Figure 18-6). In the Menus area, click the New button to add a menu. Call it "File," which is the usual location for the Print command (Figure 18-7).

5. In the Menu Items area to the right, click the New button to add a menu item called "Page Setup...." Note that when a command will display a dialog box, it is customary to indicate this by adding an ellipsis to the command name; on the Macintosh, this is obtained by typing Option-semicolon.

   In the Script pop-up menu, choose "Page-setup.scr" (Figure 18-8).

Figure 18-8: Select your script in the Script pop-up menu of the Menu Items area.

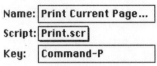

Figure 18-9: You can add a keyboard command.

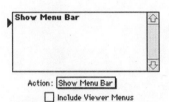

Figure 18-10: Show the Menu bar with an action in the Startup script.

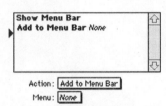

Figure 18-11: You can also add the File menu item to the menu bar with a script.

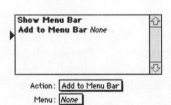

Figure 18-12: Assign the startup script to the project in the QuarkImmedia Preferences.

6. Follow the same steps to add a "Print Current Page…" command which accesses "Print.scr." (We'll use this terminology to indicate that printing is restricted to one page.) In the Menu Items area, click the New button Add Print Current Page to the Menu Items under Page Setup and select the script, Print.scr, in the Script pop-up menu.

   To create a keyboard command for the Print action, enter Command-P in the Key field (Figure 18-9). Keep in mind that providing keyboard equivalents, especially well-established ones like this, makes your project easier to use for a wider variety of users.

   We've put the Page Setup command first because it always precedes the Print command in the File menu. Again, you want to follow standard practice to build on your users' experience with other programs to successfully navigate your project.

Display the Menu

7. We'll use scripts to activate the menu you just created. In the Script panel, modify the Startup.scr script. If your project doesn't already have such a script, create one now. Add two actions at the beginning:

■ For the first action, choose Menu Bar | Show (Figure 18-10). This causes the menu bar to display when the project is run.

■ For the second action, choose Menu Bar | Add Menu, and specify the "File" menu made in step 4 (Figure 18-11). This displays our menu on the menu bar.

   This script is run when the project is first opened. If your project didn't already use a startup script, specify one in the QuarkImmedia Preferences (Figure 18-12).

Test & Print

8. Use the QuarkImmedia | Engage command, or press the F15 key to test this modification of the project.

Note the appearance of the menu bar and the two commands in the File menu (Figure 18-11). Test them out on both page 1 and page 2 of the project.

When finished, disengage by pressing Command-Q or the F15 key.

Problems?

If your project doesn't seem to work right, try running the finished project located on the Companion CD-ROM. It's located in the Exercise folder, in the folder called Exer18-1.

In QuarkXPress, you simply open the project called Done18-1.qxd. You can engage the project to see exactly what is intended. And you can click on any of the scripts and study the settings in the Script panel or in the MenuMaker dialog box to guide you in locating any place you may have gone astray.

Moving On

While the movement, sound, and interactivity of our project is what captures the interest of our viewers, the nonmoving, nonspeaking, inactive medium of print rounds out the project's responsiveness by giving viewers hard copy to refer to at a later time, away from the computer.

The print action is limited to printing out the current page, the unformatted contents of a text box object, or an EPS graphic. Like other actions, it can be accessed from a script, menu, or user interaction with an object or button.

So far in our study of Immedia, we've looked at how to construct our project and add multimedia features. In the next few chapters, we turn our attention to the preparation of our project for presentation once it's been completed. Next up—the mechanics of exporting a project from Immedia into stand-alone capability.

chapter 19

Exporting a Project

Once you've finished your project, what do you do so that others can see it? Just as most people aren't going to have QuarkXPress to look at XPress documents, most people won't have QuarkImmedia to look at Immedia projects. You'll need to put your project in an exported form.

There are three forms of export for QuarkImmedia:

- ■ Standard export—exports all elements of the project in one file, either with or without an embedded QuarkImmedia Viewer.

- ■ CD-ROM—exports a project in two parts: one file to be copied to the user's hard drive and another for the CD-ROM. Viewers can be embedded in CD-ROM projects, as well.

- ■ Internet—many files: all of the elements in the first page are exported in one file. All other pages and the individual media objects on them are exported as separate files. This allows access to the first parts of the project while the rest are being downloaded. Viewers cannot be embedded in Internet files.

QuarkImmedia™ Viewer 1.01
Figure 19-1: The Quark-Immedia Viewer is free—you can distribute it with your projects.

Exported projects can't be opened and used without the Immedia Viewer. It's possible to embed a Viewer in the standard CD-ROM projects—although this adds heft to the files' size, users won't have to locate or open the Immedia Viewer independently. Internet files, however, can't have an embedded Viewer—they must be looked at with an independent QuarkImmedia Viewer.

The Viewer is free and freely distributable (Figure 19-1). You can get it from the Quark Web site (www.quark.com). If you want, you can put it on your own disk, CD-ROM, or Web site. We will explain how to use the Viewer and customize it for your own use in the next chapter.

Should you embed a Viewer in your project? This really depends on the audience. Will potential users have the Immedia Viewer? Are they savvy enough to download one from the Internet? Do you want to distribute a Viewer with your project? Again, it's important to anticipate what your audience will expect and want to deal with.

There is a significant limitation to using embedded Viewers. Projects that contain them can't be viewed on any platform other than the one for which they're designed. You can't look at a project with an embedded PowerPC Viewer on a 68000 machine. You *can* look at a project with an embedded 68000 Viewer on a PowerPC—all PowerPCs can read 68000 files, but they run slower than native PowerPC files. No matter what Mac you've got, you can't look at a project with an embedded Windows Viewer. It's important to think of the platform that your audience will use to view your project before embedding a Viewer.

Projects without an embedded Viewer can be read on any platform as long as the user's got an Immedia Viewer. Right now, there are three separate Viewers for Macintosh—PowerPC, 68000, and one which can be used on both. The Windows Viewer can be used on both Windows 95 and Windows 3.1.

For a Web server to recognize exported QuarkImmedia projects, it must be able to support the Immedia MIME (Multipurpose Internet Mail Extensions) type. Check with your Internet provider to see if the server is properly configured before posting your projects. Use the following settings to configure a server:

> *Action: Binary*
> *Suffix/Extension: .imd*
> *Type: ODOC*
> *Creator: QORN*
> *MIME/subMIME: application/immedia*
> *Application: QuarkImmedia Viewer*

QuarkImmedia Usage

We've been talking about QuarkXPress in contrast to QuarkImmedia throughout much of this book and tend to lose sight of the fact that Immedia is an extension to XPress. You will encounter many of the same issues working with both forms of Quark.

Before QuarkXPress files are printed, they're changed into a raster image that the printer can read and print. That's the role of a RIP (Raster Image Processor). Immedia does the same. All pictures and all text in basic objects are rasterized when exported.

As you most likely know, graphics files don't actually become part of a QuarkXPress file. XPress creates links to any files and places a low-resolution preview within the document. Immedia does the same—not just with graphics, but with other media elements as well. You must make sure the links are correct before you export a final product, just as you do with QuarkXPress before you print.

In XPress, the Picture Usage dialog box in the Utilities menu helps you check the status of imported graphics. The corresponding usage dialog box for Immedia, the QuarkImmedia Usage dialog box, is found under the QuarkImmedia menu (Figure 19-2). It will be grayed out if there aren't any active media elements in the project.

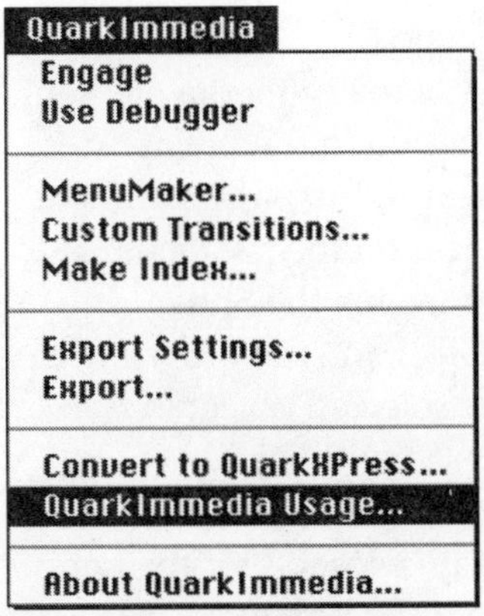

QuarkImmedia
Engage
Use Debugger

MenuMaker...
Custom Transitions...
Make Index...

Export Settings...
Export...

Convert to QuarkHPress...
QuarkImmedia Usage...

About QuarkImmedia...

Figure 19-2: Access the QuarkImmedia Usage dialog box from the QuarkImmedia menu.

In the QuarkImmedia Usage dialog box, shown in Figure 19-3, you'll find a list of all the sounds, movies, cursors, animations, printable EPS files, AppleScripts, and linked projects used in your project. Pictures, however, are still listed in the Picture Usage dialog box. The Quark-Immedia Usage dialog box, like the Picture Usage dialog box, displays objects by name, and gives their location, type of file, and status.

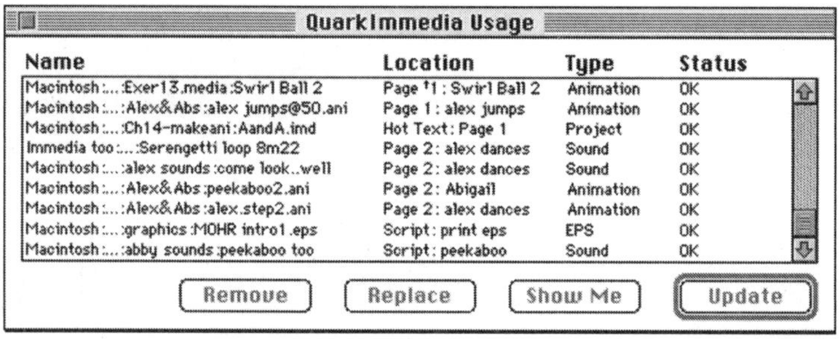

Figure 19-3: The QuarkImmedia Usage dialog box lists all media elements used in a project.

The Name column in the scrollable list displays the path to every media element used in the project as well as its name. Highlight a name to make changes, which you can do with the Remove, Replace, Show Me, and Update buttons at the bottom of the dialog box.

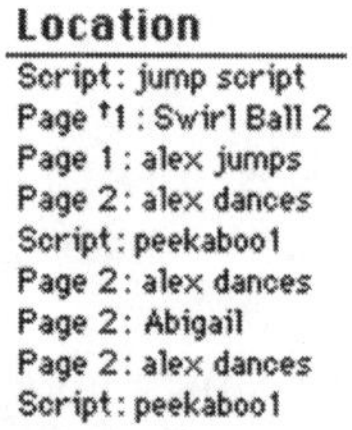

The page location in the project of every media element, AppleScript, or linked project is shown in the Location column (Figure 19-4). A dagger next to the page number indicates that you can find the object on the pasteboard. If you want to see a file in its location, click the Show Me button. Immedia will select the object, move your view to the page where it is, and place the selected object in the upper-left corner of the window.

To find out what type of object an element is, look at the Type column. Every media object is defined by type here.

Check the Status column to see if the link to a file is OK or if the file is missing, has been modified, or is no longer used in the project. If the status is OK, you're fine. There's nothing more you have to do.

Location

Script: jump script
Page †1 : Swirl Ball 2
Page 1 : alex jumps
Page 2 : alex dances
Script : peekaboo1
Page 2 : alex dances
Page 2 : Abigail
Page 2 : alex dances
Script : peekaboo1

Figure 19-4: The Location column shows you where every media element is in the project.

If the status is Missing, you'll need to locate the object or project and re-establish the link to Immedia. If the Status Column indicates that a file has been modified, you'll want to locate and update it also. To do this, click the Update button (or hit Return), which will open a dialog box in which you can locate the file or another one of the same type (Figure 19-5). Highlight the file and click Open in the dialog box and the file will be updated or replaced.

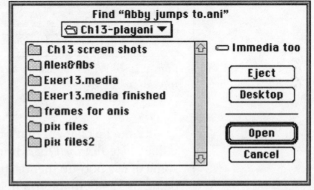

Figure 19-5: The Update button opens a dialog box that allows you to re-establish the link to a missing file.

The words Wrong Type in the status column indicate that the media type has been changed since it was first placed in the project—maybe you've changed an EPS file to a PICT in Photoshop or converted a WAV sound file to AIFF in SoundApp. You'll need to update the file the same way you do for a missing or modified file—use the Update button. You can't use the Update button to replace a file with one of a different type in QuarkXPress, but you can in Immedia. Immedia, however, also has a Replace button that opens a dialog box to locate a replacement file (Figure 19-6) for any media element. Click the Open button in the dialog box to substitute a new file.

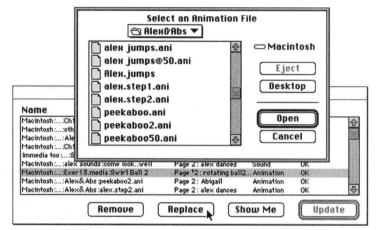

Figure 19-6: With the Replace button you can substitute files of one type for another.

Any media element that's been used once in a project will be listed in the QuarkImmedia Usage dialog box and some of the pop-up menus. If a media element is no longer being used—perhaps you deleted the action that controlled it—the element's status will be indicated as Unused in the status column. You can remove it completely from the project by clicking the Remove button in the lower left (Figure 19-7). An element with a status of OK (and not Unused) will be replaced with default selections or None.

Figure 19-7: The Remove button will delete an object from a project.

▌ Export Settings

After you've checked all media elements, there are still some things to do before you export your project. First check the export settings, which you can define separately for the different types of exports.

Pull down the QuarkImmedia menu to Export Settings (Figure 19-8). This dialog box has two panels—Compression and General. The Compression panel has pop-up menus for compressing all instances of sound and video in the project. The General panel is used mainly for CD-ROM and Internet export, to name auxiliary files, and to set parameters for changing monitor settings.

The settings you choose here will only affect the type of project selected (Standard, CD-ROM, or Internet) in the Settings pop-up menu shown in Figure 19-9. Each type of export has different requirements and constraints. You'll probably have different settings for each export type.

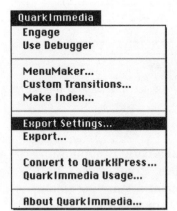

Figure 19-8: Use the Export Settings command to access panels for setting export parameters.

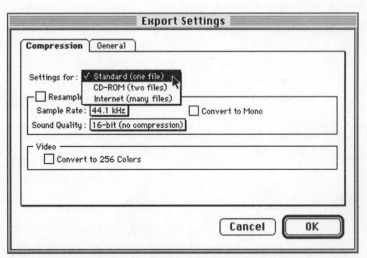

Figure 19-9: Select the type of export to apply settings in the Settings pop-up menu of the Compression panel.

You use the Compression panel to set compression for sound and video (Figure 19-10). All other media elements are compressed in Quark's proprietary format and you can't modify the settings for them.

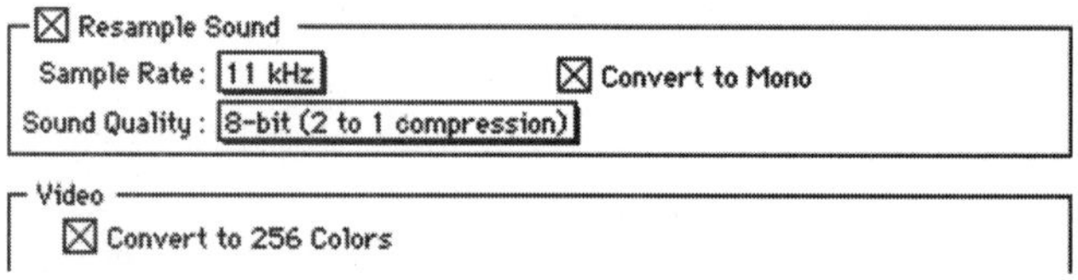

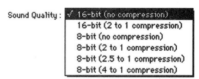

┌─☒ Resample Sound ──────────────────────────────────┐
│   Sample Rate : │11 kHz│   ☒ Convert to Mono │
│   Sound Quality : │8-bit (2 to 1 compression)│   │
└──┘
┌─ Video ───┐
│   ☒ Convert to 256 Colors   │
└──┘

Figure 19-10: Compress the sound and video files in your project in the Compression panel.

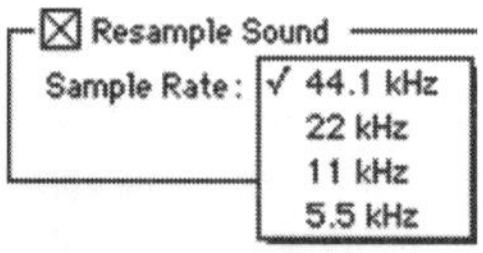

In Chapter 8, "Sound," we talked briefly about sampling and bit depth for sound files. To compress sound you generally lower the bit depth and sampling resolution. Check the Resample Sound check box to do this, then choose compression levels in the Sample Rate and Sound Quality pop-up menus (Figures 19-11 and 19-12). Another way to diminish the size of sound files is to convert them from stereo to mono—there's a check box next to these pop-up menus to do this.

┌─☒ Resample Sound ───┐
│ Sample Rate : │√ 44.1 kHz│
│   22 kHz │
│   11 kHz │
│   5.5 kHz │

Figure 19-11: Compress sound by choosing a lower setting in the Sample Rate pop-up menu.

Sound Quality : ┌─────────────────────────────┐
                │ √ 16-bit (no compression)   │
                │   16-bit (2 to 1 compression) │
                │   8-bit (no compression)   │
                │   8-bit (2 to 1 compression) │
                │   8-bit (2.5 to 1 compression) │
                │   8-bit (4 to 1 compression) │
                └─────────────────────────────┘

Figure 19-12: Lowering the bit depth will also compress sound files.

High-quality uncompressed sound can be sampled as high as 44.1 kHz at 16 bits. The sound quality of music compressed to 22.05 kHz and 8 bits is acceptable when played on most computers, and speech usually sounds fine at this rate. Sound can be resampled to as low as 5.5 kHz and 8 bits with 4 to 1 compression, but the sound quality won't be very good at these levels. You'll need to try different sampling rates to find out which ones work best for your specific sound and project.

QuickTime movies are played by the system, not the project, which means they can be played with thousands or millions of colors. To obtain smaller file sizes, you can reduce the number of colors in the movie to 256. In the Video area of the Compression panel, just check Convert to 256 Colors (refer to Figure 19-10). The QuickTime movie will then take up less disk space and may play more efficiently on slower computers. Immedia doesn't apply any other kinds of compression to QuickTime movies, assuming that they have been compressed in the application that created them.

TIP

Compression makes file sizes smaller, and small size is critical for Internet use. But with compression you often sacrifice quality. The more a sound file is compressed, the worse it will sound. Video compression can lead to banding and image degradation. It's essential to test your compressed files before distributing your project.

The settings in the General panel for Export Settings shown in Figure 19-13 are mainly for Internet and CD-ROM projects.

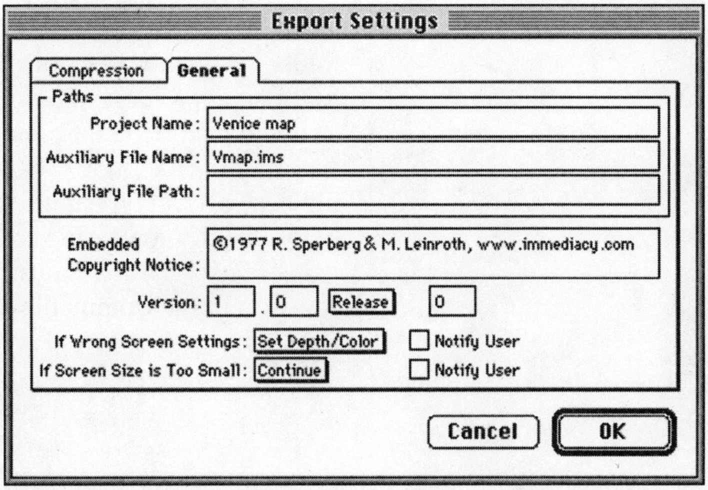

Figure 19-13: Use the fields in the General panel to name files for Internet and CD-ROM exports.

Place the name of the project in the Project Name field. This is the name that will be displayed in the Quark-Immedia Viewer. Files exported for Windows must be named with an .imd extension.

Naming QuarkImmedia Files for Windows Export

Until the most recent version of Windows, Windows 95, all Windows files had to be named in a specific manner—eight letters, a period (usually pronounced "dot"), and a three-letter extension to indicate the file type. In Windows 95 you can use file names with up to 255 characters. Not all applications support this, however. It's best to stick with the earlier Windows format when you save any files that will be viewed on Windows machines.

The Auxiliary File Name field tells the Viewer the name of the second or auxiliary CD-ROM file. If the export is meant for Windows computers or the Internet, auxiliary files must have an .ims extension. Type the path to auxiliary CD-ROM files in the Auxiliary File Path field starting with the name of the CD-ROM and following with any folders. Separate all names in the path with slashes: CD-ROM name/folder/folder.

If you want to associate a copyright notice or any other special information (63 characters or less) with your project, you can type it into the Embedded Copyright Notice field. A user can access this in an exported project using File | Get Info (Figure 19-14). Text typed here will show up in the Comments field.

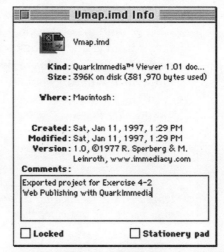

Figure 19-14: Embedded notices will show up in the Comments field.

There's no reason to change any of the settings in the Version fields or pop-up menus. If you click on the pop-up menu that displays Release, you'll see listings for previous versions of Immedia. The release version of the Viewer can't read projects created by some beta or any alpha versions of Immedia.

The last two fields in the General panel let the Viewer know what to do if the screen settings of the user's monitor aren't correct. Immedia expects a monitor to have 256 colors and be at least as large as a project. If the settings are different, you have several choices of what to do.

The QuarkImmedia Viewer will automatically try to change the settings on a viewer's monitor to 256 colors. It won't even play projects on monitors with less than 256 colors. You'll need to tell the Viewer what to do if the color depth isn't right (Figure 19-15). If you leave the If Wrong Screen Settings pop-up menu set at Set Depth/Color, the

Viewer will change the monitor color bit depth from thousands or millions of colors to 256. To prevent the Immedia Viewer from changing the monitor color setting, choose Continue, which will leave the settings unchanged, or Quit, which will cancel opening the exported project. Check the Notify User check box to provide the user with a dialog box warning of the problem (Figure 19-16).

Figure 19-15: If the monitor color settings don't match, the Viewer can be instructed to change them.

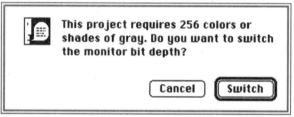

Figure 19-16: The QuarkImmedia Viewer will warn of incorrect monitor settings if Notify User is checked.

If Screen Size is Too Small: Continue | Quit

Figure 19-17: The Viewer must also be instructed what to do if the screen is too small.

If the screen size of the user's monitor is smaller than the size designated in Project Setup, you'll need to tell the Viewer what to do (Figure 19-17). Choose Continue in the If Screen Size is Too Small pop-up menu to go ahead and play the project. The Viewer will crop the project on the right side and the bottom. Using Quit in this pop-up will cancel the opening of a project. Immedia will refuse to open it if the user tries to do that again. There's also a Notify User check box to give the user a warning (Figure 19-18) that the screen size is too small.

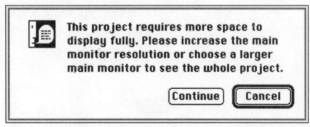

Figure 19-18: The Viewer can display a warning if the screen size is too small.

Exporting a Project

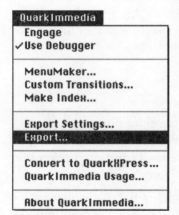

Figure 19-19: Use QuarkImmedia | Export to open the Export dialog box.

You're now ready to export your project. Just pull down the QuarkImmedia menu to Export (Figure 19-19) and open the Export dialog box (Figure 19-20). You can give your project a name in the Save Export File field, and choose the Export Format: Standard (one file), CD-ROM (two files), or Internet (many files), from the Export Format pop-up menu below. If you put a check in the Embed Viewer check box, you'll get a pop-up menu to select a platform.

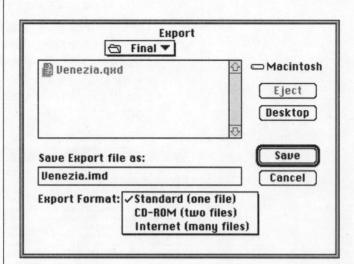

Figure 19-20: Select the Export Format of a project in the Export dialog box.

If you're exporting a final product, you'll want to check the Full Compression During Export check box. It takes longer to export a project with this option selected, so don't bother using it if you're just testing your project.

TIP

There's a handy way to find out the size of your exported projects as well as how long it will take for the different elements of CD-ROM and Internet projects to download. Hold down the Option key when you click Save in the Export dialog box and you'll get a text file identifying the individual exported files and their sizes. With Internet projects, this will even show you the times it will take to download each file on 28.8 kbps modems and T1 lines.

Exercise 19-1

For this exercise we'll use one project for different types of exports to see how they differ. We used Exer14-2, which has several animations, scripts, and cursors, but any project you have with a variety of media elements will work nicely.

1. Open your project. Check all of the media elements with the QuarkImmedia Usage dialog box (Figure 19-21). Update any if needed. It's a good idea to take a look at the Picture Usage dialog box to make sure that all the pictures are linked and none need to be updated.

	QuarkImmedia Usage		
Name	**Location**	**Type**	**Status**
Macintosh:...:other stuff:alex sounds:hard to do	Script : jump script	Sound	OK
Macintosh:...:Exer13.media:Swirl Ball 2	Page †1 : Swirl Ball 2	Animation	OK
Macintosh:...:Alex&Abs :alex jumps@50.ani	Page 1 : alex jumps	Animation	OK
Macintosh:...:alex sounds :come look..well	Page 2: alex dances	Sound	OK
Macintosh:...:peekaboo.ani	Page 2: Abigail	Animation	OK
Macintosh:...:Alex dances.ani	Page 2: alex dances	Animation	OK
Macintosh:...:Abby jumps.ani	Page 2: Abigail	Animation	OK
Macintosh:...:peekaboo too	Script: peekaboo	Sound	OK
Macintosh:...:Serengetti loop 8m22	Script: Alex1	Sound	OK

[Remove]   [Replace]   [Show Me]   [Update]

Figure 19-21: Check all media elements with the QuarkImmedia Usage dialog box.

2. Use the Remove button to take out any media elements not in use in the project—they're labeled "Unused" in the Status column.

3. Next, check the export settings, as shown in Figure 19-22. If you're exporting for Standard export, the only thing you may want to consider is resampling sound (and video if you have any QuickTime movies). Try an export with no compression and resampling set to 22.05 kHz or 11.025 kHz to see if there's a difference in audio quality.

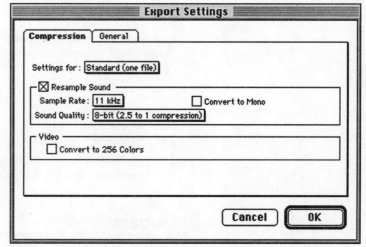

Figure 19-22: Try out different sound and video compression settings in the Compression panel of the Export Settings dialog box.

4. For Internet export, make sure you identify the project name with the .imd extension and auxiliary files with the .ims extension (Figure 19-23). Try resampling sound to the lowest sampling rate and most compression.

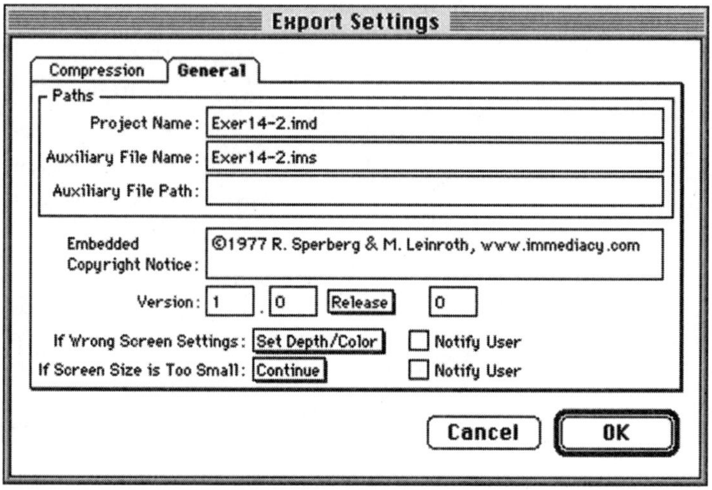

Figure 19-23: Enter the proper suffixes for Internet projects in the General panel.

5. Export your project. Hold down the Option key while you click Save and you'll get a text file with all of the files, their compression, and, for Internet projects, download times.

Exercise 19-2

You can tell the QuarkImmedia Viewer what to do if the user's monitor settings aren't what it expects. We've created an exercise that demonstrates transitions and is perfect to test this—its size is 1600 X 1200 pixels. Not too many monitors can handle that!

1. Open Exer19-2.qxd in the Exer19-2 folder on the Companion CD-ROM. Pull down the File menu to Project Setup and check the size of the project. Make sure that it's 1600 pixels wide and 1200 pixels high.

2. Use QuarkImmedia | Export Settings to open the Export Settings dialog box. Then go to the General panel and take a look at the two pop-up menus for checking monitor settings—If Wrong Screen Settings and If Screen Size is Too Small. You can leave them at the default settings, Set Depth/Color and Continue, but check each of the Notify User check boxes (Figure 19-24).

If Wrong Screen Settings: [Set Depth/Color]   ☒ Notify User
If Screen Size is Too Small: [Continue]   ☒ Notify User

Figure 19-24: Set the warnings for monitor settings in the General panel.

3. Export your project, with or without an embedded Viewer, and see what happens when you open it. You should get error messages for each of the settings.

4. Now go back to the Export Settings dialog box in your QuarkImmedia project. Change the settings on both pop-up menus to Quit. Uncheck the Notify User check box.

5. Export your project and try to open it. The Viewer won't open the project. It appears to do nothing, which can be very disconcerting to users.

6. Return to your document and check both Notify User check boxes.

7. Export your project and test it. What do you see this time?

Moving On

Exporting, putting your project into a form that a user can look at, is the final step in creating an Immedia project. There are three kinds of exports you can make—Standard, CD-ROM, and Internet.

Before you export, you must check to make sure that all media elements are correctly used in your project. Use the QuarkImmedia Usage dialog box to do this. You'll also want to look at compression settings, and for CD-ROM and Internet projects, the names for the primary and auxiliary files.

To look at Immedia projects a user must have the QuarkImmedia Viewer. In every export but Internet, you have the choice of embedding a Viewer or not. The next chapter will take you through the steps in configuring and using the Viewer for both Macintosh and Windows computers.

chapter 20

Using the QuarkImmedia Viewer

You've completed your project and it's so good that you want to share it with the world. But many of the people who you want to enjoy your projects probably won't have the QuarkImmedia XTension or even QuarkXPress. So how do you distribute your work? Quark has created the QuarkImmedia Viewer to make it easy for anyone to look at Immedia projects.

The QuarkImmedia Viewer has versions for different platforms. Currently there are release versions for Macintosh and Power Macintosh. A beta version for Windows is shipping with the program, and it won't be much longer before the Windows version will be released.

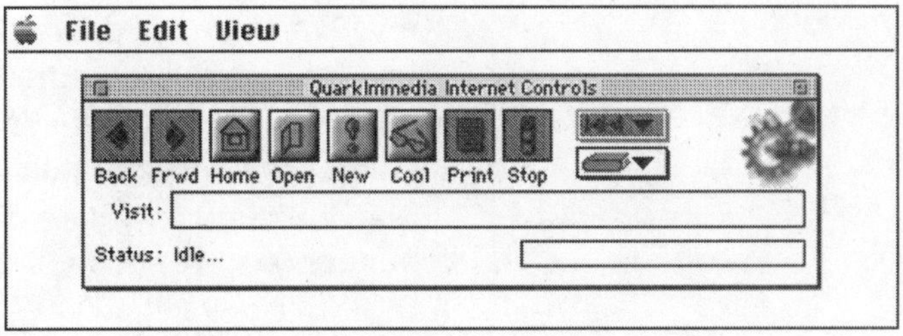

Figure 20-1: The QuarkImmedia Viewer for Macintosh.

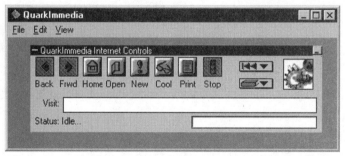

Figure 20-2: The beta version of the Immedia Viewer for Windows.

As you learned in Chapter 19, "Exporting a Project," you can embed the Viewer in any standard or CD-ROM project, but not in projects for the Internet. It's convenient for the people who will look at your projects to receive them with embedded Viewers, since they won't need to find (or launch) their own. But that's not a perfect solution. A Windows user can't look at a project that has a Macintosh Viewer in it, and vice versa. When you export a project with an embedded Viewer, it is restricted to that platform. However, if you export a project without embedding the Viewer, then it can be viewed by Windows and Mac users as is, using the version of the Viewer for their platform. This is certainly something you'll need to consider when you export your finished projects.

Obtaining the QuarkImmedia Viewer

If you don't have a copy of the QuarkImmedia Viewer, you can download it for free from Quark's FTP server. ftp://ftp.quark.com/immedia/viewers/macos/ mv101en.hqx will download the Macintosh Viewer and ftp://ftp.quark.com/immedia/viewers/win/wiv102b4.exe will download the beta version of the Windows Viewer.

It takes approximately 4½ minutes to download the Mac Viewer if you use a 28.8 kbps modem or about 5 minutes and 45 seconds if you use a 14.4 kbps modem. For ISDN users, the Viewer downloads in approximately 1 minute; for T1 users, approximately 20 seconds.

The QuarkImmedia Viewer Menus

The Immedia Viewer is quite easy to use. It opens like any Mac or Windows program. There are only three menus: File, Edit, and View.

The commands to open, quit, or exit the Viewer are found, as they are in most programs, under the File menu. Use the File | Open command to access standard and CD-ROM projects that don't have the Viewer embedded in them. This command leads to the Select a QuarkImmedia Project directory dialog box. Locate an Immedia project on your hard drive, CD-ROM, or external drive and click the Open button to open it (Figures 20-3 and 20-4).

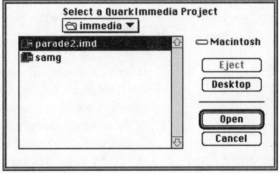

Figure 20-3: The Open command leads to the Select a Quark-Immedia Project directory dialog box for standard and CD-ROM exported projects.

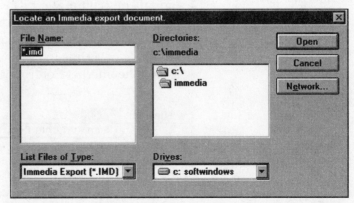

Figure 20-4: Opening a project in the Windows Viewer works the same way.

Figure 20-5: Opening an Internet project uses a different Open menu item.

There's a special open command for opening Internet sites: Open URL (Figure 20-5). This opens the Open URL dialog box (Figure 20-6). Type an Internet address into the URL field, click OK and, if your system has Internet access, the Immedia Viewer will locate the URL and open the project associated with it.

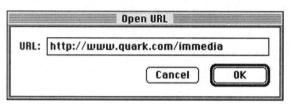

Figure 20-6: Type an Internet address into the Open URL dialog box.

TIP

Immedia uses HTTP (HyperText Transfer Protocol), one of several communication protocols on the Internet. A full URL (Uniform Resource Locator, the address for a Web site) identifies which protocol is being used by placing it in front of the address followed by a colon and two slashes: http:// www.quark.com/Immedia. In Immedia, you can type in just the Web address (www.quark.com/Immedia) and the Viewer will know you're using the HTTP protocol.

Figure 20-7: Commands in the Edit menu can be used for user input text.

Cut, Copy, Paste, Clear, and Select All are under the Edit menu (Figure 20-7). These are useful for changing editable or user entry text boxes.

The View menu is quite simple. It has only one command, Show/Hide Internet Controls. This opens and closes the Internet Control palette (Figure 20-8).

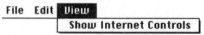

Figure 20-8: Use the View menu to make the Internet Control palette visible.

Internet Control Palette

The Internet Control palette, a floating palette, is handy for navigating and checking on the progress of your connection with the Internet (Figure 20-9).

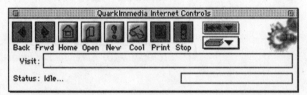

Figure 20-9: You can use the Internet Control palette instead of menus to navigate the Web.

To get to any Immedia Web site, just type the URL into the Visit field. In the Status area just below, you can monitor what the Viewer is doing—whether it's idle, connecting, or downloading a site. There's a progress bar to the right that will let you know how much of a connection has been downloaded. There's also a little animation, the Network icon, in the upper right area of the page. When the gears are moving, the Viewer and the network are communicating.

To the left of the Network icon are two pop-up menus. The top one, the QuarkImmedia URL History button, lists the sites you've visited in the current session, with the most recent at the top. Choose any option from this pop-up menu to return to that site.

The pop-up menu with the book icon underneath the URL History button is the Bookmark button (Figure 20-10). You can easily save the address, or URL, of a site when you're visiting it. Just click the Bookmark pop-up menu and select the Add to List command. The name and URL of the site are saved as a bookmark. Select any name on the pop-up menu, and the Viewer will call up that site.

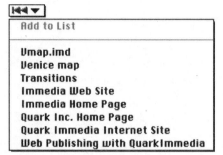

Figure 20-10: Access your favorite sites from the Bookmark button.

Use the buttons along the top of the Internet Control palette to go to specific Web sites. The Back and Frwd buttons take you "back" to the last site you visited and then "forward" to the site you're on. Obviously Frwd is only accessible after you've backtracked.

Clicking the Home, New, and Cool buttons in the Internet Control palette will take you to the URLs you've entered in the Home, New, and Cool fields in the preferences. You'll see how to do that in a moment.

The Print button sends a bitmapped image of the current page to your printer at screen resolution. You might have noticed that there's no Print command in the File menu. Unless a project has a special print command in its menu, using the Print button is the only way to print an Immedia page.

Click the Stop button to cancel the current request to the Viewer. This is not the button to push when you want to close the Viewer. Do that with the Quit command.

Bookmarks & Preferences

You now know the commands and buttons to use to navigate the Web. There are other commands to customize what the Viewer can do.

It's easy to modify your bookmarks. The command Edit I Edit Bookmarks opens the Edit Bookmarks dialog box (Figure 20-11). Here you'll find all your bookmarks

listed by name in the Bookmark scrollable list. Click a
name in the list to display that site's address in the URL
field. To change a listing, highlight the name in the
scrollable list, and enter a new name into the Name or
URL field.

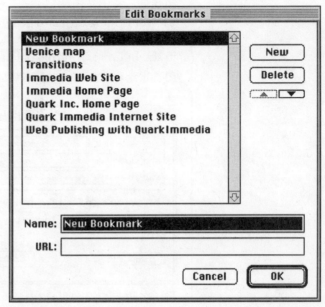

Figure 20-11: You can easily edit your bookmarks in the Edit
Bookmarks dialog box.

There are two buttons to the right of the Bookmark
scrollable list. The New button adds a new entry to the
Name field in the scrollable list, giving it the default label,
"New Bookmark." Just replace that with the name you
want to give the bookmark and enter the URL in the URL
field, and the new entry is added to the list. Use the Delete
button to erase a highlighted entry.

The two arrow buttons under New and Delete make it
easy to reorder the sequence of bookmarks in your list.
Highlight a bookmark and then click on the down arrow
to move the bookmark toward the bottom of the list or on
the up arrow to move it toward the top of the list.

Internet Preferences

Like QuarkXPress and QuarkImmedia, the preferences for the QuarkImmedia Viewer are in the last section of the Edit menu.

Use the Edit | Preferences | Internet command to open a dialog box that provides several ways to customize your Viewer (Figure 20-12). The URLs area has fields to enter URLs for the Home, What's New, and What's Cool buttons in the Internet Controls palette. When you click the buttons by those names in the palette, the Viewer goes to the sites.

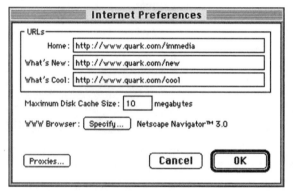

Figure 20-12: It's easy to customize your Viewer for the Internet.

The Viewer downloads pages and objects from a site to the disk cache, a part of your hard drive temporarily set aside for the Immedia Viewer, until it is ready to display them. Complex sites with movies, sound, or lots of scripts may require a larger disk cache. You can easily change the size of the cache in the Maximum Disk Cache Size field.

TIP

Downloaded information is saved in the disk cache until you fill it up or quit the Viewer. When you request a site you've recently visited, the Viewer looks first in the disk cache and then out on the Internet. You may be surprised sometime when you've disconnected from your service but still can move back and forth among the pages of the sites you've just seen!

Configuring Your Browser

When you install the QuarkImmedia Viewer, a README file tells you exactly what you need to do to configure your HTML browser to work with the Immedia Viewer.

In Netscape Navigator, the Options|General Preferences command displays a tabbed dialog box whose panels display a variety of preference settings. Access the Helper panel to add the QuarkImmedia Vewer as a helper application.

In the Helper panel, click the New button to add a new helper application. Specify the MIME type as "application" and the MIME subtype as "immedia." In the Extensions field, enter **imd**. To complete the designation, click the Browse button, which calls up a dialog box to locate the QuarkImmedia Viewer on your hard drive. Choose "Launch Application" as the appropriate action.

Microsoft Internet Explorer uses similar controls to specify the same settings. The Edit|Options command opens the Options dialog box. Use the Add button in the Helpers area to get the Configure File Type dialog box.

Enter a name to identify the Viewer in the Description field. QuarkImmedia will do nicely. Specify the MIME type as "application/immedia." In the Suffixes field enter **imd**.

In the How to Handle pop-up menu, all choices except Save as a File appear dimmed. If you click the Choose button next to the Helper Application field and locate the Immedia viewer, Save as a File will change to Use a Helper Application and display QuarkImmedia in the appropriate field. You'll have to enter **QDOC** in the File Type field.

The QuarkImmedia Viewer is designed only for Web sites created in QuarkImmedia. What does it do when you type in the URL for a site written in HyperText Markup Language (HTML)? You can configure Immedia to hand the URL over to your preferred HTML browser. Click the

Specify button in the WWW Browser field to open the Select a Browser dialog box and locate your browser. When the Immedia Viewer accesses an HTML site, it will automatically give the URL to your browser to display.

Conversely, it's a good idea to configure Immedia as a helper application for your HTML browser. When it encounters Web sites created in Immedia, the browser will hand over control to the Immedia Viewer. Configuring helper applications is usually done in the browser's preferences.

A number of networks have firewalls to prevent unauthorized access to software and files on a server or the computers and terminals attached to the network. The Proxies button opens a dialog box in which you enter the names of any servers you use to access networks outside of your own.

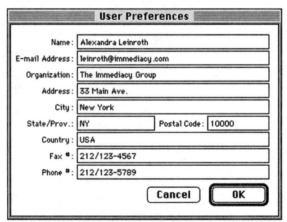

Figure 20-13: Enter identifying information about yourself in the User Preferences dialog box.

The User Preferences dialog box has a number of fields for information identifying yourself (Figure 20-13). You can design Immedia projects to access this information and write it to a file on your server where the information can be used in databases and other programs.

America Online & CompuServe Browsers
If you're an America Online or CompuServe subscriber, you will be able to use the QuarkImmedia Viewer if you can configure your connection to use other Internet applications. AOL users should contact America Online for exact instructions. CompuServe has online instructions for configuring PPP for use with Internet applications.

For those concerned about an Immedia project providing an entry for viruses, programs, or applets which might harm their system, the Security preferences can give some warning of changes being made to the files on your computer. You can also restrict all incoming information and scripts to a specified area or disk.

Moving On

For standard and CD-ROM exports the QuarkImmedia Viewer is quite simple, with only a few commands that you need to be concerned with. For Internet use, the Viewer has more options and is customizable.

The Internet Control palette gives you access to information about the state of the Viewer as well as recent and favorite Web sites. With Bookmarks and Preferences dialog boxes, you can add more information and capabilities.

Although the QuarkImmedia Viewer uses the HTTP protocol, it does not use HTML. The Viewer can be configured to open an HTML browser such as Netscape Navigator or Microsoft Internet Explorer, which will display the HTML-created site. Conversely, HTML browsers can be configured to open QuarkImmedia to display Immedia sites.

Now that you know how to use the Viewer to look at Web sites made with QuarkImmedia, it's time to learn how to optimize your sites for Internet delivery. In the next chapter we'll look at how to design Internet sites in QuarkImmedia and some of the special capabilities Immedia has for Internet projects.

chapter 21

Internet Controls

In the last chapter we looked at ways to navigate the Internet or an intranet using the QuarkImmedia Viewer's Internet Controls palette. What if you want more control? Can you build navigation into the buttons and objects of your project? Can you direct the user's path to and from your project? Definitely yes. Immedia has several Internet navigation actions that can be used in a project just like any other actions.

Perhaps even more useful are Immedia's capabilities of sending and receiving information. There are actions to send documents to users on your Intranet or at other Web sites. You can also have documents sent to your server, utilize the information in databases and applications, and send information back. You aren't limited to mouse clicks and text fields when you communicate with your users on the Internet.

Internet Navigation Controls

The Internet submenu of the Action pop-up menu has actions that you can use to guide the navigation of your users on the Web (Figure 21-1). Like all of the actions we've looked at, they can be assigned to user events and scripts. This means you can design Web projects to look like standard or CD-ROM projects.

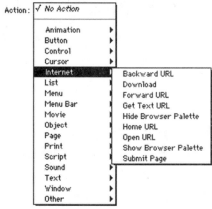

Figure 21-1: The Internet submenu of the Event and Script panels' Action pop-up menu.

Three of the buttons on the Internet Controls palette can be linked to actions in the Internet submenu of the Event and Script panels' Action pop-up menu. Backward URL, Forward URL, and Home are simple actions. There are no additional pop-ups or fields associated with them.

Action: [Backward URL]

Figure 21-2: The Backward URL action will send users to the site last visited.

- **Backward URL.** This will take the user back to the project previously visited. It's useful if you send users to another project or another part of the Internet and want to get them back to your project. When you use this button, users don't have to type in the URL (Figure 21-2).

Action: [Forward URL]

Figure 21-3: Forward URL returns users to the site where they used the Backward URL command.

- **Forward URL.** If users arrive at a page using Backward URL, Forward URL will return them to the page they left (Figure 21-3).

Action: [Home URL]

Figure 21-4: Home URL uses the URL entered in the Viewer preferences.

■ **Home URL.** This will send the users to the URL specified as Home in the preferences of their Viewers. If you have control over your users' Viewer preferences, you can define a URL as Home. Then, to send your users to that site, you only have to use this simple action (Figure 21-4).

TIP

Each page of an HTML site has its own URL. An Immedia project, however, is a unit with only one URL. An Internet action will send the QuarkImmedia Viewer to the first page of a project unless the action has fields in which you can indicate a specific page.

■ **Open URL.** This is the action that will give a Web address to the Immedia Viewer, enabling it to take the user to other Internet locations. When you select this action, you'll be able to select from two methods of entering the URL in the Method pop-up menu:

Action: [Open URL]
Method: [Enter URL]
URL: [http://www.quark.com]
Page: [1]
Return to: [Start of Project]

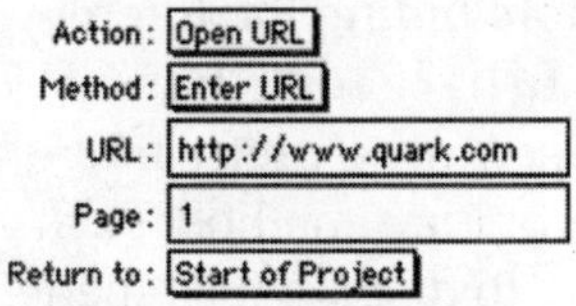

Figure 21-5: With Enter URL you put the URL into a field on the Event panel.

● **Enter URL.** When you choose this in the Method pop-up menu, Immedia will provide you with a field in which you can type a URL of an Immedia project (Figure 21-5). You can also indicate which page of a project you want to access in the Page field. The Return to pop-up menu lets you specify whether a Backward URL action or the Back button in the Internet Control palette will return the user to the current page or the start of the project.

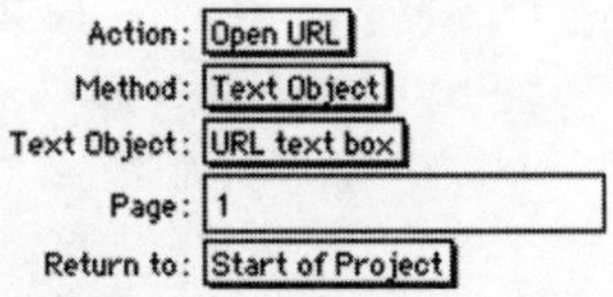

Action: [Open URL]
Method: [Text Object]
Text Object: [URL text box]
Page: [1]
Return to: [Start of Project]

Figure 21-6: Use Text Object to read a URL from a text box object, even user-entry text boxes.

● **Text Object.** This action will read text from any type of text box object—Simple Editable, Scrollable, Editable and Scrollable, or List (Figure 21-6). Editable and list text boxes offer users a way to type in a URL of their choice.

The Text Object pop-up menu for this action will give you a list of text box objects in the project from which it will read the URL. If the

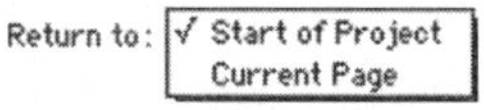

Return to: √ Start of Project
Current Page

Figure 21-7: The choice you make in the Return pop-up menu will tell the Viewer where in your project to go when using the Backward URL action.

Action: Hide Browser Palette

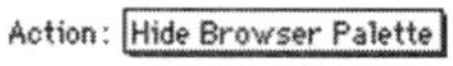

Figure 21-8: Hide the Internet Controls palette with the Hide Browser Palette action.

Action: Show Browser Palette

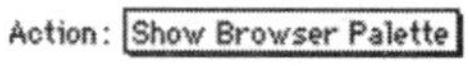

Figure 21-9: Use Show Browser Palette to bring the Internet Controls palette back into view.

text box is editable, the user can enter a URL directly. In the Page field you can indicate which page of the project specified by the URL the Viewer will go to. As with Enter URL, the Return pop-up menu gives you the choice of Current Project or Start of Project to choose where in the current project the user will return (Figure 21-7).

Immedia has a major advantage over HTML browsers, at least from a designer's point of view—the project doesn't have to be contained in a browser window. You can sweep all extraneous stuff off the screen, even hide menu bars. Of course, the QuarkImmedia Viewer does have its own palette, but even it can be dragged to the side of projects, if there's room. Your project can give a solo performance on the user's monitor.

There is a way to hide the Browser palette, leaving only your project displayed on the monitor. All it takes is a simple action in the Internet submenu: Hide Browser Palette (Figure 21-8). And it takes just one action to bring the palette back: Show Browser Palette (Figure 21-9).

You'll want to think carefully before hiding the Internet Controls palette. Most users expect to have some type of control over navigation—Internet users are a pretty independent bunch. You may want to provide a method, such as a keyboard command or a button, to display the palette again or allow the user to leave the project.

Internet Protocols With the Immedia Viewer

HTTP (HyperText Transfer Protocol) is not the only way to communicate on the Internet. There are four other protocols currently in use: FTP or file transfer protocol (ftp://), mail (mailto://), Usenet News (news://), and Gopher (gopher://).

➡

Almost any type of Internet document can be accessed with Open URL or Submit Page. Users can link to HTML projects using http:// with a URL, obtain software from FTP sites using ftp://, even send e-mail messages with mailto:// Users will need HTML browsers to read these projects. As we mentioned in the last chapter, the QuarkImmedia Viewer can be configured to hand off to an HTML browser.

Sending & Retrieving Text Over the Internet

In Chapter 16, "Text Box Objects," we explored user-entry text boxes, and ways of sending and retrieving text with QuarkImmedia. On the Internet, the Viewer must be given a specific URL and Internet protocol to send any text information. Read Text File and Write Text File don't provide a way to do this.

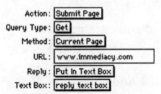

Figure 21-10: Use Submit Page to write files and send information to applications on Internet servers.

The Internet action Submit Page (Figure 21-10), like Write Text, enables the collection of information from a project or from the user's Viewer preferences, and sends it to a Web server. You can gather almost anything: survey information, requests for information, order forms, even the date entered in the user's Viewer preferences. The Submit Page action will send the following to a designated URL:

- The text in any editable text boxes on a page.

- Items that have been selected in pop-up menus and lists.

- The status of grouped and ungrouped buttons.

As you do with Write Text File action, you create editable or scrollable and editable text box objects in which users can type information and URLs. The Submit Page action requires that you specify a series of options in pop-up menus that accompany this action:

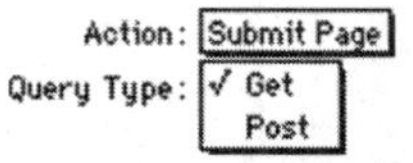

Figure 21-11: Query Type refers to the method by which information is sent to a Web server.

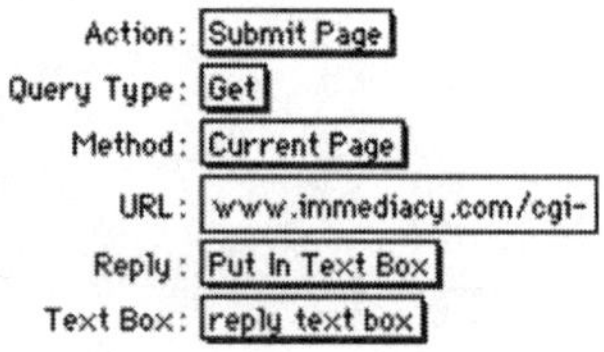

Figure 21-12: The URL for Submit Page is the CGI application or script that will process the information.

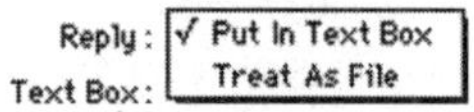

Figure 21-13: Tell the CGI application where in the user's project to return the processed information.

Figure 21-14: Use Get Text URL to retrieve ASCII files from other Web sites.

■ **Query Type.** To send this information to a server you must select a Query Type, either Get or Post (Figure 21-11). The method you'll use depends on how your systems administrator has configured your server.

■ **Method.** Do you want to send text from the current page or other pages in your project? The Method pop-up menu allows you to choose either the current page or another page, identified by number or name.

■ **URL.** You must provide a URL in the next field, the address of the software application that will process the information (Figure 21-12). You'll most likely use the HTTP protocol, so the URL will start with http://, but you can use other Internet protocols if you want.

■ **Reply.** After the CGI application has processed the information, it will send a reply to the QuarkImmedia Viewer. The Reply pop-up menu gives you a choice of what to do with the information the server returns. Use Put In Text Box to select a specific text box object which you must identify in the Text Box pop-up menu, or use Treat as File to write the file to your hard drive (Figure 21-13).

With Submit page, you're able to gather information from a project and send it on the Internet. How do you retrieve information from the Internet? Use Get Text URL to retrieve ASCII files (Figure 21-14), and Open URL to read other kinds of files. Like Open URL, Get Text URL provides two options in the Method pop-up menu—Enter URL or Text Object. If you choose Enter URL you must type an address into the URL field, then identify a text box object to receive the information in the Destination pop-up menu. You can use Text Object to provide users with a way to type in their own URLs.

Submissions to a Web Server

Information sent with HTTP protocol can easily be retrieved and used in software programs and databases. After the information is processed, an ASCII text reply will be sent to the QuarkImmedia Viewer that originated the information. A Web server will need software to do this. Most Web servers use a CGI (Common Gateway Interface) application, which can be written in a number of programming languages, to do this.

In HTTP, which both HTML browsers and the Immedia Viewer use, there are two ways to send information to a server—Get and Post. Get can only handle 256 characters, so Post is usually preferred.

If you plan to use the Submit Page action, speak to your Web administrator before you start to find out the method used and any special configurations needed. Since interacting with software on servers can lead to security problems, Web administrators are sometimes restrictive about the CGI programs used.

Action: Download
Type: Sound
Sound: harmonics.SND

Figure 21-15: The Download action can send files to the QuarkImmedia Viewer's cache.

The previous actions help a user navigate the Web and send or retrieve information on the Internet. The last action in the Internet submenu, Download, is used to send files to the QuarkImmedia Viewer's cache before they're needed by the project, so they'll be ready when called (Figure 21-15). With the Download action, you can specify what kind of file to retrieve in the Type pop-up menu—Animation, Movie, or Sound. Each choice presents you with a pop-up menu to select the specific file. The Download action is extremely useful. With careful planning you can design a project so that all large files are downloaded before any of the pages on which they're used; this way you can avoid making users wait for downloads. Any dead time in a project is a reason for users to leave your site and go elsewhere, so plan your projects carefully.

QuarkImmedia, HTML & the Web

The World Wide Web was created by Tim Berners-Lee in 1990 to facilitate the exchange of research and technical information among scientists and engineers who worked on a variety of incompatible platforms at CERN, a European center for research in nuclear physics. Because communication on the Web is based on ASCII text files, it doesn't accommodate many of the concerns of graphic designers—fonts and precise layout, for example. In fact, until Mosaic (the first graphic interface for the World Wide Web) appeared in 1993, almost all Web communication was completely text.

In the HTML browser that has evolved from Mosaic, the user, not the designer, has control over font choices, type size, and even color. The user also has control over the size of the browser window, thereby making exact layout difficult, if not impossible. There is no way, other than designing pages as one big graphic, to specify exact fonts and layout in an HTML browser.

With Immedia, you do have control over all of the elements of a page—all basic text objects and pictorial information are rasterized at export. Immedia creates one big picture file for each page. This means that the size of Immedia pages may be larger than HTML pages.

Designing for the Internet

Navigating the Internet through a modem can be slow. Corporate intranets, on the other hand, are fast. An Ethernet can transfer information as fast as 10 megabytes per second (mbps). This is seven times as fast as a T1 line and over 350 times as fast as a 28.8 kilobytes per second (kbps) modem. Designing for corporate intranets won't require much accommodation for bandwidth. But Immedia projects that will be downloaded with modems must be designed carefully.

A rule of thumb in HTML design is that 1K of information takes 1 second to download and display over a 14.4 kbps modem, the typical modem used for individuals to surf the Net. Most adults find their attention wandering after 20 or 30 seconds of waiting for an image or page—that's not much, only 20 to 30K of text or graphics! If your projects will be accessed by modem, it's essential that you design them to minimize download time.

TIP

Immedia has a built-in way to gauge download times conveniently. If you hold down the Option key while clicking the Save button during export, Immedia will create a summary of your project in a separate text file called Export Statistics. It identifies all exported elements and their approximate download times over 28.8 kbps modems and faster T1 lines.

So what takes up the most room in an Immedia project? Basically all of the graphic and media elements—movies, animation, graphics, and sound.

It's a good idea to compress most of your media elements before importing them into Quark. Immedia compresses all graphics and media elements, except sound and video, when exporting a project. It will compress movies and sounds if you select these options in the Export Settings dialog box. When compressing elements of a project, Immedia tries all the methods at its disposal and uses the one that gives the most compression, not necessarily the best image or sound quality. You may get better results from compression software designed for the specific media type.

To further slim down your project, avoid busy images and page-size photographs. Graphics with flat areas of color compress much better than images with lots of texture. The fewer colors used in a project, the smaller file sizes will be. Photoshop or DeBabelizer can reduce colors in a project for you.

Adobe Photoshop is useful for reducing image size and color bit depth, the number of colors used in a project. Equilibrium's DeBabelizer is also an excellent image-compression product and is used by most multimedia and Web production professionals. DeBabelizer has the capability of batch processing groups of images, something that Photoshop was unable to do before the most recent update, version 4.0.

For movies, programs like Adobe Premier and Terran Interactive's Movie Cleaner Pro will give excellent compression.

Reducing Color Using Color Palettes

A major way to reduce file size is to reduce the number of colors used in a project. Designers who create graphics for HTML pages know that images converted to Indexed Color using 256 colors have smaller file sizes. It's important to consider your color palette before jumping into the design of a project. Choices made early can prevent frustration at the end.

While Immedia will convert all graphic elements (except QuickTime movies) to a single palette of 256 specific colors, there are ways to obtain even more color reduction. In Photoshop, use the Mode|Indexed Color command to open the Indexed Color dialog box. Here you can select the color resolution or number of colors in a project, which is expressed as bits/pixel. Once you've converted an image to indexed color, use Mode|Color Table to open an dialog box in which you can see the color palette and save it to use in your project.

Equilibrium's DeBabelizer was designed to convert graphics to different file formats and color palettes. By pooling groups of images, it can create what it calls a superpalette, a palette that contains the best group of colors to use to display all of the images. When saved, the palette can also be used for projects in Immedia.

When a project is exported, all of the elements of the first page, and all of the buttons, cursors, and scripts used in a project are put together in one package and sent to the QuarkImmedia Viewer. It's important to choose these elements wisely to avoid excessive download times. Minimize the number of buttons and cursors in your project. If you can use objects as buttons or the default cursors, then do so. Also, keep the number of colors in a project to a minimum.

Movies, sound, and complex animation are the elements that require the most time to download. Unless you're on a corporate intranet, avoid digital video and complex animation in QuickTime. Instead use Immedia's animation capabilities, especially sliding objects and Item on a Path animation. If you must use movies of complex animation, put them in another project and give the user a choice of looking at them or not.

Exercise 21-1

Looking at projects created by others is an important part of learning. That's why we've put so many exercises in this book and included several other projects on the CD. There is also a growing number of Internet sites made in QuarkImmedia. In this exercise, we'll make a project that will take you on a quick tour of some of them.

1. Using File | New | Project, open the New Project dialog box. You don't need to make this project very large, we made ours 480 X 320 points. Leave the other settings at the defaults—Background color black, check Visible When Inactive, Project Window None, Position Center on Screen. Check Automatic Box and select Text in the pop-up menu.

    The project is a large text box. We'll add some text and a pop-up menu for navigation.

2. Select the text box created when you made this project. Open the Text Box Specifications dialog box using the Item | Modify command. Make the background color for the text box black. Change the setting in the Vertical Alignment pop-up menu to Center.

3. Using Item | Frame, put a 1-point black border around the text box. To make the border gray, select 50% in the Shade pop-up menu.

4. We're going to add text—type **QuarkImmedia Web Site Tour** in the text box. To make the text easy to read, use a bold font. We've used 14-point Futura Bold, but you may choose any font and style you'd like. Color the text white and make sure that the paragraph alignment is centered.

5. Let's add another line of text and then place a pop-up menu between the two lines of text. To make sure that there's enough room for the pop-up menu, create some space between the first and second lines of text. Use Style | Formats to open the Paragraph Formats dialog box and enter **90 pt** in the Space After field.

6. Type the words **Back**, **Forward**, **Browser**, and **Quit**, all separated by tabs. Using Style | Tabs, space these words evenly across the page.

Figure 21-16: Text and a pop-up menu will provide the navigation for this project.

7. Let's create a pop-up menu. Make a text box 270 X 20 points and place it in the center of the page. Figure 21-16 shows you what the project should look like at this point.

8. In the Object panel, make this text box a pop-up menu object and name it web sites.pu. We don't have a menu or title for this object yet, so leave the other pop-up menus related to this object as they are (Figure 21-17).

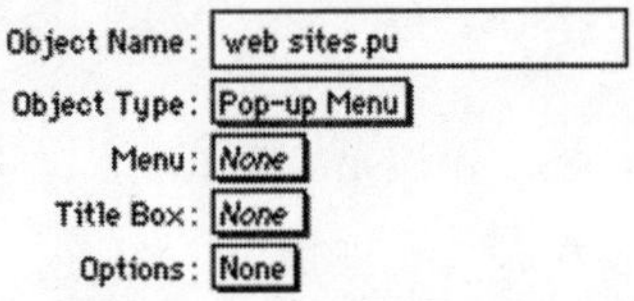

9. Each item that we place in the pop-up menu will have to have a script. Go to the Script panel and click the New button to create one. The first script will be for the Web site we've made to accompany this book. It's called Web Publishing With QuarkImmedia, but that's too long to fit in a pop-up menu. Our domain name is www.immediacy.com, so let's name this script Immediacy (Figure 21-18).

10. For the action, select Open URL. In the Method pop-up menu, select Enter URL and type our URL, **www.immediacy.com**, into the URL pop-up menu. To direct the QuarkImmedia Viewer to the project for this exercise, add a slash after the URL and enter the name of the project, ex22.imd. Figure 21-19 shows you what this should look like.

11. We can direct the Viewer to a specific page in a project. Page 2 relates to this exercise, so enter **2** in the Page pop-up menu. The next pop-up menu identifies the page in this project the user will return to as a result of clicking the Viewer's Back button. You can leave it set at Start of Project.

12. On the following page is a list of sites we've found interesting. Create a script, naming it the name in the first column and entering the URL in the second column into the URL field. You can speed up your work by duplicating this script and changing the name and URL for each site.

Object Name: web sites.pu
Object Type: Pop-up Menu
Menu: None
Title Box: None
Options: None

Figure 21-17: The text box will be a pop-up menu.

URL: .immediacy .com/ex22.imd

Figure 21-18: Create a script to take the user to our Web site.

Open URL Enter URL, "www.imm...

Action: Open URL
Method: Enter URL
URL: www.immediacy.com/ex2
Page: 2
Return to: Start of Project

Figure 21-19: The URL contains the name of the project as well as the address of the Web site.

We've given you the full URL for all of these sites. You can omit the protocol, http://, if you want. The Immedia Viewer will understand what to do.

Web Site	URL
Buttons	http://www.quark.com/buttons/buttons.imd
The Immedia Place	http://www.diac.com/~ptogel/i-place/i-place.imd
Quark Prototype Site	http://www.quark.com/prototype/prototype.imd
The Spice Web	http://channel3.vmg.co.uk/spicegirls/immedia/spicegirls.imd
Taterhead	http://www.quark.com/taterhead/taterhead.imd
Togel Mania	http://www.diac.com/~ptogel/immedia/home.imd
Van Goertze & Van Hove	http://www.uslink.net/~vgvh/vgvh.imd
WebTricks	http://www.quark.com/webtricks/webtricks.imd

Table 21-1: Some interesting Web sites.

Are you wondering why we haven't included the QuarkImmedia Web site in this list? Your QuarkImmedia Viewer comes with preset defaults for the Home, New, and Cool buttons. Home is set to the QuarkImmedia Web site, www.quark.com/immedia (Figure 21-20). When you make a script to send the Viewer to the QuarkImmedia Web site, you can simply use the action Home and the Viewer will get the URL from the Internet preferences.

13. Make a new script and name it QuarkImmedia. Then select Home in the Action pop-up menu.

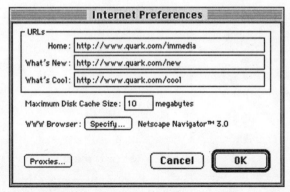

Figure 21-20: In the User preferences, Home is defined as the QuarkImmedia Web Site.

We have our scripts. Now it's time to put them together in a menu.

14. Use the QuarkImmedia | MenuMaker command to open the MenuMaker dialog box. In the Menus area, click the New button to create a new menu; name it Immedia sites.

15. Click the New button in the Menu Items area to create a new menu item for each script. Name each item in the Name field with the name of the script. Then select the script in the Script pop-up (Figure 21-21). When you've entered all the scripts, click OK or hit Return. Don't hit Return before you've entered all of the scripts—you'll close the dialog box!

Figure 21-21: In the MenuMaker create individual Menu Items for each script.

Figure 21-22: Select this menu in the Menu pop-up.

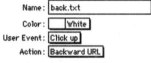

Figure 21-23: For the word, select the Backward URL Action.

Figure 21-24: Use Forward URL as the Action for the Forward hot text.

16. We have the menu and it's a simple action to attach it to the pop-up menu object we made earlier. Go to the Object panel and select Immedia sites in the Menu pop-up (Figure 21-22).

17. Save the project, naming it Websites.qxd. Engage, using QuarkImmedia | Engage or F15, to test the project. You won't be able to access any of the Web sites until the project is exported, but you will be able to see if the menu items appear in the pop-up menu.

Let's now turn our attention to the text under the pop-up menu. We can make each word interactive and assign actions to them that will aid the user in navigating the Internet.

18. Select the first word in the line, Back, and go to the Hot Text panel. In the Name field, name this text back.txt. For the Click up user event select Internet | Backward URL in the Action pop-up menu. When the user clicks this word, the Viewer will go to the site previous to this one (Figure 21-23).

19. Select the second word in the line, Forward. In the Hot Text panel name this text forward.txt. For the Click up user event select Internet | Forward URL (Figure 21-24). When the user clicks this word, the Viewer will go to the site the user was on when he or she clicked Back.

20. Select Browser and name it browser.txt in the Hot Text panel. For the Click up user event select Internet | Show Browser Palette in the Action pop-up menu. The user can easily close the Internet Controls palette, and this command will open the palette again.

21. If users do close the Internet Controls palette, they will need a way to quit this project. Select the word Quit. Name it quit.txt in the Hot Text panel and select Other | Quit in the Action pop-up menu.

22. Save the project. To test this project on the Internet, you'll have to export it. Use QuarkImmedia | Export Settings to open the Export Settings dialog box.

23. In the General panel, enter the name of this project, QuarkImmedia Web Site Tour, in the Project Name field. This is the name that will be saved if the project is bookmarked, not the name of the exported file, so you aren't restricted to legal file names with .imd extensions (Figure 21-25).

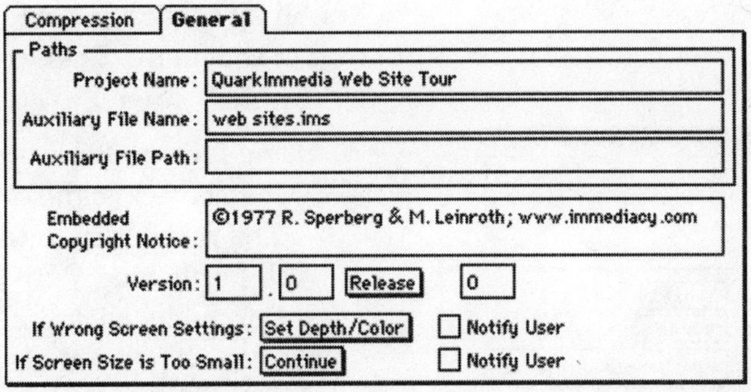

Compression	**General**

Paths

Project Name : QuarkImmedia Web Site Tour

Auxiliary File Name : web sites.ims

Auxiliary File Path :

Embedded Copyright Notice : ©1977 R. Sperberg & M. Leinroth; www.immediacy.com

Version : 1 . 0 Release 0

If Wrong Screen Settings : Set Depth/Color ☐ Notify User

If Screen Size is Too Small : Continue ☐ Notify User

Figure 21-25: Make sure to check Export Settings before exporting your project.

In the Auxiliary File Name field enter web sites.ims.

24. Export your project. Make sure that you add the .imd extension to the file name so users with a Windows Viewer can read your project. In the Export Format pop-up menu select Internet (many files) (Figure 21-26).

Save Export file as:

Websites.imd

Export Format: ✓Standard (one file) CD-ROM (two files) Internet (many files)

Figure 21-26: Select Internet (many files) when you export the project.

25. To test your project, open your QuarkImmedia Viewer. Use the File | Open command to open the project. If you have Internet access from your computer you can visit these sites.

Exercise 21-2

Navigation commands in the menu bar are a good choice if you want to give users the ability to return to your site at any moment or go to any URL of their choice without the Internet Controls palette obstructing their view of your project.

You must make scripts for each command you want placed in the menu. Then use the MenuMaker in the QuarkImmedia menu to create the menu items.

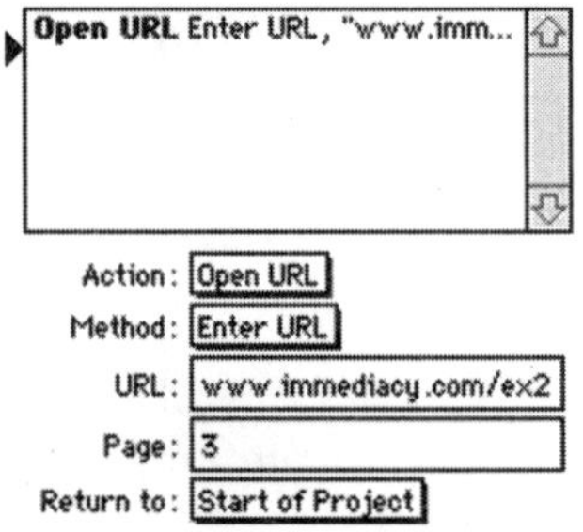

1. Using File | New | Project, create a new project 512 pts X 384 pts. Leave the other settings at the defaults.

    The first script in the menu will take users to the Web Publishing With QuarkImmedia site. In the Script panel, click the New button to make a new script and name this script Go to Immediacy.scr (Figure 21-27). To attach a URL to this command, we'll use the Open URL action, which you can select in the Action | Internet pop-up menu.

2. Since we want this URL to be permanently attached to the command, select Enter URL in the Method pop-up and type in the URL for this exercise, **http://www.immediacy.com/ex22.imd**, in the URL field. This time we'll send the users to page 3, so type **3** in the Page field.

3. To let the Viewer know to send users back to this project when they click the Back button, select Current Page in the Return to pop-up menu.

The next script will call up a floating palette in which users can type in the URL of their choice. You can create this on the pasteboard for page 1, so it will be downloaded with the first page and users can access it immediately.

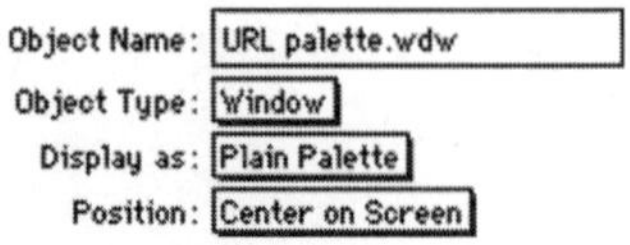

4. Make a text box 300 points wide and 100 points high on the pasteboard for page 1. This will be the floating palette, so define it as a plain palette window and name it URL palette.wdw (Figure 21-28).

5. In the window create another text box, this time 200 points wide and 25 points high. This will be the text box in which users can enter their desired URL, so

Action: Open URL
Method: Enter URL
URL: www.immediacy.com/ex2
Page: 3
Return to: Start of Project

Figure 21-27: Create a script to go to the Immediacy site.

Object Name: URL palette.wdw
Object Type: Window
Display as: Plain Palette
Position: Center on Screen

Figure 21-28: Create a floating palette for users to enter URLs.

name it URL box.txt and define it as a text box object. In the Display as pop-up menu, select Editable and leave the other pop-up menus at their default settings.

So that this text box will show up on the palette, give it a 1-point frame using the Item | Frame command.

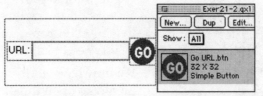

Figure 21-29: Add a button from the button library to send the URL to the QuarkImmedia Viewer.

6. We'll use a button to send the information to the project when the users have typed in the URL. We've made one for you and put it in the button library for this exercise, Exer22-2.qxl. Open the button library and drag the button onto the window. It should be labeled Go URL.btn (Figure 21-29).

7. Now for the command to notify the Viewer that the user wants to go to another URL. This will be an action for the Click up state of the button, so make sure the button object is selected and choose Click up in the User Event pop-up menu of the Event palette.

8. In the Action pop-up menu, again select Open URL. This time, select Text Box in the Method pop-up menu and enter **3** in the Page field. Once again, choose Current Page in the Return to pop-up menu (Figure 21-30).

9. Time to create the script that will open this window. In the Script panel, click the New button to create a new script. Name this script Go to.scr. In the Action pop-up menu select Open Window and identify this window, URL palette.wdw, in the Window pop-up menu.

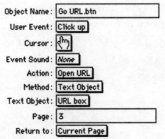

Figure 21-30: At Click up, the button will send the Viewer to the new URL.

Users may want to access the full functionality of the Internet Control palette, so we'll make the last item on the menu a command to open it.

10. Create another script in the Script panel. Call this one Show Browser.scr. Then select Show Browser Palette from the Internet submenu in the Action pop-up menu.

11. We do want to provide a way for users to leave the Viewer. Create another new script and call it Quit.scr. In the Action pop-up menu select Other | Quit. That's all you need to do.

12. We now have all the elements we need to create the menu. So open the MenuMaker using QuarkImmedia | MenuMaker. Click the New Button in the Menus area to create a new Menu. Call it Internet. In the Menu Items area click the New button to create the first menu item.
    a. We want www.immediacy.com to be the first choice in the list, so type **Immediacy** in the Name field. Select the script you wrote to do this, Go to Immediacy.scr, in the Script pop-up menu.
    b. The next command to show up in the menu will be Go to, which will open the URL palette. Click the New button again to add a menu item and type **Go to** in the Name field. This time select Go to.scr in the Script pop-up menu.
    c. To add the script that will present the Internet Control palette to the user, click New in the Menu Items area once more and type **Show Browser** in the Name field. Select Show Browser.scr in the Script field. You've created the commands that we wanted to put in this menu, so click the OK button and return to the project.

13. Finally, we'll add the script we made to quit the project, Quit.scr. The Menu Items area should look like Figure 21-31. Click OK to leave the MenuMaker.

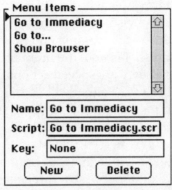

Figure 21-31: Menu items in the menu bar will enable the user to navigate the Internet.

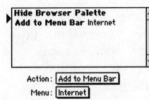

Figure 21-32: A script will hide the Internet Controls palette and add your menu to the Menu Bar.

14. The last thing we need to do is make sure that the Internet Controls palette isn't showing when the project opens. To do this we'll need one more script, so return to the Script panel and click the New button one final time. Name this script Project Entry.scr. In the Action | Internet pop-up menu, select Hide Browser Palette from the Internet submenu. Then add an action to add the menu to the Menu Bar (Figure 21-32).

Internet commands don't work in Engage mode. To test this completely, you'll need to export the project and go online using the Viewer. The project itself doesn't need to be put on a Web server. You or any other user can access it from a hard drive, so make a standard export and embed a Viewer if you want.

Moving On

Keep in mind that transferring information is one of the major strengths of the Internet. There's enough bandwidth for people who want cinematic animation and sophisticated visual entertainment on TV or in the movies. But to access information and update published information in a timely fashion, the Internet's by far the best way.

There are special actions that will control the Internet browser—either embedding URLs or allowing users to type in their own. If you want to hide the Internet browser, there's an action to do that. As well, there are commands with which you can send text information to Web servers and retrieve text files from other sites on the Web.

Ethernet-based intranets have little problem handling some of the complex graphics that sophisticated professionals create. But designing for optimum viewing at lower bandwidth is a little trickier with T1 and ISDN lines and a challenge for modem-based Internet access.

When designing for low bandwidth, think small—small project pages, small graphics, small media elements. Take advantage of anything that will lead to small file sizes.

With this chapter, we've finished the basic techniques section of the book. You now have the tools to create, export, and view your projects as well as to facilitate the users' viewing of them. For a great number of the projects you'll create, these may be all the tools you need.

There is more to Immedia—more than we can fit into this book. We do want to introduce you to a few of these advanced concepts. In the next chapter, we'll go over the actions of the Control submenu that provide programming-like options to Immedia projects.

chapter 22

Advanced Features

Immedia is designed to be easy to learn—its processes are structured so you don't have to be a programmer to do neat things in your projects. Still, programming isn't all bad. When you get Immedia to do one thing when a window is onscreen and another when it's not, or to delay starting some action until a video or audio clip finishes playing, that requires programming. And we have the rudiments of programming in Immedia, located in the Control submenu (Figure 22-1).

Scripts are just lists of actions. They're not programs. However, when we use the Control submenu actions, each line of a script serves as a line of programming. And the three basic programming constructs that we have appear in our scripts in pairs: If/End If, Loop/End Loop, and While/End While. Their names reflect how they work:

- Do this IF something is true (or false).

- Keep doing this, repeatedly.

- Do this WHILE something else is happening (or not yet happening).

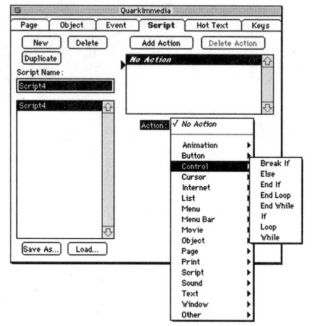

Figure 22-1: The Control submenu.

Using Control commands involves choosing If testing, While testing, or basic looping; setting up some sort of test; and then coming out of the loop or test.

It may sound complicated, but once you can use the Control submenu to guide your scripts, your projects can behave more responsively and be less complicated onscreen, because more is going on behind the scenes.

▌ The Constructs

The first thing you must know about the If/End If, Loop/ End Loop, and While/End While constructs is that they come in pairs. You put in one action to officially begin the construct and then another End action that says "all done." And in between these two actions you put in the action(s) you want to perform.

If you forget the End action, when you attempt to work with another script or in another panel (anywhere else but right in that script), you will get a reminder that you've committed a scripting faux pas and you must correct it right away. Immedia won't let that script go until you do.

If Testing

If testing follows one of two forms. The first looks something like this:

> If condition A holds true,
> Then perform one or more actions.
> Otherwise, skip these actions and jump to what
>   follows.
> Always finish up by stating that the If construct
>   is now ended.

Here's an example of when you might use this. The user clicks on a picture in your catalog and you want to open up a window with a description and pricing information. What if they've already clicked on six other pictures? Do you want to have seven windows piled on the screen all at once? With If testing, you would do something like this:

> If there's a window open onscreen,
> Close this window.
> End if.
> Now open the window with the information just
>   requested.

The alternate form simply goes one step further and tells Immedia what to do if the condition being tested turns out not to be true:

> If some particular condition holds true,
> Perform one or more actions.
> Otherwise perform these alternate actions.
> State that everything is officially ended.

The "otherwise" appears in the guise of an Else command, so you might see this alternate form referred to as If/Then/Else.

As you can see, If and End If always appear in pairs, at the beginning and end of the If statement. The Else is optional. The If action always tests if something is true, and then follows the actions that occur if it's true. If it's not true, the script can either go to other actions, following an Else action, or just end things, with the End If action.

Tests

What kinds of things can be tested in an If statement? Here's a list of conditions you'll find in the Is/Has pop-up menus (Figure 22-2):

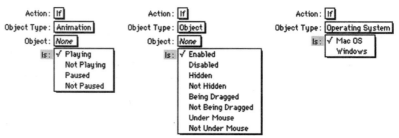

Figure 22-2: The Is/Has pop-up menus.

- With an animation or movie—is it playing or paused? (and the opposites—not playing or not paused?)

- With a button—is a button on or off? Enabled or disabled? Hidden or not hidden?

- With an editable text box object—is it empty or not empty?

- With an object—is it being dragged (or has that finished)? Is it underneath a mouse pointer or not? Is it enabled or disabled? Is it hidden or not hidden?

- With a script—is it running or not? Is it enabled or disabled?

- With a sound—is it playing or finished playing? Is it paused or not?

- With a window—is a window open or not?

- With the computer's operating system—is it the Macintosh OS or Microsoft Windows?

- With a page—is this specific page the current page or not?

- With a download—is it a specific animation, video, or sound?

- With lists—is the list empty or not? Is no item selected? Is the first or last or some other item selected? Has the selection changed?

In most of the tests, you can specify whether something is happening, or whether it's not happening—*Is a video paused? Is it not paused?* Although it makes this list longer, it simplifies your testing because you can establish exactly the condition you want to match.

The Is/Has tests listed here are the same conditions you test in While and Loop.

While/End While

The While/End While action pair isn't that different from If testing. But instead of your deciding to initiate some actions based on the test, this construct *continues* actions based on the test.

For instance, in your project you can allow a user to drag objects around the display. You use a While test this way:

While the user is dragging this picture,
Play a particular sound.
When the dragging stops, stop the sound.

The conditions you test for are the same as with If statements. The actions you put in between the While test and the End While statement continue only as long as the condition is being matched. Then the script proceeds to the next action.

▌Looping

Use the Looping construct to repeat an action or series of actions indefinitely. In between the Loop and End Loop actions, you position a Break If test, which specifies when to stop the loop. Break If tests the same things an If test does.

For instance, in a kiosk-type situation you might want to alternate two audio pieces as the background sound until a user clicks somewhere and starts some action— play a video, go to a different page, run a script, whatever activity would be launched from that screen. Your Loop script would look something like this:

> Loop.
> Play sound 1.
> Now play sound 2.
> Break if the script that plays the video
>   introduction starts.
> Break if the user goes to another page.
> Anything after this End Loop action isn't part of
>   the loop.

Note that you need at least one Break If statement in between the Loop and End Loop actions. Otherwise you'll make an endless loop.

If you want to break out of a loop by user activity like clicking, you need to use the Allow User Interaction command before the loop.

Allow User Interaction

Basically, this command says, *Don't ignore user clicks while scripts are running.* Otherwise, Immedia will simply wait to deal with any user clicks or whatnot until it's finished processing any actions and all the scripts are finished running.

If two scripts are running simultaneously, they both must include Allow User Interaction statements. If it's missing in one of those scripts, that will naturally prevent the user click from being allowed anywhere at all at that time.

> **TIP**
>
> *The corollary action to Allow User Interaction is Flush User Events. Over the Internet, and on a slow computer, there may be a delay between the click that triggers some action and the action taking place. If the user clicks repeatedly while waiting for things to happen, those clicks go into a queue for processing when the project catches up. But the click after the action has taken place may not have the same meaning as before—clicking on a go-to-next-page button might mean "go to page 2" for the first click, but after the project performs that action, a click in the same place would mean "go to page 3" and the user would leave page 2 before getting to see it. The Flush User Events action takes those clicks out of the queue.*
>
> *Where would you use this action? With the example just cited, it could appear in the page entry script for page 2. Or you might want it in the scripts that run with a play/pause/resume button. This could prevent a second click of frustration from stopping a movie that has finally started.*

Nesting

You can put these testing constructs inside each other. Inside the test that determines whether a script is running can be another test for whether a movie is playing or whether the project is still on the first page.

Just remember to include the End action for this second test—and it goes *before* the End action of the first test. Nesting looks like this:

```
If the Who-we-are script is playing,
Play Company-fight-song background sound.
    If Company-History page is current,
    Play Company-cheer sound.
    End the If test for the page.
End the If test for the script.
```

You can use nesting to build tests for three conditions (or more). As it stands, If/Then/Else statements branch one way if the tested condition is true, and another if it's not true. In that second branch, you can put another test. For example, on the payment section of an order form, the first test might ask, *Are you paying by check?* The yes answer jumps to a page with pay-by-check questions. The no answer means a credit-card payment. So following the Else action you'll want another If test: *Are you using Visa?* which takes you to the Visa page if true and the MasterCard page if not.

Let's see how these tests work in action.

Exercise 22-1

In this exercise, we'll work with the scorekeeping project created in Chapter 16, "Text Box Objects." We had a user-entry box there for the name of the person submitting the competition results. This box was to be filled in automatically from the Viewer preferences. But if that field is blank, we won't know who has submitted the results. So we'll make a window asking the user to complete the box and only open the window if the user attempts to quit the project without supplying a name.

Set Up

1. Open the Scorkeep.qxd project from Chapter 16, "Text Box Objects," or Exer22-1 in the Exercises folder on the Companion CD-ROM.

Please enter your name in the Observer field so we know who supplied this information.

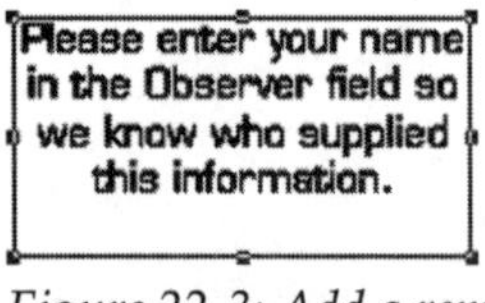

Figure 22-3: Add a reminder box to the pasteboard.

2. Go to page 2 of the project and add a text box on the pasteboard. Make it 2 inches wide by 1 inch high. Enter this text, in 12-point bold type: **Please enter your name in the Observer field so we know who supplied this information** (Figure 22-3).

   Define the text box as a standard window object, called "Reminder.wdw," as shown in Figure 22-4. It should show up in the center of the screen. Include Window Title and Include Close Box should be checked.

Object Name : | Reminder.wdw |

Object Type : | Window |

Display as : | Standard |

Position : | Center on Screen |

⬜ from left   ⬜ from top

☒ Include Window Title :

| Reminder |

⬜ Remember Window Position

☒ Include Close Box

Figure 22-4: Define as a window object.

Adding an If Test

Currently, when a user finishes entering information, clicking the Done button activates the All done.scr script, which writes the contents of the date, time, and score-keeper name fields to a text file, and then quits the project.

We'll add a test to see if the field is empty or not, then either proceed with closing down, or open the reminder window.

3. In the Script panel, edit the All done.scr.

At the beginning of the script, add a *No Action* placeholder. Replace the placeholder with the Control | If action.

Set Object Type to Editable Text, specifying Score reporter.tbo as the text box object we're interested in.

Set the Is pop-up menu to Not Empty (Figure 22-5).

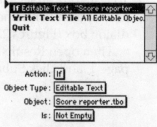

If Editable Text, "Score reporter...
Write Text File All Editable Objec
Quit

Action : | If |

Object Type : | Editable Text |

Object : | Score reporter.tbo |

Is : | Not Empty |

Figure 22-5: Edit the All done.scr to test whether the name field is not empty.

If Editable Text, "Score reporter...
▶ Write Text File All Editable Objec
Quit
Else
Open Window "Reminder.wdw",...
End If

Action: [Open Window]
Window: [Reminder.wdw]
Transition: [Default]
Sound: [None]
Trans. Time: [0]

Figure 22-6: The completed script.

4. Below the Quit command, add three *No Action* place holders.

- Replace the first with the Control I Else action.

- Set the next action to Window I Open, specifying Reminder.wdw.

- Replace the last place holder with the Control I End If action (Figure 22-6).

5. Save this project as Reminder.qxd.

Here's what happens—when the user clicks the Done button, that triggers this script. If the box is not empty, the information is written to the text file and the project quits. If it is empty, the reminder window opens. Since it has a Close box, the user can remove it from the screen. Whether or not the box is filled in, clicking the Done button repeats these steps again.

Test

When you use the Engage command, Immedia puts the name of the automatically entered field in boxes whose information is supplied from the QuarkImmedia Viewer preferences. So we can't test this feature by using Engage. Instead we'll need to export the project and use the Viewer to see how this works.

6. Use QuarkImmedia I Export to create a Results.imd project.

7. To test your project, launch QuarkImmedia Viewer and delete your name from the User Preferences dialog box (Figures 22-7 and 22-8).

Then open Results.imd. Enter information on page 1, and click Submit, which takes you to page 2.

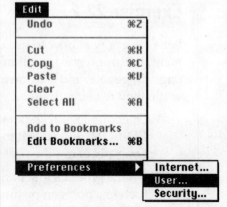

Figure 22-7: Edit | Preferences | User submenu.

User Preferences

Name :	
E-mail Address :	sgiotto@immediacy.com
Organization :	The Immediacy Group
Address :	75 Prospect Park West 1B
City :	Brroklyn
State/Prov. :	NY Postal Code : 11215
Country :	USA
Fax # :	212-572-4914
Phone # :	212-572-2252

Cancel   OK

Figure 22-8: User Preferences in QuarkImmedia Viewer.

Note what happens now. The observer name field is empty. Clicking the Done button will call up the Reminder box. Only when information appears in the box will clicking on the Done button quit the project. (In a more finished version of this project, you would want to collect this information first, before allowing users to enter scores, and put in a Cancel button to let unauthorized visitors exit without supplying their names.)

▊ Exercise 22-2

Let's look now at how to use the While/End While statement. In this exercise, we'll make some graphics on our page draggable, and play an appropriate sound for each while they're being dragged.

1. Open the Exer22-2.qxd project from the Companion CD-ROM, and save it to your local hard disk as Drag-pix.qxd.

2. On the project's first page, there are three graphics, each in a polygon picture box so they are silhouetted.

   The boxes are already defined as basic objects, named Songbird.obj, Skillet.obj, and Red car.obj (Figure 22-9).

Figure 22-9: Three graphics comprise three objects.

Sneak Preview

For the Click down user event for each graphic, we want to make the box draggable—pressing the mouse button over the image allows us to drag it to a different spot on the page. While we're dragging, we want a sound to play that's appropriate to the graphic.

The songbird is already set up so you can see how this works.

3. Engage the project and attempt to drag each object. When you drag the bird, chirping sounds play. Disengage and return to the project.

Making the Conditional Scripts

In the Script panel, you can study the Songbird.scr script. We will make similar scripts for the skillet and red car.

As we put together this script, we'll add a number of actions until there are seven altogether. We'll add them in a logical flow, so inserting the *No Action* place holders will occur in the middle of the script, according to the placement of the insertion triangle. Before we test things out, we'll review the sequence of the script actions.

4. Make a new script, called Skillet.scr.

5. To begin, we'll use Other | Allow User Interaction. This will allow Immedia to pay attention to the mouse while it's processing the various actions (Figure 22-10).

Figure 22-10: Choose Other | Allow User Interaction as the first action in the script.

6. Make Skillet.obj draggable by choosing Object | Drag, and specifying this object.

The last action in this script should turn this off, so make it now—Object | Stop Drag (Figure 22-11).

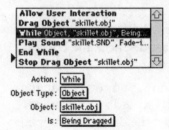

Figure 22-11: The Object Drag action allows users to drag the object around the screen.

7. Now for playing the sound. Add three place holders.

With the first place holder, choose Control | While. We want to test whether our box is being dragged, so in the Object Type pop-up menu choose Object, and in the Is pop-up menu choose Being Dragged. Specify the Skillet.obj (Figure 22-12).

Each While action is paired with an End While action. It's a good idea to put this in your script at the same time so you can keep track of things. Change the third place holder to Control | End While.

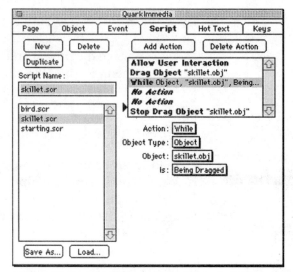

Figure 22-12: The While action will test whether the object is being dragged.

```
Allow User Interaction
Drag Object "skillet.obj"
While Object, "skillet.obj", Being...
Play Sound "skillet.SND", Fade-i...
End While
Stop Drag Object "skillet.obj"
```
Action: Play Sound
Sound: skillet.SND
Fade-in sec.: 0
☒ Loop

Figure 22-13: Inside the While statement is the Play Sound command.

```
Drag Object "skillet.obj"
While Object, "skillet.obj", Being...
Play Sound "skillet.SND", Fade-i...
End While
Stop Sound "skillet.SND", Fade-o...
Stop Drag Object "skillet.obj"
```
Action: Stop Sound
Sound: skillet.SND
Fade-out sec.: 0

Figure 22-14: Put the Stop Sound command outside the While statement.

The middle place holder will be our action: Sound | Play. Specify Skillet.snd. Check the Loop option (Figure 22-13).

8. If you engaged the project now, you could drag the skillet and the frying sounds would begin playing, but they wouldn't stop when the dragging stopped. We have to add an action for that, after the completion of the While/End While statement.

Following the End While action, insert a *No Action* place holder and set it to Sound | Stop, specifying Skillet.snd (Figure 22-14).

9. Making a similar script for the red car can be done by simply duplicating the Skillet.scr script, renaming it, and substituting the red car object and car sounds for the skillet object and frying sounds of the Skillet.scr script.

Duplicate Skillet.scr and rename this duplicate Red car.scr.

In the Drag Object and the While Object actions, replace the references to Skillet.obj with references to Red car.obj.

In the Play Sound and Stop Sound actions, replace references to Skillet.snd with references to Motor.snd.

10. Let's make one addition to this script. Insert a *No Action* place holder as the second action. Choose Sound | Play and specify Beepbeep.snd (Figure 22-15). Each time you begin dragging the red car, you'll start out with a horn beeping and then loop the motor-revving sound.

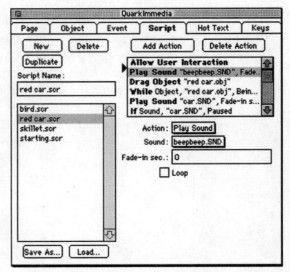

Figure 22-15: Insert a command to play a horn beeping each time the user begins to drag the red car.

11. For the Click down user event for the Skillet.obj, choose Script | Run, and specify Skillet.scr.

Similarly, for the Click down user event for the Red car.obj, choose Script | Run, and specify Red car.scr.

12. Save and engage the project.

Wrap Up

When we want our project to interact intelligently with the user, varying its responses as conditions change, the Control submenu provides the power to institute tests of what's going on onscreen.

The If/End If, While/End While, and Loop/End Loop constructs enable our action list to mimic programs, without our really needing to learn programming.

Over the course of this book, you've learned how to use the broad range of Immedia's features, from the simplest actions, like setting up a trigger to go to the next page, to playing videos and sound tracks, to creating animation that can make the screen swirl. (And your head whirl!) Windows and palettes and menus attest to your ability to make Immedia projects behave in line with users' expectations of computer interaction. Creating forms, changing content on the fly, sending information over the Internet: publishing today places many more demands on the content provider, and Immedia is here to help.

Enjoy your work with Immedia!

Appendix A

About the Companion CD-ROM

The CD-ROM included with your copy of *Web Publishing With QuarkImmedia* contains exercise files and software programs that complement the book.

Installation

Each software program resides in its own directory on the CD-ROM. The exercises are found in the Exercise folder, which also has subfolders named after the chapters of the book in which the exercises appear.

To install either of the two Macintosh software programs, simply go to the Programs Folder on your Macintosh desktop (after inserting the CD-ROM) and launch the desired program's installer. **Note:** there is no Windows software on the CD-ROM. At the time of printing, the final version of the QuarkImmedia Viewer for Windows was not yet available. You can, however, download the beta version of the Windows Viewer for free from the Quark Web site at http://www.quark.com.

Completed projects can be run from the CD-ROM. To use the exercises, copy the desired folder from the CD-ROM to the hard drive. See the corresponding chapter in the book for information on how to use the exercises on the CD-ROM. Each exercise folder contains files used in the construction of the project, as well as finished and exported versions for your study.

Software Descriptions

■ **QuarkImmedia Viewer Demo 1.01 (Macintosh version)**   The QuarkImmedia Viewer is a stand-alone application that allows those without access to QuarkXPress or QuarkImmedia to view Quark-Immedia projects. You can export projects in a platform-independent format viewable with the QuarkImmedia Viewer, or you can embed a copy of QuarkImmedia Viewer right in your exported project. See Chapter 21, "Internet Controls," for information on how to customize the Viewer for navigating the Internet.

■ **QuarkXPress Demo Version 3.32r5 (Macintosh version)**   An integrated publishing package that allows you to combine pictures, text, typography, writing, editing, and printing—in one package. The QuarkImmedia demo extension is part of this QuarkXPress demo version. This is a save-disabled version. You will be able to try out all of the exercises and create your own projects in both QuarkXPress and QuarkImmedia but you won't be able to save them. If you'd like more information about XPress or need to learn it, see Appendix B, "QuarkXPress References," for a list of books about the program.

Note: You may have to use Apple QuickTime and/or Sound Manager in conjunction with the Quark software described above. If you do not already have it, you may obtain QuickTime at http://www.quicktime.apple.com/ on the World Wide Web. Sound Manager 3.2 is built into System 7.5.3 and later.

QuarkImmedia Projects

■ **"Connect With QuarkImmedia" and "Launch Brochure"**   These are two completed projects that demonstrate what you can do with QuarkImmedia. They are in their own folders.

Technical Support

Technical support is available for installation-related problems only. The technical support office is open from 8:00 A.M. to 6:00 P.M. Monday through Friday and can be reached via the following methods:

Phone: (919) 544-9404 extension 81

Faxback Answer System: (919) 544-9404 extension 85

E-mail: help@vmedia.com

FAX: (919) 544-9472

World Wide Web: http://www.vmedia.com/support

America Online: keyword *Ventana*

Limits of Liability & Disclaimer of Warranty

The authors and publisher of this book have used their best efforts in preparing the CD-ROM and the programs contained in it. These efforts include the development, research, and testing of the theories and programs to determine their effectiveness. The authors and publisher make no warranty of any kind expressed or implied, with regard to these programs or the documentation contained in this book.

The authors and publisher shall not be liable in the event of incidental or consequential damages in connection with, or arising out of, the furnishing, performance, or use of the programs, associated instructions, and/or claims of productivity gains.

Some of the software on this CD-ROM is shareware; there may be additional charges (owed to the software authors/makers) incurred for their registration and continued use. See individual program's README or VREADME.TXT files for more information.

Appendix B

QuarkXPress References

We have written this book for those who already use QuarkXPress, but if your grasp of XPress leaves something to be desired, check out some of the source material available on XPress:

- Joe Grossman, *Looking Good With QuarkXPress: The Designer's Companion for Mac & Windows* (Ventana). This book comes with a Companion CD-ROM filled with useful ancillary material.

- Elaine Weinman, *Visual Quickstart QuarkXPress* (Peachpit Press).

- David Blatner & Eric Taub, *The QuarkXPress Book* (Peachpit Press).

- Diane Burns & S.Venit, *The Official QuarkXPress Handbook* (Random House Electronic Books).

- QUI, the international QuarkXPress user group, is a terrific resource for those who work with XPress. QUI can be reached at PO Box 170, Salem, NH 03079; telephone (603) 898-2822, fax (603)898-3393.

Online Resources

Quark has both HTML and Immedia pages on its Internet site, www.quark.com. In the technical support area, a "related sites" links page points you to other sites of interest.

- The Online Companion for Joe Grossman's *Looking Good With QuarkXPress* (www.vmedia.com/vvc/onlcomp/lgwquark/index.html) has a QuarkXPress and desktop-publishing resource link page.

- One of those included in that list is Bob Gale's XPresso Bar (www.halcyon.com/bobgale/xpresso.html), with many tips, references, and links.

- Frank Romano, the godfather of electronic publishing, has a Web page at www.rit.edu/~spmswww/frank/index.html that includes QuarkXPress tips and other source material.

Index

Q

http://www.vmedia.com

VENTANA

Official Netscape LiveWire Book

$49.95, 700 pages, illustrated, part #: 382-4

Master web-site management visually! Now even new webmasters can create and manage intranet and Internet sites. And experienced developers can harness LiveWire's advanced tools for maintaining highly complex web sites and applications. Step-by-step tutorials cover all LiveWire components. Learn to design powerful distributed applications—without extensive programming experience.

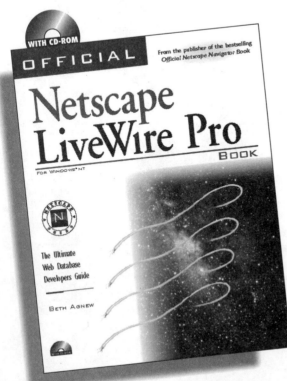

Official Netscape LiveWire Pro Book

$49.99, 700 pages, illustrated, part #: 624-6

High-end database management and connectivity techniques highlight this examination of LiveWire Pro, featuring sophisticated site development and mangement skills that ease the task for webmasters. Learn to maintain databases, update links, process online orders, generate catalogs and more. The CD-ROM features all the code from the sample applications in the book.

VENTANA

Official Netscape SuiteSpot Book

$49.99, 640 pages, illustrated, part #: 502-9

Integrate your intranet with Netscape's power tools!
Here's all you need to set up, configure and manage
an intranet using any or all five Netscape SuiteSpot
servers. With thorough coverage of each server, you'll
learn to choose the SuiteSpot servers that best fit
your needs. Follow step-by-steps to maximize the
myriad advanced features and build an integrated
intranet with SuiteSpot. Or get to know its features
and benefits before you invest.

Official Netscape ONE Book

$49.99, 500 pages, illustrated, part #: 632-7

Your ONE-Stop Reference for Internet/intranet
Solutions. Netscape's Open Network Environment (ONE) provides the tools and technology
for developing versatile applications with cross-
platform functionality. This in-depth guide helps
you harness ONE to create integrated Web
solutions that balance ease of use with economy
of resources—both financial and human. Learn to
master the basic tools, streamline development
with Internet Foundations Classes (IFC) and
much more. The CD-ROM features all the code
examples from the book; complete step-by-step
plug-in example.

VENTANA

Macromedia Director 5 Power Toolkit

$49.95, 800 pages, illustrated, part #: 289-5

Macromedia Director 5 Power Toolkit views the industry's hottest multimedia authoring environment from the inside out. Features tools, tips and professional tricks for producing power-packed projects for CD-ROM and Internet distribution. Dozens of exercises detail the principles behind successful multimedia presentations and the steps to achieve professional results. The companion CD-ROM includes utilities, sample presentations, animations, scripts and files.

The Comprehensive Guide to Lingo

$49.99, 700 pages, illustrated, part #: 463-4

Master the Lingo of Macromedia Director's scripting language for adding interactivity to presentations. Covers beginning scripts to advanced techniques, including creating movies for the Web and problem solving. The companion CD-ROM features demo movies of all scripts in the book, plus numerous examples, a searchable database of problems and solutions, and much more!

Shockwave!

$49.95, 400 pages, illustrated, part #: 441-3

Breathe new life into your web pages with Macromedia Shockwave. Ventana's *Shockwave!* teaches you how to enliven and animate your Web sites with online movies. Beginning with step-by-step exercises and examples, and ending with in-depth excursions into the use of Shockwave Lingo extensions, Shockwave! is a must-buy for both novices and experienced Director developers. Plus, tap into current Macromedia resources on the Internet with Ventana's Online Companion. The companion CD-ROM includes the Shockwave plug-in, sample Director movies and tutorials, and much more!

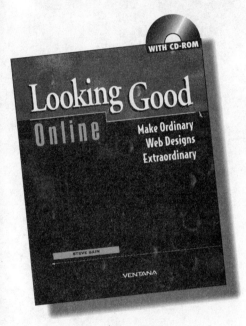

VENTANA

Interactive Web Publishing With Microsoft Tools

$49.99, 818 pages, illustrated, part #: 462-6

Take advantage of Microsoft's broad range of development tools to produce powerful web pages, program with VBScript, create virtual 3D worlds, and incorporate the functionality of Office applications with OLE. The CD-ROM features demos/lite versions of third party software, sample code.

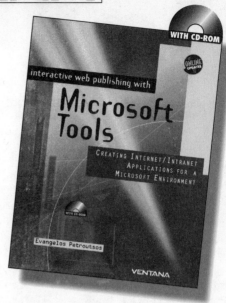

Web Publishing With Microsoft FrontPage 97

$34.99, 500 pages, illustrated, part #: 478-2

Web page publishing for everyone! Streamline web-site creation and automate maintenance, all without programming! Covers introductory-to-advanced techniques, with hands-on examples. For Internet and intranet developers. The CD-ROM includes all web-site examples from the book, FrontPage add-ons, shareware, clip art and more.

Microsoft Internet Studio Publishing

$49.95, 500 pages, illustrated, part #: 358-1

Harness the power of Microsoft's versatile multimedia publishing system! Learn to deliver dynamic interactive applications across multiple platforms. Features enhanced design techniques, content linking and onscreen title creation. The CD-ROM features include titles, graphics, sound files, templates, free utilities and more!

VENTANA

HTML Publishing on the Internet, Second Edition

$49.99, 700 pages, illustrated, part #: 625-4

Take advantage of critical updates and technologies that have emerged since this book's bestselling predecessor was published. Learn to create a home page and hyperlinks, and to build graphics, video and sound into documents. Highlighted throughout with examples and templates, and tips on layout and nonlinear organization. Plus, save time and money by downloading components of the new technologies from the Web or from the companion CD-ROM. The CD-ROM also features HTML authoring tools, graphics and multimedia utilities, textures, templates and demos.

The HTML Programmer's Reference

$39.99, 600 pages, illustrated, part #: 597-5

The ultimate professional companion! All HTML categories, tags and attributes are listed in one easy-reference sourcebook, complete with code examples. Saves time and money testing—all examples comply with the top browsers! Provides real-world JavaScript and HTML examples. The CD-ROM features a complete hyperlinked HTML version of the book, viewable with most popular browsers.

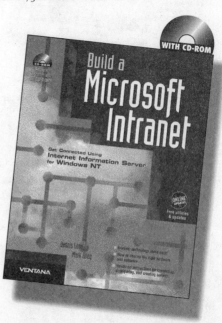

VENTANA

Online Marketing with Netscape

$34.99, 544 pages, illustrated, part #: 453-7

The perfect marketing tool for the Internet! Learn how innovative marketers create powerful, effectove electronic newsletters and promotional materials. Step-by-step instructions show you how to plan, deisgn and distribute professional-quality pieces. With this easy-to-follow guide, you'll soon be flexing Netscape Navigator's marketing muscle to eliminate paper and printing costs, automate market research and customer service, and much more.

Official Netscape Guide to Online Investments

$24.99, 528 pages, illustrated, part #: 452-9

Gain the Internet investment edge! Here's everything you need to make the Internet a full financial partner. Features an overview of the Net and Navigator; in-depth reviews of stock and bond quote services, analysts, brokerage houses, and mutual fund reports. Plus a full listing of related financial services such as loans, appraisals, low-interest credit cards, venture capital, entrepreneurship, insurance, tax counseling, and more.

Official Netscape Guide to Internet Research

$29.99, 600 pages, illustrated, part #: 604-1

Turn the Internet into your primary research tool. More than just a listing of resources, this official guide provides everything you need to know to access, organize, cite and post information on the Net. Includes research strategies, search engines and information management. Plus timesaving techniques for finding the best, most up-to-date data.

TO ORDER ANY VENTANA TITLE, COMPLETE THIS ORDER FORM AND MAIL OR FAX IT TO US, WITH PAYMENT, FOR QUICK SHIPMENT.

TITLE	PART #	QTY	PRICE	TOTAL

SHIPPING

For orders shipping within the United States, please add $4.95 for the first book, $1.50 for each additional book.
For "two-day air" add $7.95 for the first book, $3.00 for each additional book.
For orders shipping to Canada, please contact our Nelson Canada at 800/268-2222 to place your order:
For orders shipping outside the United States and Canada, phone 800/332-7450or
Email: vorders@kdc.com for exact shipping charges.
Note: Please include your local sales tax.

SUBTOTAL = $ _____

SHIPPING = $ _____

TAX = $ _____

TOTAL = $ _____

Mail to: Media Group Customer Service • International Thomson Publishing • 7625 Empire Drive • Florence, KY 41042
☎ **800/332-7450 • fax 606/283-0718**

Name _____

E-mail_____ Daytime phone _____

Company _____

Address (No PO Box) _____

City_____ State_____ Zip_____

Payment enclosed ___VISA ___MC ___ Acc't # _____ Exp. date_____

Signature _____ Exact name on card _____

Check your local bookstore or software retailer for these and other bestselling titles, or call toll free:

800/332-7450

8:00 am - 6:00 pm EST